Craft Class

Craft Class

The Writing Workshop in American Culture

Christopher Kempf

Johns Hopkins University Press

Baltimore

Johns Hopkins University Press
2715 North Charles Street
Baltimore, Maryland 21218-4363
www.press.jhu.edu

Library of Congress Cataloging-in-Publication Data
Names: Kempf, Christopher, author.
Title: Craft class : the writing workshop in American culture /
    Christopher Kempf.
Description: Baltimore : Johns Hopkins University Press, 2022. |
    Includes bibliographical references and index.
Identifiers: LCCN 2021026628 | ISBN 9781421443553 (hardcover ;
    acid-free paper) | ISBN 9781421443560 (paperback ; acid-free paper) |
    ISBN 9781421443577 (ebook)
Subjects: LCSH: Creative writing—Study and teaching—United States. |
    Writers' workshops—United States.
Classification: LCC PE1405.U6 K46 2022 | DDC 808/.042071073—dc23
LC record available at https://lccn.loc.gov/2021026628

A catalog record for this book is available from the British Library.

*Special discounts are available for bulk purchases of this book. For more
information, please contact Special Sales at specialsales@jh.edu.*

Contents

Acknowledgments

Like the workshops that appear in these pages, this book has been a collective labor.

I owe a special debt of gratitude to the Department of English Language and Literature at the University of Chicago. Thank you to Bill Brown for recognizing the potential of this material and, through countless conversations about the theoretical and historical framing herein, for guiding me toward realization of that potential. Thank you to Frances Ferguson for pushing this project toward more complicated thinking and for providing an inspiring, if inimitable, model of what scholarship and teaching can look like. And thank you to Srikanth Reddy for advice on how to shape and contextualize this work, for helping me conceive of the book as a broad cultural history, and for invaluable encouragement in both my scholarship and creative writing. For their work in ensuring that the department functions as smoothly as it does, I am grateful to Robert Devendorf, Angeline Dimambro, Lex Nalley Drlica, and Hannah Stark. For conversations which informed this book in innumerable ways, I would like to thank to Tim DeMay, Maud Ellmann, Rachel Galvin, Jacob Harris, Lauren Michele Jackson, Heather Keenleyside, Steven Maye, Deborah Nelson, Julie Orlemanski, Joshua Scodel, Richard So, Brandon Truett, Kenneth Warren, and Rosanna Warren. Thank you to the Andrew W. Mellon Foundation and the Hanna Holborn Gray Fellowship for the time and financial resources that made this book possible. And thank you to my UChicago students in both English and Creative Writing, all of whom I have learned a great deal from.

At the University of Illinois, I am grateful to Tim Dean and Ramón Soto-Crespo for their friendship, mentorship, and the model of their scholarship. And I would like to thank the graduate MFA students at Illinois for demonstrating, more persuasively than I could in any scholarly book, the richness and even excellence of the workshop system.

An earlier version of this book's first chapter appeared under the same title in *American Literary History* 32, no. 2 (Summer 2020): 243–72, and is used by permission of Oxford University Press. An earlier version of this book's second chapter appeared under the same title in *English Literary History* 88, no. 1 (Spring 2021): 225–50, and is used by permission of Johns Hopkins University Press. Thank you to Gordon Hutner, Douglas Mao, and the editors, staff, and anonymous reviewers at both journals for their stewardship of my work. Thank you, too, to the anonymous reviewers with Johns Hopkins University Press, whose comments allowed me both to clarify and to widen the argumentative scope of this project. Thanks to Kathryn Marguy and Juliana McCarthy at JHUP and to copyeditor Gillian Robinson. And thank you to my indefatigable editor, Catherine Goldstead, whose initial faith in and continued support of the book has been tremendously heartening.

Finally, I would like to express my gratitude to the staff of Houghton Library at Harvard University, especially Dale Stinchcomb; to the Josef and Anni Albers Foundation, especially Brenda Danilowitz and Amy Jean Porter; and to the staff of the North Carolina Western Regional Archives, especially Sarah Downing.

This book would not exist without the support of Corey Van Landingham, my first and final reader. Thank you.

This book is dedicated to the memory of Eavan Boland, who, as she so often put it, ran "a critical workshop"—and who changed my life.

Craft Class

Introduction

Work is never enough done.
—VIRGIL, *GEORGICS* (TRANS. KRISTINA CHEW)

This is a book about work.

More accurately, it is a book about how and why work is invoked as a metaphor for literary production across the late nineteenth and twentieth centuries.

In disarticulating this metaphor—prying apart its constitutive elements to make it speak—I am especially concerned with that form of literary production we know as the creative writing "workshop." Where does this term originate, I ask, and to what ends is it used? How do literary techniques such as imagery, dialogue, structure, texture, and tone come to be thought of as writing "craft," as strict technical construction with the bricks and mortar of language? Most importantly, what is at stake—aesthetically, socially, economically—in the figuration of literary production as craft labor?

The answers to these questions, it turns out, lie in a period of American history during which work itself changed in dramatic ways. Though modern forms of manufacturing had been transforming the nature and meaning of labor since the Civil War, a number of interrelated factors combined around the turn of the twentieth century to accelerate the industrialization of the American economy. As the nation's evolving industrial enterprises began to harness and exploit revolutionary new technologies, the entrepreneurial capitalism of robber barons like Andrew Carnegie gave way to scaled, vertically integrated, scientifically managed, and otherwise rationalized corporate structures. The 1910 opening of Henry Ford's Highland Park assembly line, for instance—itself influenced by Frederick Winslow Taylor's earlier time-and-motion studies at the Midvale Steel Works—was merely the most iconic instantiation of changes which saw nearly 10 million workers added to the American manufacturing sector between 1870 and 1920. In turn, new financial and research institutions emerged which specialized in accruing the vast economic and intellectual resources necessary to maintain these industrial-corporate behemoths. Between 1900 and 1928, the number of American stockholders rose from 4.4 million to 18 million. This group was guided in its financial undertakings by new ratings agencies like Moody's and Standard and Poor's, which abetted the founding of research laboratories at firms like General Electric (1901), DuPont (1902), Eastman Kodak (1913), and AT&T (1925). At the same time, a distinct "professional-managerial class" was tasked with coordinating the increasingly complex operations that sustained this new economic regime. Churned out in ever-greater numbers by the nation's educational system, this class of salaried mental workers developed modern managerial methods to regulate everything from hiring and payroll to disciplinary procedures to workflow and workspace organization.[1] By the turn of the century, what political theorist James Burnham termed the "managerial revolution" was underway—or, to invoke a description popularized by economic historian Alfred D. Chandler Jr., the invisible hand of the free market had been replaced by "the visible hand of management." As I will relate, Chandler's synecdochical sleight of hand had major implications for the creative writing workshop.[2]

Beneath that hand, of course, American workers bridled, rebelling in many forms against substandard wages, hazardous working conditions, and what laborers and concerned observers perceived as a generally dehumanizing division of industrial labor. Emerging contemporaneously with those transformations that constituted a "second industrial revolution," therefore, were two initiatives which sought to redress the increasing disenfranchisement of American workers in distinct ways. The first and most well-known of these initiatives was the American labor movement. Galvanized by economic changes that disproportionately affected the working class, large-scale industrial unions began to wrest power and membership from more restrictive craft unions like the American Federation of Labor (AFL). The "One Big Union" of the Industrial Workers of the World, for instance, was founded in 1905 after a secret meeting of diverse workers previously excluded from the AFL. Three decades later, in 1935, the Congress of Industrial Organizations opened its doors to millions of other unskilled laborers, workers who had manned the lines and swept the shop floors on which a new industrial-corporate regime had been built. Equally at odds with that regime, and perhaps more relevant to the history of the writing workshop, was an American Arts and Crafts movement which looked back to its British counterpart in order to develop an alternative to industrial manufacturing. Inspired by craft ideologues like John Ruskin and William Morris, American Arts and Crafts initiatives proliferated across the late nineteenth century, from the Society of Arts and

Crafts, Boston (1897) on the East Coast to the California Bungalow style promoted by architectural firms like Greene and Greene (1894) on the West Coast. Across these initiatives, craft practitioners advocated for holistic labor practices, discriminating technique, small-scale production, and respect for craft materials, offering a bold, if not wholly original, challenge to accelerating industrialization. Though the American labor and American Arts and Crafts movements were made up of diverse and sometimes irreconcilable elements, and though the legacy of both remains mixed, they nonetheless provided a platform and meaningful ideological agenda with which to address the ever more dire state of American workers.[3]

It is within this context, as Barbara Foley, John Marsh, Christopher Nealon, and other scholars have shown, that American literary modernism took shape, with modernist writers responding in multiple forms to the "labor problem" wracking the nation's economy. One of those forms was the creative writing workshop, a practice—and, as I show, a discourse and value system—which mediated key ideological tensions rending American culture across the late nineteenth and twentieth centuries. Throughout this period, the term "workshop" was taken up by diverse factions of writers and educators in an effort to reframe literary production as a particular, politically determined mode of labor. Two interrelated processes characterized this effort. First, the adoption of a craft lexicon, including "workshop," supplied a set of values by which to reorient institutions of higher education and, in so doing, to alter American literary theory and practice. Second, writers affiliated with early workshops used them to stage a wider social and economic intervention, mobilizing literary craftsmanship to rethink the meaning and ramifications of labor. They did so, as I have suggested, at a time when those meanings were very much in flux.

In this volume, I endeavor to reconstruct an already heavily scaffolded literary and historical epoch around the creative writing workshop, that site which parsed, protested, and often helped to produce new industrial-corporate and later informational-corporate economies. Despite growing scholarly interest in creative writing, the discipline's central practice and sole institutional form has remained invisible. Why has this been the case, I ask? Where is the work on workshop? For there is nothing inherent in creative writing that precludes students from practicing it in a "salon" or "studio" or "seminar." There is nothing in the discipline that necessitates craft-based pedagogies over approaches based on affective response or literary history or even poetic theory. With the rise of the workshop system in American culture, however, work and writing were welded together like steel plates. What fissures does that weld seal shut?

Toward a "Craft Ideal" of Creative Writing

Figurations of literary production as labor were hardly original to the writing workshop, of course, reaching back as they did to the ancient Greek understanding of *poiesis* as an effort in "making" or "creating," a concept as integral to classical-era poetics as it remains to contemporary creative writing.

While Plato viewed the poet's work as an inferior form of "manufacture"—"third in order from king and truth," he says, thus inimical to the well-being of the republic—Aristotle understood the poet as a "maker of likenesses," whose "well-constructed" work supplied an aspirational model of civic virtue.[4] Roman poet Horace echoed Aristotle's view of poetry as ethically instructive, linking the genre even more closely with manual labor than had his Greek predecessors. The didactic "Ars Poetica" invokes a number of craft practices as analogues for poetic composition, as Horace advises would-be writers to "put the badly turned lines back on the anvil," to "polish" poems "ten times over to satisfy the well-pared nail," and to invest "labor and time" toward "poems that deserve preserving [. . .] in smooth cypress." Horace understood his own writing, moreover, as a "fashion[ing]" of "painstaking songs," labor evident in his lapidary, tightly crafted odes and epodes.[5]

Similar figurations recur repeatedly across Western literary history, from medieval texts understood by monks and scholastics as "*opera Dei*"—intellectual work on par with agricultural and other manual labor—to Edward Young's eighteenth-century distinction between the "original composition" of the inspired poet and "a sort of *manufacture* wrought up by those *mechanics*, *art* and *labor*, out of pre-existent materials not their own." A cornerstone of Romantic aesthetics, Young's *Conjectures on Original Composition* compares poetry to manual labor in order, ultimately, to reject such comparisons, privileging organic or "spontaneous" writing over and against work too carefully crafted. "A *genius* differs from a *good understanding* as a magician from a good architect," Young argues. "[T]*hat* raises his structure by means invisible; *this* by the skillful use of common tools. Hence genius has ever been supposed to partake of something divine."[6]

Though analogies between work and writing endure into the twentieth and twenty-first centuries—in New Critical notions of the well-wrought poem, in Black Mountain field poetics, in the braided poetries of writers like Jorie Graham and Linda Gregerson—I focus in this book on the first time the term "workshop" is used in the context of creative writing pedagogy. That occurs at Harvard University in 1912, when drama professor George Pierce Baker establishes an institution for the writing and production of plays which he names, advisedly, the 47 Workshop. Like many of Boston's cultural elite at the time—including fellow Harvard professors Charles Eliot Norton and Herbert Langford Warren, then dean of the School of Architecture—Baker had close ties with the American Arts and Crafts movement, in particular its instantiation as the Society of Arts and Crafts, Boston (SACB). A who's who of the city's Brahmin class, the SACB was the nation's preeminent craft institution, publisher of the influential national journal *Handicraft* and sponsor of a range of exhibitions, gallery shows, and handicraft shops in Boston and beyond. As I argue below, Baker's 47 Workshop borrows significantly from American Arts and Crafts ideology. Specifically, Baker adapts what I identify as a "craft ideal" that animates both the SACB and the American Arts and Crafts movement generally; in its simplest form, this ideal maintains that the worker's engaged, expressive labor should at the same time adhere fastidiously to technical standards like those enforced by preindustrial guilds. In terms later popularized by Thorstein Veblen, the American Arts and Crafts craft ideal reconciled an instinct for "idle curiosity"—the pursuit of knowledge as a "self-legitimating end of endeavor in itself"—with an "instinct of workmanship" described by Veblen as a "proclivity for taking pains," a discipline which served to temper the worker's expressive impulse.[7]

This craft ideal recurs across a number of American Arts and Crafts initiatives. The SACB journal *Handicraft* enshrines in its founding statement, "Principles of Handicraft," the development of "individual character in connection with artistic work" while simultaneously advocating for "thorough technical training, and a just appreciation of standards." Gustav Stickley's *The Craftsman* maintains that in craftwork "interest and a pleasurable excitement are awakened in the workman," but also recommends a revamped system of "primary education" to elevate the worker's "general intelligence." Both aspects of the American Arts and Crafts craft ideal find expression in a 1903 editorial by Harvard art professor and SACB member Denman Ross, who explains in *Handicraft* that "the artistic impulse which would lead us to produce good and beautiful work is fruitless, so long as it is divorced from manual and technical training."[8] In the 47 Workshop, too, Baker and his colleagues tempered the expressive labor of the playwright with those standards maintained by work committees regulating everything from makeup to set design to stage lighting. Undoing the division between manual and mental labor, 47 Workshop productions were further subjected to intensive technical critique from their audiences, with audience members themselves selected only after rigorous screening. Like the American Arts and Crafts movement generally, the

47 Workshop mobilized this craft ideal as a challenge to an evolving industrial-corporate economy; specifically, Baker employed the Workshop both as a means of disrupting an increasingly utilitarian Harvard curriculum—one geared toward churning out a rising professional-managerial class—and as a proving ground for well-crafted dramatic productions that might supplant the commercial fare of Broadway. "The play's the thing," Baker stressed, succinctly articulating his approach to drama as a constructive process—as "stagecraft" in every sense of that word.[9]

In tracing the history of creative writing to an American Arts and Crafts craft ideal, this book advances a distinct genealogy for the discipline, one that departs in important ways from standard scholarly accounts. Most significantly, by attending to the cultural resonances of the notion of workshop, I foreground the wider aesthetic, social, and economic consequences involved in the figuration of writing as craft. Focusing on sites where the relation between labor and literature was explicitly contested—Baker's 47 Workshop, feminist novelist Meridel Le Sueur's workshops at the Minnesota Labor School, poet Robert Duncan's pedagogy at Black Mountain College—I chart the implications of craft rhetoric as it evolves across the late nineteenth and twentieth centuries. If workshop begins, for Baker, as an alternative, nonrationalized discourse and mode of labor, by mid-century it functions to reinscribe the very professional-managerial ethos that Baker opposed. As an evolving industrial-corporate regime yields around mid-century to new informational-corporate economies, or what management consultant Peter Drucker designated the "knowledge economy," an explosion in graduate creative writing programs helps consolidate the authority of elite educational institutions.[10] Specifically, such programs transcode professional-managerial soft skills—linguistic facility, social and emotional discernment, symbolic fluency—in the language of manual labor. At the same time, workshop ensures the university's power as the central licensing agency in literary culture, transforming the creative writing classroom into a closed guild through which literary apprentices pass on their way—quite literally—to master status. Despite creative writing scholar Mark McGurl's contention that craft rhetoric served merely as a postwar pedagogical "adjustment"—a modification which "separate[d] the question of talent and originality, which cannot be taught, from the question of technique, which can"—I argue that the practice of craft engages major transhistorical issues involving labor, education, and aesthetic and economic production.[11] How have we lost sight of these issues? How have scholars of the discipline ignored the fact that creative writing—unlike the composition and literature departments adjacent to it, unlike journalism—is practiced within a workshop, with all that that term entails?[12]

Indeed, from Laurence Veysey's 1965 *The Emergence of the American University* to Eric Bennett's 2015 *Workshops of Empire*, scholars of creative writing have been remarkably unified in eschewing critical analysis of the workshop's broader imbrication of knowledge and power. Though these figures and others identify various influences on the discipline, they universally regard writing pedagogy as a passive formation that merely reflects—rather than shapes, intervenes in, and contributes to—the consolidation of larger economic forces. For Veysey—the first to attend to creative writing, albeit briefly, in the context of the American university—the discipline emerges around the turn of the century out of a utilitarian or professionalizing impulse at institutions like Harvard and New York University. "The dominant characteristic of the new American universities," Veysey argues, "was their ability to shelter specialized departments of knowledge," departments which "represented vocational aspirations" and which realized the "desire for a practical version of higher learning."[13]

In her 1993 *A History of Professional Writing Instruction in American Colleges,* Katherine H. Adams draws on Veysey's work in order to track the emergence of creative writing more narrowly to advanced composition courses that were themselves part of an emphasis on professional education. "Like agriculture, engineering, home economics, and other fields, writing began to be viewed as a set of skills to master in college and apply in specific careers," Adams explains. "Teachers thus began to approach writing through its professional manifestations, primarily as creative writing, magazine and newspaper writing, business writing, and technical writing."[14]

A second line of thinking finds creative writing descending from nearly the opposite impulse. For Gerald Graff, creative writing was part of a broader movement to install more cultural criticism that might oppose the narrow specialization of philology, biography, and professional writing, modes of inquiry so-called generalists perceived as overly scientific and contributive to a growing utilitarianism in literary study. Advocates of creative writing, Graff argues, "saw themselves as the upholders of spiritual values against the crass materialism of American business life, of which the 'production' ethos of the philologists was for them only another manifestation."[15] Graff's student D. G. Myers likewise argues that creative writing begins with the objection of cultural critics to more professional forms of scholarship. "Creative writing arose in opposition to the German research ideal," Myers contends, "and as such it was originally conceived not as a *Wissenschaft*—a medium for producing and expanding knowledge—but as a *Bildung*, a way of cultivating students' appreciation of the literary art."[16] Despite his identification of creative writing as a constructive practice, Myers demurs on engaging writing craft more directly, documenting the institutional history of the discipline but forgoing closer assessment of its ideological and material effects.

What makes McGurl's 2009 *The Program Era* such an important contribution to creative writing scholarship is its sidestepping of this rigid genealogical binary. For McGurl, creative writing enters mainstream education neither through specialized professional pedagogies nor more cultural forms of literary study, but as part of early twentieth-century progressive education, a movement that found in the discipline a conducive medium for students' self-expression. "Responsive to a growing concern that institutions, left to their own devices, make for problematically 'institutional' subjectivities," McGurl explains, "progressive educators worked to re-gear American schools for the systematic production of original persons—more than a few of whom would actually become the most celebrated form of the self-expressive individual, the writer."[17] Creative writing craft enters McGurl's narrative only belatedly, therefore, as part of an effort within postwar writing programs to impose constraints on writers' unfettered expression. In McGurl's words, "the need for such an adjustment in progressive creativity doctrine became pressing when, as creative writing entered the professional-vocational domain of graduate education, its sponsors and practitioners began to care more for the quality of the works created than for the quality of the educational experience of which they are the occasion."[18] The result, McGurl explains, was a form of "programmatic self-expression" which reconciled "disciplinary rigor" with "self-expressive creativity," an institutional habitus that would come to characterize the practice of creative writing throughout the Program Era and into the present, from Ithaca to Irvine, from Providence to Palo Alto.

Though much of what follows is indebted to McGurl's groundbreaking reassessment of creative writing, one fundamental claim of this book is that what McGurl calls "programmatic self-expression" in fact embodies an earlier ethos integral to creative writing workshops both then and now: an American Arts and Crafts craft ideal. As I have indicated, that ideal promoted fastidious—if not quite "programmatic"—adherence to technical standards while also allowing for the craftsman's engaged, even expressive labor. Extending McGurl's lines of inquiry to Left and working-class literature, including writing produced within craft-based workshops, I argue in this study that creative writing emerges less from the expressivist ethos of progressive education than from the constructivist ethos of the

American Arts and Crafts movement, an initiative which reflexively foregrounded the formal and material construction of texts and textiles, poetry and pottery.[19] Indeed, Baker's pedagogy in the 47 Workshop establishes an anti-expressive ethos that recurs throughout the subsequent history of creative writing. From Baker student John Dos Passos and his notion of "the writer as technician" to Robert Duncan's submission to the material resistances of language, the writers I take up in this book insist that the literary artist's expressive impulse be tempered by the imposition of external constraints, whether formal, material, or spiritual. As craft sociologist Richard Sennett describes, this tempering of expression is a hallmark of craft practices; "resistance and ambiguity can be instructive experiences," Sennett notes, since "to work well, every craftsman has to learn from these experiences rather than fight them."[20] From this perspective, the well-trafficked debate as to whether the writing workshop stifles individual genius—whether master of fine arts (MFA) programs simply reproduce *ad infinitum* the "workshop lyric" or "McPoem"—seems strikingly moot. This is their very purpose.[21]

If Gerald Graff argues, therefore, that American literary study is marked by disciplinary conflicts that fail "to find visible institutional expression," I show how those conflicts were mediated by, and indeed found expression within, the creative writing workshop.[22] Extending an American Arts and Crafts craft ideal, workshop reconciled self-expression and technical rigor, coordinated antithetical concerns over beauty and utility, and refracted, reproduced, and sometimes resisted broader economic transformations across the twentieth century. Recovering the craft legacy of creative writing, in other words, helps us read the workshop as a transitional institution, one which resisted the hegemony of new industrial-corporate and informational-corporate regimes even as, in other ways, it labored those regimes into existence.

In the transitional role it played in the evolution of the American economy, the writing workshop seems prefigured by the historical workshop it metaphorizes, itself a transitional space between craft and industry, past and future. Before the "workshop," in other words, was the workshop.

Reworking Craft: A Critical History

"Craft" itself remains an amorphous term, designating simultaneously a set of ideologies, a system of knowledge, and work practices that have continuously evolved over time. In this book, I employ the term in two ways, drawing on historical and theoretical conceptions of craft in order to delineate as sharply as possible its invocation within and implications for the creative writing workshop.

First and most rigidly, "craft" designates a craft ideal, referring to that ethos which tempers the craftsman's expressive labor with technical rigor. Describing this ideal, craft theorist Howard Risatti treats craftsmanship as "existing with the realm of *poiesis*" since in it "technical skill and creative imagination come together."[23] The second sense in which I employ "craft" is more capacious, connoting a cluster of interrelated values, practices, attitudes, and affects. Craft in this second sense names a traditional way of making via hand labor that informs the craft object. Craft names a "desire to do a job well for its own sake," in the words of Sennett, the "special human condition of being *engaged*."[24] As C. Wright Mills explains in his 1951 *White Collar*, in craft "[t]here is an inner relation between the craftsman and the thing he makes, from the image he first forms of it through its completing, which [. . .] makes the craftsman's will-to-work spontaneous and even exuberant." It is Mills whose definition of craft speaks most closely to the more expansive sense in which I invoke the term. In craftsmanship, as Mills describes it, "there is no ulterior motive in work other than the product being made and the processes of its creation. The details of daily work are meaningful because they are not detached in the worker's mind from the product of the work. The worker is free to control his own working action. The craftsman is thus able to learn from his work [. . .] There is no split of work and play, or work and culture."[25] For Mills, craft practices are characterized by the autonomous self-absorption that render work akin to children's play, and it is helpful to remember that Mills began to explicitly theorize craftsmanship at precisely the moment D. W. Winnicott, among others, began to study the absorptive and inherently fulfilling processes of childhood imagination. That Mills turns to craft in the immediate postwar era is indicative too, as I will show, of the broader institutionalization of craft rhetoric like "workshop," for Mills was hardly alone in looking back to an idealized mode of labor at a historical moment when such labor seemed all but irrelevant to the American economy.

In its conceptualization of literary craftsmanship, the writing workshop invokes many of the values Mills describes, with "details of daily work"—sound and lineation, character development and narrative structure—closely related "in the worker's mind" to the final "product." The historical institution from which the workshop draws its name, though, rarely witnessed this kind of labor. Despite its misassociation with earlier forms of guild craftsmanship, the proto-industrial workshop marked a transition between skilled hand craftsmanship and the alienated work of the factory; indeed, in many cases, workshop labor was characterized by machine production, thorough subdivision of labor, and employee management practices strikingly reminiscent of later economic eras. Speaking to the transitional nature of workshop, a site which endured from the feudal era through to the nineteenth century, Marilyn Palmer explains that "many of the buildings traditionally classified as workshops made some use of power, as in the engineering workshops where lathes and presses were driven from overhead line-shafting." Workers could still "control the rhythm and intensity" of their work, describes Palmer, "something that became impossible under the factory system," but workshops also depended on the "subdivision of the production process into a number of distinct operations, each of which could be carried out by different operatives."[26] Alert to its transitional nature, both Karl Marx and Veblen devote significant attention to the workshop as a key site in the development of modern capitalism. Within his discussion of surplus value in the first volume of *Das Kapital*, Marx finds in the workshop the "decomposition" of holistic craft labor into "successive manual operations." "This workshop, the product of the division of labor in manufacture," Marx continues, "produced in its turn—machines. It is they that sweep away the handicraftsman's work as the regulating principle of social production."[27] Veblen echoes Marx's narrative in arguing that in the workshop, craftsmanship "passes over into the regime of the machine industry when its technology [has] finally outgrown those limitations of handicraft [. . .] that gave it its character as a distinct phase of economic history."[28] Far from some medieval other to capital, workshop names a critical waypoint in capitalist development, a juncture as contested in sixteenth-century textile shops as it remains in the creative writing classroom.

The misassociation of workshops with craft labor—a mixed metaphor at the very heart of creative writing—is attributable, according to craft scholars, to a nineteenth-century Arts and Crafts movement which idealized craft labor at the expense of historical accuracy. Edward Lucie-Smith's influential 1981 *The Story of Craft* exemplifies this line of thinking. "Neither piece-work nor factory conditions were unknown to the European Middle Ages," Lucie-Smith reminds us, "though the late medieval guild system was so frequently idolized by Ruskin and his disciples." It is a mistake, Lucie-Smith goes on, "to talk of an innocent pre-industrial age followed by a corrupt industrial one. If there was ever a departure from a kind of pre-technological Eden, it took place so gradually in many crafts that those who were departing did not notice the fact."[29] Glenn Adamson ratifies Lucie-Smith's position in his 2013 *The Invention of Craft*, contending that "craft was invented *as an absence*. It came into being as a figure of cancellation, an 'X' marking a spot that never existed."[30] Less commonly acknowledged among craft scholars is the extent to which Arts and Crafts adherents in fact recognized the economically nuanced and historically plastic nature of craft practices, including the transitional role of workshop. To cite one example, William Morris explains in "Art Under Plutocracy" that commercialism "destroyed the craft system of labor, in which, as aforesaid, the unit of labor is a fully instructed craftsman [and] supplanted it by [. . .] the workshop-system, wherein, when complete, division of labor in handiwork is carried to the highest point."[31] If craft scholars unfairly stereotype craftsmen themselves as poorly historicizing, doe-eyed naïfs, they likewise tend to denigrate the American Arts and Crafts movement as simply a meliorist initiative, one designed to ease workers into, and distract them from, new and more demanding regimes of labor. For T. J. Jackson Lears, American Arts and Crafts programs drew back from "fundamental social change" or the creation of a "truly alternative culture," instead adjusting workers to "bureaucratic hierarchies" by providing therapeutic outlets for their otherwise suppressed creativity.[32] For Leslie Greene Bowman, craft objects were "packaged [. . .] into a consumer proposition," while for Eileen Boris craft "could never generate a truly oppositional culture."[33] In charging its adherents with both historical ignorance and capitalist collusion, craft scholars ignore the wide variegation within the British and American Arts and Crafts movements, downplaying the far-reaching effects of those movements, including the writing workshop.

Just as this book challenges standard genealogies of creative writing, then, on another front it rethinks interpretations of late nineteenth and early twentieth-century craftsmanship—from pottery shops to community theater—that view craft initiatives as mere apologist practices, vents for pent-up social and economic resentment. "American craft leaders quickly lost sight of religious or communal frameworks of meaning outside the self," Lears contends. "Like many of their British counterparts, they allowed their quest for wholeness to center on the self alone. [. . .] In part a reaction against therapeutic self-absorption, the revival of handicraft ultimately became another form of therapy for an overcivilized bourgeoisie."[34] Evocative of Stephen Greenblatt's more nuanced theory of subversion and containment, Lears's caricature could not be further from the communal craftsmanship of initiatives like Baker's 47 Workshop.[35] Forgoing a morality tale between craft and industry, I will reveal the dynamic give-and-take between craft adherents and the forces of industrialization they opposed; a second fundamental claim of this book, therefore, is that not all non-radical responses to the plight of American workers constituted containment or what Lears calls "accommodation," a with-us-or-against-us mentality that too easily abandons the vast middle ground in which the majority of cultural formations play out. While Baker's opposition to an evolving industrial-corporate economy stopped short, for instance, of the early radicalism of his student John Dos Passos—and certainly never attained the level of commitment demonstrated by a writer like Meridel Le Sueur—Baker pointedly and repeatedly challenged the priorities of that economy as well as of the professional-managerial ethos that underwrote it. Tracking creative writing as its alternative potential is absorbed, though never anesthetized, within evolving industrial- and informational-corporate economies, I contend that the term "workshop" names a meaningful struggle over workers' self-determination, a struggle that manifests in a number of worker-writer initiatives programmatically written out of standard histories. Though in hindsight that struggle can seem like a *fait accompli*—with horse-and-buggy craftsmanship inevitably overtaken by the piston-powered engine of change—I argue that the struggle was a profound one, that a number of workshops generated significant aesthetic and economic labor during this period, and that the value of that labor has been underappreciated.

For if craft adherents like Morris idealized pre-industrial labor, they did so in response to a historical moment in which craft skills and knowledge were increasingly expropriated for the benefit of an economic elite. As Harry Braverman, Michael Denning, Richard Donkin, and others make clear, the emergence of industrial-corporate economies—or what has passed as "managerial capital" or "rationalized corporate structures"—depended to a large degree on the abstraction of technical knowledge that was formerly the province of craft laborers.[36] "Not only did the Taylorism of modernity accentuate the division between [. . .] mental and manual labor," Denning argues, "but it created entire industries and classes built on 'mental labor' and the appropriation of the skills of the craftworker."[37] As new forms of abstract, technical, administrative, and professional labor emerged alongside increasingly complex economic enterprises, craft privileges and epistemologies were gradually stripped away. In the words of Braverman, "the capitalist consolidated his powers in society and demolished the juridical features of pre-capitalist social formations." Specifically, "the breakup of craft skills [. . .] destroyed the traditional concept of skill and opened up only one way for mastery over labor processes to develop: in and through scientific, technical, and engineering knowledge."[38] As I argue below, that mastery was facilitated by institutions of higher education, and in particular by creative writing workshops, which dismantled craft and reconstructed it in their own epistemological image.

If accelerated in the late nineteenth century, the expropriation of craft knowledge had proceeded apace for hundreds of years, beginning with the exposure of craft mysteries—from *misterium*, Latin for "professional skill"—once bound securely in so-called "craft books." Circulated within pre-industrial guilds, these texts cloaked the mysteries of forging and sword-smithing, of lace-weaving, woodworking, and shoemaking, in self-protective jargon. Texts such as Vannoccio Biringuccio's sixteenth-century *De la pirotechnia* and Benvenuto Cellini's *I trattati dell'oreficeria e della scultura*, for example, were the forerunners of literary craft books like Mary Oliver's *A Poetry Handbook*, maintaining technical standards and regulating admission to guilds and workshops.[39] While Adamson traces the exposure of craft mysteries to Diderot's 1751 *Encyclopédie*, one might just as easily date the process to the Baconian scientific method of the early seventeenth century.[40] Criticizing the continued separation of mental and manual labor, Francis Bacon, acting in his capacity as Lord Chancellor, emphasized how crucial the tacit knowledge at the heart of guild craftsmanship was to British imperialism. Craft-based ways of making and knowing, Bacon declared in his 1620 *Novum Organum*, constituted "literate experience" that must be inspected, described, and institutionalized so that proper use might be made of it. Modeling the notion after craft epistemologies, Bacon described literate experience as a "kind of sagacity," an exclusive disposition which, if "put in writing," might advantage both Britain and her colonies.[41] Bacon thus sought to expropriate both the content of craft practices and their form, as well as the ethos with which those practices were carried out. His call for the public exposure of craft resulted in a number of texts written exclusively for learned audiences, the kind of philosopher-scientists with whom Bacon associated in his various courtly roles. In his 1662 *Silva*, gardener John Evelyn cautioned that he "did not altogether compile this Work for the Sake of our Ordinary Rusticks (meer Forestors and Woodmen), but for the more Ingenious, the benefit and diversion of Gentlemen, the Persons of Quality."[42] Craft books also began to be written, however, for wider audiences of curious workers. Joseph Moxon's 1678 *Mechanick exercises* discussed skills such as blacksmithing, joinery, and carpentry "in workmen's phrases and their terms explained."[43] A hydrographer and mathematician from Cornhill, Moxon explicitly framed his *Mechanick* as a response to Bacon's call for the demystification of craft.[44] "The Lord Bacon, in his Natural History, reckons that Philosophy would be improved by having the Secrets of all Trades lye open," he writes. Moxon himself agreed, "not only because Experimental Philosophy is Coucht amongst them," but also because "the Trades themselves might, by a Philosopher, be improv'd."[45] An explicit challenge to guild control of craft labor, Moxon's *Mechanick* earned him election to the Royal Society the very year of its publication.

On the one hand, such a text might be understood as democratizing labor practices, with Moxon believing, perhaps nobly, that all British culture owed to and might benefit from craft experiences made literate. "That Geometry, Astronomy, Perspective, Musick, Navigation, Architecture, &c. are excellent Sciences, all that know but their very Names will confess," Moxon reasoned. "Yet to what purpose would Geometry serve, were it not to contrive Rules for Handy-Works? Or how could Astronomy be known to any perfection, but by Instruments made by Hand? What Perspective should we have to delight our Sight? What Musick to ravish our Ears? What Navigation to Guard and Enrich our Country? Or what Architecture to defend us from the Inconveniences of different Weather, without Manual Operations?"[46] For Moxon, as for Bacon before him, craft practices undergirded nearly every aspect of cultural and scientific experience, making the exposure of craft secrets nothing less than a matter of national security. As Kathleen Biddick has demonstrated, so integral was the exposure and dissemination of craft practices to British imperialism that by the nineteenth century, craft books instructing would-be Gothic architects were retooled for use in tropical colonies in India and the Americas. One such text, the 1855 *Instrumenta Ecclesiastica*, included designs and tracing patterns for everything from door handles to coffin lids, while another included blueprints for churches and cathedrals, part of a trans-Atlantic craft network ripe for scholarly research.[47]

On the other hand, it is a short leap from Bacon and Moxon's abstraction of craft skills for the benefit of a scientific elite to something like Taylor's expropriation of craft ways of making and knowing under scientific management. Helen Clifford argues as much in her local history of London workshops. "It may be no coincidence," Clifford writes, "that it is from [the seventeenth century] that the power of the guilds began to decline, and the forces of innovation (as applied to organization, methods of manufacture, and product types) began to be felt."[48] Bacon himself seems to anticipate precisely this shift in craft practices, calling the exposure of craft secrets a "*traductio*"—a "transfer" or "translation." As in any financial exchange, much indeed was being transferred.[49]

That term also, of course, carries in its history another association relevant to the abstraction and redeployment of craft epistemologies. From the Latin for "to lead along as a spectacle," "traduce" refers to those forms of scorn in which wrongdoers were paraded before their accusers within the medieval or early modern square. "[T]*raductio*," in this sense, connotes a type of public defamation or slander. The word is related to "traitor."[50]

Craft University

It would be impossible, admittedly, to date the expropriation of craft—and the attendant transformation of work into the drudgery experienced by the majority of global workers—to a single historical moment. Certainly by the nineteenth century, however, craft knowledge had passed from closely regulated guilds and workshops to factory management offices, research laboratories, and those financial markets which underwrote them. The exposure of craft mysteries, Glenn Adamson has argued, "was infused with the triumphal logic of modern technology."[51]

As I have noted, the installation of that technology required a professional-managerial class capable of coordinating rationalized and ever more bureaucratic industrial-corporate enterprises. The American university was the primary production site, therefore, for a new cadre of executives whose work it would be to instrumentalize craft knowledge.[52] Scholars across a range of disciplines have recognized the integral role of the university in the evolution of industrial- and informational-corporate economies. Historians Barbara and John Ehrenreich describe the university as the "reproductive apparatus" of the professional-managerial class. Performance theorist Shannon Jackson explains that the "modern concept of 'discipline' [. . .] arose when the discursive strain of professional expertise met the exigencies of a restructuring university." Sociologist Daniel Bell reads the university as the "axial structure" in economies organized around "intellectual technology."[53] Indeed, the integration of the university within broader corporate regimes was explicitly promoted by the US government throughout the late nineteenth and twentieth centuries, from the Morrill Land-Grant Acts of 1862 to the 1980 passage of the Bayh-Dole Act, which cleared the way for the patenting and marketing of university research.[54]

By midcentury, the writing workshop itself served as a key distribution point for those professional-managerial discourses on which the American economy depended. As craft-based pedagogies became quite literally incorporated into higher education, migrating from labor schools to experimental arts colleges like Black Mountain to postwar MFA programs, craft was not simply commodified, but tactically redeployed in the service of—and as rhetorical cover for—hegemonic cultural and economic practices. In the workshop, those practices were rewritten as neutral and even antiquated labor, with similarities between the writing workshop and its historical predecessor suggesting that the former, too, constituted a pivotal site in the expropriation of craft epistemologies. As Richard Sennett explains, "in a workshop, the skills of the master can earn him or her the right to command, and learning from and absorbing those skills can dignify the apprentice or journeyman's obedience."[55] The master of the writing workshop, of course, is the published author who serves as instructor, a figure whose charismatic presence— not to mention cultural cachet and professional connections—can "dignify" by association the work of his or her students. For Sennett, moreover, the craftsman's workshop is "one site in which the [. . .] conflict between autonomy and authority plays out."[56] Within the creative writing workshop, would-be writers are asked to cultivate individual expression while demonstrating expertise in those techniques promoted by the authoritative master, a balance at the heart of the American Arts and Crafts craft ideal. And the way student-writers demonstrate their expertise is the MFA thesis or undergraduate portfolio, akin to the masterpiece by which craft apprentices become journeymen. Even such a notorious shibboleth as "show, don't tell" originates in the proto-industrial workshop, as the master's visual demonstration provides a model for the apprentice's work. If Pierre Bourdieu argues, then, that "the culture [the university] transmits is largely that of the dominant classes," that culture comes packaged in the MFA era in a falsely nostalgic lexicon evocative of work practices the university itself has helped to render obsolete.[57] The workshop poem or short story shares discursive space with the craft IPA or "hand-loomed" Pottery Barn rug; in this space, one economic practice transcodes itself in the language of another, just as right-wing corporatism continuously rewrites itself in the language of populism.

This function of workshop takes on added significance when one considers the still exclusionary structure of American higher education. Despite much-publicized efforts to democratize the university through affirmative action and other diversity initiatives, a number of factors have combined in the late twentieth and early twenty-first centuries to render a college education—to say nothing of a graduate degree—as inaccessible now as it was in the nineteenth century to vast segments of the working class. Owing to the rise of debt-based financial aid, a decline in federal Pell Grants for low-income students, and massive state disinvestment in public universities, social class has become the single most insurmountable barrier to higher education, to the point that a mere 6 percent of low-income students earn a bachelor's degree by their twenty-fourth birthday.[58] As Christopher Findeisen, Juliana Spahr, and Stephanie Young have shown, moreover, low-income students remain 17 percent less likely to major in the humanities than their classmates, while nearly three-fourths of MFA graduates come from expensive debt generator programs that offer, at best, appallingly limited funding packages.[59] Like the university which houses it, and like the proto-industrial workshop with which it is associated, the creative writing workshop perpetuates cultural and economic frameworks hospitable primarily to its core constituency: the professional-managerial class. "Access to the game," Peter Sacks explains, "is determined by an elaborate, self-perpetuating arrangement of social and economic privilege."[60] Such legitimation of social difference would be unremarkable, of course, were it not for the rhetorical positioning of creative writing as somehow antithetical to an otherwise professional curriculum—as socially neutral, good old-fashioned work.

What makes creative writing such an effective instrument in the crafting of class relations, however, is not only that it justifies social difference as a kind of professional technique, but that it disguises the operation of economic capital as cultural distinction. As Bourdieu notes of mass-produced couture craft—YETI coolers and Pendleton blankets being, as of this writing, two conspicuous examples— "nothing is more distinctive, more distinguished, than the capacity to confer aesthetic status on objects that are banal or even 'common.'"[61] While instructors of creative writing will reminisce fondly about their most talented students, these instructors will also tell you that there is hardly anything more "banal or even 'common'" than the majority of student writing. Yet these same instructors, myself not excepted, continuously peddle notions of student writing that idealize their work as rigorous craftsmanship—not paperwork toward a fungible credential, but careful construction in language. This study thinks through the slippage in that metaphor. For creative writing may indeed prove more culturally distinctive than systems engineering or supply chain management, but the vast majority of student-writers—at the graduate no less than the undergraduate level—both descend from and ultimately find work as professional-managerial laborers. For Natalia Cecire, the university's privileging of professional-managerialism is linked with the rise of Big Science within the midcentury university, a disciplinary shift which prompted the emergence of experimental or more "scientific" aesthetic traditions like conceptual art and Language poetry.[62] Though what follows is significantly indebted to Cecire's work, a third major claim of this study is that not only experimental but mainstream creative writing responded to, facilitated, and in rare cases critiqued the entrenchment of professional-managerial values. Like myriad other erstwhile challenges to American capitalism, writing craft was absorbed and rearticulated in academic-*cum*-corporate form, its fate paralleling that of the Language school itself, as well as of contemporaneous class- and race-based critiques levied within an academic New Left.

The writing workshop was only one manifestation, though, of a widespread fascination with craft rhetoric around the midcentury, rhetoric which exploded precisely at the time a new informational-corporate regime was entrenching itself at the heart of the American Century. C. Wright Mills's 1959 *The Sociological Imagination*, for instance, advocates craftsmanship as an idealized model of flexible thinking integral to the sociologist's work. "Be a good craftsman," Mills advises would-be sociologists. "Avoid any rigid set of procedures [. . .] let theory and method again become part of the practice of a craft." Balancing the sociologist's expressive labor with technical "perfection," Mills's sociologist embodies an American Arts and Crafts craft ideal and carries it forward into an unexpected context. "The most admirable thinkers within the scholarly community you have chosen to join do not split their work from their lives," Mills insists. "They seem to take both too seriously to allow such dissociation."[63] Admirable in its invocation of pre-industrial work as an antidote to modernity, Mills's white-collar craftsmanship at the same time ensures that mental laborers internalize the professional-managerial ethos of the university. While the proto-industrial workshop did serve, in some cases, as the home of the miller or textile-maker or blacksmith, the obscuring of boundaries between work and leisure also means that mental laborers, like most university employees, never punch out, that they are susceptible at any moment to the midnight phone call or emergency email. This infiltration of work into every aspect of existence looks far less insidious when it goes by the name of "craftsmanship."

In this way, Mills's sociologist figures forth what William H. Whyte three years earlier had called "the organization man," that figure whose internalization of corporate values—especially a guild-like sense of corporate belonging—"is like nothing so much as the Middle Ages." The challenge for organizations "is to *re-create* the belongingness of the Middle Ages," Whyte explains. "What with the Enlightenment, the Industrial Revolution, and other calamities, the job is immensely more difficult than it was in those simpler days. But with new scientific techniques, we can solve the problem. What we must do is to learn consciously to achieve what once came naturally. We must form an elite of skilled leaders who will guide men back, benevolently, to group belongingness."[64] Whyte's striking deployment of craft rhetoric reveals how evolving economic regimes not only abstracted and expropriated craft epistemologies but forced them back upon American workers as New Age corporate communalism. And it is a short step from Mills's sociologist to the practice of "managerial craftsmanship" promoted by policy analyst Eugene Bardach in a 1998 Brookings Institution report with the insipid title *Getting Agencies to Work Together: The Practice and Theory of Managerial Craftsmanship*. "[T]he leader manipulates her followers as a craftsman would manipulate her materials," Bardach explains. "To put it another way, *craftsman* and *materials* are roles in a system of strategic interactions, not personal attributes, talents, or conditions of individuals."[65] Though it would be difficult to find more succinct testimony to the expropriation of craft skills by a professional-managerial elite, Bardach's rhetoric is indicative of a wider redeployment of craft rhetoric across the twentieth century.

Of course, craft skills and practices were also incorporated quite materially into the university in the postwar era. Spurred by the passage of the GI Bill in 1944, programs in studio craft proliferated in the late 1940s and early 1950s, part of the same institutional hospitality to the arts that resulted nearly contemporaneously in the establishment of creative writing programs at schools like Iowa, Johns Hopkins, and Cornell. In their early years, programs in studio craft fostered self-expressive creativity among a neophyte student body of returning GIs, an expressivist ethos exemplified dramatically in sculptor and Black Mountain instructor Peter Voulkos. Voulkos "might have seemed an eccentric figure," Adamson explains, "but he spoke for a large number of the young people who were entering the craft scene in the late 1950s. This generation had been educated in the new university programs, and they had different expectations from those who were oriented to design for industry."[66] The expressivist era of studio craft was short-lived, though. As Adamson and other craft scholars relate, by 1960, programs in craft had begun to clamp down on undisciplined self-expression, with textile designer Jack Lenor Larsen describing such work as "directionless irresponsibility—ideal soil for that kind of parasitic, fruitless individualism that impedes our cause."[67] Gradually, craft came to be redefined as a fine art, its products destined for galleries, museums, and other high-end commercial outlets. "The general pre-war concept of craft as local, amateur, handmade functional goods," Caroline M. Hannah explains, "made room for a new perception of craft as sophisticated, unique, handmade design objects that were aesthetically attuned to the contemporary tastes of a national urban/suburban market."[68] Though studio craft cuts through this book only glancingly, its redefinition as a fine art was symptomatic of and perpetuated an inherited academic contempt for craft discourses. That contempt is neatly demonstrated in the 1970 decision to rebrand the Museum of Contemporary Crafts first as the American Craft Museum and then, in 2002, as the Museum of Arts and Design, the latter effectively obliterating the legacy of craft in the United States.[69]

It is this contempt for craft, which continues to connote for most audiences a penchant for backwoods kitsch and flea-market rubbish, that has contributed in part to scholarly disregard for the craft legacy of creative writing. This book attempts to recover that legacy. For as craft was abstracted into pedagogy and denatured into fine art, it was also taken up by a range of creative writers who found in it a value system by which to think through and sometimes redress broader economic transformations. "[E]ven as the popularity of pottery (part of the craft movement of the 1960s) lay behind its displacement from the field of art," Bill Brown has argued, "the literary register nonetheless reanimates the vitality of craft as vernacular modernism [. . .] with all its utopian longing."[70] Ignoring links between creative writing and other forms and theories of making, scholars have ignored both the economic ramifications of the discipline and how creative writers themselves reappropriated craft lexicons. In contrast, this book charts a somewhat digressive path through craft ideologies and institutions—Le Sueur's proletarian modernism, the visual arts pedagogies of Josef and Anni Albers—in order to situate workshop itself within an expansive craft culture. Though the American Arts and Crafts movement had fizzled out by the 1930s, the craft ideal it promoted would be taken up in multiple forms across the twentieth century, cast and recast in the foundry that was the creative writing workshop.

Incorporating diverse forms, genres, and media—from undergraduate theater productions to proletarian novels to avant-garde visual art and the writing pedagogies it inspired—I seek to restore a holistic, historically nuanced vision of that workplace. In doing so, I counteract the tendency in creative writing scholarship not only to disregard the discipline's craft legacy but to focus almost exclusively on American fiction. While MFA workshops themselves contributed to the growing popularity of literary fiction across the twentieth century, I attend in the second half of this book to modes of poetry which reflexively theorize themselves as craft objects, drawing as they do on the tradition of the *ars poetica* and on the capacity of poetry to foreground its formal and material construction. In Robert Duncan's experimental field poetics, in Gertrude Stein's and Ezra Pound's poetry craft books, in Margaret Walker's finely crafted worker portraits, we find the self-conscious treatment of creative writing craft and of that crafting space, the workshop, becoming increasingly integral to American literature writ large.

Work Schedule

My opening chapter, accordingly, returns to the first creative writing "workshop" to use that name: the 47 Workshop led by George Pierce Baker at Harvard University from 1912 to 1924. Drawing on extensive archival research, I reconstruct the procedures of Baker's workshop and illuminate the craft ideology informing them. For if his adoption of the term marked a calculated effort to slot arts pedagogies into Harvard's increasingly utilitarian curriculum—here, Baker insisted, was serious labor in the useful and remunerative discipline of stagecraft— "workshop" also signaled Baker's ties to a craft movement *comme il faut* among Boston's elite. As I have suggested, Baker translated an American Arts and Crafts craft ideal into both the form and content of the 47 Workshop, challenging the mass-cultural productions of Broadway and extending a broader Arts and Crafts opposition to regnant industrial-corporate economies.

In order to understand that intervention—to grasp the social work of workshop— I turn in the second half of the first chapter to a pair of dramatic texts developed under the influence of the 47 Workshop. The first, Baker's 1930 *Control: A Pageant of Engineering Progress*, pointedly challenges the priorities of emergent industrial-corporate enterprises, leveling a sharp critique of those economic forces that would subsume aesthetic, spiritual, and ecological considerations under pecuniary motives. Written for the fiftieth anniversary of the American Society of Mechanical Engineers, *Control* manages the difficult feat of celebrating innovation while warning its audience against the surrender of pre-industrial values. Similarly, Baker's student John Dos Passos found in craft a set of values by which to oppose Broadway theater and at the same time reconsider the implications of American capitalism. Examining his three-act play *Airways, Inc.*, I show how Dos Passos adjusts the American Arts and Crafts ideology promoted by his former teacher, imagining the transformation of intellectual labor from a kind of craftsmanship to a mode of technical engineering. Produced in 1929 at the New Playwrights Theater, *Airways, Inc.* routes its politics through representations of labor and laborers, staging the obsolescence of craft and the rise of new bloodless "technique." At this point in his career, Dos Passos is still working out the aesthetic and economic implications of these metaphors, but close treatment of *Airways, Inc.* reveals the foundation of a modernist technical aesthetic which, refined in Dos Passos's landmark 1935 essay "The Writer as Technician," will significantly influence his development as a novelist and cultural critic.

In the second chapter, I contextualize Dos Passos's "The Writer as Technician" within the 1930s literary Left in order to show how the American Arts and Crafts craft ideal cleaves into opposing ideological factions. Writers of the first faction, like Dos Passos and *Partisan Review* editors Philip Rahv and William Phillips, viewed the writer as a technician whose ultimate responsibility was rigorous adherence to the standards of modernist technique. A second faction of the literary Left, in contrast, organized around Mike Gold's *New Masses*, promoted the self-expression of proletarian writers otherwise unschooled in the literary arts. For both factions, aesthetic and ethical values manifested through competing representations of the worker-writer, what we might schematize as a "top-down" (writers as workers) versus a "bottom-up" (workers as writers) binary. Tracking the dual inheritance of American Arts and Crafts ideology, I show how debates internal to the 1930s Left supplied key rhetoric that would influence later creative writing workshops, particularly the pedagogical promotion of imagery—metonymized as "show, don't tell"—which had the effect of suppressing overtly political writing.

These debates fenced out a discursive field, within which the majority of 1930s writers plied their craft. In this chapter, I examine one of those writers, Meridel Le Sueur, as a study in how craft lexicons informed literary production during an era in which the relationship between labor and literature was sharply contested. A creative writing teacher at the Minnesota Labor School, backed by the Works Progress Administration (WPA), Le Sueur remains an underappreciated figure in literary critical appraisals of the 1930s, her career as a feminist and proletarian writer embodying significant intellectual tensions with the 1930s Left. Le Sueur herself was an outspoken critic of the "inhuman" leftism she associated with Dos Passos and *Partisan Review*, and her pedagogical and documentary work with the WPA, including her 1937 textbook *Worker Writers*, extends Gold's expressivist values.[71] At the same time, Le Sueur's fiction complicates any potentially reductive notions of proletarianism, revealing self-consciously modernist aspirations in its virtuosic joining of realist and lyrically experimental modes.

How and why, I ask in this chapter, have proletarian workshops—those taught by Le Sueur, as well as workshops organized by John Reed Clubs and other leftist initiatives—been written out of standard histories of both modernism and creative writing? What does that omission reveal about our own present-day disciplinary practices?

If the American Arts and Crafts craft ideal cleaves into opposing factions of the 1930s Left, it also reemerges whole at Black Mountain College in 1933, where—in poetry and pottery workshops, on the college farm and kitchen detail—students' self-expression was tempered by the resistances of craft material. At Black Mountain, students and faculty understood craft as a self-annulling discipline, a way of sublimating the expressive ego in and through materiality. What I call in the third chapter Black Mountain's "spiritualized craft ideal" operated on two distinct registers. First, Black Mountaineers viewed the worker's labor as a spiritual process in its own right, drawing on American Arts and Crafts ideology which held that intimate engagement with material facilitated freer, more authentic expression. Second, submission to material allowed the craftsman to embody formally—in language, textile patterns, and agricultural work, for example—a higher, more spiritual order of creation, to access a universal plane foreclosed by more egoistic forms of making.

As an American Arts and Crafts craft ideal migrates from labor schools to an experimental arts college, it comes to inform the work of key Black Mountain figures, including visual artists Josef and Anni Albers and poet Robert Duncan. Each of these figures conceived their pedagogies and creative practices in terms resonant with craft overtones, describing artistic creation as submission to material resistances in the service of a higher prerogative. "Articulation in visual form," Josef Albers called this anti-expressivist ideal. "Meaningful form," his wife Anni termed it. For Duncan, it was "significant craft," a process wherein immediate engagement with the materiality of language manifested in aesthetic form a metaphysical order of creation. While most scholars link Duncan to Black Mountain through his association with rector Charles Olson, I contend in this chapter that Duncan's "significant craft" extends and transforms the objectives of Black Mountain College itself.[72]

Recognizing at the same time that its spiritualized craft ideal was not merely a set of metaphors, I attend too to the Black Mountain work program in farming and construction, a labor initiative central to the aesthetic experience and financial solvency of the college. Steeped in wide-ranging research in the Black Mountain archives, this chapter treats the 1940 construction of the Bauhaus-inspired Studies Building as the literalization of—and as a limit case in—the practical viability of significant craft, the capacity of actual work to open onto a higher, spiritual experience. Black Mountain's work program, I show, prompts us to ask what happens when "significant craft" loses its significance, when work simply does not work.

While previous chapters focus on educational institutions in which the relationship between labor and literature was especially contested, my fourth chapter examines the creative writing "craft book" as a generic institution which mediated between literary producers and an evolving print marketplace. It did so through figurations of writing as work. Whereas fiction craft books frame story and novel writing as forms of fungible labor, poetry craft books insist that poetry itself constitutes more than "mere craftsmanship," that it remains a spiritual expression facilitated by—though irreducible to—technical facility.[73] Balancing the writer's self-expression with fidelity to craft techniques, the poetry craft book gives new discursive life to the American Arts and Crafts craft ideal. In similar fashion, poetry craft books help parse the relationship between nineteenth-century formalism and emergent modernist vernaculars, staking out a kind of genteel or middlebrow aesthetic appealing to a wide range of audiences. As I reveal, however, modernist writers themselves adapted the craft book as a way of advancing their own distinctly avant-garde projects, among them Gertrude Stein's 1931 *How to Write* and Ezra Pound's 1934 *ABC of Reading*.

Though early twentieth-century craft books oppose poetry to the marketplace, poetry comes to look more and more like work—and not particularly spiritual work—as creative writing takes up shop in the postwar university. If craft rhetoric helped consolidate the authority of elite educational institutions, the craft book was instrumental to that process, rewriting the university's professional-managerial ethos as meaningful manual labor. Scholars of the discipline have ignored the economic implications of creative writing craft, but a craft book such as Richard Hugo's 1979 *The Triggering Town* suggests those implications clearly. "Creative writing belongs in the university for the same reason other subjects do," Hugo writes. "[B]ecause people will pay to study them."[74] As I demonstrate, *The Triggering Town* offers a rich diagnostic of the institutional habitus of postwar creative writing, modeling an ambivalence that extends to Hugo's contemporaneous poetry collection, *31 Letters and 13 Dreams*. Poetic craftsmanship may arrogate economic and cultural authority to the university, Hugo argues, but it also allows working-class writers an *entrée* to those professional discourses on which economic success depends.

Finally, a substantive coda gestures to the implications of literary craftsmanship at the first and most prestigious of the postwar programs in creative writing. For the Iowa Writers' Workshop was hardly the first to use that name, and scholars of the program have overlooked the importance of writing craft in facilitating what was, at Iowa, nothing less than an institutional and ideological coup. Specifically, I contend in this coda that creative writing craft provided legitimating language for an insurgent attempt—Irving Babbitt's New Humanism—to transform literary study at the university level and to reconceive the relation between literary study and Western democracy. At Iowa, "workshop" worked double-time, figuring creative writing as a rigorous discipline while disciplining writers toward responsible civic participation. New Humanists like Babbitt, therefore, could be said to prioritize that aspect of an American Arts and Crafts craft ideal which tempered the craftsman's self-expression with rigorous adherence to technical standards; for Babbitt, those standards were supplied not by modernist aesthetics (as they were for John Dos Passos), nor by the resistances of craft material (as they were at Black Mountain), but by an inherited literary tradition and the cultural values that entailed from it.

Perhaps unsurprisingly, the New Humanist craft ideal figures prominently in the work of two poets who studied at Iowa at the height of New Humanist influence there. For Workshop director Paul Engle, disciplined poetic craftsmanship enacts aesthetically, and constitutes a kind of training toward, the self-discipline necessary to maintaining cultural, political, and moral superiority in the Cold War era. Mobilizing New Humanist thought in the service of a postwar liberal consensus, Engle's writing posits a lossless translation from the work of the poet to the work of mental and manual laborers, workers who carry out "the daily acts / Of life in work and word" that underwrite American civilization.[75] Less sanguine about the virtues of poetic and civic discipline, Engle's advisee Margaret Walker examines in her MFA thesis *For My People* how New Humanist thought, including narrowly conceived poetic craft, inhibits the well-being of writers and workers alike, in particular writers and workers of color. If craft discourses rely on the mediation of individual expression—inevitably shaped by, channeled through, and articulated via disciplinary techniques—such discourses necessarily abstract from embodied experience, processes which have major implications for more expressive, identity-based writing.

Workshops of Modernism

As this brief overview indicates, a fourth fundamental claim of this volume is that the invocation of work as a metaphor for literary production significantly informs the theory and practice of American literary modernism. In addition to constructing a distinct genealogy for creative writing, rethinking scholarly assessment of the American Arts and Crafts movement, and emphasizing the economic consequences of MFA-era poetics, this book reassesses American modernism through a labor studies lens, documenting the remarkable variegation within— yet shared craft ethos of—a body of writing traditionally relegated to the margins of modernist studies. Extending the work of scholars like Barbara Foley, Paula Rabinowitz, John Marsh, Christopher Nealon, and Cary Nelson, I make visible in this book how worker-writers crafted a labor modernism later eclipsed by a monolithic high modernist practice.[76] While American literary modernism may have appeared retrospectively as a rarefied retreat from social engagement and mass culture, the writers I examine constitute part of what Joseph Harrington describes as a broader "modernist effort to shift the social form" of early twentieth-century literature, an effort that Lawrence Rainey, in turn, finds materialized through "intervenient institutions that connect works to readerships, or readerships to particular social structures."[77] From Baker's and Dos Passos's experimental stagecraft to Le Sueur's proletarian modernism to Stein's parody of the craft book, the American Arts and Crafts craft ideal supplies the motivating logic for a series of worker-writer initiatives that might also be thought of as workshops of modernism.

Part of a scholarly New Labor History, this book is motivated by Nelson's conviction that literature is "continually articulated and rearticulated in terms of power," a cultural domain "that is constantly being reformed and repositioned."[78] The creative writing workshop is a principal site within which that reformation played out, revealing how major modernist concerns—the relation between aesthetic and political avant-gardes, notions of the artwork as a constructed object, the tactical retreat from and engagement with broader publics—were seen as inextricable from questions of labor and working-class identity. Recovering a richer sense of how modernism was crafted in creative writing workshops, moreover, is key to understanding how those institutions function in the postmodernist era—their influence on a surprisingly postmodernist writer like Hugo, for instance, or their implications for the increasing number of young writers who continue to hone their craft in MFA workshops.

For the MFA industry is a booming one. As of this writing, the creative writing clearinghouse *Poets & Writers* lists 158 graduate MFA programs, 64 low-residency programs, and thousands of residencies and conferences for aspiring writers. The most established of these conferences, the annual meeting of the Association of Writers & Writing Programs (AWP), boasts an attendance exceeding 12,000, with 800 exhibitors marketing their wares in the popular "book fair," itself a throwback to the medieval marketplace. Each year, between 3,000 and 4,000 student-writers graduate from MFA workshops, passing from apprenticeships to master status, their professional credentials—if few job prospects—securely in hand. What's more, with the rise of the creative writing PhD, those masters now face five more years of graduate study in order to compete for academic jobs. Though I am skeptical of such programs, I do not particularly feel the weight of claims that the workshop system separates American literature from a wider public, nor do I share the seemingly widespread conviction that the workshop homogenizes contemporary writing, as my reading of Hugo's work makes clear. Rather, by reconstructing the craft legacy of creative writing, I seek to clarify precisely what we talk about when we talk about workshop—how the institution functions in the postwar university and what, precisely, the nature of its investment in young writers is.

Similarly, while I am sympathetic to the economic challenge levied by the Arts and Crafts movement, my interest in craft is motivated neither by wistfulness for bygone eras nor idealizing notions of manual labor as somehow more authentic than other forms of work. This book is motivated, rather, by future-nostalgia for an age we have not yet labored into existence, an age in which those values associated with craft—engaged labor respective of technique and materials, infused with the spirit of play—might be extended to all labor undertaken by our globalized workforce. That age is not yet our own. In the words of Alain de Botton, "we are now as imaginatively disconnected from the manufacture and distribution of our goods as we are practically in reach of them, a process of alienation which has stripped us of myriad opportunities for wonder, gratitude, and guilt."[79] Our ability to imagine a different age depends on attuning ourselves to discourses of labor and class currently unfashionable among literary scholars. As Sacks argues, most Americans "embrace the prevailing view that class no longer matters much. Race matters. Gender matters. [. . .] But class barely registers in our collective unconscious, the social equivalent of a psychological disorder deeply buried in a patient's history." Le Sueur scholar Constance Coiner echoes Sacks, contending that "[d]espite its place on the now-familiar list of race, gender, class, ethnicity, and sexual orientation, class is often the least addressed of these issues. [. . .] Indeed, few students seem even to *see* class markers."[80] This book, therefore, seeks to restore to visibility economic and cultural practices that function most insidiously precisely when they remain invisible. For "workshop" may designate one class among others in the curriculum, but it also names the ongoing operation of class itself.

Like the plowman's turning at the field's edge, then, this book turns back to previously tended historical terrain in order to cultivate what scholars of American literature have left fallow. "Now the farmer turns / the plow the other way," Virgil writes in the *Georgics*, "and once again / he works the land and gives order / to the fields."[81] This study is an attempt at such order.

Chapter One

The Play's a Thing

The 47 Workshop and the Crafting of Creative Writing

In a letter dated September 1, 1912, drama professor George Pierce Baker recommended the term "workshop" for an experimental course in playwriting he had been planning with former students at Harvard and Radcliffe—the first time that term, now ubiquitous, was used in the context of creative writing pedagogy.[1] "What better place than this," Baker wrote Elizabeth McFadden from the Coole Park home of Lady Gregory, "from which to write you of *The Workshop*, for that is what it seems to me we could call our experiment! 'Experimental Theatre' seems to me too grand."[2]

Baker's letter possesses the force of spontaneity, its author alighting upon "workshop" as if moved, in the aging baronial manor at Coole Park, by some occult Celtic numen. In fact, his adoption of the term represented the culmination of months of intensive labor, Baker having scoured the Continent that summer researching the new stagecraft then sweeping European theaters. In Germany, Baker had seen designer Mariano Fortuny's revolutionary lighting apparatus, as well as innovative *Drehbühne* (revolving stage) and *Schibebühne* (sliding stage) technologies. In London, he documented the use of mechanical devices to subdivide the cramped English stage. Sketching these contraptions and others—mobile screens, an expanding proscenium arch—at the Abbey Theatre in Dublin, Baker added a simple note in his looping, nearly illegible scrawl: "adapt."[3] True to his word, Baker would incorporate much of this stagecraft in the workshop he and his students envisioned: an innovative, technologically advanced dramatic practice, the sophistication of which was belied in the nostalgic tone he adopted for McFadden. "As I write, a soft Irish rain silts down outside," Baker wrote. "[I]n this high room lined with books, Mr. Yeats is answering his mail. [. . .] Lady Gregory has been playing with her grandson, who in his jersey suit of Irish green looks like a gnome. I go on toward Belfast and the Ulster players tomorrow."[4] On such a note, imbued with the elegiac calm of the Twilight, Baker sounded the birth of a new and revolutionary pedagogy, to be called "workshop," that would dramatically reshape the theory and practice of creative writing.

Baker's goals for his own workshop were comparatively modest—namely, to "try out" the plays of Harvard and Radcliffe undergraduates, crafting them into stage productions and "workshopping" those productions for critical audiences.[5] Central to this vision was the concern, shared by Baker and his students alike, that workshop plays distinguish themselves from the "sordid commercial tone" of Broadway, a concern registered clearly in McFadden's appeal to craft rhetoric. In contrast to the formulaic productions of Broadway, the workshopped drama would be a labor of love, fulfilling as an end in itself but fastidiously technical as well in its integration of turn-of-the-century stagecraft. "Equipping [. . .] students with the power to work happily," McFadden wrote from the Hotel Charlesgate in Boston, "and inspiring them with high ideals for their work seems to me to be a greater 'result' than enabling them to put money in their pockets and to drink of the heady wine of Broadway." In her own workshop-by-mail with Baker, McFadden noted likewise that her mentor's encouragement had "changed the work itself from a drudgery" to a "keen delight in accomplishment [. . .] worth while to me from the sheer pleasure of the doing."[6] Conspicuous throughout her decade-long correspondence with Baker, McFadden's craft rhetoric was hardly incidental. The theatrical intervention both she and Baker anticipated necessitated an approach to stagecraft as a total art, a form in which playwright, producer, scenic artist, electrician, and stage mechanic might "labor until the stage is fitted to represent life as the author sees it."[7] Only, Baker believed, through the "total development of the drama as a form" would American audiences learn to appreciate more than Broadway spectacle and cabaret excess.[8] Baker's workshop would thus serve a pedagogical function not only for its members, but for a wider theater-going public whose taste it endeavored to elevate; indeed, by the middle of the century, the well-crafted realist drama would be a dominant mode, one first forged in the experimental crucible that came to be known, after Baker's Harvard course of the same number, as the 47 Workshop.

Like the more famous workshop that succeeded it in Iowa City, key to the influence of the 47 Workshop was the dissemination of its ideals by Workshop acolytes, many of whom went on to found a range of experimental little theaters across the country, among them Eugene O'Neill's Provincetown Players and Agnes Morgan's Neighborhood Playhouse on the Lower East Side.[9] In this chapter, I examine one of those endeavors: the New Playwrights Theater founded by Baker student John Dos Passos. In doing so, I delineate an arc that extends from the American Arts and Crafts movement—of which the 47 Workshop, with its privileging of the well-crafted drama, was a part—through a more radical literary leftism committed not so much to pre-industrial forms of labor as to the writer's work as a technician within an industrial-corporate regime. Reading plays from both writers as self-reflexive treatments of literary craftsmanship, I suggest that despite differences in their ultimate objectives, Baker and Dos Passos adopted the language of craft for similar reasons. In the first place, both found in craft a set of values by which to reposition American drama within its institutional settings—for Baker, the immediate milieu of Harvard University; for both writers, the wider context of Broadway theater. In the second place, both Baker and Dos Passos recognized the craft production of literature as a way to rethink the meaning and ramifications of industrial-corporate labor; while Baker's opposition to industrialism stopped short of his student's early radicalism, he, too, pointedly and repeatedly challenged the priorities of an industrializing economy, cautioning against the surrender of pre-industrial values in a 1930 pageant written for the American Society of Mechanical Engineers (ASME). As craft rhetoric entered institutions of higher education, the workshop itself became a laboring force in American culture.[10]

One critical tenet of this chapter, then, holds that the earliest creative writing workshop, so called, endeavored to produce a non-commercial culture steeped in Arts and Crafts values; though neither Baker nor the 47 Workshop quite harbored revolutionary ambitions, we might understand both as equipping artistic laborers with the tools for reworking regnant cultural formations, in particular by rivaling the sentimental and often shoddily produced mass theater. This chapter therefore challenges interpretations of American anti-modernism that view early twentieth-century craftsmanship as a means of easing workers into new and rationalized modes of labor. In T. J. Jackson Lears's influential reading, craft revivalists "promised not social transformation but therapeutic self-renewal within a corporate structure of degraded work and bureaucratic 'rationality.'"[11] Baker, I argue, promised something else entirely, mobilizing craft lexicons in the service of a genuinely collective and oppositional, if not anti-capitalist, movement. *Pace*

Lears, I offer that not all non-radical culture need count as "accommodation," an overly reductive framework that ignores the nuance within those cultural formations Lears indicts.

A second and more substantial tenet of the chapter is its claim for a distinct genealogy of the discipline of creative writing, a history that begins in a genre since expelled from standard creative writing curricula: the drama. In tracing how Dos Passos's leftist stagecraft evolves from the Arts and Crafts impetus of the 47 Workshop, I reconsider Mark McGurl's contention that creative writing begins in the classrooms of progressive education. McGurl's curious statement that the term "workshop" seems "odd when [. . .] used to describe George Pierce Baker's playwriting classes at pompous old Harvard" is somewhat misleading, the result of a selective history that reads forward into midcentury creative writing programs an aesthetic and institutional complexity that predates them.[12] Neither neutral nor arbitrary, the term "workshop" coordinated a network of conflicting values, signaling as it did so the affiliations of creative writing with an American Arts and Crafts movement to which, in its instantiation as the Society of Arts and Crafts, Boston (SACB), Baker had material and ideological ties. As I demonstrate throughout this book, that movement would play a major role in the conception and institutionalization of creative writing, including in Baker's own creative writing pedagogy.

Most significantly, the 47 Workshop adapted what I term an American Arts and Crafts "craft ideal" which reconciled the craftsman's expressive labor with the kind of technical standards enforced by pre-industrial guilds; as craft ideologues promoted them, such standards worked to discipline or temper the craftsman's expressive impulse. As the SACB journal *Handicraft* described it, craft was rooted in "thorough technical training [and] a just appreciation of standards," yet carried out by "an intelligent man, whose ability is used as a whole, and not subdivided for commercial purposes."[13] For Baker, the self-expression of the playwright was tempered by the workshop's collective stagecraft, as work committees for scenery painting and stage lighting, for instance, ensured the maintenance of rigorous technical standards—on these committees, the playwright became merely one worker among others. "When [the playwright] has assisted in lighting," Baker believed, "he will be less likely to ask the light man to provide the atmosphere and the subtler gradations of feeling which it is his business to provide by his text."[14] Balancing self-expression and technical rigor, and undoing the division between mental and manual labor, the American Arts and Crafts craft ideal in turn reconciled the conflicting values of beauty and utility, fostering within an industrial-corporate regime "the love of good and beautiful work as applied to useful service."[15] In Baker's case, workshop supplied the rhetorical cover to slot aesthetic production into Harvard's increasingly utilitarian curriculum; in doing so, Baker hoped to transform a mass theater industry in which commercial considerations had long entailed the de-privileging of aesthetic standards.

Baker himself was well-connected within that industry. The "father of modern American playwrights," as his obituaries called him, Baker remained throughout his life a close associate of New York theater managers who looked to him for the material techniques and ideological framework—and, of course, the writers—of a new mode of dramatic realism.[16] This chapter documents that work.

The 47 Workshop

"Pulchritudo cum Utilitate": Society of Arts and Crafts, Boston

Throughout what craft historians refer to as the Craftsman period of the 1890s, the Society of Arts and Crafts, Boston (SACB) remained the largest and most active organization in a rapidly expanding American Arts and Crafts movement.[17] A leader in craftsmanship since the Colonial era, Boston was fertile ground for the movement, its adherents drawn from a closely knit network of educators, architects, artists, and idlers that comprised the city's cultural elite. Interlinked by marriage and board memberships, these "craftsmen"—among them Astors, Longfellows, Coolidges, Searses, and Warrens—further sought to parlay their families' economic prosperity into cultural capital, defining standards of beauty and utility and enforcing those standards through a variety of institutional endeavors.[18] This was a Brahmin class, and one with strong ties to Harvard University. Among the Harvard faculty affiliated with SACB were Herbert Langford Warren, dean of the School of Architecture; Denman Waldo Ross, a lecturer on design theory; and professor of fine arts Charles Eliot Norton, the first president of SACB and a close friend of John Ruskin over the last decade of the nineteenth century. Baker's strongest link with SACB was Craftsman member Henry Hunt Clark, a professor at Boston's Museum of Fine Arts School and an expert in staging and set design for the 47 Workshop. It was likely Clark who convinced Baker to seek financing for a theater building among SACB's well-heeled elite. "They have given us our Art Museum," Baker wrote of this group. "Is there no one who by his skill as a leader and organizer [. . .] will establish a theater?"[19]

Heterogeneous in ethos and ambition, SACB endorsed multiple craft initiatives, from manual training programs integrating aesthetic and vocational education to an experimental Handicraft Shop near Boston Common, where, as in

medieval guilds, craftsmen working collaboratively could benefit from one another's technical expertise in lacemaking, silverwork, and other craft practices.[20]
SACB also attempted a quasi-transcendentalist community designed to broaden
"the intelligence of both the farmer who becomes a craftsman and the craftsman
who turns in part farmer." "We would be much interested," a 1910 editorial in
Handicraft implores, "to learn of any instances of the actual working out of this
plan."[21] As the editorial's tone suggests, many of these schemes eventually—or
immediately—failed, a fact which has led critics to read American Arts and Crafts
as a dead-end venture, unable to develop a "truly oppositional culture,"[22] co-opted
by corporate interests and "packaged [. . .] into a consumer proposition,"[23] and
contributing, where it did come to institutional fruition, to a stratified education
system with "different subjects for different classes" of citizen.[24] "What began as a
critique of art and labor under industrial capitalism," Eileen Boris argues, "turned
into a style of art, leisure activities, and personal and social therapy."[25] Common
among these postmortems, which are not entirely inaccurate, is a tendency to
think of institutions like SACB in terms of their opposition *to* and accommodation *of* an evolving industrial-corporate regime, a framework first proposed by T. J.
Jackson Lears in his account of turn-of-the-century anti-modernism. For Lears,
as I have suggested, American Arts and Crafts represented an "accommodationist" platform designed to "fit individuals into [. . .] bureaucratic hierarch[ies]" by
providing a therapeutic outlet for otherwise suppressed creativity; craft ideologues drew back, therefore, from "fundamental social change" or the imaging of
a "truly alternative culture."[26] In what follows, I reconsider such crisp binaries, a
form of hindsight moralism that ignores how "opposition" and "accommodation"
exist almost always—and certainly in the case of SACB—as mutually constitutive
processes.

For among the lasting contributions of the American Arts and Crafts movement was its maintenance of a craft ideal which held self-expressive craftsmanship to rigorously technical standards. Such an ideal sought to integrate, in other
words, what Thorstein Veblen called the "instinct for idle curiosity" with the
"instinct of workmanship," the latter a "proclivity for taking pains" that served to
discipline the artist's expressive impulse.[27] First SACB president Arthur A. Carey
articulated this craft ideal in an address to SACB members in November of 1901.
While encouraging craftsmen to "execute designs of their own" and to cultivate
"imaginative pleasure" in their work, Carey at the same time sought "to counteract the popular impatience of law and form and the desire for over-ornamentation
and specious originality." SACB, Carey maintained, should "insist upon the ne-

cessity of sobriety and restraint, of ordered arrangement, of due regard for the relation between the form of an object and its use."[28] This synthesis of self-expression
and technical rigor is further suggested in SACB procedures for evaluating—in
juried exhibitions, live demonstrations, and gallery shows—the adherence of craft
objects to standards of beauty and utility. While judges attended meticulously to
basic design elements—shape, line, color, balance, scale, and intensity—they also
employed linguistic metaphors as a way of assessing a work's "expression," prizing
unstudied or "vernacular" work, as one nineteenth-century critic put it, over objects viewed as "affected," "pretentious," or "strained," all terms original to SACB
judges.[29] Effective craft, Lewis Day wrote, entailed "the translation of natural
[. . .] form, not merely into the language of art, but into the dialect of some particular handicraft. We detect in it the homely accent of sincere workmanship."[30]
In detecting this accent, SACB judges insisted that all exhibition productions
carry the name of their maker, often inquiring as to how craftsmen conceptual-
ized their products and what they sought to express in them. It was this craft ideal
that Baker translated into the operation and objectives of the 47 Workshop, where
the expression of the playwright was shaped and honed by workshop critics who
doubled as stagehands, set managers, and costume makers. Just as workers in the
SACB Handicraft Shop worked collaboratively on the chasing of silver tea ser-
vices, 47 Workshop members labored over proper lighting techniques—frosted or
bare bulbs, spot or floor angling—and how most effectively to block actors with
respect to their illumination.[31]

Equally integral to Baker's pedagogy was the reconciliation, in SACB terms, of
"Beauty with Usefulness"—specifically, his effort to adjust aesthetic production
to the imperatives of an increasingly utilitarian or professionalizing system of
higher education. More than simply a "Boston society shibboleth," as Lears holds,
the reconciliation of beauty and utility constituted SACB's most prominent form
of opposition to industrialization, its standards disseminated nationwide as part
of the organization's work to elevate public taste in Boston and beyond.[32] As craft
ideologues analyzed the way craft objects functioned, parsed the materials they
were made from, and discerned the manner of their construction, they viewed
their mission as itself a pedagogical gambit, laying a foundation for economic reorganization by re-educating the American public. These critics utilized an array
of national journals like *Handicraft* and Gustav Stickley's *The Craftsman*, as well as
public workshops and outreach programs, to teach consumers to demand greater
refinement from the products they purchased, advocating a product's handcrafted
beauty, as well as its price, as indication of its utility. And while that term, "utility,"

had accrued a wide variety of meanings by the late nineteenth century—from designating anything with beneficial consequences to connoting short- and long-term commercial success—craft adherents also repurposed the word to include the hand-manufacture of objects and the maintenance of a salutary lifestyle. Among its other accomplishments, American Arts and Crafts wrested "utility" from its commercial and industrial connotations. The official seal of SACB testifies to its anti-industrial impetus, the phrase "Pulchritudo cum Utilitate" forged in Gothic letters below a designer's calipers, a claw hammer, an architect's pen, and an artist's brushes and palette—here in miniature was Baker's stagecraft, a unity of the expressive arts held to rigorous technical standards.

To be sure, the American Arts and Crafts movement was at least partly animated by nostalgic ideology, one never "fully linked to a Progressive politics," as Wendy Kaplan diagnoses.[33] But its effort to integrate expression and technique into a craft ideal—as well as its commitment to the reconciliation of beauty and utility—constituted meaningful if non-radical opposition to the degraded quality of life under an industrial-corporate regime. Such a movement paved the way, moreover, for more political modernisms of the 1920s and '30s—including Dos Passos's literary leftism and the experimentation of Black Mountain College, both taken up in this book—and defined clear and consequential parameters of aesthetic production for the institutions within which those modernisms were crafted. Baker's 47 Workshop was one such institution, its invocation of that term signaling its affiliation with Arts and Crafts ideology while simultaneously providing the rhetorical cover with which, at Harvard, to legitimate the study and production of the drama.

"Pompous old Harvard"

"Whatever new courses in the drama you may teach, George, it is for your work in argumentation that Harvard pays you."[34]

So spoke Harvard president Charles W. Eliot to Baker in 1900, when the latter had first introduced a course in drama that twelve years later would become the 47 Workshop. Eliot's statement unequivocally indicates the values of the university he sought to transform, prizing as he did the work in logic, rhetoric, and argumentation that had made Baker a guru-figure of sorts among turn-of-the-century businessmen. Baker's *Principles of Argumentation*, a handbook of persuasion devoured by the nation's corporate elite, had single-handedly won Baker promotion to assistant professor in 1895. Though Baker was married to Eliot's niece, the two would maintain an uneasy alliance throughout their time at Harvard, with Baker perpetually weathering his superior's efforts to divert his dramatic investments along more profitable lines. Eliot's comments are indicative, too, of the difficulty Baker would face in adapting a course in dramatic production—English 47 and its attached Workshop—to Harvard's utilitarian elective system; as Baker keenly perceived, such a system significantly imperiled the role of the arts in higher education.

In employing a craft lexicon as what I have called "rhetorical cover," Baker was responding to a broader utilitarian movement that had been gaining influence in American education since the end of the Civil War. "Almost every visible change" during this period, writes Laurence Veysey, "lay in the direction of concessions to the utilitarian type of demand for reform."[35] The elective system was only the most iconic of these concessions, which included at Harvard the creation of an official graduate school, expansion of the faculty in newer, more professional disciplines, and subdivision of the responsibilities of the president into dozens of specialized offices, precursor to the byzantine administrations of our own era. In theory, of course—and as its reputation leads one to believe—the elective system constituted a liberalizing force in higher education, empowering students with greater agency over their learning and loosening the grip of so-called "classical" pedagogy. Indeed, by the time Eliot's reforms were implemented fully in 1899, the sole mandatory requirements at Harvard consisted of freshman English and a course in either French or German which, in the administrative jargon of the era, could be anticipated at the preparatory level.[36] That we imagine, however, that such changes led to the flourishing of ceramics courses—or to doe-eyed bohemians reading Rousseau or conservatories of aspiring Schoenbergs—testifies to how shrewdly Eliot peddled the elective system as fostering "the natural bent and peculiar quality of every boy's mind," trumpeting "the happiness of the individual" as "sacredly regarded in his education."[37]

Nominally promoting individual freedom, in practice the elective system subordinated that freedom to the needs of an industrializing nation, de-emphasizing a well-rounded education—a phrase Eliot loathed—in favor of professional-managerialism. "In his freedom," writes Veysey, "the student was supposed to become a trained expert in some special field," with emphasis given to newer disciplines in engineering and the applied sciences.[38] Eliot himself was fond of metaphorizing these transformations. "To reason about the average human mind as if it were a globe, to be expanded symmetrically from a center outward, is to be betrayed by a metaphor," he wrote in 1869, the year of his inauguration. "A cutting-tool, a drill, or auger would be a juster symbol of the mind."[39] The imagery is telling of the ultimate values behind what Eliot called "the new education." Geared toward professional specialization rather than humanist breadth, such a curriculum was intended to produce those well-trained experts on whom, according to social efficiency adepts like Veblen, an evolving industrial-corporate regime would depend. Industrialization, Veblen wrote, inherently "lends itself to systematic control under the direction of industrial experts, skilled technologists, who may be called 'production engineers,' for want of a better term."[40] Time and again, Eliot's comments betray his subordination of liberal to utilitarian imperatives. "[T]o make a good engineer, chemist, or architect," he wrote, "the only sure way is to make first [. . .] an observant, reflecting, and sensible man, whose mind is not only well-stored, but well-trained also to see, compare, reason, and decide."[41] Even the practice of creative writing at Harvard, an occasional pursuit in advanced composition courses, prioritized professional forms like the newspaper article, the magazine feature, and the technical memo.[42] In his inaugural address, Eliot waxed poetic about the potential of this new education, declaring that "when millions are to be fed [. . .] the single fish-line must be replaced by seines and trawls, the human shoulders by steam-elevators."[43] One professor at New York University put it even more succinctly—"[t]he college has ceased to be a cloister and has become a workshop."[44]

Baker felt the deleterious effects of this utilitarian impetus quite sharply. As I have suggested, he rightly perceived that his work in the drama was considered "second best," as Eliot put it, in comparison with more profitable endeavors, and his 1905 proposal for a course in dramatic technique was initially rejected by one faculty member as an "absurd interpretation of the elective idea."[45] Only when Baker rebranded the course as a response to growing demand for professional training in the drama—and only when he'd adopted the craft rhetoric implicit in "workshop"—was his proposal finally accepted; his pedagogy was not, as Baker once again stressed, the avant-garde insurrection of "experimental theater," but serious labor in the useful and remunerative discipline of stagecraft. Due to lecture at the Sorbonne the following year, Baker would offer English 47: The Technique of the Drama for the first time in 1908–1909, the year of Eliot's retirement. While his decades-long pursuit of a theater building would never prove successful, Baker found greater encouragement for his dramatic work under Eliot's successor, A. Lawrence Lowell. Rolling back many of Eliot's more utilitarian reforms, Lowell declared at his own inauguration that "the college ought to produce not defective specialists, but men intellectual and well-rounded, of wide sympathies and unfettered judgment."[46] Eliot, no doubt, was appalled.

While a scholar like Gerald Graff argues, then, that the turn-of-the-century conflict between liberal and vocational education—between beauty and utility, we might say—failed to find "visible institutional expression," that conflict was expressed in many forms, among them a craft rhetoric and practice, called "workshop," which mediated between aesthetic production and the utilitarian impetus of the new education.[47] Tracing creative writing to "pompous old Harvard" in 1912, and to Baker's redeployment of American Arts and Crafts ideology, reveals an essentially anti-expressive ethos at the very foundations of the discipline—one predicated, we have come to believe, on the writer's self-expression.

THE PLAY'S A THING: THE 47 WORKSHOP

On the evening of Thursday, January 23, 1913, the 47 Workshop staged its first production at Agassiz House, Radcliffe College, an otherwise unremarkable three-act play written and produced by W. Fennimore Merrill, another of Baker's former students. Titled *Lina Amuses Herself* (figure 1), the play was rudimentary in comparison with later workshop productions, its single largest expenses running to $14.00 for flowers, $8.36 for construction of the stage, and $3.28 for unspecified "damages from flashlight."[48]

Despite its humble beginning, the 47 Workshop would dramatically reshape American theater, providing a crucible within which the realist, psychologically insightful drama would first be forged. Indeed, when the 47 Workshop closed shop in 1924, a "literary awakening" had taken root among American audiences akin, according to Wisner Payne Kinne, to the nineteenth-century development of the novel.[49] Other critics, too, have understood the revolution in American drama with reference to nineteenth-century fiction, noting that the emphasis on characterization in Henry James, for instance, contributed to the illumination of psychology and social forces under dramatic realism. Characters in the drama, summarizes Gerald Berkowitz, "were affected by the world they inhabited."[50] If the idea seems basic, fundamental to American drama as a whole, its obviousness is a testament to how successful Baker's effort was to elevate public taste through education, a mission he shared with American Arts and Crafts initiatives like SACB. By the time Baker decamped for Yale in the fall of 1926, the 47 Workshop had become a household name, lauded in venues as diverse as *Science*, the *Saturday Evening Post*, and *New Masses*. Baker "has raised to the level of the other arts an art that was considered unworthy of college or university attention when he

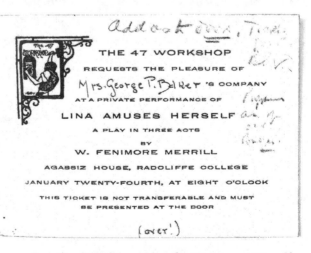

Figure 1. Top: Opening day program for *Lina Amuses Herself*, the first production of the 47 Workshop, January 23, 1913. Bottom: Invitation to *Lina Amuses Herself* for Mrs. George P. Baker. *Courtesy of the Houghton Library, Harvard University.*

started," Jackson Gardner wrote in the *Boston Daily Globe*. "He has made the production of plays a study just as significant in modern life as is the study of poetry, of painting," Gardner went on, "yes, just as significant as the study of business or industrial engineering."[51] The Workshop had done its work.

Just as it reconciled aesthetic production to utilitarian education, the 47 Workshop mediated between Harvard playwrights and an American entertainment industry that had long privileged commercial success over aesthetic integrity. Major blockbusters from the 1910s, for example, included George M. Cohan's farcical melodrama *Seven Keys to Baldpate* (1913) and Irving Berlin's *Watch Your Step* (1914), the latter adapting Verdi into syncopated dance-tunes. As these works suggest, Broadway plays from this period tended toward melodrama, light sentimentalism packaged in familiar, economically safe formulas. Built to facilitate the early twentieth-century star system, Broadway drama reinforced the era's belief in upward mobility, an escapism cultivated in a dazzling array of nickelodeons, chorus lines, folies, and cabaret shows at venues like Rector's and Murray's Roman Gardens.[52] Moreover, the theater faced serious competition from a booming film industry that offered consumers cheaper and more accessible mass entertainment. Baker opposed these modes, but he did not ignore them. What Baker valued in such fare, rather, was its ability to "amuse and entertain," what he called—in a slightly different sense than I have used the term—its "utilitarian" function. In unpublished lecture notes, Baker distinguishes between the "utilitarian" and "ethical" functions of the American drama, counterposing to its entertainment value the genre's ability to employ "situation, dialogue, character not as ends in themselves, but as means of inculcating a thesis." For Baker, both functions were integral to successful drama. Only by synthesizing "the technique and the artistic self-respect of the Ethical School," he wrote, with "the understanding of audiences that belongs to the Utilitarian, can lasting and great drama come."[53] Baker's dramaturgy, in other words, functioned as a kind of "stretching device," plying dramatic form until it simply contained and expressed more than conventional drama.[54]

The mode resulting from such stretching was dramatic realism, the psychological depth and social complexity of which necessitated "almost perfect technique" and promoted, therefore, the "total development of the drama as a form." More than mere truckling to one's audience (to use Baker's term) or didactic politicizing, dramatic realism entailed a well-crafted drama that included attention to scenery, music, stage mechanics, costumes, lighting, writing, directing, and even ushering. While Broadway stages had consisted of either extravagant spectacles or simple backdrops for larger-than-life stars, the realist stage would assume a defining power in service of what Baker called "the just representation of life."[55] In their excellent history of interbellum American drama, Jordan Miller and Winifred Frazer detail one example of how dramatic realism was facilitated by and necessitated an innovative new stagecraft. They are worth quoting at length in order to demonstrate how crucial a craft like lighting became to the realist mode. "Now," they write, "the stage technician could produce startling realistic illusions. [W]hile darkening the auditorium was not unknown with the gas, electric lighting could instantly place the house in total darkness; as a result, the actors abandoned the custom of playing outward to a visible audience and turned inward to each other on the fully illuminated stage. The movement and stance of their characters became more natural, more representational [. . .]"[56] Baker knew well the dramatic potential of lighting techniques. When he first wrote to McFadden of "*The Workshop*," he had recently completed a tour of European theaters where lighting and electrical innovations had been dazzling audiences for several years. And Baker himself had experimented in the simulation of natural light with Mariano Fortuny's revolutionary cyclorama dome; mounted behind the stage, Fortuny's dome gave the illusion of an expansive sky on which the stage artist, by painting a system of reflective mirrors, could simulate clouds, rainfall, and even eclipses. "We still think too much in terms of candles and gas," Baker wrote in 1925. "The university theatre should not only train young electricians to lighting as real, as delicate, as suggestive as possible, but should abet them in all desired technical and imaginative experiments. Many an electrician thinks technically in watts and amperes, but not in terms of the imagination. Others riot in imagination, but are not properly based technically. Here, as elsewhere in the theatre, the leap inspired by imagination should be taken from a sure footing in technique."[57] Yoking inspiration and imagination—terms redolent of self-expression—to the discipline of stage technique, Baker's comments point once more to the affinities of the 47 Workshop with Arts and Crafts ideology, a value system that understood craft as the dynamic imbrication of expressive labor and technical standards. If the expressiveness of dramatic realism necessitated a revolutionary stagecraft, it was that stagecraft, Baker implies, that made dramatic realism possible in the first place—on the stage as elsewhere, form had become indissolubly bonded to content.

In its attention to the aesthetic possibilities unique to dramatic form, the 47 Workshop might seem to anticipate what Clement Greenberg, after Gotthold Ephraim Lessing, would famously term modernist "medium specificity," the idea that "to restore the identity of an art object the opacity of its medium must be emphasized."[58] Somewhat paradoxically, though, Baker found that "the special-ization of the time had come even into the drama" most noticeably in the genre's incorporation of virtually every other art form—its maintenance, as he put it, of "the long-established relationship" between music, dance, poetry, painting, and architecture, as well as among mechanical arts like lighting and sound engineer-ing.[59] This integrative art was not merely a response to the dictates of dramatic realism, however. It was also the practical extension of Baker's courses in the history and technique of the drama, including a course on Shakespeare attend-ing to Inigo Jones's stage architecture, the Elizabethan printing industry, the ge-ography of London and its environs, curtain technologies, royal patronage, and the psychology of English as opposed to Continental audiences. Key to Shakespeare's mastery of the early modern drama, Baker taught, was his command of cutting-edge stagecraft. The powerful structural irony at the beginning of act 3, scene 2 in *Romeo and Juliet*, for instance—when Juliet, unaware that Romeo has been banished, declares that she will "cut him out in little stars," so firm is her love—is enhanced by concealing Juliet's bedchamber behind the curtains of the inner stage, immediately opened after Romeo's banishment.[60] As he understood it, Baker's work was to teach stagecraft through attention to space, sound, color, light, and shadow, properties as meaningful as the play's text itself. "I would like to know more about lighting," one student wrote to Baker, "for I can see that it has *body* as well as spirit and must be reckoned with as *material* the same as any other plot substance."[61]

In this light, Baker's dramaturgy looks less like modernist medium specificity than like Wagnerian *Gesamtkunstwerk*, that "total work of art" in which all other modes found their apotheosis. "The highest conjoint work of art is the *Drama*," Richard Wagner had written in 1849, explaining that drama "can only be at hand in all its *possible* fullness when, in it, each *separate branch of art* is at hand in *its own utmost fullness*."[62] For Wagner, whose work Baker knew and admired, that fullness had only ever existed in the amphitheaters of ancient Greece, where choral, architectural, poetic, and rhythmic artists brought forth together an "ideal expression" that managed at the same time to sublimate those arts within "the only rule- and purpose-giver, the Dramatic Action."[63] Absent from the world stage since Aeschylus, the *Gesamtkunstwerk* had fallen victim, Wagner held, to precisely that medium specificity Greenberg would identify: the arts "unlinked from the united chain" until contemporary drama became one more "industrial undertak-ing" of men "who have yesterday conducted a speculation in grain and tomorrow [. . .] a 'corner' in sugar."[64] There is much of Wagner in Baker's dramaturgy, from the craft-like disciplining of the expressive arts to the barbed objection to commercial theater, to Wagner's mandate that "the *Scene* has firstly to comply with all the conditions of 'space' imposed by the joint dramatic action." At the same time, Wagner wrote, "it has to fulfill those conditions in the sense of bringing this dramatic action to the eye and ear of the spectator in intelligible fashion. In the arrangement of the *space for the spectators*, the need for optic and acoustic understanding of the artwork will give the necessary law, which can only be observed by a union of beauty and fitness in the proportions."[65] This was Wagner in 1849—but this was also, almost verbatim, Baker's work six decades later, whose stagecraft, employed in the service of the realistic drama, could be said to be "medium-specific" only insofar as its medium included virtually every other.

The organization and operation of the 47 Workshop, accordingly, reflected its commitment to drama as a total art. Indeed, later creative writing craft—with techniques focused on structure, sound, movement, texture, and tone—might be considered abstractions of or formal metaphors for material practices first institutionalized in Baker's workshop. Workshop plays were written, in most cases, by individual playwrights in English 47, itself a workshop-style course based on reading, critiquing, and revising student plays, and which met, Kinne reports, "around a large round table that soon became a symbol of the course"—and of every workshop since.[66] Once Baker selected it for staging, a play passed to set designers in the 47 Workshop proper, among whom a competition was held to determine the overall aesthetic of the staged production; as part of this competition, designers were required to submit sketches, models with costumed figurines, and even architectural schematics for lighting and stage backgrounds. Soon after, the play would be distributed to the producer for rehearsals, its schematics doled out to electricians, properties managers, and carpenters "to be made up out of stock," Baker wrote, or—in rare cases when the Workshop's vaults proved wanting—"to be newly built." These groups represented merely a fraction, however, of what the Workshop's constitution called its "Artistic Workers"—dozens of students, alumni, Boston citizens, and drama aficionados organized into work committees, with assignments ranging from acting and shifting scenery to subscribing, prompting, and makeup (figure 2).[67]

For Baker, as for later creative writing pedagogues, the collective technical standards enforced by these committees served as a check on the playwright's expressive ego. "In thinking that any part of the labor that goes to the making of his finished product is beneath him," Baker wrote, "[the playwright] impairs the

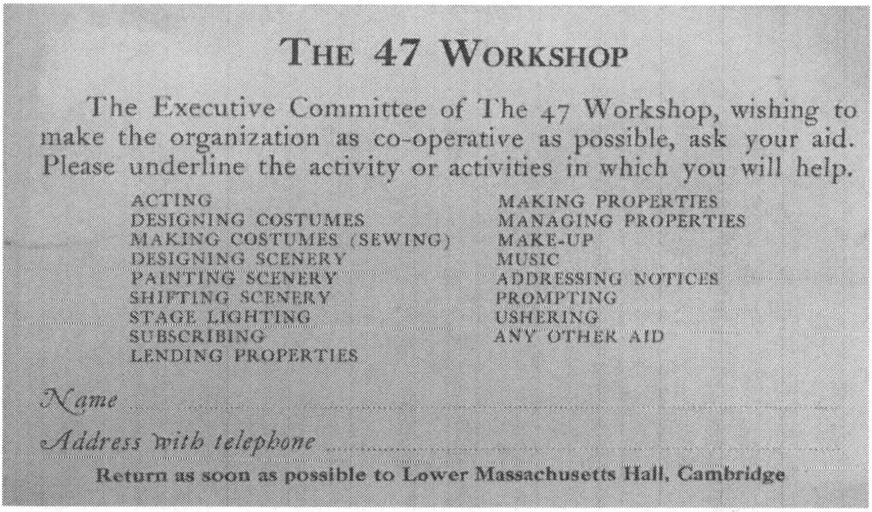

THE 47 WORKSHOP

The Executive Committee of The 47 Workshop, wishing to make the organization as co-operative as possible, ask your aid. Please underline the activity or activities in which you will help.

ACTING
DESIGNING COSTUMES
MAKING COSTUMES (SEWING)
DESIGNING SCENERY
PAINTING SCENERY
SHIFTING SCENERY
STAGE LIGHTING
SUBSCRIBING
LENDING PROPERTIES

MAKING PROPERTIES
MANAGING PROPERTIES
MAKE-UP
MUSIC
ADDRESSING NOTICES
PROMPTING
USHERING
ANY OTHER AID

Name

Address with telephone

Return as soon as possible to Lower Massachusetts Hall, Cambridge

Figure 2. 47 Workshop work committees. *Courtesy of the Houghton Library, Harvard University.*

value of his work. The genuine artist will have learned his craft or crafts as well as his art."[68] A signet that adorned the Workshop's programs symbolized the collaborative nature of these practices: four masked Pierrots representing author, actor, artist, and audience.[69] Such emblems would have been familiar to craft ideologues, who since William Morris had deployed similar logos, crests, and insignias as a way of signaling inclusion in the closed guild of the craft workshop.

For Baker, the workshopping of plays for critical audiences was integral to the maintenance of stagecraft standards, an effort, like SACB's juried exhibitions and like guild specifications before them, to present to the public and to Broadway managers only the most well-crafted of Harvard dramas. Beginning in 1915, archival records include extensive applications for Workshop membership, in particular statements of interest and experience in drama as well as letters of recommendation embossed with the letterheads of Boston's elite. These applications suggest the popularity of the 47 Workshop within those same circles that constituted the membership of SACB. "I am trying to move heaven and earth to get two tickets to the 47 Workshop play for this week," a Mrs. Walter B. Kahn wrote to Baker in 1921, "and I have been told that to achieve this stupendous result you are the only person to turn to." With regrets, Baker declined.[70] For those who passed muster, however, Workshop staffers kept meticulous attendance records, noting the number of complimentary tickets actually used and issuing warnings to audience members with unexcused absences or outstanding critiques. "The Executive Committee respectfully reminds you that membership in the 47 Workshop involves [. . .] a written criticism of every performance attended," the standardized admonishment read (figure 3, top). "None has been received from you this season. [. . .] Will you not cooperate?"[71] When one audience member failed to show, he mailed a handwritten note explaining that he'd suffered a flat tire on the way to the performance. "It is only honest to tell you that I came to the Workshop in a shameful way," he wrote (figure 3, bottom). "I am afflicted with a Ford."[72]

The exchange neatly allegorizes the way craft production was threatened by an evolving industrial-corporate regime, but it also demonstrates that it was serious work to workshop those plays that made it on stage. Audience members were required to hand in written comments—ranging in length from cursory note cards to multiple-page essays, and in tone from adulatory to withering—within a week of viewing any given play; while these critiques were signed "as a guarantee of good faith," Baker frequently removed the signatures before passing them on to individual playwrights.[73] Workshop audiences adhered to meticulous rules as well, regarding everything from their applause to their wardrobe—"no evening dress," Baker stipulated, no flowers across the footlights—so that even casual observers showed up, we might say, in the costumes of workers.[74] A century before the phrase would take off among early modern materialist scholars, Baker emphasized repeatedly that "the play's the thing," and every aspect of the 47 Workshop experience was oriented toward the optimal crafting of that thing.

Like the proto-industrial workshop to precede it, therefore, and like an American Arts and Crafts movement which hearkened back to it, the 47 Workshop was a transitional institution, adjusting liberal to utilitarian education, mediating between Harvard and Broadway, and, by fusing self-expression with fastidious stagecraft standards, preserving the craft ideal within an industrial-corporate economy. Also like its historical predecessor, the 47 Workshop provided a site within which, as sociologist Richard Sennett describes, "to face or duck issues of authority and autonomy," subordinating the artist's autonomy not to the authority of a master, but to a collective.[75] For Sennett, medieval and pre-industrial craft fostered an "engaged material consciousness," precisely the ethos Baker's dramaturgy cultivated in reminding students, for example, that light contained both spirit and body.[76] These affinities between the 47 Workshop and its namesake are succinctly suggested in the insignia printed on Workshop letterhead (figure 4). Within the frame of a cast-iron bracket adorned with Art Nouveau scrollwork, a hooded

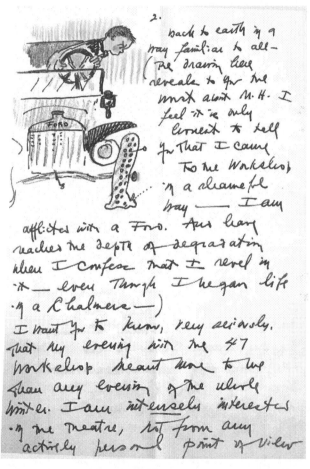

Figure 3. Top: Standardized note of warning to delinquent
members of the 47 Workshop. Bottom: "I came to the
Workshop in a shameful way—I am afflicted with a Ford."
Courtesy of the Houghton Library, Harvard University.

Figure 4. 47 Workshop letterhead. *Courtesy of the Houghton Library, Harvard University.*

medieval engraver wields a hammer and chisel. Hammer raised nearly outside the frame, the engraver holds chisel to stone, his torso swollen, bicep flexed. This worker, forever anonymous, is dressed in the apron of his labor. He is ready to craft.

Control

Setting the Stage: Pageantry, Baker, and the ASME

Though realist drama had proven the main beneficiary of Baker's work, it was the pageant form, more than any other, that captivated him as an opportunity to achieve the "total development of the drama," making up in technical sophistication what it lacked in psychological insight.

An effort to revitalize drama as a popular form distinct from commercial entertainment, pageantry had been inspired by the British Arts and Crafts movement under John Ruskin, who in 1882 had called for a revival of the medieval mystery pageant and early modern masque as vehicles for pre-industrial values. In the United States, pageantry became wildly popular between 1905 and 1925, the genre embodying an anti-modern impetus both in its form and mode of production and in its frequent depiction of a halcyon age of craft labor and religious conviction, characteristically realized through scenes of medieval Europe and the colonial United States.[77] Employed not only by anti-moderns and artistic innovators but by civic leaders, social workers, political activists, and educational reformers, pageantry was viewed as a vital form of participatory democracy, one uniquely suited for breaking down barriers of race and class and, like the Abbey Theatre and Bayreuth opera festivals, for the promotion of civic identity.

Like the theorists and practitioners of American Arts and Crafts, moreover, pageant enthusiasts held the genre to rigorous technical standards, organizing the American Pageant Association in 1913 in order to enforce "professional expertise" in the pageant's cutting-edge stagecraft.[78] Baker's own 1921 pageant depicting the Pilgrims' landing at Plymouth Rock had featured massive chorus ensembles, a parade of historical floats, and even a reconstructed *Mayflower* in Plymouth Harbor, all lit with the "most sensitive and flexible electrical equipment that has ever been used for a dramatic performance out-of-doors." Writing in *The New Republic*, Oliver Sayler raved over the lighting in *The Pilgrim Spirit*, noting that the pageant "saves the intimate scenes from the disaster which usually befalls them by cutting out of the night a small and sharply outlined rectangle of brilliance, for the world and all like a prison cell or a ship's cabin"; the pageant's lighting technician, Sayler went on, "belongs to that rare type, the engineer who is also [an] artist."[79] As a genre, the pageant's total stagecraft—especially evident in Baker's pageantry, but also, for instance, in the famous *Paterson Strike Pageant* of 1913—facilitated its characteristic integration of myth, fable, pastoral, and history in a kind of social allegory, its technical possibilities making it an important platform for a wide variety of early twentieth-century social reforms.

It was the success of *The Pilgrim Spirit*, with crowds overflowing the ocean-front grandstands and 50-cent seats selling for $10 apiece, that drew the attention of the American Society of Mechanical Engineers, which approached Baker in early 1929 to write and direct a pageant celebrating the organization's fiftieth anniversary.[80] Baker's association with the ASME seems curious, perhaps, given his earlier ties with SACB and given the former organization's interest in mass production and industrialization. Led by the era's most prolific technical innovators, the ASME consisted of precisely those "professional scientifically trained mind[s]," as its official history describes them, produced by an ever more utilitarian education system, and like that system, the ASME instilled in its members the "qualities of leadership in the processes of production, so that the engineer is often also a business man."[81] Moreover, in bringing together "designers and managers of the producing machine shop" with "engineers of production [in] factories and power plants," the organization helped reengineer the workshop in the image of the industrial manufactory, serving as a key site for the expropriation of craft epistemologies.[82] Baker had wandered far, it may seem, from an American Arts and Crafts movement dedicated to anti-modernism and to the "intelligent man, whose ability is used as a whole, and not subdivided for commercial purposes."[83]

Yet if the specifications enforced by the ASME, regulating everything from plumbing fixtures to power plant systems, contributed to the growing influence of an elite professional-managerial class, they also represented an effort to maintain technical, craft-like standards within an industrial-corporate regime. That effort, undertaken alongside post-bellum industrialization, had been a response to ubiquitous mechanical failures in the second half of the nineteenth century, rampant among modern equipment powered by steam pressure. Enforcement of technical standards seemed especially urgent in the wake of the 1905 disaster at the Grover Shoe Factory in Brockton, Massachusetts, where, on the morning of March 20, a boiler exploded in the factory's basement, rocketing upward through three floors and killing 58 people in the ensuing conflagration. Widely covered in national newspapers, the disaster prompted the ASME to develop a "Boiler & Pressure Vessel Code" regulating the production and maintenance of steam-pressurized equipment, legislation that was later incorporated into US law.[84] Baker might, therefore, have recognized in the ASME an attempt to translate into an industrial context that aspect of a craft ideal which emphasized workers' fastidious adherence to technical standards—and Baker himself had long held his students to precisely those standards.

Regardless of his feelings toward the ASME, Baker relished the opportunity—and certainly the financial backing—to further realize the possibilities of dramatic form. Titled *Control*, his pageant was staged at the Stevens Institute of Technology (SIT) in Hoboken the weekend of April 5, 1930, and tracked the development of the ASME from its founding in 1880 through the present moment in mechanical engineering. In doing so, it warned against the perils of industrialization and urged the reconciliation, through craft standards, of beauty and utility. For the most elaborate production of his career, Baker returned to an idea that had been his life's work—namely, that the well-crafted drama offered a way to rethink the meaning and ramifications of labor in an industrial context, specifically by modeling in aesthetic form more engaged, socially responsible work. To recall Lears's terminology, *Control* reads as "accommodationist" and "oppositional" at once, its complexity betraying the limitations of such a framework and asking us, in place of moralistic evaluation, to hold both possibilities in mind simultaneously. *Control* itself deftly negotiates these possibilities, making it an important, if not obvious, text in American anti-modernism.

Control

As reported by *Science* in its coverage leading up to and succeeding the ASME's fiftieth anniversary, *Control* was to serve as the culmination of a weekend of activities that opened with a toast from Charles Schwab at the Roosevelt Hotel in New York and concluded three days later at the Chamber of Commerce in Washington, DC, no small engineering feat in its own right.[85] Baker himself had decamped for Yale four years earlier, after that institution had agreed to build the theater so long denied him at Harvard, complete with a carpenter shop, a paint studio, a sewing room, and electricians' gantries. The production crew for *Control*, therefore, came almost entirely from Yale's Department of Drama, including lighting technician Stanley R. McCandless and visionary design student-turned-professor Frank Poole Bevan as costume designer.

Demonstrating humanity's increasing control over the natural environment, the pageant is composed of a series of vignettes drawn from pivotal moments in the history of engineering, from James Watt's creation of the steam engine to George Stephenson's floating of a railroad across Chat Moss. One vignette, detailing the invention of electric light, takes up the life of Thomas Edison at precisely the moment he manages to balance the distribution of electricity across a city block—to control bodily, Baker might say, the spirit of illumination. "Hey! Look at the rest of the street," a bystander shouts in wonder. "[A]ll up and down it is lighted just the same!" And Edison, in language that might have been pulled from 47 Workshop notes, explains that while the "best incandescent lamp requires 138 foot-pounds of energy per second," his own "new light requires but 39.6 foot-pounds," describing luminous expression in terms of its technical standards.[86] These historical vignettes come nested within an overarching *bildungsroman* revolving around the figure of Control, one of four allegorical characters—the others being Conversion, Intelligence, and Imagination—whose coming-of-age represents broader civilizational development. It is Control, as his name suggests, who provides the narration linking the pageant's multiple vignettes, relating, for example, that "within a year George Stephenson, the man whose motto was 'Persevere,' got a bill through Parliament [and] successfully drove across Chat Moss his engine, the Rocket." Its dialogue pulled from historical records, *Control* thus functions as an origin story for that early twentieth-century professional turned out in increasing numbers by American universities, a Veblenesque expert who had become, as Mature Control declares near the pageant's conclusion, "a controlling force" in American culture.[87] At the same time, Mature Control makes explicit the pageant's most prominent theme, reminding the audience of engineers that "ever with use and power Beauty comes"—by now a familiar refrain.[88]

As with dramatic realism, the pageant's historical material required an approach to drama as a total art, one drawing significantly on the new stagecraft that was just beginning, owing to Baker's efforts, to take root in the American theater. "Obviously," Baker wrote in a preface to the pageant's typescript, "much of the material [illustrating] the remarkable development of mechanical engineering in the past fifty years, and the growing sense in such work that beauty may and must be combined with utility and power, have demanded the use of the motion picture instead of tableaux." Moreover, as the pageant celebrated the increasing influence of the mechanical engineer, "it has seemed wiser to do without a band or orchestra, and to substitute electrical reproduction."[89] In its very form, and like Wagner's *Gesamtkunstwerk*, *Control* enacts the celebration of technological innovation that is its subject, incorporating film sequences, dramatic lighting effects, music from Antonín Dvořák's *New World Symphony* and Felix Mendelssohn's *A Midsummer Night's Dream*, a "march of the schools" with standard-bearers from 26 universities, and Bevan's sumptuous costume design, at once classic and futuristic. The allegorical figure of Conversion (figure 5), for instance, one of Bevan's most compelling costumes, is rendered with the pageant's characteristic angularity; dressed in toga-like robes and a headdress reminiscent of ancient laurels, the figure sports a kind of gear or sprocket for a chestplate and, in place of one hand, an electrical capacitor sparking like a torch—an almost weapon-like prosthesis. Mediating between what Baker called the "ethical" or thesis-driven drama and "utilitarian" mass entertainment, *Control* is quite simply both at once: the well-crafted dramatic production.

The new stagecraft employed by Baker figures most prominently in the pageant's opening and closing scenes, multimedia tableaux bookending the development of Child Control into Mature Control and, more generally, the evolution of human civilization. Preceding its vignette-like accounts of Watt, Stephenson, and others, *Control* opens at the dawn of human existence, a filmic montage depicting great rivers, seascapes, forests, and lava flows, out of which appear tool-wielding Neanderthals walking ever more upright through the mist. From behind the projection screen, a procession of SIT student actors moves across the stage: Egyptians, Assyrians, Greeks, all bearing items such as rugs, mantles, costumes,

CONVERSION
Costume Design by F. P. Bevan

Figure 5. Frank Poole Bevan's design for the character Conversion in Baker's *Control. Reprinted with permission from the American Society of Mechanical Engineers.*

and pottery. Important in this procession is the fact that, as humans evolve, so too do their tools, from primitive stoneware to increasingly aestheticized craft objects; the pageant's opening sequence thus positions the ASME not as some modern force for industrialization but as a natural, almost organic, stage in human development. The illumination soon after of the pageant stage proper—"*strong, although not extremely strong light*"—represents more than a literal enlightenment.[90] In the same way, the pageant's conclusion situates films of modern dams and bridges as visual backing for a climactic paean to the potential beauty of industrial engineering. "Ever growing in beauty," chant the figures of Control, Conversion,

Intelligence, and Imagination—a kind of Greek chorus—after which Beauty herself emerges in a "great glow of light and color," proclaiming herself the child of Imagination and Mature Control.[91] Even as the movement itself had begun to die out, Baker translates American Arts and Crafts values into an industrial context, urging the reconciliation of beauty and utility and enacting that union in his stagecraft. As Beauty retreats offstage, no less telling an opera than Wagner's *Siegfried* fades away. Appearing via "special equipment loaned by Electrical Research Products," President Herbert Hoover delivers a closing exhortation to the pageant's audience, the first notes of "America the Beautiful" echoing through the theater.[92]

The climax would look farcical today—something out of Kubrick, perhaps—but its most remarkable feature is the way it positions the entire history of engineering as culminating in the present place and time, "America the Beautiful" being accompanied by film footage of the New York skyline shot from across the Hudson River in Hoboken. As they left the auditorium at SIT that night, Baker's audience of mechanical engineers would have stared out at exactly that scene, viewing the city—its electrical lights and roaring subways, its untold wonders of engineering—as an inheritance toward which all human history had been tending. It is a triumph of the "total work of art" that as its audience members exit it they also enter it, finding the work itself suddenly turned inside out. But the pageant's evolutionary arc, as Baker treats it, is not ultimately a natural or foreordained trajectory; rather, the present industrial-corporate regime has been midwifed by those educational institutions through which its beneficiaries have passed. "Come now the Schools," declares Control halfway through the pageant. "Come the Departments!" And on cue, standard bearers from 26 universities—from MIT to the University of California—process down the aisles in a fourth-wall shattering "March of the Schools."[93] Just as Baker used the 47 Workshop as a means of elevating public taste in the drama, *Control* represents higher education as critical in raising an emergent professional-managerial class of engineers above mere utilitarianism. The contemporary moment in engineering may be the result of an eons-long evolutionary arc, Baker suggested, but it is no more inevitable—or unalterable—than the Broadway spectacle.

THE CRAFTSMAN AND THE TECHNICIAN: CRAFTING CREATIVE WRITING

Like *The Pilgrim Spirit* before it, *Control* is a fascinating example of the historical pageant, a genre underappreciated despite its importance across the early twentieth century. While *The Pilgrim Spirit* dutifully participated in the genre's project of buttressing national identity, *Control* was less sanguine about that project, at least insofar as American identity was defined by mass production and the commercialism of Broadway drama. Craft rhetoric and practice was key to Baker's challenge of that commercialism, as it was to his critique of the wider industrial-corporate regime that lay behind it. Though craft labor itself had become a moribund proposition, Baker's work in the pageant and 47 Workshop helped institutionalize craft as an aesthetic practice, ironically laying the foundation for another soon-to-explode industry: the MFA.

My genealogy for that industry, traced back to Baker, parallels and extends the genealogy developed by Mark McGurl in *The Program Era*. For McGurl, creative writing originates as an aspect of progressive education, facilitated institutionally by an elective system that emphasized "the student's interest in his studies and the diversity of those interests (and abilities) from student to student."[94] As creative writing entered graduate institutions dominated by the New Criticism, the progressive emphasis on individual expression became a concern secondary to "the classically modernist value of impersonality," an aesthetic formalism achieved through the discipline of writing craft; the result was a creative mode which McGurl, somewhat archly, calls "programmatic self-expression."[95] McGurl's narrative is a compelling one, not least for its attention to how postwar aesthetic formations formally encode the program within which they are produced; the restrained short stories of Flannery O'Connor, for example, with their efficient narrative structure and rigorous impersonality, embody a "masochistic aesthetics of institutionalization" in which writing craft holds the whip to the erstwhile expressive artist.[96] By refocusing, however, on Left and working-class writers, including those affiliated with craft-based workshops, this book adds another layer of complexity to McGurl's argument, revealing how influences beyond the university shaped creative writing as an ideological practice. Before midcentury creative writing programs institutionalized "programmatic self-expression," that mode characterized an ideal of aesthetic production upheld by the American Arts and Crafts movement, for whom proper craftsmanship adhered to rigorously programmatic standards while also allowing for engaged, even expressive, labor. More narrowly, as the elective system developed at Harvard—where the first workshop came to fruition and where other forms of creative writing had been taught in composition courses since 1880—it served less as an instrument for individual freedom than as a means of adapting higher education to the needs of an industrializing nation.[97] Whether the objective was composing fiction, journalism, or drama, creative writing was rarely understood as self-expression—it was vocational training.

Like his Harvard professor, John Dos Passos turned to the drama as a means of opposing such vocationalism, seeking at the same time to rectify the lapsed standards of American audiences. As Baker's affinity with the American Arts and Crafts movement yielded to Dos Passos's more idiosyncratic leftism, the drama continued to bridge what Baker called the "utilitarian" and "ethical" functions of the theater, so that "the problems of the sociologist, the questions that beset the psychologist, the pathologist, the philosopher, open[ed] out before the dramatist."[98] Indeed, Dos Passos's dramatic productions skewed as heavily toward ethical content as anything yet seen on the American stage, eschewing both pageantry and realist characterization in favor of direct critique of American capitalism. While middle-class audiences ignored these productions, having few qualms with a roaring American economy, Dos Passos's early experiments in the drama would prove integral to his subsequent efforts to reengineer the novel; in both genres, Dos Passos refigured the writer not as a craftsman but as an engineering technician, a literary designer whose critique of industrialism rested on his adherence to modernist technical standards. Examining his little-known play *Airways, Inc.*, I argue that Dos Passos's notion of "the writer as technician" emerges out of and reworks American Arts and Crafts ideology—in that play, the craftsman at last exchanges his hammer for a drafting set.

John Dos Passos and *Airways, Inc.*
"BETWEEN HIGH MASS [. . .] AND BARNUM AND BAILEY'S CIRCUS":
NEW PLAYWRIGHTS THEATRE

Before his fiction vaulted him into the literary spotlight, John Dos Passos participated intimately in an experimental Little Theater Movement stocked with Baker acolytes and 47 Workshop alums. As part of the New Playwrights Theatre, Dos Passos endeavored to create a cooperative, craft-based theater that might, through integration of the dramatic arts, supplant Broadway commercialism and the broader economic regime which underwrote it. As in the 47 Workshop, Dos Passos's commitment to the new stagecraft eventuated from the kind of material he wanted to stage, namely, "the side of the American mass myth that the musical comedies leave out."[99] Dos Passos himself, who had contemplated a career in architecture at Harvard, was particularly interested in the possibilities of staging and set design. While New Playwrights was short-lived, running only from 1927 to 1929, as a direct inheritance of Baker's legacy it might be viewed as part of a wider process of experiment and exploration that transformed American drama during the first decades of the twentieth century. For Baker, as I've suggested, one crucial aspect of the well-crafted drama was its reconciliation of the theater's "ethical" and "utilitarian" functions, a union Dos Passos explicitly adapted in *Airways, Inc.*, joining what he called the "serious" and "box-office" halves of the American entertainment industry.[100] At the same time, *Airways, Inc.* retools the Arts and Crafts values promoted by his former teacher, as the character of Professor envisions the evolution of mental labor from craftsmanship to a kind of technical engineering. Dos Passos's playwriting has been critically neglected, but it reveals, once again, how craft rhetoric and practice reoriented early twentieth-century literature within its institutional context; in turn, the American theater offered a way for craft practitioners to stage a wider intervention in labor and culture. Finally, renewed attention to Dos Passos's drama helps clarify how the discipline of creative writing evolved as it migrated from the American Arts and Crafts movement into a leftist campaign with its own distinct, and decidedly more radical, ambitions for the creative writer.

No archival evidence exists linking Dos Passos explicitly with the 47 Workshop, though he seems by several accounts to have taken at least one other Baker offering at Harvard, most likely The Technique of the Drama, prerequisite to the 47 Workshop proper.[101] Many of Dos Passos's closest friends, moreover, were Workshop participants, including Edward Massey, who would later direct Dos Passos's play *The Moon is a Gong* for the Harvard Dramatic Club, a group closely affiliated with the 47 Workshop. Produced in 1925, that play was Dos Passos's first effort at the well-crafted drama, an elaborately staged work combining "box-office" elements such as burlesque and syncopated music with "serious" content drawn from tragedy, surrealism, and leftist critique. The play was a failure—a patchwork of various modes, compositionally uneven, overly sentimental—but it convinced Dos Passos that audiences needed further exposure to experimental theater in order to grasp its social import. A year later, and ten years after graduating from Harvard, Dos Passos undertook his own pedagogical initiative in founding New Playwrights, one of a number of little theaters operating in the East and West Villages. Like many of those ventures, New Playwrights held that the American entertainment industry had become little more than a prop for "the imperialist prosperity myth."[102] The drama, Dos Passos wrote, "oughtn't to be expected to pay any more than an artgallery or a library. [. . .] If the theater doesn't become a transformer for the deep high tension currents of history, it's deader than cockfighting."[103] New Playwrights would thus draw its material from and appeal directly to the industrial and white-collar working classes, rejecting Broadway audiences consisting, as Dos Passos put it, of "literary-minded people who seek in culture a dope to make them dream that they live [. . .] in a Louis Quinze drawing room."[104]

For Dos Passos, direct appeal to the working classes required a startling new stagecraft, the end goal of which was less dramatic realism than "something between high mass in a Catholic church and Barnum and Bailey's circus."[105] Integrating elements of mass theater with Bertolt Brecht-like estrangement (though Dos Passos was unfamiliar with Brecht's work), New Playwrights sought to involve its audiences materially in the productive labor of the drama, fostering what Dos Passos called an "active working audience" similar to that of the 47 Workshop; breaking the fourth wall, for example, represented for Dos Passos what Michael Fried has termed a uniquely "theatrical" strategy, one that distinguished the genre not only from the "absorption" of dramatic realism but from rival forms like film and radio.[106] "The movies have made the theatre of the transparent fourth wall unnecessary and obsolete," Dos Passos wrote. "The camera and screen can transport the audience into circumstances, in the ordinary sense, real. [. . .] The theatre can only bungle at it clumsily. Therefore, if the theatre is going to survive, it has got to find for itself a new function."[107] As in the 47 Workshop, stagecraft was not an end in itself but a means of realizing the drama's form and purpose; so integral was this stagecraft that when Dos Passos spoofed New Playwrights in his novel *Most Likely to Succeed*, he rechristened it the Craftsman's Theater. A first step, he wrote elsewhere, "towards realizing a revolutionary theatre seems to me to be to work with new tools."[108]

Fittingly, the idea of craftsmanship would figure prominently in the last play New Playwrights produced. In *Airways, Inc.*, Dos Passos juxtaposes various forms of craft labor with an evolving industrial-corporate regime and the systems of financial speculation subtending it. Eyeing the ramshackle construction of a new suburban development, one of the play's protagonists, simply named Dad, laments the inhumane nature of mass production. "Maisonettes knocked together out of laths and plaster and enamel paint and kindlin' wood," Dad complains, "and no place for an old man in them, no place for a tired man without a job."[109] If Dad waxes nostalgic over a bygone era of craftsmanship, however, *Airways Inc.* ultimately stages the evanescence of that ideal, imaging new forms of labor for worker and writer alike. As Dos Passos keenly perceived, the era of the writer-as-craftsman had passed.

"WE WORKED IN THOSE DAYS": *AIRWAYS, INC.*

Directed by 47 Workshop alum Massey, *Airways, Inc.* was produced at New Playwrights in the spring of 1929. Among the features of the play's innovative stagecraft were its incorporation of film and radio, an "interlude" style of action in which events occurred simultaneously throughout the theater, and most importantly its use of a thrust rather than picture-frame stage, an apron having been extended over the orchestra pit in order to bring the action nearer the "active working audience" that Dos Passos sought. That audience, in turn, was afforded a glimpse of the labor undergirding aesthetic production, with costume and scene changes made in full view, and with actors breaking character to assist in the handling of stage equipment. The play itself opens with a meditation on the evolving nature of American labor, juxtaposing carpenters' work on an unfinished suburb with emergent regimes of finance and industry. As the "sound of sawing and hammering" reverberates, "two real estate men, IRVING BLOOMSTEIN and EMANUEL KLEIN enter [. . .] looking about them with an appraising air."[110] The pun, like the anti-Semitism, is obvious, though the neighborhood appraised by Bloomstein and Klein is also surrounded by the industrial plants of the "Swastika Refrigeration Company"; Dos Passos figures craftsmanship as uniquely American labor threatened by new European economies. It is those professional-managerial economies, a consortium of interlocking financial and industrial interests, that imperil and ultimately destroy the lives of the working-class Turner family, six figures living together in a dilapidated cottage hunkered in the shadow of nearby factories. Martha Turner, for instance, becomes involved along with her fiancé Walter in a carpenters' strike that halts construction on the unfinished development; a stand-in for Sacco and Vanzetti, executed two years earlier, Walter is eventually electrocuted after being framed for shooting a sheriff's deputy during a riot between police and strikers. Eddy Turner, Martha's brother, attends night school in the hope of getting work as a union carpenter, eventually abandoning this dream in order to become a shoe salesman, a job that leaves him more time for leisure activities like "see[ing] a good picture for a change."[111]

The play's central figure—most actively engaged with its economic antagonists, and thus serving as a mouthpiece for Dos Passos's political agenda—is Elmer Turner, an ace pilot modeled after Charles Lindbergh, whose coming-to-consciousness as a worker constitutes the play's primary action. At the beginning of the play, however, Elmer remains blissfully ignorant of class struggle, mocking Martha and Walter for their participation in the strike and signing on as a celebrity promoter for Bloomstein's rapacious All-American Airways, Inc. Such promotional partnerships were common for pilots in the early years of commercial aviation, perceived, as pilots were, as icons of class, quality, and respectability; Lucky Strike cigarettes gained notoriety through endorsements not only from pilots but from ground crews and air-traffic controllers as well. "The cachet of aeronautical association," Roger Bilstein writes, extended from "'Wings' brand shirts to [. . .] typewriters designed especially for air travelers, but obviously highly desirable for the average consumer who wanted only the best."[112] Like many early airlines, All-American was ostensibly founded, as one of its board members states, to "fulfill a great scientific and patriotic duty"—namely, to serve the military-industrial complex by "turn[ing] seventy-five bombing planes over to the government at twenty-four hours' notice." The true purpose of All-American, however, is speculative, to "not be devoid of profit to the stockholders."[113] Elmer himself aspires to become one of those stockholders, longing for a financial stake in the 51 percent of stock the board apportions among itself—the board, for its part, refuses Elmer, relegating him to the status of common laborer.

Just as Elmer harbors dreams of economic self-sufficiency, he also longs for the autonomy to construct his own airplane, to "build my boat," as he puts it, blueprints in hand, eyes wide with an optimism woefully misplaced in midst of the corporation's initial public offering.[114] At the time, aircraft manufacturing still drew heavily on craft techniques, requiring, Bilstein explains, the "time-honored vocations of cabinetmakers, tinsmiths, coppersmiths, and even seamstresses. The careful work they lavished on each 'plane' imparted to it an individuality compounded of skilled craftsmanship, knowledge, and love." A plane like Boeing's open-cockpit PW-9, for instance, required workers to wield foot-long needles as they hand-stitched linen fabric across wings and fuselage.[115] So fastidious was the craftsmanship of airplane-makers that journalist Stuart Chase was put "in mind of the builders of Chartres" when he encountered such craft, naming the very structure which a century earlier had inspired the founders of the original Arts and Crafts movement.[116] In the same way, in other words, that the play juxtaposes carpentry with those economic forces that imperil it, so too does it image in Elmer the expropriation of craft epistemologies and worker autonomy, gesturing toward new assembly-line techniques that would soon dominate the airline industry and every other. "It is sad," wrote Chase, "to think of mass production hanging like a sword of Damocles" above the heads of craftsmen.[117] Tracking the industrialization and financialization of aircraft manufacturing, *Airways, Inc.* stages anew the confrontation between authority and autonomy that Sennett identifies at the heart of the craft workshop; as in the 47 Workshop, Elmer's autonomy as a craft producer—of aircraft rather than stagecraft—is held in check by the collective authority not of an audience, but of an executive board. As one of All-American's executives says of Elmer while he wrangles for a portion of the company's stock, "Don't mind him," denying Elmer's potential status as a mental laborer.[118]

Because that board consists of the same financial magnates who underwrite the play's real-estate market, Elmer is eventually tasked with air-dropping Chamber of Commerce pamphlets over the construction strike led by his sister and brother-in-law. "I don't see that it hurts the strikers any," Elmer rationalizes to Martha. "They're paying a hundred bucks an hour for doing the trick."[119] It is during one of these runs that Elmer, having already lost financial and manufacturing autonomy, loses control of his aircraft as well, entering a tailspin and crashing offstage, ultimately fracturing his spine and becoming paralyzed for the remainder of the play. If the crash paralyzes him physically, however, it also awakens Elmer to the urgency of the class struggle being waged by Martha and Walter. "They don't give a damn about me or aviation or anything," Elmer recognizes of the executive board, propped up in his convalescent bed. "All they see is a chance to scoop up some easy cash." Later, his resentment becomes personal. "It isn't right the way they won't let me have anything to do with All-American," he says. "Every time I ask Dave about it, he just kids me along."[120] By the play's end, Elmer has become so outraged that Martha mistakes him for her executed fiancé, the implication being that Elmer too, after his literal and metaphorical coming-to-consciousness, will now take up the mantle of proletarian rebellion. Elmer's conversion to working-class resistance thus follows the familiar model of the hero's awakening to his class positionality, a model common among proletarian cultural forms of the 1920s and '30s. "In these texts," Barbara Foley writes, "the protagonist's espousal of—or at least growth toward—revolutionary class consciousness embodies in microcosm the change that is occurring, and must continue to occur on a larger scale, in the working class."[121] In the figure of Elmer, Dos Passos asks his "active working audience" to envision itself as exactly that.

It was in part the ease of Elmer's conversion that contributed to the critical and financial failure of *Airways, Inc.*, which ran for less than a month before the entire New Playwrights project collapsed. Many critics described the play as a hodgepodge of leftist ideals, citing its apparent lack of dramatic unity and the failure of its narrative threads—particularly its romantic and political plots—to converge meaningfully.[122] New Playwrights member Mike Gold was more optimistic, finding in *Airways, Inc.* indication that "the American chaos could be conquered," and that simply ignoring such injustice "was no longer [Dos Passos's] answer to the cruelty men have done with the help of Machines."[123] In *The New Republic*, Edmund Wilson thought the play the best New Playwrights had ever produced, though he found Dos Passos "less expert as a dramatist than as a novelist."[124] No small part of Dos Passos's expertise in the novel, though, owed to the experimental techniques he pioneered on stage, including the interlude-style juxtaposition of related narratives and the collagist language pastiches that would become the newsreels of *Manhattan Transfer* and the *U.S.A.* trilogy. These techniques are most apparent in Dos Passos's treatment of a character known only as Professor, a former Eastern European revolutionary who acts as the play's narrative voice, contextualizing its working-class strife within a global newsscape. "Riots in Poland, mobilization ordered in Jugo-Slavia," Professor narrates during the fever pitch of the strike. "So many bottles of nitroglycerin on a shelf. [. . .] A scuffle and they all drop."[125] If such techniques proved effective on the page, theater-going audiences found them disorienting, a distraction from an interpersonal drama that was itself never fully realized, its characters tending toward types rather than realistic personalities.

The figure of Professor is integral to the play's transition from halcyon craftsmanship to industrial-corporate manufacturing. Looking back wistfully on an era of fulfilling labor, Professor seems in part a winking allusion to Dos Passos' own professor, George Pierce Baker, describing a time when "work, worked, we worked in those days for the instruction of the people, worked. [. . .] Every time I moved it was pleasure, the twist and untwist of my arms . . . We were unloading melons [. . .] then they slipped from my hands into another man's hands."[126] Seated in one scene in what the stage directions refer to as a "Morris chair"—a callback to the founder of the original Arts and Crafts movement—Professor is given some of the play's best lines in set-piece speeches about the dignity of craft labor and the perils of industrialization. "The world was a huge ball then," he romanticizes, "the universe a mighty harmony of ellipses, everything moved mysteriously, incalculable distances through the ether. We used to feel the awe of the distant stars upon us. All that led to was the eighty-eight naval guns, ersatz, and the night airraids over cities. [. . .] Nowhere is far anymore. Distance has snapped back in my face like a broken elastic."[127] Citing the classic image of machine-age planned

obsolescence, Professor is key to Dos Passos's rethinking of the meaning and ramifications of labor in an industrial context. While Baker confronted an evolving
industrial regime with a reminder of the aesthetic potential of labor, Dos Passos
recognized that beauty itself had become obsolete, vanished, along with human
wonder and awe, in a world of perpetual warfare and outsized industrial-corporatism.
The image of labor with which *Airways, Inc.* concludes is decidedly postlapsarian.

Yet Professor does not simply revel in nostalgia for craftsmanship, but looks
forward as Dos Passos did to new modes of labor for worker and writer alike. In
his own conversion at the play's end, Professor exhorts the audience to "make
ourselves machines" in order to confront the injustices of industrialization, turning "our hearts into dynamos, our blood into electric current." While Elmer will
never fly again, his work toward proletarian revolution necessitates that his body
itself become the honed, hardened instrument he controls. "Look at my hand,"
Professor commands. "The soft twitching flesh is drying up into steel. [. . .] Man
is the last machine we must invent."[128] For Dos Passos, cultural producers in particular needed to become efficient experts whose labor might organize and direct
the wider mass of American workers; the writer, Dos Passos argued, was a "technician just as much as an electrical engineer is."[129] Coordinating disciplines and
discourses, the work of the writer-technician drew on that aspect of an American
Arts and Crafts craft ideal which stressed the worker's adherence to technical
standards—in this case, the standards of modernist aesthetics. Being able to "put
the words down on paper" no more made one a writer, in Dos Passos's view, "than
the fact that he can scratch up the ground and plant seeds in it makes him a
farmer, or that he can trail a handline overboard makes him a fisherman."[130]
Nearly half a century after Eliot's reforms in the name of utilitarian education,
Dos Passos's technician is the very image of the "cutting-tool, a drill, or auger" by
which the former had described his ideal student. Dos Passos learned more at
Harvard, it would seem, than the craft of playwriting.

I have suggested that the discipline of creative writing, in particular the lexicon and practice of workshop, began with a craft ideal adapted from the American Arts and Crafts movement, a group for whom craftsmanship proper consisted
of engaged, even expressive labor which simultaneously adhered to technical
standards like those enforced by pre-industrial guilds. Renewed attention to Dos
Passos's early work in the drama reveals how his influential figuration of "the
writer as technician" grew out of this context, stressing technical standards while
downplaying—even explicitly challenging—more self-expressive aesthetics. The

"programmatic self-expression" that scholars have read as a distinguishing fea-ture of postwar creative writing programs predates those programs by nearly fifty years, originating not in the MFA but in the American Arts and Crafts movement and, soon after, under an entirely different acronym: the CPUSA.

Chapter Two

A Vast University of the Common People

Meridel Le Sueur and the 1930s Left

In the summer of 1934, as record-breaking heat waves throttled the Plains states and the Great Depression deepened to its nadir, writer Meridel Le Sueur served chicken dinner to 3,000 strikers at the headquarters of General Drivers Local 574 in Minneapolis.[1] A volunteer in the union's Women's Auxiliary, Le Sueur would document her work over the succeeding months in a series of essays in the Communist Party-affiliated *New Masses*, detailing firsthand a strike of Minneapolis transportation companies that brought to a halt virtually all trucking activity in the Twin Cities and which, by the time it was resolved, would dramatically reshape the organization and objectives of American labor relations. "I found the kitchen organized like a factory," Le Sueur wrote. "Nobody asks my name. I am given a large butcher's apron. I realize I have never before worked anonymously."[2]

Until that summer, as significant to US history as the summers of 1863 or 1968, labor advocacy had revolved almost exclusively around the craft-based unions of the American Federation of Labor (AFL), reformist orders of construction tradesmen, railway workers, and other skilled laborers eager to defend the traditions and privileges of so-called craft unionism. With the passage of the National Industrial Recovery Act, however, and in particular its protections for collective bargaining, the Minneapolis Truckers' Strike became one of several labor initiatives to mobilize unskilled workers across a range of industrial occupations, organizing those workers into non-exclusive industrial unions. Recognition of such unions was a key objective in related labor actions that summer among West Coast longshoremen, Toledo auto-parts workers, and the diverse coalition of truckers, paint-ers, cab drivers, and iron workers who banded together in Minneapolis to agitate for rights denied them under the more conservative craft unionism of the AFL.

It was the high degree of coordination across these worker groups that dis-tinguished Minneapolis as a labor initiative, with workers picketing key intersec-tions at the city limits, turning back commercial deliveries, and commandeering food and medical supplies from non-union vehicles. Other roving picketers, di-rected by radio from strike headquarters, crisscrossed the city in "flying squad-rons," massing at contested flashpoints and vanishing before authorities could respond. At strike headquarters, Le Sueur and other members of the Women's Auxiliary staffed kitchens, managed commissaries, and assisted in a makeshift hospital for wounded strikers, all while raising funds, intervening with relief boards and government officials, and marching alongside their sons, husbands, and fellow workers. Additionally, a union newspaper, *The Organizer*, marshaled first-person reportage to encourage, entertain, and apprise workers of the latest in strike negotiations. Despite differences in language, culture, and background—and despite their disparate experiences across multiple industrial occupations—Minneapolis strikers displayed a remarkable unity of method and purpose, forg-ing themselves into an effective force for labor rights.

By July, their tactics had taken a toll. Under increasing pressure to resolve the strike, Minneapolis administrators forced a confrontation between strikers and city police, endeavoring to move a cargo truck through crowds of picketers in Minneapolis's downtown Market District on the sweltering afternoon of July 21. As onlookers sweated in the Minnesota heat, the truck inched away from its load-ing platform and proceeded slowly up Hennepin Avenue. When strikers blocked the vehicle with their own open-bed pickup, police officers opened fire into the massed workers, killing two and wounding fifty in the ensuing chaos. Soon after, Local 574 managed to secure higher wages, improved working conditions, union recognition, and collective bargaining rights in the vast majority of Minneapolis trucking firms, a landmark victory for advocates of industrial unionism and a clear indication that laborers across multiple occupations could work together for wide-ranging reforms.[3]

Inaugurating a new era in labor relations, the Minneapolis Truckers' Strike immediately gained recognition as an unprecedented instance of cross-class col-laboration, as intellectual labor leaders harnessed "the native militancy of the masses" and taught mass-production workers "to fight for their rights and [fought] with them." Writing soon afterward in *The New International*, James P. Cannon singled out this aspect of the strike as a harbinger of future developments in the labor movement. "In other places," Cannon wrote, "strike militancy surged from below and was checked and restrained by the leaders. In Minneapolis it was organized and directed by the leaders."[4] Based out of New York City, Cannon was a leading administrator of the Trotsky-influenced Communist League of America (CLA), and with other strike leaders made up what novelist Charles Rumford Walker labeled a "brain core of military operations" working out of strike headquarters.[5] There, as Cannon described, "a group of determined militants, armed with the most advanced political conceptions, organized the workers in the trucking industry, led them through three strikes within six months and remain today at the head of the union."[6] Indeed, the strike headquarters itself—located, ironically, across from the swank Minneapolis Club—proved an apt testament to the *savoir faire* of strike strategists: a nerve center of sorts, strewn with Trotskyist pamphlets, tangled in telephone wires, and cluttered with the detailed cartography of picket locations and incident reports. The Minneapolis Truckers' Strike, in other words, was both a labor action and a cross-class pedagogical initiative, with East Coast intellectuals instructing midwestern workers in the theory and practice of labor militancy, and with working-class strikers contributing on-the-ground intelligence and their own local knowledge of Minneapolis and its politics.

It was this cross-class exchange—between "teamsters and Trotskyists," as one historian puts it—which for Cannon and others constituted the "meaning" of Minneapolis and allowed strikers to outmaneuver not only their employers but virtually every layer of meliorist government intervention, from city police to President Franklin D. Roosevelt.[7] Gaining momentum over the long summer of 1934, the Minneapolis coalition seemed even more remarkable given that much of the 1930s Left remained riven by factional debates between precisely those groups that the coalition unified: on the one hand, intellectual theoreticians, and on the other, advocates for an autochthonous, militant proletarianism. Falling out along Trotskyist and Stalinist lines, these debates would try allegiances, rend cultural institutions, and strain long-held friendships. While their ability to sidestep such debates was integral to the success of Minneapolis strikers, elsewhere— and with equally lasting consequences—these debates would prove far more difficult to ignore.

"The philosopher goes to work": A critical prologue

Organized around Le Sueur's literary and political work in Minneapolis, this chapter contends that the Left cultural debates of the 1930s—debates about the role, representation, and function of literary leftists in particular—constitute the fracturing of a prior craft ideal dominant in the early twentieth-century American Arts and Crafts movement. As I have described, that movement promoted craft as workers' engaged, even expressive labor combined with fastidious adherence to technical standards; in the words of craft adherent Denman Ross, in craft "the philosopher goes to work and the working man becomes a philosopher."[8] While one legacy of the American Arts and Crafts movement lies in the subsequent experimental modernism of Falling Water, the Eames Lounge Chair, and Black Mountain College, in another future, splitting apart like a parallel universe or frayed wire, the movement bifurcates into opposing camps within the literary Left, each of which in its own way translates the anti-modern animus of Arts and Crafts into 1930s cultural politics.

One such faction, organized around John Dos Passos and *Partisan Review* editors Philip Rahv and William Phillips, understood the writer as a "technician" whose responsibility lay not in "the fight for social justice," but in adhering to modernist aesthetic standards. "The aims of the technician," Dos Passos wrote, "insofar as he is a technician and not a timeserver, [are] the development of his material and of the technical possibilities of his work."[9] In contrast, a second faction of the literary Left, organized around Mike Gold's *New Masses*, fostered insurgent working-class consciousness embodied in the self-expressive proletarian writer, a figure Gold himself virtually imagined into existence. While Dos Passos's technician hewed closely to the standards of his art, cultivating that state of mind "in which a man is ready to do good work," Gold's proletarian literally expressed himself in "jets of exasperated feeling," his class obligations leaving him "no time to polish his work."[10] Each faction advanced its cultural politics through distinct representations of the worker-writer, what we might schematize as a top-down (writers as workers) versus a bottom-up (workers as writers) dialectic. Drawing on a cultural geography mapped by Jeff Allred, Shannan Clark, Terry Cooney, and others, I attend in this chapter to what Laura Rigal has called the "cultural production of production," those representational strategies through which—in addition to strikes, slowdowns, and union organizing—the American labor movement articulated itself, sometimes contradictorily.[11] For in addition to marking the fracturing of a prior craft ideal, the opposed factions of the 1930s literary Left manifested a tension within the word "craft" itself, a word which came in the fourteenth century to be associated with mental acuity, but which, in its original Old English, signified manual power and physical strength.[12]

Playing out across a range of journals, lecture circuits, and writers workshops—

from those affiliated with Party-backed John Reed Clubs to Works Progress Administration (WPA)-sponsored workshops like Le Sueur's at the Minnesota Labor School—debates between literary technicians and proletarians were part of a wider contradiction in leftist theory between mental and manual labor; as Michael Denning reminds us, "the emergence of 'culture' as a distinct region depends on a social surplus, extracted through exploitative labor relations."[13] Reading the 1930s Left as a dual inheritance of American Arts and Crafts ideology, however, I show how Left debates provided key rhetoric that influenced later conceptualizations of creative writing craft, in particular a prohibition on didactic politicizing metonymized in that infamous workshop cliché: "show, don't tell." For scholars of creative writing, "show, don't tell" originates with the New Critical disciplining of self-expression in the name of modernist impersonality, a discipline enforced through the stringencies of literary craftsmanship.[14] As Barbara Foley notes, though, the critique of didacticism in fact begins within the 1930s Left, where a range of writers expressed reservations about policies dictated from Communist Party cultural bosses.[15] "The function of a revolutionary writer is not to suggest political platforms and theses," Gold argued in defense of proletarian realism, "but to portray the life of the workers."[16] Before there was the Program Era, in other words, there was the literal program of the Communist Party.

Examining Le Sueur's creative writing pedagogy and literary production from this period, I show how leftist writers staked out distinct positions within a discursive field opened up by more theoretical polemics. In their rhetorical figurations of the worker-writer, Gold and Dos Passos constituted two poles along a spectrum of possible figurations; in practice, leftist writers operated inconsistently and heterogeneously between these poles, interrogating ossifying theoretical categories and promoting diverse views of working-class writing. Le Sueur's career embodies significant tensions within the literary Left, but it also reconstructs a prior ideal of literary craftsmanship which otherwise fragments across the 1930s. Specifically, while her pedagogical and documentary work with the WPA frames cultural production as an autochthonous "bottom-up" opposition to economic exploitation, grounding literary agency in proletarian expression, her fiction complicates any reductive notion of "proletarianism," revealing self-consciously modernist aspirations in its virtuosic joining of realist and experimental modes. That proletarian culture exhibited significant modernist influences—indeed, that proletarianism *was* modernist in many cases—has by now been widely recognized.[17] Rarely acknowledged, however, is how modernist proletarians like Le Sueur not only challenged regnant theoretical binaries, but explicitly positioned themselves as inheritors of a craft ideal, literary craftsmen who insisted that modernism itself was built through craft labor.

Blacklisted throughout the immediate postwar era for her continued Party affiliation, Le Sueur experienced a revival of interest in the changed political climate of the 1960s and '70s, her early novels republished by Minneapolis-based West End Press and heralded by scholars for their contribution to the feminist and regionalist traditions in proletarian writing.[18] This scholarship constitutes an important first step in reappraising Le Sueur's legacy, but it tends to marginalize her contribution to Left culture in ways that reinscribe the gendered and regionally biased divisions of literary labor that prevailed throughout the 1930s. Indebted to but departing from this work, I situate Le Sueur at the nexus of 1930s literary and political culture. Specifically, I read her as a major figure of the 1930s Left who, in retheorizing the relationship between labor and literary production, actively engaged the era's most pressing questions. Just what kind of work is writing? On whose behalf does the poet punch in?

Ultimately, the critical intervention I propose in this chapter is threefold. First, I contend that debates about the role, representation, and function of leftist writers constitute the splitting of a prior craft ideal that had reconciled self-expression and technical rigor. More importantly, by making visible workshops programmatically written out of scholarly histories, I show how Left cultural debates and WPA-endorsed pedagogies influenced later workshops ostensibly organized around New Critical principles. Finally, in order to make that argument, I resituate Le Sueur at the center of the 1930s Left, reading her reconstruction of craft as a significant influence on US literary and political culture—for Le Sueur was simply everywhere in the 1930s, her CV a record of those alphabet agencies that dramatically reshaped American life throughout the Great Depression, from CLA-organized picket lines to WPA- and WEP-backed writing workshops to FWP research offices. I work here to make that alphabet meaningful.

Crafting the Literary Left: American Writers' Congress, 1935
"The Writer as Technician"

Since the collapse of his short-lived dramatic career, culminating with the failure of *Airways, Inc.* in 1929, Dos Passos had periodically sought respite from New York's *Sturm und Drang* in the bright, Bacardi-tinted environs of Key West, at that time still an isolated enclave of artists, idlers, Portuguese fisherman, and Bahamian rum-runners. Wintering with his wife, Kate, at their bungalow at 1401 Pine Street, Dos Passos would pass the days "licking my wounds, fishing, eating wild herons and turtle steak, drinking Spanish wine and Cuban rum and generally remaking the inner man."[19] It was Dos Passos, reportedly, who first informed Ernest Hemingway of the charm and restorative seclusion to be found in the removes of Key West, where, sometime in April 1935, the two writers enjoyed one another's company while cruising the Dry Tortugas, fishing for tarpon in the Gulf Stream, and drinking in barroom shacks beneath the stars and coconut palms. That month, amid the pastel-colored cocktails that swim through his letters of this period, Dos Passos completed his essay "The Writer as Technician," mailing the typescript up the coast to be read into the record at the first annual American Writers' Congress, held April 26–28 at Mecca Temple near Central Park.

Organized by the League of American Writers, a Party front, the Congress was a who's who of literary leftists, among them Malcolm Cowley, James T. Farrell, Langston Hughes, and Meridel Le Sueur, who delivered a paper on a movement she called "proletarian regionalism," arguing that "nowhere in America are the ravages of *laissez faire* colonization so apparent as in the Middle West."[20] Originally wary about participating in the Congress, Dos Passos changed his mind after learning from Edmund Wilson of increasingly unmanageable rumors regarding his growing conservatism. "It is being rumored," Wilson wrote, "that you are 'rubbing your belly' and saying that 'the good old Republican Party is good enough for you.'"[21] In response, Dos Passos begrudgingly contributed an essay on leftist aesthetics and the role of the artist in social crises. This was, after all, an era when rumor mattered, when writers constantly shifted allegiances among a range of acronymic organizations, and when an ill-advised comment at a cocktail party or a poorly placed editorial might lastingly damage one's chances for personal and professional success. Eager to remain publishable within a literary culture dominated by the Left, Dos Passos nonetheless used the occasion of the Congress to air his objections to the "middleclass communism of the literati," contributing what he described as "a little preachment about liberty of conscience [. . .] that I hope will queer me with the world savers so thoroughly that they'll leave me alone for awhile."[22] That "The Writer as Technician" arrived in New York a dead letter, however—too late to be read into the record that weekend, or stashed away in Congress offices, perhaps—suggests the tenuous position Dos Passos already occupied with respect to the Left. That position was adumbrated in an essay that served as Dos Passos's coming out as a literary independent, a "technician," as he put it, an ex-leftist at the age of 39.

One of the central claims underlying Dos Passos's rhetorical figuration of the writer as technician was that his adherence to modernist aesthetic standards entailed the writer's disentangling himself from ulterior political commitments. The essay opened, accordingly, with Dos Passos's own self-emancipation. "A writer," he declared, "must never, I feel, no matter how much he is carried away by even the noblest political partisanship in the fight for social justice, allow himself to forget that his real political aim [. . .] is liberty. A man can't discover anything, originate anything, invent anything unless he's at least morally free, without fear or preoccupation insofar as his work goes."[23] Free to attend exclusively to the imperatives of his work, the literary artist sought to realize the formal ideal latent in his material, and did so, Dos Passos believed, through fastidious adherence to technical standards. The technician's state of mind was a state of "selfless relaxation, with no worries or urges except those of the work at hand."[24] One of the reasons Dos Passos so cherished the isolation of Key West, geographically instantiating the intellectual remove he sought for his writing, was his ability to attune himself there strictly to the dictates of his material, to work "without tripping over that damn Party line."[25]

Privileging modernist technique over self-expression, Dos Passos's technician embodies that aspect of an American Arts and Crafts craft ideal which promoted technical standards like those enforced by pre-industrial guilds. Objecting to the inferior quality of mass-manufactured commodities, craft idealists cultivated, as the journal *Handicraft* described, "thorough technical training, and a just appreciation of standards," supporting "good and beautiful work" through the kind of juried exhibitions sponsored by the Society of Arts and Crafts, Boston.[26] At such exhibitions, Beverly Brandt explains, craft critics "examined the basic design elements—shape, color, and texture—and their component parts, namely line or form; hue, value, and intensity; pattern and surface finish."[27] It is this emphasis on technical rigor that Dos Passos adapts in "The Writer as Technician," stressing "the need for clean truth and sharply whittled exactitudes"—"even if he's to be killed the next minute," Dos Passos writes, "a man has to be cool and dispassionate while he's aiming his gun."[28] Decades later, Dos Passos would elaborate on this Hemingway-esque metaphor for the impersonality of technique, contending in *National Review* that an "expert hunter [. . .] forgets himself," letting "all his senses come awake to respond to the frailest intimations." Skilled marksmen, Dos Passos argues, "are able to forget who they are and become for the moment just an eye and ear and a gun."[29] Likewise, the Arts and Crafts practitioner submitted himself to the imperatives of clay, wood, metal, and textile, cultivating precision and discrimination in his labor, keywords that recur like totems throughout craft literature from the late nineteenth and early twentieth centuries.

For all his pretension to the disinterested realization of aesthetic form, how-ever, represented in the reserve of the patrician hunter, Dos Passos's technician nonetheless retains a social function: to serve as part of an intellectual vanguard and, by properly calibrating American culture, to organize the attitudes and af-fects of the working class. The technician "molds and influences ways of think-ing," Dos Passos writes, "to the point of changing and rebuilding the language, which is the mind of the group."[30] One of the contradictions inherent in Dos Passos's conception of literary craftsmanship is that the figuration of "writer as technician" names a double operation, signaling the writer's fastidious adherence to technical standards while paradoxically pointing to his role as an engineer of American culture. "In his relation to society," Dos Passos writes, "a professional writer is a technician just as much as an electrical engineer is."[31] It is at this point in the essay, having invoked not only hunters and technicians, but scientists, en-gineers, inventors, day laborers, and car mechanics, that Dos Passos's metaphors begin to indicate the challenge in adapting a wider contemporary fascination with technocracy to the theory and practice of literature. Popularized by sociolo-gist Thorstein Veblen, technocracy itself was premised on the idea that the disin-terested efficiency engineer, rather than the profit-driven tycoon or nationalistic statesman, was best positioned to resolve increasingly complicated global prob-lems like underproduction, inefficient distribution, and unemployment. "The material welfare of the community," Veblen wrote in *The Engineers and the Price System*, "is unreservedly bound up with the due working of this industrial system, and therefore with its unreserved control by the engineers, who alone are com-petent to manage it." Like Dos Passos's technician, Veblen's engineer attended exclusively to the dictates of his work "as it should be done," requiring "a free hand, unhampered by commercial considerations."[32] Dos Passos's technician car-ries over into literary production the disinterest of Veblen's engineer, whose lib-erty allows the economic system, in this case, its fullest formal realization. In Dos Passos's rendering, however, the literary technician possesses something of a split consciousness, faithful to modernist technique while simultaneously engaged—precisely through this technique—in the reengineering of culture.

In his excellent study of Depression-era documentary, Jeff Allred situates Dos Passos's technician as part of a broader "cultural technics" of the 1930s, an exten-sion of the "principle of engineering beyond narrowly technological concerns to the social and cultural realms."[33] For Dos Passos, though—who knew, admired, and even plagiarized Veblen—the figure of the technician owed less to a vogue for technocracy than to his own longtime interest in craft.[34] Though "The Writer as

Technician" has the force of a manifesto, and though it marked a dramatic shift in Dos Passos's relationship with the Left, its technician constituted an evolution in the craft rhetoric that had animated some of Dos Passos's earliest writing. In a previous chapter, I show how Dos Passos allegorizes this evolution in his 1929 play *Airways, Inc.* That same year, reviewing *A Farewell to Arms* in *New Masses*, Dos Passos praised the novel as a "firstrate piece of craftsmanship by a man who knows his job," comparing it to a "piece of wellfinished carpenters' work." Hemingway's prose style struck Dos Passos as "terse and economical," with each phrase "bear[ing] its maximum load of meaning, sense impressions, emotion."[35] Metaphorizing the literary text as craft object—the joists of a Key West bungalow, perhaps—Dos Passos's descriptors suggest an even more uncompromising commitment to the writer's technical independence than he would come to advocate in "The Writer as Technician," where his technician works double time as an engineer of culture. Despite his freedom from the Party, that is, Dos Passos's technician is far more socially engaged than the craftsman he earlier brings to life in his review; what Dos Passos values in Hemingway is neither his "cultural technics," properly calibrating American working-class culture, nor the anticipatory imaging of social revolution—and certainly not the self-expression of some probing interiority turned outward—but his ability to "work ably with his material and his tools and continually push the work to the limit of that effort."[36] Such an evolution, from disinterested craftsmanship to the technician's modicum of social engagement, complicates the critical tendency to find in Dos Passos's career a clean trajectory from the idealistic leftism of New Playwrights Theatre to the neoconservatism of *National Review*; while many erstwhile leftists followed precisely this trajectory, Dos Passos's own career delineated a far more erratic arc.[37]

Yet Dos Passos's review of *A Farewell to Arms* takes his commitment to literary craftsmanship one step further, finding in Hemingway's prose a "hangover from the period of individual manufacture that is just closing"—exactly that period that the American Arts and Crafts movement had tried to resuscitate. Advocating craftsmanship as "the privilege of any workman," whether in "novelwriting, the painting of easelpictures, [or] the machinebuilding trades," Dos Passos laments that "most of the attempts to salvage craftsmanship in industry have been faddy movements like East Aurora and Morris furniture and have come to nothing."[38] By 1929, when Dos Passos was writing, the journals *Handicraft* and *The Craftsman* had been defunct for over a decade. In 1915, the same year that craft furniture-maker Gustav Stickley declared bankruptcy, Roycroft founder Elbert Hubbard died in the sinking of the *Lusitania*. John Ruskin had been dead since 1900, William

Morris since the last century, and the American movement that looked to their example had become, at the hands of the roaring twenties, an irrelevant and underfunded proposition. "[C]raftsmanship is a damn fine thing," wrote Dos Passos, but "the drift of the Fordized world seems all against it. [. . .] It's getting to be almost unthinkable that you should take pleasure in your work, that a man should enjoy doing a piece of work for the sake of doing it as well as he damn well can."[39] As major American Arts and Crafts initiatives died out, the movement fragmented into a series of cultural formations with varying degrees of allegiance to its craft ideal. While architects like Julia Morgan and Frank Lloyd Wright incorporated craft, somewhat affectedly, as architectural style, other artists found in craft production a set of metaphors by which to rearticulate literary labor, whether, in Gold's case, as an expression of proletarian experience or, as with Dos Passos and *Partisan Review*, as adherence to technical standards.

Dos Passos's embrace of the technician was not, however, without profound regret for the evanescence of the craftsman, a figure he memorialized in one after another of the biographies scattered throughout his *U.S.A.* trilogy. While many critics have read the trilogy's quasi-documentary aesthetic as the kind of literary engineering that Dos Passos's technician might well produce, the novel's biographies sound a strikingly elegiac note for a waning era of craft. In his treatment of Henry Ford, Dos Passos parodies his own tendency toward portmanteau as an effect of the assembly line, describing "the Taylorized speedup everywhere [. . .] adjustwasher, screwdown bolt, reachunderadjustwasherscrewdownreachunderadjust until every ounce of life was sucked off into production and at night the workmen went home grey shaking husks."[40] When Ford himself retires to Massachusetts, he attempts to undo these effects. "[H]e had the new highway where the new-model cars roared and slithered and hissed oilily past (*the new noise of the automobile*), moved away from the door," Dos Passos writes, "put back the old bad road, so that everything might be the way it used to be, in the days of horses and buggies." Dos Passos's portrait of Orville and Wilbur Wright, similarly, contrasts the industrialization of the airplane with nostalgia for the brothers' workshop in Dayton:

[N]ot even the headlines or the bitter smear of newsprint or the choke of smokescreen and gas or chatter of brokers on the stockmarket or barking of phantom millions or oratory of brasshats laying wreaths on new monuments can blur the memory of the chilly December day two shivering bicycle mechanics from Dayton, Ohio, first felt their homemade contraption whittled out of hickory sticks, gummed together with Arnstein's bicycle cement, stretched with muslin they'd sewn on their sister's sewingmachine in their own backyard on Hawthorn Street in Dayton, Ohio, soar into the air above the dunes and the wide beach at Kitty Hawk.[41]

The note of wistfulness is unmistakable here, Dos Passos's prose moving across time and place to join craft labor, in a single finely constructed sentence, to its own obsolescence.

Though Dos Passos's technician constituted a necessary makeover of the craftsman that embodied his earlier ideal of literary labor, Dos Passos would find himself literally and rhetorically *persona non grata* at the American Writers' Congress, where on opening night the editor of a magazine calling itself *Marine Workers' Voice* wondered aloud whether the intellectuals in attendance "want to starve today or not." "Because if they don't," Hays Jones declared, "they have got to do certain things, and that is to come down to the place where they have a market." Jones himself seemed to perfectly occupy that place, no more so than when he crowed that if "professional" writers like Dos Passos "don't take the invitation we'll give them an ultimatum. They can go on writing about the dead," Jones declared, "until finally we have to shove them into the grave and cover them up with the dirt."[42] These, in 1935, were the stakes.

"Jets of exasperated feeling": On Proletarianism

The long summer of 1934, witness to the great industrial strikes in Minneapolis and elsewhere, played witness too to a groundswell of young writers declaring themselves proletarians in the magazines of the Left, promoting themselves in a variety of cultural institutions that included writers' workshops, lecture circuits, art exhibitions, dance troupes, and even parade committees. Influenced by the *proletkult* values of the Soviet Union's ultra-revolutionary Third Period—a six-year period from the crash of 1929 to the Popular Front of 1935—these young writers militantly agitated for economic revolution and for an accompanying shift in social and cultural values. Eager to prove their mettle as class warriors, proletarian artists descended *en masse* on the American Writers' Congress in April of 1935, as much of an in-scene for the literary Left as today's Association of Writers and Writing Programs (AWP) conference remains for the MFA industry—and one which, given his allergy to *causes célèbres*, Dos Passos may have done well to avoid.

For among the papers delivered that weekend—Alexander Trachtenberg on the leftist publishing industry, Langston Hughes on Black proletarianism—one common line of inquiry was the more or less explicit critique of Dos Passos's disinterested technician, a whipping boy of sorts by which proletarian writers demonstrated their commitment. In contrast to Dos Passos's view that the writer should preserve his autonomy, French poet Louis Aragon celebrated "the chain" that bound him to the working class and which "hired philosophers had taught [him] to deny."[43] While Dos Passos viewed intellectual liberty as a precondition of the writer's ability to "discover anything, originate anything, invent anything," novelist and recently minted Guggenheim Fellow Jack Conroy decried a "desperate striving for novelty of phrase and imagery" that ended in a "semi-private terminology almost unintelligible to the masses." The worker-writer, Conroy went on, in a clear jab at Dos Passos's portmanteau, "must learn to express himself as clearly and as simply as he can," but in so doing he "will not find it necessary to concoct weird hybrids of words or to coin new words."[44] Most prominent among Dos Passos's detractors, Kenneth Burke rebuked those who would "profit by the prestige which the technological expert enjoys in the contemporary framework of values," castigating Dos Passos, without naming him, for "polarizing allegiance around the symbol of the engineer."[45] Even Le Sueur, whose talk on proletarian regionalism hewed closely to her experience in the Midwest, stressed that "the emphasis must not be simply on skill and technique, but on a new experience, a communal relationship and revolutionary ideology."[46]

Given such opprobrium, it is hardly surprising that Dos Passos preferred the boozy isolation of Key West over the certain confrontation awaiting him in Midtown; his "morally free" technician had become increasingly irreconcilable with the committed proletarian writer, a figure leftist impresario Mike Gold had conceived six years earlier. Writing in *New Masses*, Gold described a "wild youth of about twenty-two, the son of working-class parents, who himself works in the lumber camps, coal mines, steel mills, harvest fields and mountain camps of America." Gold's expressive proletarian "writes in jets of exasperated feeling and has no time to polish his work"; rather, he "knows it in the same way that one of Professor Baker's students knows the six different ways of ending a first act."[47] Grown by 1935 to a national phenomenon, Gold's proletarian writer was present not only in person at the American Writers' Congress—thousands strong, in fact, from 26 states and four foreign countries—but made cameo appearances in many of the lectures delivered that weekend. Le Sueur would explicitly echo Gold in describing a regionalist movement organized around the "growing yeast of the revolutionary working class arising on the Mesabi range, the wheat belt, the coal fields of Illinois."[48] Despite Gold's invocation of Baker, his proletarian marks a clear departure from the craft of the 47 Workshop, with Gold de-emphasizing technical standards in order to privilege the almost literal expression of the worker's experience. While both aspects of the craft ideal were mobilized in Baker's dramatic productions, Gold's expressivist rhetoric adapted that aspect of craft that prioritized "native or vernacular expression," as one nineteenth-century craft critic put it, over fastidious technique.[49] Stressing the craft object's origin in working-class experience, craft adherents turned to linguistic metaphors as a means of articulating their belief in expressive labor. "They advised their constituents," Brandt writes, "against producing objects 'having nothing meaningful to say,' or that made statements which might be denounced as elaborate, affected, pretentious, artificial, or strained (all their words)."[50] Under Gold's editorship, *New Masses* became a forum for expressions of working-class life otherwise neglected by mainstream publishing outlets, with Gold actively soliciting workers' editorial input and, in the columns of the *Daily Worker*, maintaining a series of "Worker's Correspondence" poems that combined letters to the editor and other not-quite-publishable material.

For Gold, all of these endeavors entailed a reorientation of literary standards toward the language and experience of the working class, a "proletarian realism," as he termed it, that dealt with the "*real conflicts* of men and women who work for a living."[51] "Write," Gold encouraged the audience of *New Masses*. "Your life in mine, mill, and farm is of deathless significance in the history of the world. [. . .] It may be literature—it often is."[52] Rejecting "scholastic jargon" that "no American could understand without a year or two of post-graduate study," Gold's commitment to proletarianism frequently manifested as class contempt for Dos Passos and other intellectuals associated with *Partisan Review*, a coterie Gold derided as a "little group of Phi Beta Kappa Trotskyites."[53] This rhetoric would become more vituperative over time, with Gold arguing at the height of the Moscow Trials that "it is easy to criticize Soviet Russia in a steam-heated New York restaurant, before a group of book reviewers and college instructors who've never shot a White Guard *saboteur* in their lives."[54] Underlying Gold's *ad hominem* invective was a critique of literary modernism as bourgeois experimentation sealed off from social and political engagement, an "art for art's sake" aestheticism divorced from the everyday lives of workers. Modernism, Gold argued, constituted the cultural epiphenomenon of a maladjusted leisure class "which has no function to perform in society except the clipping of investment coupons," and which therefore "develops ills and neuroses," causing its sufferers to "seek new sensations, new adventures constantly in order to give themselves feelings." Pathologizing modernism,

Gold traced the movement to the spiritual lassitude of neurasthenic elites. "Their life is stale to them," he wrote. "Tasteless, inane, because it has no meaning."[55] Less critically nuanced than rhetorically forceful, the proletarian objection to modernism tended to center on a handful of influential high modernists, among them the *bêtes noires* Gertrude Stein—a "literary idiot," Gold said—T. S. Eliot, James Joyce, and Marcel Proust, who represented "the worst example and the best of what we do not want," a "master-masturbator of the bourgeois literature."[56] In contrast, Phillips and Rahv thought it a mistake "to assume that [Proust's] values are the values of bourgeois ideology," since his novels exhibited "many insights into bourgeois social relations that are far removed from the way the normal bourgeois sees them."[57] Was not Eliot's "autumnal sensibility," Phillips asked, "a kind of comment on the state of society?"[58] Didn't Rimbaud's poetry "stand up off the page?" Dos Passos implored.[59]

These schisms—between modernists and anti-modernists, mental and manual laborers—manifested in a variety of forms and with varying degrees of intensity across the literary Left of the 1930s, but they also curiously replay similar debates that had wracked the American Arts and Crafts movement earlier that century. Unfolding in the SACB journal *Handicraft*, those debates had centered in large part on the relationship between craft movement leaders and craft workers, the former consisting of wealthier intellectuals like Harvard professor Charles Eliot Norton, who provided the movement's theoretical framework and financial backing. While Norton and others viewed aesthetically savvy, well-connected intellectuals as an elite *avant garde* justly tasked with shaping the values and vision of American Arts and Crafts, another faction of the movement militantly promoted socioeconomic reorganization as integral to craft's continued viability, advocating for everyday craftsmen to assume positions of social authority. Painter and Harvard professor Denman Ross suggested the tone of these debates in a 1903 editorial, contending that "knowledge of art, which means aesthetic discrimination and judgment, is found, generally, among the people who do no work, people who study works of art, collect them, and talk about them, but produce nothing." In contrast, "the people [. . .] who are able to work and do work, have, as a rule, no discrimination, no judgment, no standards."[60] Emphasizing technical standards and fidelity to the work of art itself, Ross's position anticipates that of Dos Passos thirty years later, while Mary Coffin Ware Dennett, a women's rights activist who was prominent in SACB circles, foreshadowed the simple, forceful invective of Gold when she declared that "there is the lover of art on one side of the field, the lover of humanity on the other."[61] Neither faction proved long for the world, but the vitality of the debate, raging for months across *Handicraft* and other fora, indicates the seriousness with which craft ideologues viewed the movement's potential.

Likewise, the scope and vitality of the American Writers' Congress suggested a movement in the heyday of its influence, one that had dominated the Left in the years following the crash and which seemed poised, riding a groundswell of working-class support, to revolutionize American culture and politics. In fact, Gold's proletarianism proved a short-lived affair, supplanted mere months after the Congress by a shift in Soviet cultural policy toward the broad, cross-class alliance of the Popular Front. Despite its relatively brief tenure, however—and despite Gold's vitriol for high modernists like Proust—proletarianism constituted a vital movement within modernist ideology. More than simply the project of "making it new," proletarianism shared with modernism a cluster of interrelated values like forcefulness, simplicity, spontaneity, expressiveness, and masculinity— this last, sometimes, to the point of misogyny—while also influencing quintessential high modernists like the William Carlos Williams of *Paterson*. Though later overshadowed by unfavorable literary historiography, labor modernism constituted a proving ground for major modernist concerns such as the relation between aesthetic and political *avant gardes*, revealing modernism itself as intimately related to those values championed at the American Writers' Congress.

After three days of talks on everything from "social trends in modern drama" to "the writer in a minority language," novelist James T. Farrell, fresh off the success of his *Studs Lonigan* trilogy, rose to propose that the Congress conclude with a communal rendition of the *Internationale*. It was a fitting end to what must have seemed like a glorious weekend of proletarian fervor, and it was an act that would have sickened Dos Passos: thousands of literary "proletarians," free enough from work to spend the weekend in Midtown, singing their allegiance in lyrics imported from the Commune by way of Moscow. Nonetheless, and as Henry Hart reported in the minutes, "this was done."[62]

Reprogramming

Outlining cultural debates internal to the 1930s Left matters not only because those debates fenced out the discursive field within which writers like Le Sueur operated, but because they also shaped many of the values institutionalized in midcentury creative writing workshops organized around ideas of literary craftsmanship.

Examining the rise and proliferation of those workshops, scholars of creative writing have suggested that self-expression is rotated therein to what McGurl calls the "minor position" in relation to "values that include impersonality, technique, and self-discipline."[63] As I've suggested, however, the mobilization of craft rhetoric in the service of Eliotic or New Critical impersonality was hardly endemic to workshops organized around New Critical principles, nor was it an exclusive feature of the Program Era. Rather, such practices characterized one faction of the 1930s literary Left which found in craft, as Dos Passos had, a way to foster that "state of selfless relaxation" wherein the writer knows "no worries or urges except those of the work at hand."[64] In reading postwar writing pedagogy like "show, don't tell" as promoting a New Critical resistance to didacticism, moreover, suppressive of more expressive and identity-driven or political writing, scholars ignore how didactic poetics were in fact rebuked not just by Dos Passos and his partisans but by a range of leftist writers who otherwise took diverse positions with respect to the Party program. There was "widespread agreement among 1930s Marxists," Foley writes, "that explicit didacticism was undesirable," quoting Gold's remark that "the function of a revolutionary writer is not to suggest political platforms and theses, but to portray the life of the workers and to inspire them with solidarity and revolt."[65]

Just as my reconstruction of the 1930s Left pressures characterizations of the Program Era as uniquely craft-conscious, though, I also want to complicate the scholarly tendency to overstate the role of New Critical poetics in suppressing proletarian writing. Faulting New Critical values such as ambiguity, irony, and paradox for their exclusiveness and elitism, Foley and many other scholars re-encode precisely those values in ostensibly recovered texts. Of proletarian fiction, for instance, Foley writes that "expressions of political doctrine would be woven, blended, or otherwise embedded in the narrative," her own craft rhetoric framing didacticism as simply another rhetorical thread in the richly ambivalent tapestry of the proletarian text.[66] Cary Nelson, while excoriating New Critical pretension to an ahistorical aestheticism, nonetheless celebrates 1930s "political poetry that was experimental, rhetorically complex, and explicitly modernist."[67] And James Bloom finds proletarian texts characterized by "the density, the generic ambiguity, and the understanding of their own production [. . .] that make the most memorable writing of the past century and a half 'modernist.'"[68] In rescuing literary proletarians from charges of didacticism, these scholars ironically reinscribe in writers like Gold precisely those aesthetic values they castigate as licensing a "political witch hunt in the realm of literary and cultural history." Relatedly, these same scholars continuously collapse Dos Passos and his *Partisan Review* coterie with later New Critical aestheticism, describing an "interlocking directorate" between the two groups that worked to rationalize "a conservative and exclusionary conception of literary value."[69] To be sure, such arguments remind us that New Critical objections to leftist writing were sometimes ideologically motivated, more concerned with Cold War politics than with acknowledging stylistic affinities between midcentury and earlier, more radical writers. But New Critics rarely went out of their way to sideswipe leftist writers, and these scholarly frameworks themselves risk privileging ideology over literary history, ignoring the variegation that existed within both the 1930s Left and those New Critics who succeeded that era.

I am less interested in entertaining a morality tale about Cleanth Brooks than in showing how 1930s cultural debates, a lacuna in McGurl's otherwise remarkable project, supplied the terminology and ideological positioning for later workshops operating on New Critical principles. The question of how to reconcile political commitment with literary craftsmanship, of course, would be posed and reposed throughout the twentieth century, just as it had been posed countless times before—from Horace to Edward Young, from Plato's banished poet to Shelley's unacknowledged legislator—when the relationship between technique and expression had been brought to a crisis. The 1930s constituted one such moment, and while Gold and Dos Passos took up opposed barricades in that crisis, in doing so they opened up a cultural field in which a range of leftist writers could stake out their own positions. As I show in what follows, Le Sueur was one of the most important writers to do so.

"A vast university of the common people": Meridel Le Sueur and the WPA

WORKER WRITERS

Alongside her work in the Women's Auxiliary of General Drivers Local 574, Meridel Le Sueur promoted working-class cultural production at the WPA-backed Minnesota Labor School in Minneapolis, where throughout the mid- to latethirties she taught creative writing as part of the New Deal's Workers Education Project (WEP). While WEP objectives were manifold, ranging widely in terms of audience, ambition, and administration, Le Sueur's pedagogical aims were relatively straightforward—namely, to equip workers with the linguistic tools needed to reflect critically on their experiences as workers.

Toward that end, Le Sueur's pedagogy framed creative writing as practical labor, work her students might learn just as readily as they "learn carpentry, just like you learn to make a table or chair." Language, Le Sueur wrote, "like the plow, the chisel, the needle, the spindle, is a tool. Everyone must make this tool his or her own."[70] Le Sueur's democratization of literary culture manifested also as a critique of the exclusionary institution of the university; she encouraged her students "not [to] be afraid to write simply because you are not a University student or quit school when you were ten." Relatedly, Le Sueur followed Gold in objecting to the kind of decadent modernist literature such universities promoted, deriding Proust as a "sick nobleman who shut himself up in a cork room to remember [. . .] the fetid decay of his life." Le Sueur convicts Gertrude Stein, likewise—"with her 'Pigeons on the grass, alas'"—of writing only "for a select few," restricting "the word as a tool" for the exclusive use of elites.[71] One of many cultural formations informed by 1930s proletarianism, Le Sueur's workshops extended Gold's critique of what Le Sueur herself, at the American Writers' Congress, called *Partisan Review*'s "intellectual, inhuman, non-human" brand of Marxism; what mattered for Le Sueur was less the virtuosic craftsmanship of intellectuals like Dos Passos than writing which came "straight from the [worker's] experience [. . .] for other workers to understand."[72]

These values are outlined in Le Sueur's creative writing textbook, *Worker Writers*, a slim volume she printed and distributed to her students at no charge. Organized into five sections with titles that indicate its tone of proletarian uplift— "The Word is a Tool," "We Must Have Writers"—the book reinforces Le Sueur's pedagogical figuration of writing as practical labor, metaphorizing narrative structure, for example, as a process that "can be learned only by wrestling" with the writer's raw material, "trying it" as if it were mortar, until the structure "hold[s] and satisf[ies]."[73] Appended to these five sections as a kind of pedagogical exemplum, Le Sueur's critical reading of her own short story, "Biography of My Daughter," neatly allegorizes her proletarian values. In a column of marginal comments running parallel to the text proper, she identifies key moments in the story's formal development, noting at the conclusion of the story's opening movement, for instance, that "now we have prepared completely for the narrative problem, 'Why did Rhoda die?'"[74]

To understand that question, and to grasp how Le Sueur hardwires political commitment into creative writing pedagogy, we should understand something of Rhoda's story. Originally published in 1935 in H. L. Mencken's *The American Mercury*, "Biography of My Daughter" picks up Rhoda's narrative in the months after her college graduation, following her through several menial jobs—cooking and housekeeping for a local family, night-waitressing at a dive called Coffee Dan's—

before she finds work as a librarian under the Civil Works Administration, a New Deal initiative intended to create temporary jobs in the winter of 1933–34. When federal funding for her position runs out after two weeks, Rhoda finds herself unemployed and eking out a starvation-level existence, wandering from bread-lines to flophouses until, near madness, she is brought to a sanitarium by her college friend. It is at the sanitarium gates, Rhoda and Marie "stopping at the door at the smell of death," that Le Sueur indicates the "END OF BEGINNING," noting in the story's margins that the narrative problem—"Why did Rhoda die?"—has now been established.[75] The moment is a pivotal one, positioning Rhoda between two institutions equally "inhuman" in Le Sueur's treatment of them—equally inattentive, that is, to the imperatives of working-class experience. While it is "the university doctor himself" who, treating Rhoda at the sanitarium, ultimately contributes to her death, Le Sueur indicts Rhoda's college education too as a kind of cultural malpractice, a haute aestheticism fatally severed from workers' day-to-day reality. "'Listen,'" Marie says to Rhoda's mother in the sanitarium. "When she was graduated from the university I went to see her. There we sat and Coffman, the president, said we mustn't pay any attention he said to this shifting world, that's what he said. It's abstract science, that's what it is, go to the classics, he said, go to the good sane things of our forefathers. [. . .] [S]he died of starvation."[76]

The answer to the narrative problem of "Biography of My Daughter," then—that Rhoda died because her education denied her the proper tools for living—images in fictional form a critique that Le Sueur makes explicit in *Worker Writers* proper, where she contends that "the Universities have put a kind of halo around the written word as if it were sacred and not for common use." Le Sueur's marginal exegesis of her own story, moreover, demonstrates how her creative writing pedagogy soldered leftist critique to questions of aesthetic form. "Show the theme clearly," she admonishes her students in one marginal note. "What happened to [Rhoda] must stop happening. END OF THE MIDDLE." Like Gold, Le Sueur privileges implicit political suggestion over didactic commentary, reminding her students of the "secret" of effective writing—"don't tell about [a story's] conflict," she urges in *Worker Writers*, "SHOW it actually happening. [. . .] We should feel as if we had actually taken part in the conflict."[77] Curiously, in a proletarian workshop of 1935, of all places, we find the same creative writing pedagogy scholars have attributed to the "New Critical idea of narrative impersonality."[78] While Foley and McGurl read the "heresy of the didactic"—a phrase original to Edgar Allen Poe—as naming the restraint of the expressive ego through New Critical craft, Le Sueur follows Gold in prohibiting didacticism because it impedes the realistic portrayal of workers' experiences, hardly a concern paramount to Brooks, Robert Penn Warren, and the movement they inspired.

"A PROLETARIAN PUBLIC SPHERE": THE WORKERS' EDUCATION PROJECT

If influenced by Gold's proletarianism, Le Sueur's pedagogy was shaped equally by the institutional context in which it took place, a Workers Education Project bankrolled by the WPA from 1933 to 1942 and reaching over 60,000 students in two dozen states.[79] Le Sueur's workshop-style classroom, to cite one example of WEP influence—in which students and teacher collaboratively produced, critiqued, and revised work, sharing experiences and intellectual resources—arose not as some default writing pedagogy but out of consciously deliberated WEP protocols. These protocols encouraged discussion-based classrooms in which teachers acted as dialogic partners rather than authoritative reserves of knowledge; thus, both in its content and form, Le Sueur's pedagogy might be said to have promoted a kind of cultural egalitarianism. As with her refashioning of proletarian thought, however, Le Sueur worked within WEP parameters while revising them to accord with her own theories of working-class education; both sets of values helped determine the paradigm within which later workshops would take shape.

The sole American effort to educate workers on such a massive scale, the Workers Education Project employed over 1,000 out-of-work teachers at the height of its influence, in subjects ranging from economics and labor history to parliamentary procedure, public speaking, and creative writing.[80] In accordance with WEP protocol, unions and other community groups could request classes through a government sponsor—typically a state university or department of education—though funds were also distributed to pre-existing institutions like the Minnesota Labor School. Teachers themselves were hired, as Le Sueur was, from county relief rolls and completed a teacher-training program before taking charge of their own classrooms.[81] It seems fitting that a writer who so derided the university as an exclusionary institution found work instead in "a vast university of the common people,"[82] as she would later put it, a network of night schools, extension courses, labor colleges, summer camps, and union meetings that dramatically reshaped higher education in this country to the point, as Denning writes, that there emerged in WEP courses "an alternative intellectual world in the United States, a proletarian public sphere."[83] Intended by the Roosevelt administration as a means of critically engaging laborers in their work, WEP courses juggled multiple and sometimes contradictory objectives, all of which stemmed from the

WEP's primary mission of increasing workers' economic, social, and political literacy. In addition to extending the liberal education of workers whose schooling was cut short by the Great Depression, the WEP endeavored to provide vocational training and labor rights counseling, to enrich workers' leisure time, to strengthen home lives, and to train prospective citizens in American history and culture.

As Joyce L. Kornbluh and Caroline Ware note, WEP objectives drew heavily on the agenda of early twentieth-century progressive educators, yoking citizenship and social engineering goals to liberal education focused on self-improvement and cultural uplift.[84] Such an agenda found its classic and most influential articulation in John Dewey's *Democracy and Education*, in which the luminary of progressive education recognized that a "great majority of workers have no insight into the social aims of their pursuits," advocating an education that would uncover the "intellectual content" and "cultural possibilities" in industrial labor and "give those who engage in industrial callings desire and ability to share in social control."[85] Importantly—and seldom remarked upon in the extensive scholarship on his work—Dewey understood workers' education as a surrogate for the craft epistemologies produced and disseminated in nineteenth-century workshops. In such spaces, Dewey argued, workers' knowledge and ingenuity were honed through their direct manipulation of the tools at their command. Though Dewey believed that the "intellectual possibilities" of industrialism were greater than in previous eras, the actual conditions of industrial work precluded full realization of its educational potential. Unless workers could "saturate with meaning the technical and mechanical features" of their work, Dewey wrote, they would "sink to the role of appendages to the machines they operate."[86] Thus, the task of educating workers in the ramifications of their labor fell to progressive educators, to programs like the WEP and to teachers like Le Sueur. Though the WEP's workshop-style classroom originated in Washington, then, this format signaled the importance of workers' education as a replacement for the proto-industrial workshop, where, in Dewey's idealized view, craftsmen labored collectively at shared projects they oversaw from beginning to end. As an industrial-corporate regime cemented its influence on the American economy, the workshop became "workshop."

Indeed, its translation of the proto-industrial workshop into the context of industrial education would contribute to the most formidable difficulty and greatest controversy the WEP faced in implementing its progressive ideals. As the Congress of Industrial Organizations (CIO) and other industrial labor organizations requested an increasing number of WEP classes, with some unions even developing their own educational initiatives, more conservative craft unionists associated with the AFL objected to what they perceived as the promotion, with government funding, of revolutionary rather than reformist values. As Kornbluh notes, while AFL educational efforts focused on fostering a "craft culture" among skilled laborers—respect for technical standards, brotherhood with one's fellow workers—industrial unions advocated more radical economic reorganization, promoted racial solidarity among Black and immigrant workers, and advocated stridently for gains among women workers, causes that threatened not only the appeal and viability of craft unionism but also, according to craft unionists, destabilized the very foundation of democracy.[87] One need only glance at Le Sueur's own textbook to understand the basis for these charges. "We have to find out how to look at society," she wrote, "as being transformed by [its] dialectical opposite," describing an "inevitable movement into the synthesis, the movement and solidarity of all life."[88] "We need words," she argued, "to write the true history of the past so that we can create a true history in the future."[89] The evolving conflict between craft and industrial unionism—so volatile during the long strike-filled summer of 1934—found expression too in New Deal undertakings like the WEP, initiatives which tended to aggravate more than ameliorate existing tensions over the broader meaning and ramifications of labor. Le Sueur's rhetoric is far indeed from the business unionism of an AFL focused on the orderly maintenance of collective bargaining within existing economic structures.

Yet the WEP's implementation of workers' education faced not only ideological but practical challenges as well, among them developing pedagogies flexible enough to educate a heterogeneous student population and retaining qualified teachers who were nonetheless expected to demonstrate absolute destitution as a condition of employment. Le Sueur describes her firsthand experience of WEP hiring practices in her essay "Women are Hungry," originally published in *The American Mercury* in 1934. "[Y]ou feel very terrible going up to the capitol office building," she writes, her second-person positing a communal experience. "You've gone up there lots of times to get a position but that is different. Then you had your Ph.D. and your fur coat and the knowledge that you were going to get on in that world, and you didn't have to watch to see that your elbows did not come through and that your last pair of stockings did not spring into a run." Contrasting the New Deal's high-flown symbolism with the realities of working-class life, Le Sueur describes "the great building with the chariot of horses high above," an edifice which now "looks terrifying and you feel guilty, as if you had failed somehow and it must be your own fault."[90] The statehouse chariot, equally democratic ideal and autocratic scourge, is in turn embodied in the hiring supervisor whom

Le Sueur watches interrogate another prospective teacher, their tense exchange staging the kind of authoritative relationship Le Sueur worked to circumvent in her pedagogy. "The man was going over her application, trying to make it more definite," Le Sueur writes. "'You see, to get this, you have to prove absolute destitution,'" the supervisor explains. "'[Y]ou say you had fifty dollars left from your savings in the spring. Have you still got that? [. . .] How have you been living?'"[91] It is a testament to the teachers who endured these interviews, and to the strength of the progressive ideal for which they did so, that the WEP grew to become such a cultural force, reaching across two dozen states and nearly a decade to educate vast segments of the working class.

Increasingly imperiled as the nation's Depression-era progressivism shaded to wartime nationalism, the WEP faced ever more withering attacks from right-wing politicians eager to dismantle New Deal programming, the rhetoric in many of these attacks supplied by the AFL's own charges of radicalism within WEP classrooms.[92] While the WEP witnessed nothing like the Dies Committee attacks on the contemporaneous Federal Writers' Project, its initiatives were gradually phased out to make room for cultural and material mobilization for World War II. The legacy of the WEP would endure, however, in the increasing prominence of labor education in American colleges and universities, institutions which had begun to recognize the importance of labor in the healthy functioning of the state and which eagerly welcomed working-class students as tuition-paying customers.[93] Much of the pedagogy developed under the auspices of the WEP, moreover, would reemerge as a "pedagogy of the oppressed" during the New Left of the 1960s and '70s, rearticulated—an almost literal return of the repressed—as a combination of progressive education and liberation theology.[94]

Refiguring writing as practical labor rather than cultural capital—the kind of capital that contributes to Rhoda's death—Le Sueur's proletarianism, like Gold's, adapts the late nineteenth- and early twentieth-century emphasis on the craft worker's expressive labor, part of a prior craft ideal that fractures, as I've shown, into opposing factions of the 1930s Left. In what follows, I complicate this reading of Le Sueur's pedagogical and literary investments, since, as the "certain rules of construction" in *Worker Writers* suggest, hers was more than merely an expressivist ethos. Rather, underlying Le Sueur's advocacy of proletarian writing was a sophisticated theory of language as "the 'action' of the creative worker," a kind of performative utterance *avant la lettre* which imagined and labored into existence more just modes of being.[95] Nor, finally, did Le Sueur's pedagogy owe entirely to the immediate context of the 1930s or the imperatives of the WEP—as is appropriate for a writer who so capitalized on puns on "labor," she was born for it.

"THE 'ACTION' OF THE CREATIVE WORKER"

The daughter of radical parents active in the turn-of-the-century socialist movement, Le Sueur grew up in a greenhouse of leftist culture; her father, Arthur, was elected four times on the socialist ticket as mayor of Minot, North Dakota, and her mother, Marian Wharton, was a close associate of Helen Keller in the temperance and suffrage movements. In addition to their more overt activism with the Industrial Workers of the World (IWW), Le Sueur's parents were among the leaders of the socialist-inspired People's College in Fort Scott, Kansas, where from 1914 to 1917 Arthur served as college president alongside Eugene Debs, the chancellor of the college, and Marian administered the college's publicity department, teaching part-time in the school's Department of Plain English. Housed in a mansion near the town square, the People's College centered around a three-year course of study in US law, but also offered residential and correspondence courses in a range of subjects, from English and algebra to typewriting, public speaking, and shorthand. As in Le Sueur's workshops, leftist critique came hardwired into People's College pedagogy, and no more so than in the textbook Wharton herself authored for use in the college's English courses.[96]

Titled *Plain English: For the Education of the Workers by the Workers*, Wharton's textbook provided much of the framework for Le Sueur's pedagogy two decades later. As would Le Sueur, Wharton figures writing as practical labor, encouraging her students to "master the use of English words, the tools of your expression." "Make your notebook your workshop," Wharton enjoins her students, figuring writing as the crafting of working-class identity in the same way that her chapter prefaces, each beginning with "Dear Comrade," figure literary education as the cultivation-by-correspondence of working-class solidarity. As would Le Sueur, moreover, Wharton seamlessly encodes leftist critique into her textbook's grammatical exercises, so that a lesson on "Kinds of Sentences" asks students to explain the differences in the following sentences: "Two classes have always existed. To which class do you belong? Join your class in the struggle." Finally, Wharton challenges an elite monopoly on literary culture, reminding her students that "the best of everything is none too good for you. It is your right, your heritage, and the best in the English language will bring you into the company and comradeship of the men and women who have striven and toiled for humanity, who will talk to you of dreams and deeds worth while, who will place in your hands the key to a new world."[97] As Wharton's rhetoric of class uplift suggests, *Plain English* is less radical in outlook than *Worker Writers*, oriented more toward mechanical correctness than economic revolution. Le Sueur scholar Julia M. Allen reminds us that Wharton's pedagogical mission was empowering workers to succeed within, rather than militate against, a rapidly developing industrial-corporate regime, her students encouraged to prioritize class mobility over class warfare.[98] "Don't think this is putting on airs," Wharton writes. "It is not. It is simply demanding the best for yourself in words, as you should do in everything. We of the working class have built the world in its beauty. Why should we live in shacks, dress in shoddy, talk in slang?" For Le Sueur, in contrast, literary language was a tool for class conflict. "The English language is to be used," she wrote. "Those fighting for their daily lives today are the ones that are going to need to have that strong, sturdy language for their use."[99]

For all her working-class utilitarianism, however, Le Sueur's pedagogy revolved around a complicated, if never fully elaborated, theory of language as "the 'action' of the creative worker," a quasi-performative utterance which labored into existence more egalitarian social relations.[100] Le Sueur glosses this theory in her creative writing textbook, where "dialectical" narrative structure formally models the dialectical transformation of society. "We not only want to describe the world, we want to change it," Le Sueur taught, sounding a Hegelian note. "[W]e need a structure that includes the thesis, the antithesis, and the synthesis."[101] Fuller development of her language theory comes in a series of essays that appeared in *New Masses* in late 1934 and early 1935. In "The Fetish of Being Outside," Le Sueur describes the proletarian writer as an avant-garde force "moving in the chaotic dark of a new creation"; while Le Sueur frequently figures this action as a form of labor, in "Fetish" she borrows from the language of evolution, noting that "even the lowest forms of life are able to step out in this belief into a new element and grow a new orientated fin or organ that makes creative alignments."[102] To be sure, Le Sueur's treatment of language as action is inconsistent; at times, she anticipates J. L. Austin's notion of "performativity," while at other moments she locates linguistic action in the materiality of language or in non-narrative lyricism. What matters is not so much detangling the knot of Le Sueur's folk philosophy, but acknowledging the multiple ways in which she instrumentalizes language as a tool for proletarian empowerment.

Le Sueur's most extensive theorization of language comes in her guide to the history and culture of Minnesota, a text written and published under the auspices of Erskine Caldwell's American Folkways Series. Though unaffiliated with the WPA's more popular American Guide series, *North Star Country* reworks much of the same material that Le Sueur uncovered in her research as a staff member on the WPA's *Minnesota: A State Guide*. Le Sueur's refashioning of this material, however—especially through her figuration of language as action—suggests the deep reservations she harbored regarding the WPA's ideological tendency to frame history as a narrative of civilizational progress. Like the WEP, the WPA's Washington-based Federal Writers' Project (FWP) exerted strong editorial control over a guidebook series otherwise researched, written, and produced at the state level, its centralized policies regulating everything from tone and style—"impersonal" prose was essential, passive voice discouraged—to questions of emphasis and organization. Word allotments, for instance, were strictly enforced to ensure "balance" and "proportionality," while the guides' "tours" of each state—though that word was prohibited—were expected to follow roadways from north to south and east to west, another useful lesson in American values.[103] Most significantly, while FWP editors permitted isolated critique of localized incidents, discrete historical episodes were structured within overarching narratives of progress, so that the Minnesota guide opens by evoking the wonder of those historical processes that led Minnesota to its present grandeur: "[W]ithin the span of a single lifetime, 54 million acres of forests, lakes, rivers, and untouched prairies have been converted into an organized area of industrial cities and rich farms, of colleges, art centers, golf clubs and parks. The men and women who accomplished this were for the most part New Englanders, Germans, and Scandinavians—probably as hardy as the world has produced."[104] Tinged with racial pride, such narratives require the suppressing of the material and ideological violence underlying national progress, with Minnesota's forced displacement of Algonquin peoples converted to a "westward hegira" and centuries of cruelty toward American Indians, workers, women, and Eastern and Southern European immigrants tidily bracketed as a "long series of unappetizing affairs."[105] The account of one FWP employee, editor of the New Jersey guide, speaks to the central office's strict enforcement of this American narrative. "Our manuscripts told how Seabrook Farms had used teargas against the striking farm workers [. . .] how trichinosis was spread from the meat of garbage-fed hogs," the editor wrote. "All of this material was killed in Washington."[106] As would WEP educators, therefore, FWP writers and researchers worked within the organization's editorial parameters to produce as accurate and as democratic a guide as institutionally possible. Le Sueur, on the other hand, whose objections to this kind of editing we might well imagine, simply wrote her own book.

In one of the few scholarly engagements with the American Guide series, Christine Bold argues convincingly that FWP administrators exploited the generic conventions of 1930s documentary, masking their ideological investments as objective research. The guides' "documentary status," Bold writes, "allowed project publicizers to speak of them as 'discovering'—rather than 'creating'—American culture, thus effectively naturalizing their very selective and interested representations." Though FWP guides did not announce themselves as ideological, their narratives of civilizational progress allowed for the orderly management of differences that loomed threateningly outside the stable architecture of historiography, particularly in the 1930s. "The series as a whole," Bold writes, "is marked by a tendency to naturalize social difference—even social dysfunction—as 'local color,' part of an ultimately harmonious landscape defined as 'the nation.'"[107] *North Star Country* challenged this landscape by making visible those peoples and experiences neglected in more conventional histories. As Allred notes, documentaries like Le Sueur's worked to disrupt "overarching metanarratives" like those scaffolded throughout *Minnesota: A State Guide*, an ideological intervention Allred links to a wider modernist "aesthetics of interruption."[108] Drawing heavily from historical anecdotes, newspapers, folk songs, journals, maps, travelogues, and other archival material, *North Star Country* engages in precisely this interruption, figuring language as a technology of empire which, while historically abetting a capitalist class of bankers and land speculators, might be reclaimed as a tool for working-class enfranchisement.

North Star Country reads history, in other words, as enacting that dialectical narrative structure Le Sueur first imagines in *Worker Writers*, the documentary describing "the people" as a "story that never ends," a "long incessant coming alive from the earth."[109] Language as "the 'action' of the creative worker" is key to this "coming alive," a figuration invoked equally in wide-angle historical narration and in in-scene "showing" rendered with all the immediacy of Jamesian scenic method. Discussing French exploration of the Mississippi delta, Le Sueur depicts massively consequential history in luminous detail: "All along the rich country they stopped, and La Salle donned his ermine robe, the seals and documents were unwrapped, and they took in the name of the King the copper country, even the silk worms in Arkansas—the prairie, the forests, the river [. . .] There was no record, no ledger, and yet they were creating it. The little clerk took out his notebook and wrote in it. La Salle put down every bend and even at night calculated what wealth might be accrued from an industry using the worms of the mulberry tree."[110]

The passage is a remarkable one, figuring language as a kind of croupier that abstracts and gathers the continent to itself; here La Salle takes the copper country of Arkansas "in the name of the King" just as in Austin priest baptizes infant "in the name of" the Father, Son, and Holy Spirit.[111] If Le Sueur is critical of such procedures, her tone seems equally in awe of the reach and ramifications of language, seems to wonder at that commanding instrument La Salle wields. For implicit in Le Sueur's historiography, evocative of Lévi-Strauss's "writing lesson" among the Nambikwara, is that the imperialistic action of language might be reappropriated as a weapon for class struggle. Culminating in the Minneapolis Truckers' Strike of 1934, *North Star Country* resounds in its second half with the language of proletarian activism, with ironworkers, river-pilots, farmers, and lumberjacks crafting their own autochthonous language to describe not only their work but the wider social and economic contexts in which it takes place: "They named the machines they worked with: 'cat,' 'tractor,' 'donkey'—a small engine which yards and loads; 'hoot-nanny'—a device to hold a crosscut saw while sawing a log from underneath; and the saw itself was a 'Swedish fiddle.' [. . .] To 'Saginaw' a log is to retard the large end, and to 'St. Croix' her is to help the small end gain. The 'wobbly horrors' were what employers got in a strike."[112] In the same way that Le Sueur's pedagogy critiqued *Partisan Review*'s "inhuman" Marxism, her folk philosophy of language indicts language use abstracted from the lived experiences of working-class Americans. Language, for Le Sueur, was a material thing, her depiction of turn-of-the-century Populist meetings echoing workers in its assertion that "we must talk it over, thresh it out, winnow it down."[113] *North Star Country* was precisely that kind of winnowing.

Le Sueur's proletarian reworking of history came in for strident critique from reviewers who found her narrative "erroneous to a degree bordering fantasy." From Le Sueur, Stewart Holbrook wrote in the *New York Herald Tribune*, one "would get the impression that pretty much all of North Star country is under mortgage to fat and grinning bankers, and that most of the farms had blown away on dust storms anyway."[114] In *The Saturday Review of Literature*, Howard Mumford Jones similarly objected to Le Sueur's proletarian bias: "It is a 'folkway' to cheat Indians and be massacred by them in 1862, just as it is a 'folkway' for Minnesota gendarmes to fire into a mass of strikers. But it is not a 'folkway' to have lived a middle-class life in La Crosse, Wisconsin, as I did. In fact, 'folkways' seem to be confined to (a) the country life; (b) persons not of 'Old American' stock; (c) the proletariat."[115] The extent of these reviews, however, suggests the singular importance of a text—one of 28 in Caldwell's American Folkways series—which might easily have fallen into oblivion, a text integral to the proletarian tradition and which at the same time looked forward to postwar aesthetic strategies simplified as "show, don't tell." For insofar as the polemic of *North Star Country* relies on an aesthetic of visuality, we might understand the text as a precursor to the New Critical privileging of implicit political suggestion over didactic commentary. As a genre, William Stott explains, 1930s documentary sought to "treat [lower-class] experience in such a way as to [. . .] render it vivid, 'human,' and—most often—poignant to the audience," resorting in many cases to the photographer's camera to "show" what language could not.[116] Le Sueur's workshop lesson to "SHOW it actually happening," then, might be read not only as promoting a more immediate representation of working-class experience, but as a translation into pedagogy of her contemporary documentary work.[117]

Toward a Labor Modernism: Le Sueur the Novelist

"I BEEN A LABORING TOO": PROLETARIAN PLOTTING

Having demonstrated how American Arts and Crafts ideology informs Le Sueur's work with the WPA and related organizations, I want to close by briefly suggesting how such thinking refracts through the fiction for which Le Sueur is most widely known. In two novels conceived and written across the 1930s, but unpublished until much later, Le Sueur treats literary expression as a crucial component of proletarian self-determination, echoing Gold's call for cultural forms attentive to working-class experience. Those same novels, though, rely to an extraordinary degree on technical procedures that might most accurately be described as modernist, including but not limited to Le Sueur's theorization of language as "the 'action' of the creative worker."[118] By tracing the imbrication of these ostensibly irreconcilable aesthetic philosophies, we might gain a more detailed picture of how 1930s writers redeployed theoretical debates in the service of their own cultural and political priorities. Even as Le Sueur helps to forge a robust labor modernism, she situates herself as part of a craft tradition, advocating for labor that is respective of human needs and fulfilling for those who undertake it. In both the form and content of these novels, as I show, the workshop itself proves instrumental to Le Sueur's crafting of class.

In discussing these texts, I shift more or less vertiginously between them, making a preliminary sketch of their narrative trajectories something of a necessity.

Le Sueur's earliest novel, *I Hear Men Talking*, was composed sometime after the tumultuous summer of 1934, when, contemporaneous with the great industrial strikes, a number of smaller agrarian protests swept the Midwest, including the milk strikes and penny auctions that figure prominently in the novel's plot. Le Sueur experienced much of this unrest firsthand, incorporating such protests into *I Hear Men Talking* alongside memories of her parents' Progressive-era activism in Kansas and North Dakota. Indeed, the family at the center of *I Hear Men Talking*—the novel's protagonist, teenage Penelope; her mother Mona; and Mona's live-in boyfriend, the transient union organizer Lowell—closely resembles Le Sueur's own childhood experience, with both fictional and real families converting their homes into meeting halls for dissenting laborers. It is Lowell, acting in the role of class-conscious outsider, who spearheads the effort to organize the novel's disenfranchised farmers, providing language and practical strategies, like the climactic penny auction, with which they might more effectively protest the policies of absentee bankers and land speculators. Interwoven with this labor narrative is Penelope's own sexual coming of age, her adolescent development closely linked with her coming into class-consciousness as a worker. Near the end of the novel, as its labor and sexual narratives climax, Penelope helps the town doctor deliver neighbor Cora Fearing's baby boy; "'I been a laboring too,'" Penelope proudly declares afterward, her pun emphasizing feminine identity and working-class solidarity as mutually constitutive processes.[119] Published by the Minneapolis-based West End Press in 1984, *I Hear Men Talking* thus re-genders the proletarian *bildungsroman*, a mode dominated by male heroism and the domestication of female labor. The novel also complicates that mode with its own modernist inclinations.

In similar fashion, Le Sueur's *The Girl* reworks proletarian commitment as an intersectional working-class feminism, following its unnamed protagonist through a series of initiatory experiences that eventuate in her joining the feminist Workers Alliance. Completed around 1939 and published in 1978, *The Girl* originated in a workshop Le Sueur taught in that same organization, a Popular Front effort to mobilize unemployed workers and solicit relief funds from institutions like the WPA. "[W]e met every night to raise our miserable circumstances to the level of sagas, poetry, cry-outs," Le Sueur recalls in an afterword to the novel. "There was no tape recorder then so I took their stories down. Some could not write very well, and some wrote them out painfully in longhand while trying to keep warm in bus stations or waiting for food orders at relief offices. [. . .] This should be the function of the so-called writer, to mirror back the beauty of the people, to urge and nourish their vital expression and their social vision."[120] Though *The Girl* bears Le Sueur's imprint, it is no less a product of collective authorship than the dramas of the 47 Workshop, with Le Sueur stitching together her students' stories into a text that indeed bears the marks of group composition. Organized into three movements, the novel's lack of strong authorial control—symptomized in stilted pacing, narrative disjunction, and characterological inconsistency—renders it more akin to picaresque than proletarian *bildungsroman*. In its first movement, *The Girl* tracks its titular protagonist as she falls for a scab worker and gangster *manqué*, named Butch, in the Minneapolis tavern where she works. Following a botched bank robbery in the novel's second movement, the now pregnant Girl is arrested and turned over to a maternity home, where she meets a member of the Workers Alliance named Alice. The novel's third movement treats the Girl's dawning political consciousness. Riding out the Minneapolis winter in an abandoned warehouse, the Girl gives birth while surrounded by Alice and other Alliance militants-turned-midwives, the implication being that together the women labor forth a more emancipatory future. As Le Sueur explains, these narrative threads all tie back to her own Workers Alliance workshop. "The family of the Girl is the family of Gladys," she writes, while the "birthing of the child is the story of Natalie, who has been for thirty years or more in an asylum." And Le Sueur goes on: "Butch's death soliloquy a girl wrote down from remembering leaving her lover like that after a bootleg shootout. The bank robbery was reported by the girl who drove the car."[121]

As in her pedagogy, the expression of working-class experience occupied a central role in Le Sueur's fiction, both in *The Girl* and in its predecessor, *I Hear Men Talking*. In the latter, Penelope seems the very image of Le Sueur's worker-writers, managing the bookkeeping for the farmers' strike commissary; she "made a kind of record when one man took more than he left," Le Sueur describes, "[a]nd this she wrote down besides names that were German, Irish, English, feeling proud of the book, keeping its records as clean as she might."[122] In *The Girl*, likewise, literacy and cultural proficiency provide the foundation for proletarian empowerment, with its unnamed protagonist inducted into class-consciousness through the acts of reading and writing. Realizing that Alice is deaf, the Girl follows her lead in a remarkable textual conversation in their room at the relief home. "Alice touched my cheek and showed me a tiny flashlight she had under her pillow," Le Sueur writes. "She wrote, *Don't cry. We, the common people, suffer together*."

I didn't know what she meant. How did she know I felt sad?

She nodded and wrote again, *Nothing can hold us apart . . . See . . . even deafness,* then she wrote, *or loneliness,* and then, *or fear.*

I wrote, *How?*

We are organizing, she wrote.

I read it.

Then she wrote, *Nothing can stop us.*

After the two are temporarily interrupted by a patrolling relief worker, the Girl grows ever more enthusiastic about the organization Alice describes.

When she turned on the light again we could not write fast enough.

I wrote, *What does it do, the Workers Alliance?*

They demand food, jobs, she wrote quickly.

I looked at the word *demand.* It was a strong word. I didn't know what to write. I looked at it a long time. She looked at me, and when I looked at her she smiled and nodded, like she was going through woods and I was following her. She leaned over and the light shone through her thin hand. She put her hand under her cheek, closed her eyes which I saw meant sleep, and then she wrote in a bold hand and turned the tiny light on it.

Wake tomorrow![123]

An astounding pedagogy in labor activism, the passage contrasts Alice's physical frailty with the energy and efficacy of proletarian literacy; that efficacy is tidily suggested in the performative resonance of "demand," a form of linguistic action akin to the marriage ceremony's "I do."

The passage also marks the Girl's conversion to the cause of proletarian rebellion. Following a police raid on Workers Alliance offices, its members transport a hulking mimeograph machine to the warehouse where the Girl and other women are struggling to survive the winter. While she initially describes the machine, concealed from relief workers, as "covered with an old oil cloth and boards put over it to make it look like a table," the Girl soon comes to recognize its true potential. The machine, she narrates, sat "in the middle of the floor as if it was some kind of shrouded altar, like they covered the statues in the church, Friday before Easter rising."[124] Endowed with sacramental authority, the mimeograph machine functions in *The Girl* as the driving engine of Workers Alliance activism, employed in the printing of political leaflets as well as in the curation and preservation from generation to generation of working-class consciousness. As one organizer describes it, the machine serves as a kind of external memory drive. "We got to re-member to be able to fight," she says. "Got to write down the names. Make a list. Nobody can be forgotten. They know if we don't remember we can't point them out. They got their guilt wiped out. The last thing they take is memory."[125] So par-amount is memory in the workers' struggle for self-determination that it consti-tutes virtually their sole form of resistance to economic exploitation, to the point that their politics, and implicitly Le Sueur's, are predicated to a vast extent on anticipatory belief. "What's there to do?" the Girl asks an Alliance friend towards the novel's conclusion. "It'll be buried deep in our class," the woman answers her, "it will come out. It always comes out."[126] If literacy and literary expression are integral to Le Sueur's emancipatory working-class politics, those politics seem characterized more by deferral than defiance, at least in Le Sueur's fiction.

Yet *The Girl* also reflexively theorizes its own quite forceful intervention in class conflict. In an extraordinary passage, Le Sueur dramatizes the production of the novel on the very mimeograph machine its fictional workers employ. "Go, Sara, and get that on the stencil," an organizer says. "You can use the typewriter at the Labor Temple. [. . .] O yes, get some paper from them. Tell them about Clara and the Girl."[127] While scholars have rightly criticized *The Girl* for its essen-tialist depictions of female labor—women-workers are valued primarily for re-producing the next generation—the novel's reproductive futurity extends beyond mere human natality.[128] Within and without *The Girl*, Le Sueur links sexual with textual reproduction, the anticipatory politics of the latter borne out historically by the novel's publication nearly four decades after it was written. This link—between labor and literature, sexual and mental conception—comes full circle at the novel's conclusion, as the Girl gives birth while recalling her now-deceased lover. "He asked me before he died, Do we belong to the human race?" the Girl declares. "Some people think we don't, I told him, but we do. Yes we do. This is your face, Butch, coming back down the great river, the great dark. I was bucking like a goat, lifting like a mountain. I hear the mimeograph start. A kind of beat."[129] That "beat," of course, is both the human heartbeat and the cyclical revolution of the mimeograph, equally vital to the future of American proletarianism. Writing from that future, Le Sueur makes explicit the almost sacred power inherent in both forms of reproduction. "So the publishing of this book is wonderful," she writes in her 1978 afterword. "[T]o be made visible now by a new generation, not born yet when these women sent them a message—a hosanna, a shout of joy and strength back to those wonderful women our mothers ourselves who keep us all alive."[130] Conceived in a creative writing workshop and fictionally encoding its own collective composition, *The Girl* suggests that publication itself is the deferred birth its authors imagine.

"THE SUMMATION, THE SYNTHESIS, THE MORAL": MODERNIST MERIDEL

Though clearly indebted to Gold's proletarian expressivism, *The Girl's* self-reflexive quality betrays its significant modernist—even postmodernist—inclinations. Multiple afterwords to the novel recognize its experimental form, from Neala Schleuning's description of an "inner realism" akin to Woolf's impressionism to West End Press editor John Crawford's explanation that "Meridel has always been more interested in what she once called, quoting Joyce, 'the curve of emotion' than in the niceties of plotting."[131] Le Sueur even seems to try her hand at Joycean prosopopoeia and Dos Passos's simultaneous language pastiches. As she sits in a Minneapolis tavern, weighing an abortion, the Girl seems lifted straight from Leopold Bloom's Dublin, exterior and interior narration overlapping in complex heteroglossia. "The little pad the beer sat on said, In my old cupboard who wants bones, cried Mother Hubbard, I like Schmidt's! The radio was announcing that the White Sox made a home run. *We wont ever make a home run, ring the bell, beat the race, come in first. There's nothing to it, science is wonderful. Listen honey, don't cry. It's nothing. I'll do it. I'll do it.*"[132] Reminiscent of Joyce's depictions of Plumtree's Potted Meat as well as of Dos Passos's radio newsreels, the passage underscores the extent to which, despite her vitriol for them, Le Sueur was influenced by and adapted the work of literary modernists.

It is Le Sueur's earlier novel, though, that most demonstrates her affinities with experimental techniques she elsewhere derides. Unpublished until 1984, *I Hear Men Talking* draws on Le Sueur's folk philosophy of language as action in order to overcome what she sees as the limitations of literary realism; throughout the novel, proletarian language use "shows in terrific movement," as Le Sueur describes, shedding its husk of representation to labor as material presence.[133] The pervasive gossip that runs throughout the novel's unnamed Iowa town, for instance, appears in an extended mixed metaphor as indiscriminate animal violence, the town's "tongues clack[ing], striking flint on flint like a pack of starved wolves." "They tore what they could get their teeth in," Le Sueur writes, "tore it beyond any shred of its truth."[134] Similarly, the language of the titular "men talking" begins as a "low tight sound that gathered around an invisible object," a physical force "approaching slowly, like a season, striking down, slowly mounting from the steady flow of their words." A peripheral concern at first, the farmers' talk builds to become the primary driving action of the novel, a form of collective labor under which its word-workers strain as if "lifting some heavy invisible stone [. . .] or like men in a quarry hefting new rock, speaking serious words: produce without market, spill the milk, picket the highways."[135] Le Sueur's theorization of language as action is not merely rhetorical, however, nor restricted to the simplistic metaphorization of language as labor; rather, in its very form, *I Hear Men Talking* enacts that broader societal "movement into [. . .] synthesis" that Le Sueur envisions in *Worker Writers*, the novel's dialectical structure modeling the transformative "movement and solidarity of all life."[136]

This dialectical structure manifests in two ways: first, in interwoven narrative threads, each of which rotates around dynamic "forces [that] come into collision," and second, in stylized prose that synthesizes subjectivity and objectivity. Both Penelope's sexual coming of age and her emerging class-consciousness, for example, image broader societal transformation through interpersonal and social violence, whether through Penelope's experience of sexual assault, her labor activism, or her delivery of Cora Fearing's baby; for Le Sueur, these narratives constitute dialectical "collision[s]" which, as they build to "the summation, the synthesis, the moral," model in fictional form a broader economic and feminist revolution.[137] Yet Penelope's delivery of Fearing's baby signals too what we might think of as the novel's dialectical style, shuttling as the passage does between inner emotion and exterior action, between the lyricism of subjective reverie and the realism of objective description:

> She kept her eyes on Dr. Starry. His hands moved exact and real. He looked at her, holding her rigid to what would be expected of her. She felt something striking in her, leaving no loose ends, catching her up so she moved like the instruments he took from his bag, moved under his hands direct and keen, with joy, her movements held within the time of what was happening, cutting through, waiting upon it as if something passed from an unknown world beyond them into their hands, and they took it, threading it through them precisely and nakedly, passing it on to death if it should be, to birth if it should be.[138]

As Le Sueur would later explain, the lyricism of this passage "function[s] as part of the action," with external events "told in active prose, in contrast to the poetic and lyrical song of the girl trying to find her place."[139] As a form of action, Le Sueur's prose style shows, rather than tells about, Penelope's experience as she encounters and labors over objective reality. For as Penelope begins to understand, such reality is only ever a matrix of multiple languages, perspectives, and experiences: perpetually in flux, dialectically evolving. Toward the end of the novel, as the town's gossip takes on a life of its own, Penelope reads that matrix, "seeing then three things: what had happened, what had been said about it, and what it had become in Miss Shelley's mind, fusing together, lapping over."[140] Here, the materiality of Le Sueur's prose—fusing, lapping, like electrical soldering or textile folding—points to her theory of language as actively reworking experience, subjectivity reaching out and transforming the world with its linguistic tools.

We might, therefore, resituate Le Sueur's work at the center of that crucial interchange between proletarian expression and modernist experimentation through which, in the 1930s, almost every major writer passed. For the contradictions inherent in this work—Le Sueur's simultaneous disavowal of and deployment of modernist technique, her sometimes inconsistent instrumentalization of language—ultimately refract contradictions endemic to 1930s literary leftism. While Gold rebuked modernist "verbal acrobatics" and "sickly mental states [with] their subtleties, their sentimentalities, their fine-spun affairs," and while Le Sueur herself objected to the "beautiful and ornate sentences" of that "sick nobleman" Marcel Proust, her manipulation of literary realism corresponds with an entire spectrum of modernist innovation, from Pound's vorticism to Woolf's impressionism to Joyce's object-oriented heteroglossia.[141] Her proletarian "creative worker," in other words, seems far more closely affianced to Dos Passos's modernist technician than either might care to admit. Taken as a whole, Le Sueur's career solders together a craft ideal that runs like faulty wiring through the 1930s Left, her work fusing the writer's expressive labor with technical rigor and theoretical sophistication. More importantly, Le Sueur's proletarian modernism shows how modernism itself was forged within and against the 1930s Left to the point that major modernist concerns, like the relation between aesthetic and political *avant gardes*, seem inextricable from questions of labor and literary craftsmanship.[142]

"He wrote in wood"

If Le Sueur's career reconciles opposed aspects of an American Arts and Crafts craft ideal, those aspects manifest variously in her contradictory invocations of the word and practice of craft, one of the keywords that run throughout her work.

In *I Hear Men Talking*, craft is time and again figured as the impersonal, almost inhuman exploitation of others, a kind of cold, technical precision associated with gossip and sexual violence. A lyrical prologue to the novel figures the town's prolific gossip through synecdoche, Le Sueur describing "*all the Eyes looking [at] you—the crafty ones, the gimlet eyes, measuring and calculating [. . .] with a cunning that closed the door too close behind a man's coming in.*"[143] Similarly, Bac eyes Penelope just before he assaults her "with indifference born of craft," carefully "making no move as he knew to watch rabbits, until they sat up, revealing their white under-bodies to him, teaching him just the moment to let go at them."[144] This is, to resort to the OED, craft "in a bad sense," a "skill or art applied to deceive or overreach." Linked with "deceit, guile, fraud, [and] cunning," this is the craft of the Pharisees who in the Gospel of Mark consider "how they might take him by craft, and put him to death," the craft of Hobbes's Leviathan, who practices "that Crooked Wisdome, which is called Craft."[145] Appearing some two dozen times in the novel, the "craft" of *I Hear Men Talking* is the fastidious technical mastery which Le Sueur, in more polemical modes, associates with the inhuman leftism of *Partisan Review*, in particular its privileging of aesthetic standards over the lived experiences of the working class.

At the same time, an alternative, more positive figuration of craft—one which speaks to both aspects of the craft ideal—runs through *North Star Country*, in which Le Sueur lavishes attention on a Scandinavian carpenter living on the nineteenth-century Minnesota frontier. In one of the documentary's brilliant moments of scenic detail, Le Sueur describes how the work of Jacob the Carpenter literally expresses its maker's working-class identity. "There are people today who can tell anything that Jacob has built," Le Sueur writes. "They can tell the barns—so solid they have grown like a living body and become part of the ground. [. . .] He could not write, but he wrote in wood, and you can read the scroll of a good workman, a craftsman."[146] Yet Jacob's labor is characterized too by its demonstrable technical virtue:

> He handled all his life the lathe, the center and the spiral bit, the brace, the ax, saw, claw hammer, small augers, mallet gouges, gimlets, and the bradawl. He had in his toolbox the chisel, the iron square, the rule, and the chalk line. In his early buildings you can see the wood pins, squared off neat as you please with an ax. When he came to this country he had to get used to the woodcraft of the open fields: how to hang a gate, which is an art in itself; how to make roofs for the prairies, strong king posts to hold against the wind.

Jacob, in other words, is the prototypical craftsman of the American Arts and Crafts movement, his labor simultaneously expressive and technically rigorous. Opposed by Le Sueur to deadening and de-creative speculative discourses, Jacob's craftsmanship gives life to his frontier community, the dignity his work provides —the sense of purpose and fulfillment and vitality to be found in all genuine craftsmanship—succinctly suggested in the evolution of Jacob's work as it is linked to the life and labor of the Plains states. "When building stopped," Le Sueur writes, "Jacob became a coffin-maker."[147]

To confront craft in Le Sueur's teaching and writing is to experience, beyond the term's moral ambiguity, her conviction that modernist technical virtuosity might be enlisted in the battle for proletarian and working-class enfranchisement. Amid the schisms and cleavages of the 1930s, she looked back to a prior craft ideal that championed the individual worker as capable of meaningful material production. Her own work updates that ideal for an industrial-corporate age.

Chapter Three

Significant Craft

Robert Duncan and the Black Mountain Craft Ideal

As thousands of would-be proletarians descended on the Americans Writers' Congress in the spring of 1935, and as the cause they sought to promote overtook the country's literary and political forums, another group of artists retreated to the mountains of western North Carolina, guided by an alternate interpretation of the American Arts and Crafts craft ideal. At Black Mountain College near Asheville, craft thinking loomed largely in an avant-garde modernism which invoked craftsmanship not as an instrument of proletarian revolt, like Gold and Le Sueur, but as an exercise in self-transcendence. In ways akin to Dos Passos's literary technician, Black Mountain pedagogues conceived of craft as an anti-expressive, self-annulling discipline, a way of sublimating the ego in and through the resistances of craft material. Black Mountain's was a *spiritualized* craft ethos. As in American Arts and Crafts, the worker's labor constituted a spiritual process in its own right, maintaining an intimate engagement with simple materials that facilitated freer, more authentic expression. At Black Mountain, additionally, submission to the material allowed craftsmen to formally embody a higher order of creation, to access a spiritual plane unapproachable via more egoistic forms of making. Through craft, Black Mountain's course catalog asserted—"some kind of art-experience, which is not necessarily the same as self-expression"—students could "come to the realization of order in the world," attaining "firmer control of [themselves] and [their] environment."[1]

By 1933, of course, when Black Mountain College was founded, the American

Arts and Crafts movement had largely died out. Though the movement endures in various avatars to the present, a number of interrelated factors combined around the year 1916 to hasten the demise of major craft initiatives. That year, Gustav Stickley's movement-defining journal *The Craftsman* appeared on newsstands for the final time, swept under in the bankruptcy that had already led Stickley to shutter operations at his Morris County community, Craftsman Farms. It was Stickley, more than any other craft practitioner, who had popularized the social, economic, and aesthetic value of craftsmanship, acquainting American audiences with the philosophies of William Morris and John Ruskin (to whom the first two issues of *The Craftsman* were dedicated) and enlisting hundreds of retailers in an effort to distribute his hand-manufactured Craftsman furniture more widely. A year prior to Stickley's bankruptcy, fellow craft proponent and founder of the utopian Roycroft community, Elbert Hubbard, had died in the sinking of the *Lusitania*. Three years before that, in 1912, the influential national journal *Handicraft* ceased operations, discontinued by an underfunded and increasingly irrelevant Society of Arts and Crafts, Boston.[2]

The death dates for the American Arts and Crafts movement are potentially as numerous as the forms the movement adopted. One of the more poetic timestamps for its decline, though, might be 1913, the year that Stickley's doomed cathedral to craft, the Craftsman Building, opened in a city still buzzing over the Armory Show that had closed its doors three months earlier. While the American Arts and Crafts movement imploded for multiple reasons endemic to craft itself, its demise was hastened by the fauvist color palettes and cubist fragmentation of a show which conferred on craft an even quainter, more sepia-tinted aura than the movement had already possessed. Indeed, there is grim resonance in the fact that, as Stickley hung draperies and arranged *chaises longues* in his Craftsman Building, the art movement for which the era would be named was exploding into existence a mile away. "[T]he art event of the season," *The Craftsman* had called the Armory Show, devoting two paragraphs to the exhibition in an issue featuring articles like "What To Prune and How to Spray" and a poem, written by Margaret Widdemer in rhymed couplets, called "The House of Ghosts."[3] By 1913, the craft movement seemed exactly that.

If the American Arts and Crafts movement was moribund by the 1930s, the exigencies of the Great Depression would have a resuscitative effect on craft practices, with many Americans returning to craft not as some rarefied aesthetic endeavor—much less as a protest against modernity—but as a matter of necessity, taking up crafts like sewing, quilting, carpentry, and even architecture as a means of subsistence. As the economy contracted, Americans looked back to those skills which had empowered their ancestors to break the plains and drive the cattle and raise the roofbeams beneath which the continent had become a home.[4] Despite the limited resources of Great Depression-era America, communities of craft teaching were established in virtually every state, from rural schools dedicated to preserving indigenous labor practices to prestigious coastal institutions where craft became part of a broader arts curriculum for the nation's elite.[5] Alongside the labor colleges of the Works Progress Administration (WPA)'s Workers Education Project, moreover, craft played an integral role in a progressive education movement for which activities like carpentry, bookbinding, and weaving constituted a means of making labor "intellectually fruitful"; as progressive scion John Dewey put it, craft allowed student-workers to recover "the continuity of aesthetic experience with normal processes of living."[6] Even as the American Arts and Crafts movement died out, in other words, craft itself remained pivotal to a wide range of economic and educational institutions.

Part arts school, part labor college, part experiment in democracy, Black Mountain College adapted American Arts and Crafts ideology in numerous ways, from the pedagogy of visual artists Josef and Anni Albers to a college-wide work program to poet Robert Duncan's postwar "field poetics," described by Duncan in terms resonant with craft overtones. De-privileging lyric expression, Duncan argued that the poet's ability to access "the hidden and life-creative and destructive ID-entity underlying and overriding the conveniences of personal identity is what makes the difference between mere craft (the triviality of workmanship in and of itself) and significant craft."[7] In this chapter, I reconsider the scholarly tendency, influenced by Donald Allen's 1960 anthology *The New American Poetry*, to link Duncan to Black Mountain through his relationship with rector Charles Olson, revealing instead how Duncan's "significant craft" extends the objectives of the college at which both writers taught. Attending to these objectives—to the ways in which a craft ideal informs and is transformed by Black Mountain aesthetics—helps clarify the evolution of American Arts and Crafts principles as they migrate from lapsed craft initiatives, including Baker's 47 Workshop, through the 1930s Left and reenter the ambit of US higher education. In describing this trajectory, I have focused on the importance of craft to the writing workshop, but the artistic afterlives of American Arts and Crafts were many, and, though those afterlives would be both vitalized by and vitiated within the American university, at Black Mountain they animated diverse and conceptually sophisticated creative practices.

What Duncan called "significant craft" Josef Albers called "articulation in visual form"; his wife Anni called it "meaningful form." In dealing "with visual matter, the stuff the world is made of," Anni Albers explained, the "discipline of matter acts as a regulative force: not everything 'goes.'" The artist, therefore, must "circumvent the NO of the material with the YES of an inventive solution."[8] Examining courses in drawing, design, and weaving, including an introductory course called *"Werklehre"*—literally "work teaching" or "how to work"—I show how Black Mountain pedagogy fostered what Richard Sennett has called craft's "engaged material consciousness," promoting flexibility, experimentation, and constructive thinking through students' immediate engagement with craft materials.[9] Rather than employing paper as simply a flat material to be written upon, for instance—"whereby one side of the paper loses its expression," Josef argued—students emphasized the paper's edge by standing it, sculpting it into mobiles, twisting, sewing, and even riveting, all in an effort to short-circuit hardwired patterns of "vision and articulation." If such defamiliarization cultivated "independent thinking and [. . .] an individual style," however, that individuality differed dramatically from mere self-expression, since students' discoveries were made possible by the resistances to which they were subject.[10] "Standing between the actual and that which may be," Anni wrote, the craftsman "forego[es] his own identity in order [. . .] more impartially to interpret the potential" of his material.[11] As in the American Arts and Crafts movement, adherence to technical standards promoted more fulfilling expression, leaving the craftsman "free to follow the promptings of material."[12] Josef articulated this aspect of the Black Mountain craft ideal with characteristic directness: "a teaching method mainly concerned with self-expression," he stated, "is wrong, psychologically and artistically."[13]

For both artists, as for Duncan, submission to material resistances was a means of unlocking, or of embodying in aesthetic form, a universal spiritual order, a plane of abstract forms underlying all creation. Combining the abstraction and self-renunciation of De Stijl with Constructivist fidelity to materials, the Alberses viewed craft making as a transubstantiative process, a means of "listening for the dictation of the material" in order to "tak[e] part in an eternal order."[14] As one of Josef's students phrased it in a notebook: "God forever geometrizes."[15] And—true to form, we might say—spiritual geometries run throughout the Alberses' work from this period. In weavings and wall hangings, lithographs and machine-engraved platens, the Alberses' use of spareness and abstraction suggests a renunciatory effort toward order, a spiritual harmony re-presented in relations among line, color, and shape. Refocusing on media traditionally marginalized within art

history and theory, including work from both artists inspired by recently excavated precolonial sites in Mexico and South America, I show in this chapter how
Black Mountain's craft pedagogy translated into artistic practice. In doing so, I
chart how the Alberses' interest in craft as a spiritual discipline evolved from their
earlier work at the Staatliches Bauhaus, where craft practices had constituted
preparatory training for industrial-corporate manufacture.

Recognizing, however, that its spiritualized craft ideal was more than mere
rhetoric, I attend too in this chapter to the Black Mountain work program in
farming and construction, manual labor central to the aesthetic experience and
financial solvency of the college itself. A synthesis of progressive education and a
manual labor movement that had been dormant since 1845, Black Mountain's work
program aimed at fostering the self-discipline integral to democratic society, ex-
posing students at the same time to the spiritual benefits of manual labor. Work,
therefore—whether milking cows or making corn silage, pouring concrete or
raising wall frames—was accomplished "in perfect order," Louis Adamic reported
in *Harper's*, "even with form."[16] Treating the 1940 construction of the Bauhaus-
inspired Studies Building as a case study, I assess the practical viability of "significant craft," the capacity of actual work to open onto higher, spiritual orders.
Theodore Dreier, the *de facto* head of the work program, was remarkably sanguine about the spiritual potential of labor, recording in his journal on October 7,
1940, that "the spirit was really excellent" and two weeks later that "the spirit
was good today. We worked late and had quite a feeling of accomplishment at
the end."[17] While many students and faculty ratified Dreier's assessment, buying
wholesale into the "work mystique" that gathered around the construction of the
Studies Building, others, lampooning Dreier as the "chief Messianist of work,"
saw the program as mere drudgery, criticizing its autocratic nature and objecting
to its domination of cultural life at Black Mountain.

Literalizing a craft ideal that found in material resistances an avenue toward
spiritual order, Black Mountain's work program raises the question of what happens when "significant craft" loses its significance, when work simply does not
work. For, like the very idea of poetry as craft—from Horace's admonition to put
"badly turned lines back on the anvil" to contemporary creative writing pedagogies organized around structure, texture, and tone—the significant craft of Black
Mountain College is ultimately metaphorical, a figuration carrying over the experience of manual labor into the process of aesthetic creation, sometimes with
scant regard for the degradations of work itself.[18] "The stubble-field becomes a

poem," Black Mountain co-founder John Andrew Rice asserted in 1942, positing a lossless translation from vehicle to tenor and reminding us that that translation—from work to writing, manual to mental labor—is planted deep in the etymology of "verse": the plowman's turning at field's edge.[19]

That work was crucial to the poetics of Duncan and the Alberses, just as it animated the field poetics of Black Mountain College's last rector, Charles Olson, who in his iconic statement on "Projective Verse" imagined an equally lossless metaphor, a perfect translation from field to field. "[A]*ll* parts of speech," Olson argued, "suddenly, in composition by field, are fresh for both sound and percussive use, spring up like unknown, unnamed vegetables in the patch, when you work it, come spring."[20]

This chapter tests the fidelity of that metaphor.

Josef and Anni Albers

"The material does not err": From the Bauhaus
to Black Mountain

In a publicity statement delivered in 1923, founder Walter Gropius articulated a bold new vision for Bauhaus pedagogy, abandoning the school's earlier emphasis on craft as an artistic practice and reconceiving its workshops as a proving ground for industrial-corporate manufacture. "The old craft workshops will develop into industrial laboratories," Gropius proclaimed, creating a "new productive union" wherein the craftsman's engagement with the "entire process of production" would supply an ideal model for industrial labor. For Gropius, the craftsman's intimate knowledge of his material uniquely equipped him to create prototypes for industry, a belief that transformed the Bauhaus into one of the earliest schools of industrial design.[21]

Perhaps the most iconic of Bauhaus products, Marcel Breuer's tubular-steel chair, originated as just such a prototype, as did objects created in the pottery and furniture workshops, as well as Josef Albers's designs for bowls, teacups, and tables—all exquisitely functional, to invoke a Bauhaus keyword.[22] As Virginia Gardner Troy notes, moreover, textile prototypes were one of the weaving workshop's "most significant innovations," with Anni Albers herself keenly attuned to the importance of aesthetic integrity in mass-produced domestic objects.[23] "Utility became a keynote of work, and with it the desire to reach a wider public," Anni wrote in "Weaving at the Bauhaus," describing "a desire to take part actively in contemporary life by contributing to the forms of its objects." For Anni, originally a student under Paul Klee and Wassily Kandinsky and subsequently the director of the Bauhaus weaving workshop, craft objects were no "romantic attempt to recall a temps perdu," but a key stage in large-scale machine manufacture.[24]

Integral to this process was the craftsman's immediate engagement with material, understood by Bauhäuslers as a way of sensitizing the craftsman to—or of disciplining him with—influences beyond his control. Anni Albers's writing on design testifies powerfully to a Bauhaus craft ideal which balanced the worker's expressive labor with submission to materiality. "As the one who makes something from beginning to end and has it actually in hand," Anni wrote in "Designing," the craftsman "is close enough to the material and to the process of working it to be sensitive to the influences coming from these sources. His role today is that of the expounder of the interplay between them. He may also play the part of the conscience for the producer at large. It is a low voice, but one admonishing and directing rightly. For the craftsman, if he is a good listener, is told what to do by the material, and the material does not err." Anni returns to this materialist ethos in her 1947 "Design: Anonymous and Timeless," in which she finds "direct experience of a medium" one of the primary "justification[s] for crafts today. For it means taking, for instance, the working material into the hand, learning by working it of its obedience and its resistance [. . .] The material itself is full of suggestions for its use if we approach it unaggressively, receptively."[25] Though he wrote far less frequently than Anni, Josef Albers echoed his wife's line of thinking, warning that mass production was "doom[ed]" unless it found a way to incorporate "the best qualities of the crafts."[26] While scholars have discussed Bauhaus prototyping at great length, the transformation of this industrial impetus among ex-Bauhäuslers in the United States has been far less examined.[27] For neither Josef nor Anni, while still in Germany, yet understood the craftsman's receptivity to material as a spiritual process; rather, respecting materiality allowed craftsmen to simply produce a more functional object, one destined not for some transcendent plane of universal form but for mass production in the Weimar manufactory.

It was this industrial-corporate orientation that provoked widespread criticism from Bauhaus detractors, among them craft unionists and construction tradesmen who feared that the Bauhaus influence on industry would reduce demand for their own craft labor.[28] Even more threatening to the Bauhaus, as Peter Hahn notes, was the "hostility of the same petit bourgeois elements that were the cradle of the Nazi movement," those spurned sons of the middle classes who would themselves have trained as craftsmen in earlier eras, but who, underemployed in Depression-era Weimar, agitated for and achieved the defunding, barricading, and blacklisting of the Bauhaus and its members.[29] As the Alberses fled Dessau for the United States, they carried with them and transformed the Bauhaus emphasis on material engagement as preparation for mass manufacture. In western North Carolina, however, they were to meet with equal, if far less militant, opposition to the integration of craft and industry, challenged there by Appalachian craft revivalists who encouraged craftsmen to pursue complete independence from machine production.[30] Returning to craft in many cases as a matter of necessity, revivalist organizations like the Southern Highland Craft Guild no doubt balked at the opportunity to set their tables with Albers-designed placemats, as they could beginning in the 1940s, when the *New York Times* declared the handweaver "no arts-and-craftsy eccentric, but an important contributor to the march of industry."[31] Anni, for her part, looked with equal disregard on the Craft Guild, heaping especial scorn on its preferred overshot weaving technique; Anni viewed such techniques as sentimental, arguing that relegating textile work to obsolete methods threatened its existence in the modern world. "Crafts," she jabbed, "have a place today beyond that of a backwoods subsidy."[32]

In fact, both Josef and Anni Albers had begun to de-emphasize the importance of industrial-corporate manufacture in their craft pedagogies and practices. "Sometime between 1938 and 1959," T'ai Smith explains, Anni "began to rethink her tenure in the weaving workshop and the wider implications of that experience for her philosophy of education." In Smith's reading, Anni reconceives weaving at Black Mountain not as preparation for industry but as intellectual training for broader service to American society. "[F]unctionalism in the weaving workshop was not a dead end of utility," Smith argues, "but a way of developing new capacities for understanding and rethinking the role of textiles in the modern world."[33] In contrast, Troy finds Anni refocusing on weaving for its own sake, contending that "Albers's interest in the utilitarian aspects of weaving diminished in favor of her pursuit of the artistic possibilities of weaving."[34] Accompanying these changes, however, was an increased interest in and sensitivity toward craft as a spiritual discipline, an interest shared by Josef and Anni alike. At Black Mountain, the Alberses' Bauhaus ethic combined with the progressive values of founders Rice and Dreier, along with the ethos of American Arts and Crafts, to produce a spiritualized craft ideal, one which allowed the craftsman to transcend egoistic experience.

Of course, Black Mountain College incubated a range of experimental modernisms, as scholars like Natalia Cecire and Eva Diaz have demonstrated.[35] Assessment of its craft inheritance, therefore, might just as readily prioritize the more expressive values of Black Mountaineers such as Elaine and Willem de Kooning,

Hilda Morley, Robert Motherwell, Joel Oppenheimer, and Peter Voulkos. It was the Alberses, however, whose aesthetic ideology constituted the main line in Black Mountain thought; and that ideology, as I reveal, was nurtured within and disseminated through Black Mountain workshops, where the Alberses refined their craft pedagogies and where, with the same commitment to American Arts and Crafts values, they would hone their own creative practices.

"Ora et labora": Spiritual Pedagogies

In their flight from Nazi persecution, the Alberses and other ex-Bauhäuslers left behind certain craft values and practices incompatible with the institutions at which they landed, transposing other aspects of Bauhaus ideology into distinctly American practices. One of those practices was Josef Albers's *Werklehre* course at Black Mountain. Modeled after the preliminary course at the Bauhaus, *Werklehre*, along with Anni's weaving workshops, advocated immediate engagement with material as a means of freeing students for more creative ways of thinking—"thinking in situations," Josef called this learning. *Werklehre* itself stressed two basic forms of study as preliminary craft training: *matière* studies in the combinative possibilities of surface materials, and *material* studies in the structural properties underlying those materials.

The first, *matière* studies, prompted students to consider how things felt and how they looked like they felt, juxtaposing unlike materials in order to foreground discrepancies between physical fact and psychic effect. Combining grass and carpet swatches, light bulbs and cement, students' fiberboard-mounted assemblages aimed at a kind of textural *trompe l'oeil*, tricking the eye into perceiving similarities where none existed, what Josef termed a "schwindel."[36] Such visual defamiliarization figured prominently in Josef's other pedagogical exercises, including students' creation of fluctuating figure-ground designs, their drawing of numbers and signatures in reverse, and color collages in which a hue was made to appear variously recolored by juxtaposing, framing, or overlapping it with other colors, a technique Josef later employed in his iconic *Homage to the Square* series. In her own workshops, Anni used similar experiments as an introduction to the surface qualities of textiles, scratching paper to make it appear fibrous, for example, or "achiev[ing] the appearance of fluffy wool using feathery seeds," a means of "revitalizing our tactile sense [before] dealing with real weaving."[37] Anni's version of *matière* studies also emphasized collage-like repetition of similar elements; setting corn kernels in rows or arranging blades of grass into parallel columns allowed for a uniformity in which natural irregularities made the plainest of surfaces come alive.[38]

While the Alberses' *matière* studies focused on surface texture, *material* studies concerned the structural capacities of things in themselves, how assemblages such as paper mobiles, wooden furniture, and metal sculptures were put together and how their construction affected flexibility, tension, contraction, and expansion. Josef was especially interested in the structural principles underlying everyday objects, including pairs of scissors and the keystones of arches, instructing *Werklehre* students as to how to properly drive a nail into wood, for example, and to appreciate equally the integrity of Breuer's tubular chair and locally made Arts and Crafts-style furniture.[39] Though *Werklehre* students did "not actually make useful things," as Josef admitted, the course was "not opposed to handicraft work but [was] its very foundation."[40] As such, the end of *material* studies was what the Black Mountain course catalog, almost certainly written by Josef, referred to as "building-thinking," the cultivation of a "finger-tip feeling for material" that allowed students to assess and master the relation between structure and function, form and feeling.[41]

The ultimate objective of both forms of study was what Josef called "mental unrest," to transform "productive seeing into creative revelation." To see "grass only as an eatable vegetable," argued Josef, "that does every cow. But as soon as we see grass for instance as a carpet, or, as a fur, as an assemblage, or as a forest (suppose we have our eyes deeply enough in it), or when we see it as [. . .] many and changing colors [. . .] there enters the human being who naturally wants to be creative. [. . .] Here comes the poet . . ."[42] Re-envisioning the world as a vital material assemblage, according to Josef, allowed students to break down the scaffolding of habit and its tendency, as unthinking idiosyncrasy, to support self-expressive creation. "The aim of our art studies," he declared, "is not self-expression but articulation in visual form. Since [proper] expression is purposeful, aiming through selected means at definite effects, it is the result of self-control and mastery of medium."[43] For Anni, the resistance encountered in material engagement did not necessarily stifle expression but guided it, providing imagination "something to hold to" within the "immense welter of possibilities" available to the artist.[44] The Albersian craftsman worked against material in order to work with it.

Such pedagogical strategies were hardly unique to the Alberses, prevalent as they were within an early twentieth-century progressive education movement in which craft practices played a significant role. The Alberses' pedagogy had more in common with first-wave or Deweyan progressive education, however, than with those versions of the movement promoted by Black Mountain contemporaries. In *Art as Experience*, Dewey described artistic creation in terms strikingly similar to those used both by the Alberses and the erstwhile American Arts and Crafts movement. "That which distinguishes an experience as aesthetic is conversion of resistance and tensions," Dewey wrote. "Things in the environment that would otherwise be mere smooth channels or else blind obstructions become means, media."[45] Like the Alberses, early progressive educators advocated immediate engagement with rudimentary materials, such as Friedrich Froebel's blocks, as a precursor to more advanced "occupations" such as clay modeling, slat-weaving with paper strips, and connecting dots within a gridded field. As a schoolteacher during the first decades of the twentieth century, Josef would have been familiar with these pedagogies, particularly insofar as the work of both Froebel and Johann Heinrich Pestalozzi had been enjoying a resurgence of interest in Wilhelminian Germany.[46] If the Alberses' craft pedagogies resembled progressive notions of childhood play, however, they nonetheless insisted—as had Dewey himself, along with a number of other nineteenth-century craft idealists, among them Morris, Ruskin, and Charles Fourier—that the most instructive forms of play involved constraint. Like constraint-based artists working within contemporary Dada and later Oulipo movements, the Alberses recognized that only by confronting material resistances could student-artists achieve the self-transcendence at the heart of aesthetic experience.[47] For inherent in progressive thinking, as the Alberses well knew, was a tendency toward treating self-expression as an end in itself, with Froebel promoting children's and primitive art as legitimate artistic practices, and with subsequent educators championing freedom, spontaneity, and individuality in the progressive classroom. While Deweyan pedagogies aimed, like Bauhaus ideology, at the radical transformation of industrial-corporate production, reformers like Harold Rugg and Ann Shumaker of the Teachers College at Columbia University viewed the expressive artist as a Rousseauian holdout against modernity, expanding one aspect of progressive education—its emphasis on expression—into the movement's *raison d'être*.[48] In contrast, the Alberses maintained that "children's work is essentially no art," as Josef put it, denying such work the quality of "intuitive forming" which marked the transition from primitive expression to a "more advanced drive [. . .] for being productive," what the Alberses called "*Gestaltungstrieb*"—literally "impulse to form."[49]

Whether Anni's "meaningful form" or Josef's "articulation in visual form," aesthetic formalism played an integral role in the Alberses' spiritualization of both

Bauhaus ideology and the American Arts and Crafts craft ideal, their belief that artistic creation, facilitated by fundamental craft pedagogies, participated in and made manifest a metaphysical order. "As I see it, art today means more than technical ability or workmanship," Josef argued in 1940. "Art has become a word for something more spiritual."[50] The textural and visual gestalt of floated wefts and triple-weave palimpsests, for example, or of nested squares and colored glass and fiberboard-mounted moss and chicken-wire assemblages, became a means of unlocking the "secret life of things," that occult-like order immanent within workaday realities.[51] "The organization of forms," Anni wrote, "their relatedness, their proportions, must have that quality of mystery that we know in nature." As nature revealed itself only incompletely, however—in the structure of shells and galaxies or the arrangement of seed heads or the pinnation of crystals—the role of aesthetics was to instantiate "a wholeness that we can comprehend," a universal order labored into material existence.[52] We might understand the Black Mountain craft object, therefore, as a holdover from that utopian aspiration which Bill Brown finds embodied in the modernist "good object." Though Brown focuses on modernist potters like Herbert Read, his association of the good object with Bergsonian vitalism indicates its affinities with the theory and practice of craft at Black Mountain.[53]

For the Alberses's effort to access a higher plane of existence was part of a wider contemporary interest in translating modernist process philosophy, in particular the thinking of Henri Bergson and Alfred North Whitehead, into aesthetic form. Indeed, the Whiteheadian universe closely resembles those mobiles and assemblages constructed as part of the Alberses' *material* studies, with objects in the world (what Whitehead calls "actual entities") interconnected in a vast network both with other entities and with "eternal objects" similar to Platonic forms. Since entities constantly "prehend" one another—the way, in today's Internet of Things, thermostats and smartphones, servers and sprinkler systems signal and respond to each other—changes in one object redound throughout the entire network. More than cursory engagement with process philosophy is beyond the scope of this chapter, but it bears mentioning that an interest in the work of Bergson and Whitehead characterized a number of otherwise irreconcilable *avant gardes* at Black Mountain, including the performance art of summer teacher John Cage, whom the Alberses knew well, and the materialist poetics of poet Robert Duncan.[54] Describing what he called "the flux of things," Whitehead strikes a remarkably Albersian note, explaining that his materialist network "may be illustrated by our visual perception of a picture. The pattern of colors is 'given' for us.

But an extra patch of red does not constitute a mere addition; it alters the whole balance."[55]

Like the Alberses', Whitehead's was a spiritual materialism. He believed that objects constantly seek their own apotheosis, prehending toward those eternal objects of which they are themselves incomplete particulars. Seeking ever higher "gradations of intensity," objects can be aided in their intensification toward "satisfaction" by a greater degree of order in their immediate network. Order, in other words (what Whitehead variously calls "form" and "structure"), facilitates spiritual growth, in particular as it allows objects to convert what might prove "negative prehensions" or "*incompatibilities*" into orderly "*contrasts*." The corollaries with Albersian aesthetic experience are evident. "Blue becomes more intense by reason of its contrasts," Whitehead writes, "and shape acquires dominance by reason of its loveliness." For Whitehead as for the Alberses, moreover, the process of intensification constitutes a self-annulling experience, an object's prehending akin to the Black Mountain craft ideal in that it converts material resistances into spiritual thriving—"what was received as alien, has been recreated as private." An object's "completing" entailed "the perishing of immediacy," as Whitehead put it. "It never really is."[56] Student notes from Josef's *Werklehre* course suggest a very similar ethos. "Painting related to gambling," John Urbain wrote in 1946. "[U]se abandonment as the beginning of order."[57]

Copies of both Bergson's *The Two Sources of Morality and Religion* (1932) and Whitehead's *Adventures of Ideas* (1933) could be found in the Black Mountain College library. But while the Alberses were familiar with Bergson's more influential *Matter and Memory* (1896)—and likely knew Whitehead's systematic masterwork *Process and Reality* (1929) as well—it is reasonable to surmise that they came independently to similar ideas about material resistance and spiritual order.[58] In the last days of the Bauhaus, as Nazi authorities froze faculty payments, padlocked the school's doors, and demanded family trees from students and teachers, Josef wrote to his friend Franz Perdekamp to inform him of developments in Dessau. "One will never hear Bach on the street again," he lamented on June 10, 1933. "Only [the popular German song] '*Püppchen, du bist mein Augenstern*' or the like. Even if they dictated Wagner every day." As the nation descended into fascism, Josef "retreated to my little chamber [to] *ora et labora* alone."[59]

Prayer and labor: the Rule of Saint Benedict serves as an apt motto for the Alberses' spiritualized craft ideal. It was also a characteristically Albersian response, in the violent summer of 1933, to the very real material resistances in which, as the idiom holds, they found themselves.

"The meditative icons of the twentieth century"

Decrying the increasing purchase of fascism among the German masses—symbolized in the overthrow of Bach by "Baby, You Are the Star of My Eyes"—Josef found small comfort in the fact that the following day would be a holy day. "Pentecost remains," he wrote to Perdekamp, "and will remain, thank God."[60] The day must have been particularly meaningful to Josef, who as a devout Catholic would have appreciated the resonance of Pentecost with his own artistic practice—the Apostles, hidden away for fear of violence, receiving the Holy Spirit through the breath of Christ, himself the ultimate in-forming of spirit in matter.

Throughout his tenure there, Josef was an almost daily communicant at the small Catholic church near Black Mountain, driving himself and painting instructor Jean Charlot to mass after breakfast and, across the rest of the day, conducting his own pedagogical and creative work with monastic discipline.[61] Charlot identified early on the spiritual dimension of Josef's work, noting that it "longs for the state of repose as does a saint for unitive vision," an assessment Josef ratified in describing his effort to "create the silence of an icon." "That's what I'm after," Josef stated, "the meditative icons of the twentieth century."[62] That aspiration toward iconicity is evident even in Josef's earliest creations, assemblages made from shards of colored glass he had collected wandering the streets of Weimar, his repurposing of urban trash—a modernist trope, from Baudelaire's ragpicker to Woolf's "Solid Objects"—hardly lacking in Christological resonance. Called *"Scherbenbilder"* or "shard pictures" (figure 6), the assemblages suggest the incarnation of light in matter, their various colors, textures, and patterns unified in a single radiant body.

Josef's early glass works possess a vibrancy—even a personality, one is tempted to say—far less prominent in the abstract lithographs and engravings he created at Black Mountain, but his later "graphic tectonics" and "structural constellations" remain equally dedicated to manifesting spiritual order in formal relations. Invoking the De Stijl belief that a kind of cosmic beauty could be attained through abstraction and self-renunciation, Josef's mid-career works, produced from the late 1930s to early 1950s, share likewise in the "schwindel" of his *matière* exercises, tricking the eye in its depth perception and sense of spatial integrity, and evoking geometrically impossible dimensionalities through paradoxical overlappings and enigmatic planar arrangements. As his graphic tectonics make especially clear, Josef's mid-career works constitute critical studies in linearity, with variation in the weight of lines suggesting three-dimensional volume and their

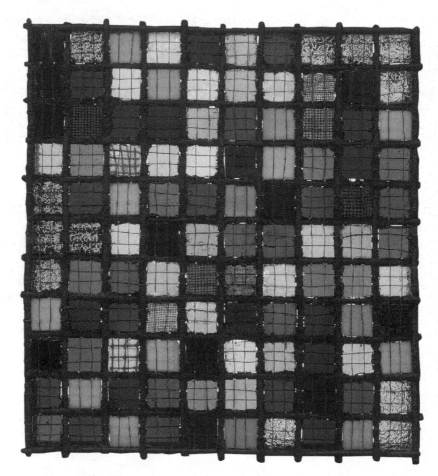

Figure 6. Above: *Gitterbild* (Grid Mounted), ca. 1921. Opposite: *Scherben im Gitter-bild* (Shards in Screens), ca. 1921. © *The Josef and Anni Albers Foundation / Artists Rights Society (ARS), New York, 2021. Photos: Tim Nighswander.*

vertiginous proximity making it difficult to discern precisely where one ends and another begins. A "breathing line," Josef called these techniques, one of the more explicit links between the Alberses' work and Black Mountain field poetics orig-inating, as Olson put it, in "certain laws and possibilities of the breath."[63] Titles like *Sanctuary* (figure 7, p. 120) and *To Monte Albán* (figure 7, p. 121) gesture to the spiritual aspiration of these tectonics, many inspired by the Alberses' journeys to recently excavated pre-colonial sites at Teotihuacán and Monte Albán, where

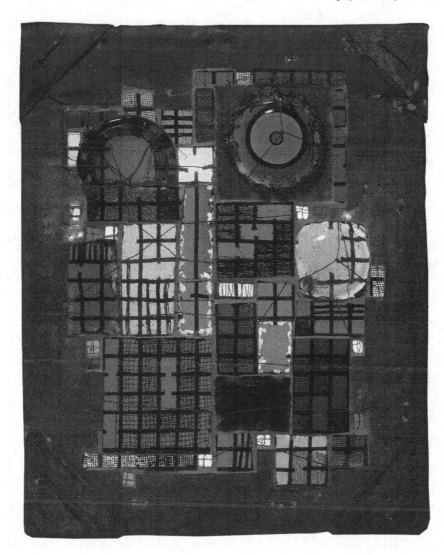

Mexican archaeologist Alfonso Caso had been unearthing vast complexes of temples and underground tombs since 1931.

Though many of Josef's graphic tectonics possess an architectural quality in their resemblance to stepped pyramids, the spiritual dimension of these works is formal, not representational; constructed with ruler and drafting pen, executed by zinc-plate lithography, the tectonics achieve unity through asymmetrical bal-

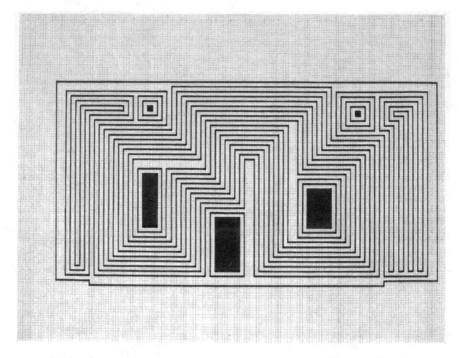

Figure 7. Above: Study for *Sanctuary*, ca. 1941–42. Opposite: *To Monte Albán*, 1942. © *The Josef and Anni Albers Foundation / Artists Rights Society (ARS), New York, 2021. Photos: Tim Nighswander.*

ance, converting what Whitehead might call *"incompatibilities"* into harmonized *"contrasts."* It seems appropriate, moreover, that the lithographs actually *hurt* us after sustained attention, straining our vision as the most familiar of aesthetic objects are rendered unfamiliar, wrenched into unstable configurations that force us to confront our own material limitations.[64]

That sense of resistance—an experience not only of the artist or craftsman but of the viewer, whose vision strains to reconcile enigmatic realities—animates Josef's later structural constellations as well: floating, apparently multidimensional assemblages that seem to prompt viewers to spin or rotate them in order to decipher their mysteries. Precisely how, we find ourselves wondering, does this plane overlap that one? Where does this line recede and that one advance? Just which direction is up? Produced between 1949 and 1951 in a series called *Transformation of a Scheme*, Josef's structural constellations employ manipulations of depth, space, and linearity similar to those he had developed in his graphic

tectonics; like those earlier works, the constellations flirt with the border between abstraction and symbolic reference, rewarding sustained attention with
their formal verve and visual dynamism. The "breathing lines" of *Transformation
of a Scheme No. 10* (figure 8, p. 122), for example, in addition to their almost material evocation of folded paper—as if these were origami pleats or the most intri-
cately unfolded of cardboard boxes—seem to resemble pre-colonial pictographs
of insects, animals, and men dancing, while *Transformation of a Scheme No. 23* (fig-

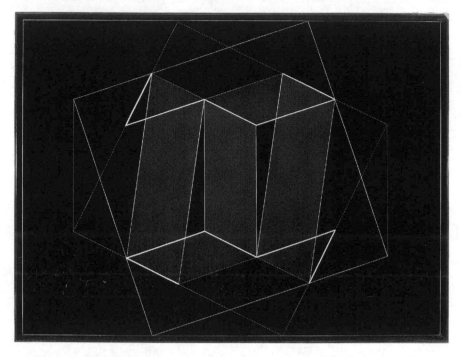

Figure 8. Above: *Structural Constellation: Transformation of a Scheme No. 10,* 1950–51. Opposite: *Structural Constellation: Transformation of a Scheme No. 23,* 1951. © *The Josef and Anni Albers Foundation / Artists Rights Society (ARS), New York, 2021. Photos: Tim Nighswander.*

ure 8, p. 123) suggests both a deconstructed swastika and the evolution of the human species, some limbed figure wheeling itself into an upright position. The planar transparency in both works, of course, ultimately proves deceptive, since the promise of seeing through the figures serves only further to disorient us— transparency as opacity. And while there seems to be a clear delineation in *No. 23* between the work's tilted square frame and the more angular geometries at the center of the piece, it remains difficult to discern whether those geometries are sinking into or emerging out of the portal the frame creates.[65] "Constellation" seems an apposite title for these works, then, since constellations themselves represent human attempts to translate distant points of light into flat planes possessed of universal meaning. "Bear," we say, or "swan" or "archer" or "eagle," and suddenly the cosmos comes alive for us. Suddenly we understand, as we say, our place in things. For Josef, the point of the structural constellations was not for

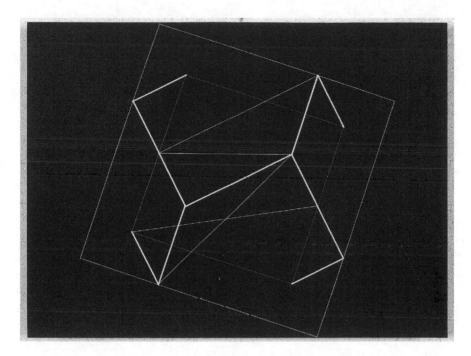

viewers to see through to resolution, but to hold irreconcilable realities in mind at the same time, to conceive those realities as paradox and potential, and in so doing to consider material resistances as egress onto spirit. Josef would have been familiar with such spiritualism—"this is my body," the Catholic priest declares, and bread becomes the savior of the world.

In a similar way, Anni's textile work during and immediately after her Black Mountain period dedicates itself to the in-forming of spirit in matter, invoking visual and textual abstraction as well as material resistance as avenues not only toward richer expression, but toward planes of existence normally foreclosed to the artist or craftsman. Joining De Stijl visual vocabularies with Constructivist attention to textile structure, Anni's work was consistent with a wider modernist emphasis on medium specificity, returning attention to the foundational horizontal and vertical intersections which for Anni elicited the weaver's freest expression. Anni's weaving deprioritized representation, therefore, in order to foreground the possibilities made available through the basic constraints of material, to "let threads be articulate again."[66] In addition to integrating new synthetic fibers like rayon and cellophane, Albers pioneered innovative double-, triple-, and open-weave structures, layering distinct planes on top of one another and interlocking, pulling away, pocketing, puckering, or flattening these planes to create three-dimensional surfaces.[67]

So-called structural weaving had first been developed by Andean weavers in pre-colonial South America, a period and form of craftsmanship studied with renewed interest in the first half of the twentieth century, when European artists looked to "primitive" cultures for more authentic, spiritually unadulterated forms of production. Abstract and handmade, Andean weaves were Gothic cathedrals, products of integrated societies in which craft labor remained both expressive and technically rigorous, fulfilling and faithful. Anni knew these cultures well. As Troy notes, she owned and consulted Max Schmidt's influential *Kunst und Kultur von Peru*—which her family's company, Ullstein Verlag, had published in 1929— and would have visited the collection of Andean textiles on display at the Berlin Museum für Völkerkunde in 1907, the largest collection of Andean work ever exhibited.[68] After her move to Black Mountain, moreover, Anni made almost yearly treks to sites of other pre-colonial cultures in Oaxaca, incorporating abstracted Zapotec architectures into her textiles, most prominently in her 1936 wall hanging *Monte Albán*.

Woven from silk, linen, and wool, *Monte Albán* (figure 9) marks one of Anni's earliest uses of supplementary weft brocade, what weavers refer to as a "floating" weft for the way a superficial weft floats above—traverses, interlocks with, loops across—the work's primary or foundational weft, allowing the weaver to inscribe independent motifs. In the case of *Monte Albán*, those motifs evoke the temples and terraces, the vast plazas and cramped burial vaults of Zapotec civilization, the wall hanging a kind of X-ray or cross-section of the site's archaeological strata.[69] Because floating wefts serve no structural purpose—one can pull them off without compromising a textile's integrity—and because they function as textural inscription, works like *Monte Albán* mark a departure from Anni's earlier emphasis on abstraction and medium specificity, rearticulating textiles as quasi-literary texts. Like her husband, Anni flirts in these weavings and wall hangings with the line between representation and abstraction, her work increasingly script-like as she seeks to manifest in material form what often seem like encrypted or occult languages.[70] Both *Haiku* (figure 10, left) and *Code* (figure 10, right), for example, gesture toward an indecipherable mystery just beyond our ken, an alien language garbled in transmission, so that as we scan what appears to be a musical score or Morse code, we apprehend only abstractly that whole of which these texts are a part.

Figure 9. Monte Albán, 1936. © The Josef and Anni Albers Foundation / Artists Rights Society (ARS), New York, 2021. Photo: ©President and Fellows of Harvard College.

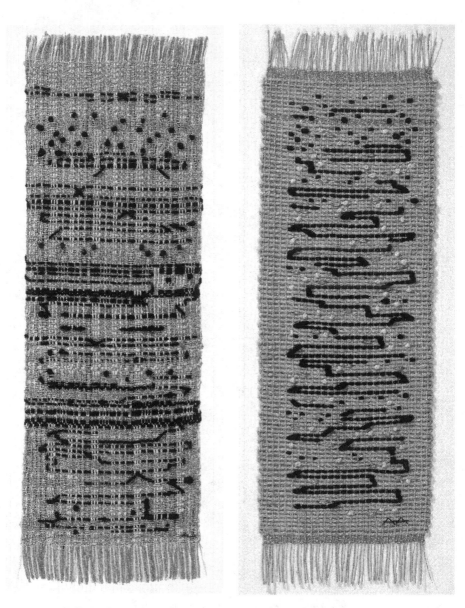

Figure 10. Left: Haiku, 1961. Right: Code, 1962. © The Josef and Anni Albers Foundation / Artists Rights Society (ARS), New York, 2021. Photos: Tim Nighswander.

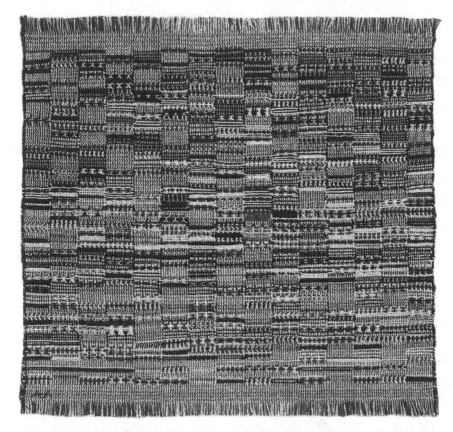

Figure 11. Open Letter, 1958. © The Josef and Anni Albers Foundation / Artists Rights Society (ARS), New York, 2021. Photo: Tim Nighswander.

Anni's textiles ask us to accept materiality as our sole point of access to a universal order beyond the expressive self. Most striking among such work is her 1958 weaving *Open Letter* (figure 11), an open weave in black and white cotton which, on close inspection, reveals several orange supplementary wefts floated across the weave proper. With multiple warps twisted together by hand, the weaving is virtuosic craftsmanship, its braids highly controlled but also remarkably various in pattern, arrangement, and color, instantiating that craft ideal at the heart of the Alberses' work. Like *Haiku* and *Code*, *Open Letter* evokes a communication scrambled in transmission, the static through which—just dimly, as on the premium channels of yore—one perceives the shadows and outlines of forms in relation, figures screened both for and from us. That the text is "open," however, suggests that it hides nothing, that it is itself the presence to which it points. The work conveys not information, but an in-formation.

Such an assumption was integral to the Alberses' craft pedagogy and artistic practices at Black Mountain College, just as it was integral to those Black Mountaineers who worked alongside and after them, from the carpenters and field hands of the work program to the "significant craft" of poet and creative writing teacher Robert Duncan. Indeed, Duncan might have been thinking of Anni's *Open Letter* when he wrote, in an essay called "Towards an Open Universe," that "[e]ach poet seeks to commune with creation, with the divine world; that is to say, he seeks the most *real* form in language." That real form, though, was "something we [only] apprehend; the poem, the creation of the poem, is itself our primary experience of it."[71]

"Open form," Duncan would call this kind of poem: field poetics. And among its other evocations, *Open Letter* recalls, I think, a patchwork grid of fields and farmland as seen from above, those vast agricultural geometries that sustain us, those verses we turn and turn.

The Black Mountain Work Program
"The rhythm of swinging machetes": Work as Spirit

Two days after returning to Black Mountain College in the fall of 1947, second-year student Harry Weitzer found himself drafted into labor on the college farm, tasked with cutting and storing silage for use as fodder during the winter ahead. "I ended up with a corn knife in hand, and not too long after, blisters," Weitzer described. "Cut, cut, cut, gather a shoulderfull of the stalks before they fell, and turn them as a bundle out of the row for the wagon crew to pick up." Prolific in the school's woodworking shop, Weitzer would go on to a distinguished career as a furniture designer and master woodworker in the Pacific Northwest, his elegant bent-wood lighting fixtures—quintessential midcentury modern—neatly embodying that Black Mountain synthesis of spirit and matter so conspicuous in Josef Albers's structural constellations and in Anni Albers's pictorial weavings. Weitzer's description of farm work testifies to Black Mountain's spiritualization of an American Arts and Crafts craft ideal. "What lovely work," Weitzer exclaimed in his memoir. "Ah, the sweet hot smell of corn juices, the just fatigue of honest work. [. . .] Then, we were in the silo under a shower of corn stomping it down, round and round surrounded by a head-spinning smell just a little better than Bourbon." Reminiscent of Sufi dervishes or the Transcendental-like farms of American Arts and Crafts, Weitzer's reverie suggests that at Black Mountain craft was a spiritual discipline, a way of subordinating ego to an order resident in even the most unassuming of material. As Weitzer put it, "we learned about more than hay that day."[72]

Farm work was only one aspect of the work program at Black Mountain, where students could fulfill their work requirement by patching roads and cleaning dishes, preparing and serving at community meals, sweeping, felling trees, and maintaining buildings, or with more craft-like tasks such as constructing furniture and weaving curtains and floor coverings. Though understood as a substitute for intercollegiate athletics, Black Mountain's work program was hardly extracurricular, closely integrated as it was with art, architecture, and weaving courses, all of which counted as credits toward graduation.[73] "As they do in craft work," wrote architecture teacher A. Lawrence Kocher, students in the work program "may learn that materials have limitations and laws of their own and that working with them requires discipline and technique."[74] In an interview in 1965, Josef Albers similarly positions the program as coextensive with other forms of learning: "I thought carpentry is a very wonderful handicraft—with the most material considered. When they made bookshelves—the boys [. . .] put the nails through the vertical board into the horizontal board. That's the greatest nonsense when it comes to carpentry, because the nails go parallel into the long grain. It falls apart. The nail has to go across the direction of the grain. [. . .] I made them 'steal' with the eyes. We had a carpenter from Black Mountain come up once a week to show them what means: thinking in wood." Josef's catchphrase is powerful shorthand for the necessity across art, craft, and work practices of attuning oneself to and respecting one's materials. Testifying equally to the continuity across these practices is an order form submitted to student Frank Rice in his capacity as manager of the college kitchen (figure 12): on one side of the form, a modest order for eggs and fruit; on the other, notes on graded weaves from Anni's workshop, including how to "make a double weave twill."[75]

The integration of work into academic learning was a hallmark of Deweyan progressive education, in which an activity like weaving was seen concurrently as artistic expression, craft labor, and vital preparation for the world of industry. In his effort to make labor "intellectually fruitful," Dewey held that the "only adequate training *for* occupations is training *through* occupations," incorporating farming, cooking, construction, and book-binding into progressive curricula and promoting foundational craft skills like folding, cutting, molding, modeling, and pattern-making.[76] In the contemporaneous manual training movement, an off-

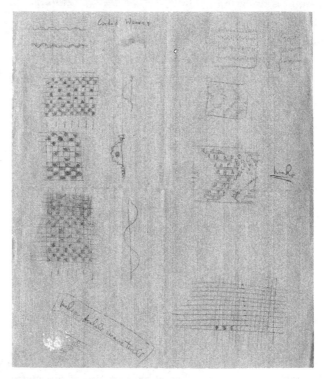

Figure 12. Frank Rice, Kitchen order form (top: side 1; bottom: side 2). *Collection of Frank Aydelotte Rice, Gift of Mary Emma Harris, Black Mountain College Project, Courtesy of the Western Regional Archives, State Archives of North Carolina.*

shoot of progressive education proper, educators like Calvin M. Woodward of the Manual Training School in St. Louis likewise joined mental and manual labor by combining courses in mathematics, science, language, and literature with instruction in carpentry, brazing, soldering, iron chipping, and other semi-industrial occupations, all intended, like the program at Black Mountain, more as liberal than vocational education.[77] Black Mountain's own work program was dedicated, in the words of program coordinator Dreier, to "showing how the liberal arts can be revitalized by being again more intimately related to the rest of life"—an objective achieved, among other ways, by clearing time for work in the exact middle of the day, between morning and evening classes. Invoking Whitehead's comment that in contemporary society "the kings are the plain citizens pursuing their various avocations," Dreier argued that "the plain citizen or the common man is a working man and his philosophy, among other things, has got to be connected with and make sense out of his work."[78]

For Dreier, making sense of work meant appreciating its spiritual potential. "What is your height?" Dreier asked in a questionnaire for work program participants. "How much do you weigh? How do you feel the next day as a result of your work at Lake Eden, especially is there a carry-over of your spiritual moods or physical well-being?"[79] Among other influences, Dreier would have acquired such spiritualism from his close friendship with the Alberses, having accompanied the couple on those trips to Oaxaca that proved so formative for the Alberses' own work. Dreier was also the nephew of Duchamp patron and Bauhaus supporter Katherine S. Dreier, a leading promoter of modernist art who organized the Co-operative Mural Workshops inspired by the Armory Show and facilitated one-man exhibitions for Kandinsky in 1923 and Klee in 1924, well before the height of their popularity.[80] Dreier's interest in the spiritualism of labor, this is to say—as many *did* say—was in part the distant and refined spiritualism of one who has never labored for a living. "Ted had this notion," mused Black Mountain co-founder John Andrew Rice, "having been born in Brooklyn Heights, and never having seen more than a few blades of grass, that there was some kind of mystical experience in touching the soil." Rice himself had grown up among Southern farmers compelled to endure the miserable work of picking cotton by hand: repetitive, often injurious labor—to pick a cotton boll, one brings all four fingers to the thumb— that left Rice's neighbors and relatives both physically and mentally exhausted. "Untoiling poets may sing of the dignity of toil," Rice wrote, but "others know there is degradation in obligatory sweat."[81] Nonetheless, Dreier proved an indefatigable worker and teacher throughout his leadership of the work program,

Figure 13. Ted Dreier leading construction on the Studies Building foundation, 1940. *Courtesy of the Western Regional Archives, State Archives of North Carolina.*

visible in myriad archival photos as he led and instructed students in their work (figure 13).

The centerpiece of Dreier's tenure as head of the work program—indeed, the most important event in Black Mountain history, excepting perhaps John Cage's legendary 1952 "happening"—was the construction from September 1940 to April 1942 of a three-story Studies Building out of stone and lumber sourced from college property. Intended to house 59 undergraduate and 12 faculty studies, two apartments, and an unfinished ground-floor space for painting and weaving workshops, the Studies Building was to be a paragon of Bauhaus modernism, designer and architect teacher Kocher having worked closely with plans drawn up by Marcel Breuer and Walter Gropius. The influence of Breuer and Gropius is conspicuous in continuous steel-sash windows that run the length of the building and in its simple corrugated facing made from modular transite panels, giving the building the distinctive linearity and clean abstraction of the Bauhaus (figure 14).[82]

Strikingly futuristic, even alien, nestled among the hills and gently rolling fields of western North Carolina, the building's cleanliness belies the extent of

Figure 14. Top: Studies Building under construction. Bottom: Studies Building completed. *Courtesy of the Western Regional Archives, State Archives of North Carolina.*

the material resistances—from financial to foundational instability—that confronted Kocher, Dreier, and other Studies Building workers. If the Black Mountain catalog for 1940–41 positioned the project as offering "specific laboratory problems for students in the Architecture and Art courses," those problems were many, including the calamitous rerouting of a mountain stream crossing the proposed site and, soon after, the discovery that a layer of loose mud underlay the entire area, requiring the driving of piles to solid substrate.[83] Rather than contract a local pile-driving company for the work, at a cost the school could hardly afford, Dreier endeavored with construction manager Charles Godfrey to rig up a homemade pile-driving machine powered by their Farmall tractor (figure 15). "He proposed to cut a 500-pound black-gum log," Dreier writes, "haul it to the top of the twenty-seven-foot tower with a steel cable that could be wound up on a wide-flanged steel pulley [. . .] on the tractor's power drive." Throwing out the tractor's clutch to release the pulley, Dreier and Godfrey watched the log plummet three stories on vertical tracks, a distance "Charlie was sure would be enough to drive any piles that we had to drive," as indeed it proved. Dreier does not quite invoke the spiritualism of labor here, but his account does resonate with Albersian craft pedagogies geared toward promoting creativity through material experience, literally embodying what Josef had called "thinking in wood." "Not only the buildings," claimed Dreier, "but the design and experience of constructing them were in a very fundamental sense works of art."[84] Initial difficulties overcome, work on the Studies Building proceeded at a blistering pace, with the Black Mountain community celebrating a topping-out ceremony—a Scandinavian rite meant to appease tree-spirits displaced in construction—as the last beam was lowered into place just before Christmas 1940.

Assisting Dreier throughout that tumultuous first year was German exile Richard Gothe, an economics PhD and master mechanic hired by Josef to assemble and coordinate teams of student laborers. Gothe was well qualified for the work. Prior to Hitler's rise to power, he had been actively involved in the popular work camp movement in the Weimar Republic, work he had continued in the US as secretary of the Work Camps for America. As in Weimar Germany, American work camps were intended not only as a means of ameliorating Great Depression-era unemployment, but as a program for teaching cooperative living, fostering community relations, and instructing youth in constructive and non-violent problem-solving—in short, as a way of espousing "the importance of 'work' in a philosophy of life and service."[85] It is easy to overlook the popularity of work camps among American youth of the 1930s and '40s, overshadowed as they were by New Deal

Figure 15. Dreier and Charles Godfrey's tractor-powered pile driver, 1940. *Courtesy of the Western Regional Archives, State Archives of North Carolina.*

programming focused on adult education and employment, as well as by those more sinister camps uncovered during the Second World War. Work camps, though, were wildly popular during this period, organized in almost every state and offering diverse experiences to those interested, from hauling coal in the anthracite fields of Pennsylvania and West Virginia to harvesting crops among migratory workers in Washington to urban labor projects in Chicago and New York. In addition to those camps organized by Work Camps for America, Quaker camps sponsored by the American Friends Service Committee were a common destination for American young people, offering, as one camper put it, that "sense of integration and purpose" so conspicuously absent elsewhere.[86] Gothe would have been familiar with these camps, and Dreier viewed them as laudable models for the work program at Black Mountain, oriented as they were toward "the springs of creative love that expand [campers'] frame of meaning, that draw, gather, and refocus [their] partial purposes and relate them to the very grain of things, to the creative life of God himself."[87] Though more explicitly Christian than Black Mountain's spiritualized craft ideal, Quaker camps likewise promoted sublimation of the ego in labor, one pamphlet describing campers' "personal claimful demands melting down and a new and living sense of fellowship with, and responsibility for, the wider community springing up." "Corporate contemplation," another pamphlet in Dreier's papers called it, a practice integral not only to Quaker camps in Reading, Pennsylvania, and Delano, California, but to the entire Black Mountain craft ideal, from the Alberses' craft pedagogy and artistic practices to summer work camps the school itself organized in an effort to finish the Studies Building on time and under budget.[88]

At the same time that traditional Black Mountain summer students were performing Bach concertos and staging Erik Satie, work campers from Black Mountain and other schools were roofing, insulating, and wiring the Studies Building, quarrying and stacking stones into landscaping walls, and creating frescoes for the wide supports underneath the building, work overseen by painting instructor Charlot (figure 16). That many of these students came from elite Eastern institutions, including Harvard, Princeton, and Sarah Lawrence, suggests that their work was not merely a matter of necessity—that some other, perhaps more spiritual purpose had driven them to the wilds of rural North Carolina. Comments from work campers and Black Mountain students and faculty bear out Dreier's conviction that the material resistances of labor constituted a spiritual discipline. Asked on his exam for matriculation into the Senior Division, "What is work [and] what is play?," Jimmie Jamieson went on for several typewritten pages before concluding with a five-word summary: "Work is play, and vice-versa."[89] In a letter to her friend, lecturer May Sarton writes with glee of Black Mountain's communal labor. "Rosalind, it is a great sight to see the trucks go down the mountains every afternoon filled with teachers and students, boys and girls," Sarton wrote. "It is something hard to describe in words to watch Straus, the ex-German psychiatrist with a wonderful head of white hair throwing rocks to a young girl who throws them to a boy who sets them in the wall which others have prepared with a bed of cement. I helped on the wall one afternoon and felt happier at the end, more whole and ready for *thought* than I have in years."[90] Summer student Ruth Lyford Sussler likewise recalled her fresco work under Charlot with the reverence of

Figure 16. Charlot at work on frescoes on Studies Building support beams. *Courtesy of the Western Regional Archives, State Archives of North Carolina.*

childhood reminiscence, comparing the labor to "cutting cornstalks in the field for silage." "The flow of energy that bristled from this gathering of souls was powerful," she admitted. "The day's work swallowed you up, carried you along in the rhythm of swinging machetes. [. . .] The excitement and energy released in this ritual of harvesting the corn gave magic to the hard physical labor taking place in the hot sun, making the work seem effortless. The importance of community manual labor as a balance to solitary thinking and artistic effort could be well understood."[91] No less powerfully than these recollections, archival photos from the work program suggest the extent to which labor functioned as a spiritual ex-

Figure 17. "The spirit of work." Top left: Student workers digging a drainage ditch, 1940. Top right: Student workers take a break, 1940. Bottom left: Brochure for Black Mountain College work camp. Bottom right: Workers at rest with Black Mountain College co-founder Rice, 1937. *Courtesy of the Western Regional Archives, State Archives of North Carolina.*

ercise at Black Mountain, with students engaged in their work as if moved by and toward some higher order, as many professed to be (figures 17 and 18). Like the Alberses' *matière* exercises, the photographs try our perception. We are unaccustomed, I think, to seeing young people in this light—shirtless, pants rolled up, muscles straining, they belong in Abercrombie & Fitch ads and Warby Parker billboards, in the gingham halo of Instagram filters and the throwback sepia of Snapchat. It is difficult, scanning the thousands of photographs housed at North Carolina's Western Regional Archives, not to be moved by the dignity of these students' labor—their work does not look pleasant, but it looks meaningful, an embodiment of American labor as "significant craft," as spirit laboring itself into existence.

Figure 18. "The spirit of work." A BMC student in the work program. *Courtesy of the Western Regional Archives, State Archives of North Carolina.*

"More burden than any brightness": On Drudgery

Not everyone at Black Mountain shared this spiritualism.

As I've suggested, the school's work program constituted a study in the practical viability of "significant craft," testing the capacities of aesthetic and pedagogical practices in which work was invoked as both idealized metaphor and romantic abstraction. Literalizing a craft ideal that found in material resistance an avenue toward spiritual order, the work program serves as a limit case for the very idea of aesthetic craft, a metaphor carrying over the experience of labor into artistic creation, sometimes maladroitly. As such, craft labor at Black Mountain helps us reassess the legacy of the American Arts and Crafts movement writ large; for if American Arts and Crafts did not explicitly prioritize submission to material, it did temper expression through inherited technical standards, upholding a view of labor as spiritually meaningful in its own right.

At Black Mountain, that spirit flared briefly then failed, fizzling out into widespread suspicion of work as an ennobling ethic. History teacher Eric Bentley complained that "labor is the curse of this world, and nobody can meddle with it without becoming proportionably brutified." Likewise provoked by the college's gospel of work, two students parodied its pretension to spiritual vitalism by posting a notice on a campus bulletin board: "WANTED: ZOMBIES FOR THE WORK PROGRAM."[92] Writing for *Harper's*, Bernard DeVoto echoed this line of thinking, arguing that "phrases like 'to experience art as a process which is also life' are mere logomachy" and that Black Mountain's work program was more fit for "jails and army cantonments" or the "labor battalions" of Hitler and Stalin.[93] As Dewey had perceived, when work does not "remain permeated with the play attitude," it becomes drudgery, disconnected from other aspects of workers' lives and preventing rather than facilitating their spiritual thriving.[94]

That drudgery took many forms at Black Mountain, from slippages of attention—the routing of a sewer uphill, the roofing of a house with grease rather than asphalt cement—to an overzealous concern for self-sufficiency that caused Dreier to "run himself ragged" gathering construction materials, determining crop rotations, and deciding whether to sell or silage the autumn harvest.[95] Notes from Dreier and college farmer Roscoe Penley indicate the meticulousness with which they managed their work, scribbled over as they are with budgets, crop ledgers, and instructions for the upcoming season: "graze cover crop of barley and vetch and plow under. (Lost hay crop due to lack of manure.) Silage corn 75 tons at $6.50 per ton $487.00."[96] Material resistances are one thing, but Dreier and Penley's notes reveal the potential of those resistances to foreclose rather than open onto spiritual order—the failure of the filament of work to ignite. Even the German exile Gothe, so integral to the efficient functioning of the work program in its early stages, ultimately proved too autocratic for Black Mountain; the former economist and master mechanic was let go at the end of the spring term of 1941. Though the work program endured through the 1940s and into the '50s, its most outspoken and effective critic would be its last: Black Mountain rector Charles Olson. Assuming the rectorship in 1951, Olson ordered all future work "to be done by hired hands," revoking the academic credit associated with the work program and refusing to perform basic community duties like washing dishes and cutting wood. "No more of this community horseshit," Olson wrote to Robert Creeley, "which, at least when there are so few people, is more burden than any brightness."[97]

Olson's shuttering of the work program met with little opposition—by 1951, few Black Mountain faculty remained to challenge him. Two years earlier, Josef and Anni Albers had decamped for New Haven, where Josef's *Werklehre* course and linear aesthetic would become hallmarks of Yale's nationally recognized Department of Design and where Anni continued work on her writing and weavings. Theodore Dreier, "chief Messianist" of the work program, had resigned that same year, objecting to faculty plans to prioritize courses in economics and the social sciences over the arts and work program. Though Black Mountain had never truly achieved the closed economy toward which its students and faculty labored, underwritten as it was by Dreier family largesse, its final desperate years dramatized how integral the Black Mountain craft ideal had been to its overall mission. Rather than sharing meals in the dining hall and living in communal dormitories, students moved into isolated cottages on the hillsides, roving old-growth forests for firewood—"Breughelesque bands of student woodsmen," Tom Clark calls them— and permitting the fields and outbuildings of the college to pass into disrepair.[98] Among the dairy herd, long a sought-after assignment in the work program, an outbreak of mastitis contributed to the death of one cow, and others had begun "to drown in [their] own shit" as a result of unmucked stables.[99] Voracious kudzu overtook even those buildings still in use. Piles of trash grew by the day in the Studies Building. Descending into spiritual lassitude, its physical plant eroding, the school became unrecognizable to those who had founded it, its entropic decline from order to disorder—from discipline to decadence, spirit to spoilage— refracting and representing in miniature wider changes in postwar American culture.

For the problems at Black Mountain were not merely material. In contrast to the optimism of students from the 1930s and '40s, readily apparent in photographs from that era, students of the 1950s reported disillusionment at many aspects of Black Mountain culture, alienated especially, they felt, from the faith in work that had dominated Black Mountain during its early years. Expressing their alienation in disheveled clothing and unkempt hair, in drinking, drug use, and insubordination, students under Olson prefigured that counterculture that would profoundly reorient American society in the 1960s and '70s, advocating individuality and self-expression in ways that would have appalled the Alberses. Returning for a visit in the summer of 1956, former student Michael Rumaker recalled a "psychotic unpredictable energy in the air," an horrific parody of the spirit that had once moved through and ordered so many of students' experiences at Black Mountain.[100] That same year, Black Mountain's last, Robert Duncan described the school and its students as "very noticeably derelict," no longer "the Black Mountain one had heard about in the late 1930s, when there was a coordination between the land and its farms and the college."[101]

Though he would teach only two semesters—one in the summer of 1954, the other in the spring term of 1956—and though Black Mountain College was by then a spiritless husk of itself, Duncan's work explicitly drew from and extended the school's craft ideal, promoting the material resistances of language not only as a more fulfilling mode of expression, but as formal egress onto universal order. By 1956, Duncan understood that this ideal had lapsed, at Black Mountain and possibly everywhere. "In the new generation," he lamented, "poets have returned to drugs, to hashish, principally marijuana, but also to heroin, to seek their highs and their being *sent*." "[T]he trip is a 'gas,'" Duncan wrote. "Well, I like poems that are a gas. But this is a gas, the spirit, that is filled with and fills itself with the world."[102] If the "psychotic energy" that Rumaker identified began, as early as the late 1940s, in the Faulkner-esque decay of an arts college in western North Carolina, it ended, as Joan Didion and others have observed, twenty years later in the French country-style mansion at 10050 Cielo Drive. It ended in the lawnmower drone of high-altitude bombers over Hanoi, and in what Duncan saw as the equally psychotic energy of the protests inspired by those bombings. Objecting to a counterculture that would replace one authoritarian ideology with another, Duncan argued to fellow poet Denise Levertov that the role of artists was not "inflicting peace on their own terms," but "acts of care in making." "The art of the poem—which has fallen into disrepair—[is] the art of long persisting and careful work," Duncan argued. "I am not talking about prisoners, blacks, children, and angry women in revolt—I am talking about those with work to do deserting their work. And our work is surely to get the words *right* . . ."[103]

Duncan's is a complicated aesthetic ethics, one which, like the values of Catholicism, cuts across contemporary political affiliations and challenges shibboleths on both sides of the political divide. At the heart of his ethics, though, is profound faith in the work of the poet—work he understood as manifesting a spiritual order too frequently neglected in the urgencies of American life. Attending to Duncan's work, both his poetry and pedagogy, reveals how an American Arts and Crafts craft ideal continued to inform the theory and practice of creative writing long after the movement itself had vanished. For in addition to invoking the Alberses' pedagogies in the visual arts, Duncan explicitly cited American Arts and Crafts practitioners like Gustav Stickley as an influence on his poetics and teaching, maintaining across these practices that the writer's expression should be tempered by the material resistance of language. Indeed, Duncan's inheritance of American Arts and Crafts ideology is particularly relevant to the disciplinary genealogy this book constructs, since in Duncan's work we witness creative writing—

and the craft ideal behind it—migrating ever closer to the mainstream of American higher education.

"The million sorties of the life code in its variations manifesting itself": Robert Duncan

"[T]REMBLING IN THE STEADINESS WORK DEMANDS":
DUNCAN AS WEAVER

Until 2012, if students of poetry were inclined to look up the poetics of the "Black Mountain School" in *The New Princeton Encyclopedia of Poetry and Poetics*, they were met with a one-line prompt to "See PROJECTIVE VERSE."[104] Though the latest edition expands on that suggestion, it continues to define the movement through Olson's influential 1950 essay and through association with *Black Mountain Review*, that journal for which Olson—in his first act as rector, with the college unable to pay faculty salaries—appointed $500 from the Black Mountain operating budget.[105]

The association of Black Mountain with Charles Olson extends to poetics scholarship which links Duncan to the school primarily through its last rector. Robert Von Hallberg finds Olson's poetic "transmission of energy" crucial for Duncan's own spiritual poetics, while Joseph Conte and Anne Day Dewey cite the poets' shared interest in collage, process-based poetics, open form, and seriality as evidence of Olson's influence on the younger Duncan.[106] Such lineages are not inaccurate. Whatever his limitations as an administrator were, Olson was a tireless editor and promoter of his friends' writing, and he remained a beloved teacher throughout his tenure at Black Mountain College, where his classes frequently went on past midnight, fueled by cigarettes and Appalachian moonshine. Olson was and remains, moreover, a titanic figure in American letters, his inexhaustible stores of energy directed perpetually to multiple outlets at once, from a groundbreaking scholarly reassessment of *Moby Dick* to an ambitious postmodernist poetics which offered a bold challenge to mainstream academic poetry. In more ways than one, Olson simply was Black Mountain.

Lost, however, in collapsing writers as distinct as Robert Creeley and Denise Levertov into Olson surrogates is a sense of the institutional identity that underlay aesthetic theory and practice at Black Mountain. Duncan himself explicitly situated his work, including his poetry workshops, in relation to the Alberses' pedagogy, explaining to interviewer Mary Harris in 1971 that he "just had what would be anybody's idea of what [Josef] Albers must have been doing. You knew that [Albers's students] had color theory, and that they did a workshop sort of approach, and that they didn't aim at a finished painting. I thought, 'Well, that's absolutely right.'" Invoking the Alberses' basic *matière* and *material* studies, Duncan describes his own courses as "work with the materials of poetry," including "five weeks of just vowels," as well as studies in pitches and stresses, consonant clusters, syllables, sounds, and junctures, a pedagogy geared like the Alberses' toward defamiliarizing linguistic material in order to break the scaffolding of habit.[107] "Only words come into [the poem]," Duncan wrote. "The tone leading of vowels, the various percussions of consonants. The play of numbers in stresses and syllables."[108] By subordinating ego to material resistances, Duncan believed, writers no less than craftsmen could achieve more authentic expression and glimpse that spiritual order moving beneath the surfaces of things. In later prose, Duncan grounds this materialism in the human body, echoing Olson's focus on the breath and Ezra Pound's on "melopoeia" in explaining that "*VOWELS* are related by position in relation to lips, velum, how the breath is emitted, articulation [. . .] our *a-I* of *tile* is a glide, between *a* (low central) and *I* (high front)."[109] "Craft here," Duncan elaborates, "is not to impose a form upon a force but to find the force, the very movement of shape, sound, and meaning, in which the form of the total process is apprehended."[110] Among Black Mountain's already disaffected student body, Duncan's pedagogy proved a hard sell. Writing to Levertov, Duncan describes having to maintain a steady supply of coffee throughout his eight a.m. class in order to keep his "would-be poets directed to the immediate task of gaining a craft."

> [A]nd they, not yet awake to the feel of the language, much less to the depths that words are filled with, are impatient of hearing the vowels and consonants, at taking soundings—I find myself already raising my own specters in their minds, as if it were their part to know how the power of a word can overwhelm the spirit, that they must at once work with the greatest discretion, knowing the finest and most exact measures in the materials at hand—the exacting of the sounds and timings, the concern for localities, melodies, and resonances of meaning—and at the same time tremble, and contain the trembling in the steadiness work demands.[111]

The passage is a remarkable encapsulation of Black Mountain's spiritualized craft ideal, firm in its conviction that immediate engagement with the material resistances of language opens onto an almost Kierkegaardian trembling, onto spirit.

That ideal was at the heart of Duncan's poetry, in particular a serial poem called

"Passages," conceived at Black Mountain and published across several of Duncan's mid-career and late collections, most prominently his 1968 *Bending the Bow*. While Duncan scholars prioritize his first and most critically acclaimed collection, *The Opening of the Field*, as Duncan's most meaningful contribution to Black Mountain poetics, it is in *Bending the Bow* that we find Duncan's most mature and sustained engagement with the Black Mountain craft ideal, the work therein addressing and explicitly modeling itself after craft practices like weaving and architecture. Though serial form and open sequences were common among the Black Mountain and San Francisco Renaissance poets with whom Duncan associated, Duncan viewed his poetics as a spiritual practice akin to Josef Albers's structural constellations, a way of entering in and manifesting universal order. "I came to be concerned not with poems in themselves," Duncan describes, "but with the life of poems as part of the evolving and continuing work of a poetry I could never complete—a poetry that had begun long before I was born and that extended beyond my own work in it."[112]

One of the earliest "Passages" poems, though, looks not to Josef's but to Anni's artistic practice as a metaphor for the operations of poetry. Duncan finds in weaving—as so many had before him, from Ovid to Olson—an apt allegory for the in-forming of spirit in language. Indeed, "At the Loom" opens by braiding together in a kind of triple-weave palimpsest Duncan's own poetic genealogy, invoking Pound, Homer, and those countless mythological sources in which weaving stands in for the procedures of language, warp and weft for the strings and crossbar of the lyre. Here is the poem's opening movement:

> A cat's purr
> in the hwirr thkk   *"thgk, thkk"*
>   of Kirke's loom on Pound's Cantos
>   *"I heard a song of that kind . . ."*
>
> my mind a shuttle among
>   set strings of the music
> lets a weft of dream grow in the day time,
>   an increment of associations,
>   luminous soft threads,
> the thrown glamour, crossing and recrossing,
>   the twisted sinews underlying the work.
>
> Back of the images, the few cords that bind
>   meaning in the word-flow,

> the rivering web
>   rises among wits and senses
> gathering the wool into its full cloth.
>
> The secret! the secret! It's hid
>   in its showing forth.

As its vertiginous allusiveness indicates, ghosting the poem like a weaving cartoon are those poetic laborers whose work Duncan carries on, the poem a laborious "increment of associations"—Pound's term for literary communities—endeavoring to fulfill the past in the present. That effort places Duncan within a tradition of process philosophy which holds, in Whitehead's terms, that entities draw on "a feeling of the world in the past" in their prehension of other entities, "inherit[ing] the world as a complex of feeling."[113] Whitehead himself picks up this apperception toward the past from the spiritual materialism of Bergson, in particular the latter's definition of spirit as "a synthesis of past and present with a view to the future." "To touch the reality of spirit," Bergson contends, "we must place ourselves at the point where an individual consciousness, continuing and retaining the past in a present enriched by it, thus escapes the law of necessity. [. . .] When we pass from pure perception to memory, we definitely abandon matter for spirit."[114] Duncan had been reading Whitehead's *Process and Reality* throughout his tenure at Black Mountain College, and soon thereafter invited Olson to give a series of lectures on the philosopher at the San Francisco State University Poetry Center, where Duncan took over as assistant director following Black Mountain's closure in 1956. Duncan's fidelity in "At the Loom," accordingly, is not necessarily to previous poetic weavers, but to the spiritual order in whose service they worked.[115] For underlying his linguistic tapestry—structuring it like warp "cords" or "set strings of the music"—is that cosmic "full cloth" whose "secret" the poem manifests. So seamlessly does the poem weave itself in with this cloth that it becomes difficult to syntactically separate the poet's "weft of dream" from the spiritual fabric to which his dreaming binds him, the immanence of spirit in matter neatly encapsulated in Duncan's paradoxical description of a secret "hid / in its showing forth." And that "showing forth," as should now be familiar, occurs through material resistances, through onomatopoeia, sonic texturing, and "twisted sinews" (or syntax) that instantiate linguistically the resistance of the weaver's fabric.

As the poem takes shape, moreover, Duncan, like Penelope, undoes his earlier weaving in order to refigure the titular loom as multiple prehistoric tools and forms of labor:

And the shuttle carrying the woof I find
    was *skutill*   *"harpoon"* —a dart, an arrow,
        or a little ship,

      navicula   *weberschiff,*
crossing and recrossing from shore to shore—

    prehistoric *skutil *skut-
      "a bolt, a bar, as of a door"
    "a flood-gate" •

If Duncan's etymological excavation continues his effort, as Bergson put it, to "touch the reality of spirit" through memory, the poem's final movement indicates the extent to which Duncan remains "bar[red]" from that spirit, cut off by the slamming shut of a prehistoric "*flood-gate*," itself resonant with mythological import. The bullet point after "*flood-gate*"—a marker in Duncan's poetics for a caesura or interval of silence—doubles down on this sense of exile, shifting the poem into a more traditionally lyric speaker whose recollection of the Trojan War includes one final metaphor for acts of weaving and writing: bending the bow.

           but the battle I saw
was on a wide plain,   for the
    sake of valor,
the hand traind to the bow,
    the man's frame
withstanding, each side

facing its foe for the sake of
    the alliance,
allegiance, the legion, that the
    vow that makes a nation
one body not be broken.

Yet it is all, we know, a mêlée,
    a medley of mistaken themes
    grown dreadful and surmounting dread,
so that Achilles may have his wrath

and throw down
the heroic Hektor who raised
the reflection of the heroic

in his shield . . .[116]

An iconic embodiment of the Black Mountain craft ideal, Duncan's archer withstands the material resistance of his bow in the same way that the weaver works against the loom's warp or the writer subordinates himself to the material of language. As Anni Albers writes of this process, "a balanced interplay of passive obedience to the dictation of the material on the one side and of active forming [on the other side] is the process of creating"—or so the ideal holds.[117]

For juxtaposed with the calibration of Duncan's archer is Achilles's unhinged expression of his egoistic wrath, the poem likewise unraveling in its final stanzas into a "medley of mistaken themes," trailing off in the loose thread of a closing ellipsis. Scholars have read the poem's close as an indictment of American involvement in the Vietnam War, a conflict Duncan saw as an abdication of spiritual and political responsibility. "Duncan's literary understanding of war as a violent struggle between victim and aggressor," argues Anne Day Dewey, "challenges the government's one-sided image of a war for national glory."[118] To delimit Duncan's imagery within a contemporary political context, however, is to ignore his meditation here on the procedures of his own poetics. If Achilles's indulgence models the loss of aesthetic discipline, Duncan's closing image also comes counterwoven with the suggestion that the spiritual potential of "significant craft" remains viable despite "surmounting dread." Duncan's repetition of the word "heroic," for instance, evokes a kind of *mise en abyme* in which—as when viewing oneself in parallel mirrors—infinity is made material in polished metal.[119] The poem's closing ellipsis, then, reads not so much as an unraveling but a continuation, a prehending, weaving the poem in with a spiritual order that always exceeds it. And the ellipsis gestures equally toward the longer poem of which "At the Loom" is a part, Duncan's serial poetics a spiritual discipline not only in the sense of a daily or iterative practice, but of a potentially endless process toward spirit. In Whitehead's materialist network, we will recall, "actual entities" were themselves caught up in this process, seeking satisfaction through ever higher "gradations of intensity," a quasi-evolutionary growth that could be abetted by greater order in an entity's immediate environment. Similarly, the individual poems of Duncan's "Passages" prehend toward, reverberate against, abrade, alter, and amplify one another in a process that Duncan calls "intensifications of Its orders." "*It*," Duncan says, the critical pronoun doubly emphasized, "is striving to come into existence in these things, or, all striving to come into existence is It."[120]

Cutting across three collections and thirty years, "Passages" constitutes what Duncan calls a "grand collage" that both models and manifests a metaphysical creation; its tapestry reveals not only a vertical core-sample of the past but a horizontal arranging of sources on the field of the page, "parts fitting in relation to a design that is larger than the poem."[121] We might identify a number of influences on Duncan's collagist aesthetic. In James Maynard's reading, Duncan's poetics owes as much to American pragmatism as to Whiteheadian process philosophy, oriented as Duncan's work is toward "conditions of plenitude and change" as described in William James and John Dewey. "Duncan's writing [. . .] continually struggles to find a poetics adequate to the pluralistic complexities of the real," Maynard contends, and can therefore "never be anything but a working *toward* the pragmatist sublime."[122] So too is Duncan's work part of a broader interest in collage among gay visual artists at the midcentury, including the combines of Josef Albers's student Robert Rauschenberg and the "translations" produced by Duncan's partner, Jess. Manipulating figure and ground, layering myth, history, and romantic iconography alongside sexual imagery and architectural schematics—all in a visual field several feet wide—Jess's translations visually model the palimpsest-like fields that structure Duncan's poetics. Jess's collage and line-drawing serves as the cover for the original Grove Press edition of *The Opening of the Field*, and Duncan frequently links their work in his essays and correspondence. "He has gone far ahead in these paintings in exploring color tones and sets (what in poetry would be vowel progressions)," Duncan writes of Jess, himself aspiring to "correlat[e] the intuitive organization of vowels with the designing organization of numbers [. . .] giving another more obscure source of measure in the poem."[123] As Duncan's own visual metaphor implies, his "grand collage" also extends and develops a Black Mountain craft ideal dedicated to mapping and enacting a spiritual order; describing his poetics, Duncan might just as easily be describing the Alberses' *matière* studies in texture and appearance, in particular the color collages in which a single color was made to appear variously recolored in relation to its neighbors. "[I]n the grand collage," Duncan writes, "signs flash green against blue, black against white, red against yellow." And "all the signs rime."[124]

Such "rimes"—happy coincidences, it may be, between Duncan's work and the Black Mountain craft ideal—flare up like sparks in archival material otherwise full of resistances. An underscored passage in John Urbain's *Werklehre* notes, for instance, points to similarities between the visual and literary arts at Black Mountain: "Passages created by juxtaposition of extremes."[125] More admissible to the court of critical appraisal, perhaps, is the fact that Duncan's workshops, in addition to adapting the Alberses' *matière* studies in surface texture, at the same time repurposed their *material* studies in structural capacity, with students examining the formal structures of various texts, including the book of Genesis. The import of such a text would not have been lost on Duncan. The book opens, in one of its competing creation accounts, with spirit "moving upon the face of the waters," and the central event in the narrative that unfolds therefrom is the divine injunction to labor "in the sweat ōf thy face" as a way of attaining that spirit again. This, anyway, "till thou return unto the ground," we are told. "For dust thou art."[126]

GHOST HOUSE; OR, "THE INDWELLING": DUNCAN AS ARCHITECT

It was Duncan's deprivileging of expression that lay at the center of his friendship-severing dispute with Levertov in the fall of 1971, with Duncan objecting that Levertov's politics intruded into and corrupted her poetry. Previously, Duncan had admired Levertov's poetic craftsmanship. "What a beautiful job you did with 'Face to Face,'" he wrote in 1964, "sharpening, so that there's a lovely pivot (that exact) in the verb 'edges' [. . .] It's exhilarating to get these articulations that ring so right. (I'm thinking of an experienced worker's hand going over the joints, fit to fit, of a cabinet)."[127] In Levertov's more recent poetry, however, Duncan found that her "verse form has become habituated to commenting and personalizing just where the poem itself begins to open out beyond the personal into your imagination of a 'you,' a 'world' or a history beyond your idea of yourself or your personal history."[128] While sustained engagement with their dispute lies beyond the scope of this chapter, the exchange highlights how Duncan's poetics inform his political ethics, in particular his objection to anything which might sway the writer from his proper work. "The moralist must always be outraged by what God finds good," Duncan writes, "for God works, as the creative artist works, not with a sense of rewards and punishments, but to fulfill the law that he creates."[129] Unfaithful to the poem's intensification of its order, Levertov's politics foreclose "any imagination of or feeling of what [. . .] greed, racism or imperialism is like," papering over with approved moral slogans the in-forming of spirit in language. "The poet's role is not to oppose evil, but to imagine it," Duncan argued. "[W]hat if Shakespeare had opposed Iago, or Dostoyevsky opposed Raskolnikov—the vital thing is that they *created* Iago and Raskolnikov. And we begin to see betrayal and murder and theft in a new light. It is a disease of our generation that we offer symptoms and diagnoses of what we are in the place of imaginations and creations

of what we are."[130] Despite the scholarly juxtaposition of "open" and "closed" poetries, Duncan's insistence on formal integrity within the field of the poem quite
closely resembles a certain New Critical aestheticism that would banish Levertov's hortatory as didactic propaganda. For Duncan, though, one imagines evil the
more powerfully to combat it, to draw into existence a metaphysical order beyond conventional notions of right and wrong; Duncan does not so much advocate evil as fidelity to that supra-moral order moving beyond us. "In the plenitude
of His powers," Duncan explains, "He works always upon the edge of arbitrary
alternatives; He could, we know, change the work if He would. But first among
His powers is His Oneness in creation: the universe is faithful to itself."[131]

While weaving constitutes one analogue for this creation, equally prominent
in "Passages," as in the pedagogy and work program at Black Mountain, is the
field of architecture, that practice which Bauhaus founder Gropius had seen as
the unity and apotheosis of all crafts. Architecture was equally integral, of course,
to the ideology of the American Arts and Crafts movement, from its invocation of
Ruskin's Gothic cathedral to an American Craftsman style promoted by Stickley
and embodied in the work of architects Harvey Ellis, Greene and Greene, and
Julia Morgan. The credo of one crafts organization, the Society of Arts and Crafts,
Boston, anticipates principal Duncan keywords in declaring its mission "to counteract popular impatience of Law and Form, and the desire for [. . .] specious
originality"; proper architecture, the SACB maintained, "will insist upon the necessity of sobriety and restraint, of ordered arrangement, of due regard for the
relation between the form of an object and its use."[132] In an interview in 1985,
Duncan echoes these SACB strictures, explaining that "I architect my poems.
[. . .] You design how people move through them and so that's [a] projected imagination already of how you're not going to live in a room, but how you're going
to go from one passageway to another. So, it's very natural that I would have a
long poem called 'Passages.'"[133] Duncan's interest in architecture was "natural" for
other reasons as well. His adoptive father, Edwin Symmes, was a practicing architect in Oakland, and Duncan's childhood home, a Mission Revival-style house on
the city's north side, reflected the theosophist faith and occult interests of his
parents, its high wooden crossbeams resembling a theosophist cathedral and its
interior balcony allowing Duncan to look down surreptitiously on his parents'
worship.[134]

Like "At the Loom," "The Architecture" functions as both a historical core
sample of previous workers in the craft and a spatial arrangement of "parts fitting
in relation," the quintessential "grand collage" imagined as architectural assem-

blage. The poem opens by quoting Stickley's 1909 *Craftsman Homes* for its description of what Duncan viewed as an ideally ordered structure:

". . . it must have recesses. There is a great charm in a room broken up in
plan, where that slight feeling of mystery is given to it which arises when
you cannot see the whole room from any one place . . . when there is
always something around the corner"

from the window-shelter

the light

the curtains of daffodil-yellow

light

beyond •

a little night music

after noon

• strains of *Mahoganny* on the phonograph

distant

intoxications of brazen crisis,

the (1930) *Können einem toten Mann nicht helfen* chorus

the procession with drum-roll

in the distance

recesst

As might by now be apparent, Duncan's is an explicit metapoetics, constantly re-figuring its own compositional procedures; here the rooms and recesses of Stickley's Craftsman-style home gesture to an elusive but ever-present whole of which they are a part, an order duplicated soon after in the poem's bookcases, their "glimmering titles arrayd [like] keys // Hesiod • Heraklitus • *The Secret Books of the Egyptian Gnostics.*" The formal order within these networks—or assemblages, or collages, or constellations, our metaphors for Duncan's work potentially as various as his own—matters for Duncan in that it allows for what he elsewhere calls the "indwelling" of spirit in material form, maintaining that "if we have not set things to rights, / the indwelling / is not with us."[135] In the passage from "The Architecture" quoted above, that spirit manifests as light flickering in Duncan's curtains, their pleats and folds offering only a glimpse of some "beyond" the poem approaches.

Similar images recur throughout the middle of the poem, where porches open onto gardens and staircases onto mysterious upper regions, all figures for the poem's "building" from material to spiritual realms.

Because the various rooms and floors of Duncan's poetics are so closely built together, that middle section demands quoting at length, beginning with another citation of Stickley:

> "Take a house planned in this way, with a big living room, its great fire-place,
>   open staircase, casement windows, built-in seats, cupboards, book-cases
>   . . . and perhaps French doors opening out upon a porch" . . .
>
> *La Révélation d'Hermès Trismégiste*
> *Plutarch's Morals: Theosophical Essays*
> *Avicenna*
> *The Zohar*
> *The Aurora*
>
> I was reading while the music playd
>
>   curled up among the ornamental cushions
>
> . . ."which links the house with the garden / and
>
>   sparkling into the jeweld highlights given forth by
>   copper, brass, or embroideries"
>
> "the staircase, instead of being hidden away in a small hall or treated as a
>   necessary evil, made one of the most beautiful and prominent features of
>   the room because it forms a link between the social part of the house and
>   the upper regions". . .
>
>   Below the house in the dark of the peppertree
>
> stript to the moonlight embraced
>
>   for the mystery's sake mounting
>
>   thru us the • garden's recesses

One cannot, in Duncan's poetics, read "garden" without hearing "*the* garden," though what seems of greater import here is that the transit from house to garden, as rendered in Stickley's interrupted prose, occurs only through those "passages" opened up by hermetic texts like *The Zohar*. Likewise, Duncan's passionate embrace provides passage for that unnamed and unnamable spirit "mounting // thru us," the subsequent bullet point serving as caesura, perhaps, but also a kind of supra-linguistic presence: a black hole, absolute matter. Returning to and inverting Genesis, Duncan recovers the garden as a home, a site not for exile but indwelling, not mourning but "mounting." Ideas of dwelling and indwelling appear too in the many images of domestic contentment that run throughout "The Architecture," from the languid afternoon strains of Kurt Weill to Duncan "curled up among the ornamental cushions," imagery that suggests an at-homeness in the universe at large. To invoke Gaston Bachelard, Duncan's architecture is a nest, a shell, a corner, "our first universe, a real cosmos in every sense of the word."[136] Whether Duncan knew Bachelard's *The Poetics of Space*, published in English in 1964—or the earlier Martin Heidegger treatise it closely resembles, "Building Dwelling Thinking"—remains unclear, but the coziness of Duncan's poem echoes both Heideggerian and Bachelardian notions of dwelling, the idea of the home as a "protected intimacy," as Bachelard put it, one of the "greatest powers of imagination for the thoughts, memories, and dreams of mankind." Both Heidegger and Bachelard understood poetry, moreover, as a means of reconstructing this cosmic ur-home; "building and thinking belong to dwelling," Heidegger wrote. "[O]ne as much as the other comes from the workshop of long experience and incessant practice."[137]

Regardless of whether he knew this work, Duncan's practice of home evinces a similar commitment to dwelling. Prior to arriving at Black Mountain in the summer of 1954, Duncan had been living with Jess in an apartment in the former Adolph B. Spreckels mansion in San Francisco, by then a rundown Greek Revival enclave for musicians, poets, and painters in the city's Pacific Heights neighborhood. Nicknamed "Ghost House"—and currently the home of romance novelist Danielle Steele—the apartment "was a place of habitation ultimately independent of time and space," as Christopher Wagstaff describes it, "where the flow of ideas and the conjunction of poetry and painting fed [Duncan and Jess] daily."[138] Returning from Black Mountain after the school's closure in 1956, Duncan moved with Jess to a sprawling Victorian at 3267 20th Street in the Mission District, stuffing the house's four floors with paintings, records, sculptures, antique Tiffany lamps, and other kitsch Victoriana, as well as massive libraries of French and modernist literature, esoteric treatises, Oz books, and fairy tales. Embodying Duncan's "grand collage," the house was the antithesis of Bauhaus architecture, far removed from the abstraction and angularity of Black Mountain's Studies Building.[139]

Of course, by the time Duncan left, the Studies Building was hardly the clean, otherworldly structure it had once been. If Bauhaus architectures are not pristine, they are decrepit, and Duncan was keenly attuned during his time there to the spiritual and material decline of all that Black Mountain had meant. "We stayed in the so-called Gropius building," Duncan recalled in an interview, "which by that time was a derelict piece of modernism—nothing looks more run down than an art moderne building ten years later. [. . .] One had only to walk about to find deserted laboratories with broken glasses and splendid kiln equipment which had just gone to ruin."[140] Soon after auctioning off the college farm and other Black Mountain property, Olson sold the Studies Building to a local gravel company, using the revenue to pay off the college's debts and refund back-salaries owed to faculty from as far back as the Rice era.

The building and former Black Mountain property remain, as then, difficult to access, nestled in an isolated valley at the end of an unprepossessing dirt road, half an hour's drive from Asheville. The property, a sign informs passersby, is monitored by closed-circuit television, its entrances flanked by what amount to guard shacks. Driving past, one can just catch a glimpse of the Studies Building through stands of oak and loblolly pines. Its corrugated transite facing, so luminous in photos from the building's construction, hardly glints in the golden, late evening light. The building seems to sink into itself at the edge of the water. Its roof slumps. Its windows are cracked. It is a Christian camp.

Mountains Beyond Black Mountain

Black Mountain's craft ideal endured beyond the school's physical decline, of course, as attention to Duncan's work helps make clear. For one, the Black Mountain School of American poetry would continue to draw on and transform aesthetic theory, as developed in the pedagogy and practice of artists like Josef and Anni Albers; Black Mountain poets share not only an affiliation with Olson and *Black Mountain Review*, but an underlying faith in the submission of artistic ego to material dictation, a faith traceable to the ethos of Black Mountain College itself. Moreover, if Olson and Duncan "failed to make major inroads into the poetic mainstream," as Christopher Beach argues, their attention to the materiality of language serves as one source for the work of major Language poets like Lyn Hejinian, Susan Howe, and Barrett Watten.[141] Indeed, much of postmodernist poetics, from John Ashbery to Rosmarie Waldrop, incorporates collage, open forms, seriality, and an attention to process first popularized at Black Mountain. To be sure, postmodernist poets rarely traffic in the kind of spiritualism that animated Duncan's work. But their investment in language as both a material and suprahuman system signals their filiation with Duncan's "significant craft," helping us trace the evolving influence of a craft ideal original to American Arts and Crafts.

In this chapter, I have shown how that ideal informs and is transformed by artists working on the avant-garde of poetry and the visual arts. Though Duncan's writing may be experimental in form and sensibility, in his poetry and pedagogy we find the craft legacy of creative writing playing an increasingly prominent—and increasingly institutionalized—role in American higher education. *Pace* Beach, the theory and practice of craft at Black Mountain, as at earlier labor schools and proletarian workshops, significantly influences the construction of an academic poetic mainstream, as I reveal in tracking the literal incorporation of craft rhetoric into the creative writing workshop. As with countless other alternatives to regnant capitalist formations, craft's erstwhile critique of industrial- and informational-corporatism becomes absorbed within and rearticulated as a professional-managerial value system. These processes can be apprehended, I suggest, within that genre most responsible for disseminating craft-based pedagogies among a mass audience: the poetry craft book.

Chapter Four

The Better Craftsmanship

Poetry Craft Books Then and Now

Intermezzo: Black Mountain Redux

Despite its aspiration to spiritual enlightenment, Black Mountain College was no paradise, even before its decline and dissolution under rector Charles Olson. "Like all Edens, Black Mountain had its serpents," wrote former student Martin Duberman, alluding, among other serpents, to the uneasy détente that prevailed between the school and a surrounding community skeptical of both its experimental ideals and progressive student body.[1] Since its founding in 1933, Black Mountain had witnessed significant extramural tensions over everything from land purchases and arts and crafts practices to desegregation and the biased policing of students' sexual practices.

Animosity between town and gown was nowhere more pronounced than in a 1945 incident involving creative writing professor Robert Wunsch. Late one evening in mid-June, Wunsch was caught *in flagrante* with a Marine in the front seat of his coupe roadster. Despite indications that the affair had been an attempt to entrap Wunsch, known to authorities as a gay man sympathetic to civil rights, Wunsch was imprisoned and charged with crimes against nature, to which he pleaded guilty. On the intervention—and probably financial campaigning—of Black Mountain co-founder Theodore Dreier, Wunsch's charge was reduced to aggravated trespass, provided he resign and leave the area as soon as possible. While it remains unclear to what extent they understood the situation, students and faculty offered little resistance to these terms. Tendering his resignation,

Wunsch left under cover of darkness soon afterward, driving west to California, where, in a grim parody of American mythology, he was last seen working under a pseudonym in a Los Angeles-area post office.[2]

That Wunsch found anonymous labor with the US Postal Service more hospitable, it would seem, than Black Mountain College points damningly to a school which promoted itself as a site of social and artistic transcendence. Wunsch's affair also raises a number of questions, integral to this book, about the relationship between educational institutions and those workers who live, move, and have their being within them. Why did Black Mountain College, in Wunsch's case, prove such a quintessential embodiment of what Mark McGurl has termed "bad institutionality," characterized by "linoleum hallways and plastic chairs," by a sense of "institutionalization as entrapment," and by gross inattention to institutional workers?[3] More generally, what pressures do institutions like Black Mountain, and the American university writ large, exert not only on their workers but on those lonely satellites who orbit at their periphery, at the very edges of their social, cultural, and economic gravity? How do institutional workers experience and aesthetically reproduce the multiple ambivalences engendered in them by their labor?

If the Postal Service constitutes the reverse image of the workshop—isolating, anonymous, its work merely distributive rather than creative—both exert powerful institutional influence and maintain in distinct ways the authority of broader economic regimes. As I will unfold in what follows, the poetry "craft book" plays a crucial role in this maintenance of institutional authority, disclosing to amateur writers the skills of the professional and in so doing inducting cohort after cohort into professional-managerial discourses. To begin in the postwar era, though, is to elide the historical evolution of the craft book itself and of those precise mechanisms, including figurations of writing as work, by which writing craft migrated discursively across the long twentieth century. As I have shown, craft lexicons originated as part of an anti-modern economic critique, passing first into leftist cultural politics and subsequently into an avant-garde modernism and experimental arts college. Like almost every other avant garde, craft was then commodified within and tactically redeployed by the professionalizing machinery of postwar higher education.

"A kind of blueprint": The Argument

In his role as workshop leader and pedagogical theorist, Wunsch coauthored in 1933 a creative writing craft book for use in his fiction workshops at Black Mountain College. Titled *Studies in Creative Writing*, and written in collaboration with Asheville high-school teacher Mary Reade Smith, the text is an otherwise unremarkable example of the genre, a mode which guided would-be writers toward authorship by providing instruction in distinct craft techniques. Massively popular across the early twentieth century, the genre took its name from its tendency to figure literary production in terms of manual labor. Wunsch and Smith, for instance, write that "the worker in any profession, if he would become a skilled craftsman, must learn to use effectively the materials peculiar to his own profession." In mechanical work, they go on, these materials consist of "bolts, screws, pistons, valves, cylinders, and a thousand and one related things. [. . .] In writing the materials are words, phrases, clauses [. . .] thoughts, and images." Early twentieth-century craft books tend especially to invoke building practices like masonry, architecture, and housing construction as corollaries for the creative process. Just as "the mason must select stones before building a structure," Wunsch and Smith describe, "students aspiring to write must gather words."[4] Wunsch and Smith's pedagogy must have seemed particularly suited to Black Mountain College, where, in addition to constructing the school's Bauhaus-style Studies Building, students designed and built their own individual studies, and where in later years they foraged for firewood in what one alumnus describes as "Breughelesque bands of student woodsmen."[5] But figurations of writing as work are widespread during this period, within craft books and within literary discourse more generally— when T. S. Eliot famously identifies Ezra Pound as *"il miglior fabbro,"* in other words, he draws on and focuses a broader contemporary fascination with craft rhetoric.

In this chapter, I contend that the invocation of manual labor in craft books means to achieve several interrelated objectives, facilitating processes of aesthetic consolidation within a print culture characterized by increasingly fluid formal and generic categories. Moreover, while craft books intended for a mass readership ultimately reinforce conservative cultural priorities, modernist craft books like those written by Pound and Gertrude Stein adapt the genre for uniquely radical ends. By midcentury, however, as the craft book becomes required reading within creative writing programs, the genre functions to underwrite the growing cultural and economic influence of the institution housing those programs. Tracing the endurance in poetry crafts books of an American Arts and Crafts craft ideal, I show how an ethos which helped George Pierce Baker challenge the utilitarian values of Harvard University comes to reinforce precisely those values within midcentury and postwar higher education. The craft book thus embodies as a generic institution a broader expropriation of craft epistemologies which this book has, to this point, tracked across educational institutions.

Examining dozens of craft books from the early twentieth century, I argue in the first section of this chapter that the appeal to metaphors of housing construction contributed in profound ways to what Joseph Harrington has called "the institutional production of the poetic."[6] Specifically, such metaphors establish and triangulate a given genre's relation to an expanding literary marketplace. Whereas fiction craft books frame the genre as a form of labor fungible within broader literary and material economies, poetry craft books insist that poetic composition involves more than "mere craftsmanship," as one text puts it, figuring poetry as a spiritual expression facilitated by (though irreducible to) technical facility.[7] In the poetry craft book, the American Arts and Crafts craft ideal finds new discursive life, with such texts balancing the writer's expressive labor with fidelity to technical standards like those enforced by pre-industrial guilds. That these texts return to residual forms of craftsmanship during this period is hardly incidental; as I establish in the introduction to this book, the emergence of new industrial-corporate economies depended on the consolidation of technical knowledge formerly belonging to craft laborers, with "entire industries and classes built on 'mental labor' and the appropriation of the skills of the craftworker."[8] Like the American Arts and Crafts movement generally, poetry craft books served not merely as a cultural intervention, then, but as an economic critique of emergent professional-managerial values, a plea that labor remain both spiritually expressive and technically masterful.

Though middlebrow poetry craft books evince strong resistance to modernist experimentation, Pound and Stein appropriate the genre to levy a similar economic critique, at the same time interrogating and transforming the craft book to advance distinctly avant-garde objectives. In the second section of this chapter, I argue that, far from some rarefied retreat from mass culture, modernist craft books engage meaningfully with mass-cultural pedagogies, deploying the tropes and topoi of the genre to rethink the function of literature—even the very nature of language—within an industrial-corporate regime. In making this claim, I follow scholars like Harrington, Lawrence Rainey, and Jennifer Wicke in contending that literary modernism was forged through tactical engagement with, rather than outright resistance to, mass culture.[9] Though these scholars and others have focused on the importance of anthologies and little magazines to modernism, the critically neglected genre of the craft book played an equally pivotal role in sorting, sifting, and producing sometimes irreconcilable definitions of the poetic. This work—namely, the tendency to oppose poetry to wider literary and material economies, common among middlebrows and modernists alike—culminates in arguably the most influential of twentieth-century craft books: Cleanth Brooks and Robert Penn Warren's 1938 *Understanding Poetry*. Extending the metaphors of housing construction found in earlier texts, Brooks and Warren argue that "the poet certainly [does] not draw up an analysis of his intention, a kind of blueprint, and then write the poem to specification. But it is only a very superficial view of the way the mind works that would cast the question into those terms."[10] It has become a commonplace that *Understanding Poetry* significantly impacted mid-century literary studies, but by situating the text in the tradition of the craft book, I show that *Understanding Poetry* in fact constitutes a literary-historical switching point, since the vast majority of postwar craft books figure poetry as precisely the kind of labor that Brooks and Warren reject. Indeed, poetry comes to look more and more like work—and not particularly *spiritual* work—as the practice of creative writing enters the university, an institution of which Brooks and Warren remained profoundly suspicious.

Analyzing one of the era's bestselling poetry craft books, Richard Hugo's 1979 *The Triggering Town*, I argue in the final section of this chapter that creative writing craft comes in the postwar period to consolidate the authority of elite educational institutions. More than a pedagogical "adjustment"—an institutional modification allowing as elusive an art as poetry to be taught in the first place—writing craft transcodes the university's promotion of professional-managerialism in the language of manual labor.[11] The writing workshop peddles that labor as craft pedagogies, soft skills necessary to the maintenance of a rising professional-managerial class. Whereas most histories of creative writing disregard its social and economic ramifications, in this chapter I traverse quite wide historical territory in order to reveal the stakes involved in reconstructing the discipline's craft legacy. By the midcentury, the craft ideal becomes—in warped form—an instrument for rewriting one economic practice in the language of another, just as American neoliberalism continues to rewrite itself in the language of populism. In what follows, I remain skeptical, however, that the incorporation of craft signals the inevitable entrenchment of the "workshop lyric," as the most common critique of the master of fine arts program (MFA) holds.[12] Rather, by reading Hugo's poetry for its disarticulation of a craft ideal, I show how the alignment of poetry and university opens space for a postmodernist poetics characterized by reflexive attention to its own institutional habitus.

Early Twentieth-Century Craft Books

"Essentially a workshop": The Advertising Craft Book

As a genre, craft books were part of a broader explosion across the early twentieth century in mass-cultural pedagogies, so-called "how-to" and "self-help" manuals marketed to upwardly mobile middle-class consumers. Though I focus on the literary craft book in particular, mass-cultural pedagogies could be found on virtually every conceivable undertaking, with such manuals especially popular in subject areas related to bodily care, cooking and domestic work, athletics and physical culture, and professional success, the latter exemplified in Dale Carnegie's bestselling *How to Win Friends & Influence People* (1936). In 1895, readers could learn social politesse in George Sandison's *How to Behave and How to Amuse: A Handy Manual of Etiquette and Parlor Games*. Readers in 1899 could brush up on urban farming in John H. Robinson's *Poultry-Craft: A Text Book for Poultry Keepers*. In 1924, aspiring bakers could turn to Fred Bauer's *Cake-art Craft: The Most Complete and Helpful Book on Cake Ornamenting Designs and Instructions Published*. Though the genre nearly lampoons itself, Pound made explicit the somewhat absurd premise of mass-cultural pedagogies, an aspirational mode promising, as he put it, "how to seem to know it when you don't."[13]

From Henry James's 1884 "The Art of Fiction" to Clement Wood's 1936 *The Complete Rhyming Dictionary and Poet's Craft Book*, literary craft books supplied courses of instruction unavailable in traditional pedagogical settings. Accordingly, these texts frequently downplay the necessity of conventional education. In *How to Write Short Stories (With Samples)*, satirist Ring Lardner notes that "when you skim through the pages of high-class periodicals, you don't often find them cluttered up with [. . .] boys or gals who win their phi beta skeleton keys." In fact, Lardner goes on, most authors "never went to no kind of a college, or if they did, they studied piano tuning or the barber trade."[14] A kind of literary apprenticeship, craft books ostensibly opened the way toward professional authorship, helping consumers enter, navigate, and eventually master what Bartholomew Brinkman has called an emergent "culture of mass print."[15] One 1929 guide for consumers "who aspire to authorship" includes appendices with lists of leading American authors of the nineteenth century, including information about the college they attended, their age at the time of their first publication, and their previous occupation. The same text includes style guides for major American magazines.[16] Another craft book, written in 1934 by magazine editor Arthur Sullivant Hoffman, reminds readers that "the market is not a market but many markets, each with its own specifications for stories."[17] The early twentieth-century literary craft book functions as one of those "intervenient institutions" which for a scholar like Rainey "connect[s] [. . .] readerships to particular social structures."[18]

As I will show, poetry craft books stridently reject the kind of market determinism evidenced in craft books for fiction and advertising. Across genres, however, craft books deploy remarkably similar tropes, strategies, and topoi. The vast majority break down creative production into constitutive craft techniques—layout and ad design, characterization and dialogue, rhyme and imagery—and provide exercises and examples to reinforce these techniques. At the same time, craft books insist that writers internalize such strategies so that they function unconsciously during the writing process. As we will see, craft books develop this line of thinking through one specific metaphor, appealing to the newly fashionable field of physical culture. The writer "is like the golfer in a tournament match," writes George Burton Hotchkiss, "who should not be giving attention to little details of grip, stance, and swing, but should be concentrating on the one task of hitting the ball straight." In *How to Write Advertising*, Howard Allan Barton reminds would-be writers that "[i]t takes a golfer twelve years to learn how to play golf and twelve more years to *forget* what he has learned."[19] As ubiquitous as athletics metaphors is the assumption within craft books of a level professional playing field, with such texts ignoring determinants of class and culture that remain hugely influential in sorting out literary losers and winners. "A rejection is not a haphazard act," cautions Edwin Wildman in his multi-genre *Writing to Sell*. "It means something definite: your manuscript needs fixing, rewriting, or it was sent to the wrong market." After his apprenticeship, Earnest Elmo Calkins maintains, "the story is merely one of rise in advertising work, until the unwilling recruit is now at the head of one of the leading agencies."[20] All that was required for amateur authors to succeed, these texts averred, was hard work and familiarity with those vocabularies employed by professionals. Accordingly, almost all craft books instruct readers on how to prepare manuscripts for submission, decoding otherwise esoteric practices into step-by-step advice. Wildman instructs readers to "use light-weight unlined bond paper of regular manuscript (not legal) size." "Clip the sheets together with an ordinary Collete, or regular steel clip," he goes on, "or fasten them together with brass fasteners through a punched hole."[21] Likewise, almost all craft books introduce readers to the patois of literary craftsmanship, from identifying "dactylic movement with anapestic phrasing" to explaining "'the dramatic method' as a difference of 'showing vs. telling.'"[22] This practice holds for advertising craft books as well. "An *em* is any given body of an individual square of any size of type," write Raymond Hawley and James Barton Zabin in *Understanding Advertising*. "An *agate* is the name of a 5 ½-point type."[23]

Though advertising craft books may appear extraliterary in relation to craft books dedicated to fiction and poetry, they demonstrate how crucial the genre was to the kinds of professionalization that prevailed across the early twentieth-century.[24] On the one hand, this induction of readers into professional discourses suggests the affinity of craft books with those texts that circulated for centuries among pre-industrial guilds. On the other hand, the language of professionalism bespeaks the genre's more recent orientation toward, and its role in creating, a new class of salaried "knowledge workers," a demographic whose ultimate function was "the reproduction of capitalist culture and capitalist class relations."[25] Advertising craft books' invocation of professional rhetoric also contributed to the instability of formal and generic boundaries within early twentieth-century print culture, for the newly conceived advertising "campaign" aspired to literary status, drawing on techniques of both poetry and fiction to secure consumer interest. Advertising was "literature which compels Action," one Chicago agency maintained.[26] "The same people who thrill and suffer and cry and grow hot-tempered over the tempests and joys of fiction," a *Printers' Ink* columnist held, "are touched and influenced by the heart which is put into advertising."[27] Indeed, Hotchkiss touts advertising as the most elevated of literary forms. "[I]t is not necessarily lower than pure literature," Hotchkiss wrote. "In some ways it is just as pure. Purer perhaps in that it contains less pessimism, less cynicism, less smut. It seldom panders to the prurient instincts. It cannot justly be charged with impairing morals. Even when it stimulates public demand by emotional appeals of the lower sort, it is not wholly bad, for human wants are not only the impulse to human progress but the measure of civilization."[28] Testifying succinctly to the entrenchment of a professional culture of mass print, Hotchkiss's polemic points equally to the blurring of formal and generic boundaries within that culture.

Across advertising craft books, the most frequently invoked comparison to advertising is fiction, with Hotchkiss declaring that "copy should be as interesting as the material for which people buy the publication."[29] Because of its position alongside short stories and novelettes, advertising had a greater likelihood of retaining consumers' interest if it employed narrative form, keeping consumers in a consistent frame of mind across multiple quasi-literary modes. Trade characters like the Quaker of Quaker Oats constitute a direct legacy of this philosophy, as does the predominance of narratives in which an unnamed protagonist overcomes obstacles like halitosis, malnourishment, body odor, fatigue, or unpopularity. Neither was poetry, though, without instructive value for would-be advertisers, particularly in the creation of slogans, jingles, and other text that might attract more attention than traditional copy. Hotchkiss's treatise on "catalytic copy" shades quickly into instruction in poetic meter, a reminder that "important words and syllables demand an accent" and that too heavily accented lines are "as bad for the purposes of an advertising jingle as for poetry."[30] As other scholars have pointed out, advertising craft books emphasize clarity and exactness of language in ways similar to Pound's imagist credos. While Pound urges "direct treatment of the 'thing,'" Barton advises "clear thought [and] clear expression of that thought."[31] Pound's advice to "go in fear of abstractions" becomes Kenneth Goode's "absolute horror of words that don't spark-tingle—buzz—flash."[32]

Yet if advertising craft books move the profession toward literary arts like fiction, and to a lesser extent poetry, they also insist that the language of advertising is useful, distinguishing proper writing from "art for art's sake" aestheticism. Advertising may have been literature, but it was not modernism. Barton, for instance, discourages amateur advertisers who see in the profession merely "the glitter and glamor of Bohemia." For such pretenders, "[t]he Atlantic Monthly, Des Imagistes, Wedgwood Pottery and the Moscow Art Players" constituted the "chief topics of conversation." And Barton was not "going to take your time in emphasizing the absurdity of this conception of advertising."[33] One advertising executive tersely expressed this widespread resistance to individual eccentricity or experimentation: the Batten, Barton, Durstine & Osborn agency (BBDO) was no "scenic background for a Personality," he warned, but "essentially a workshop," language consonant with an increasingly rationalized industrial-corporate economy. Like other early twentieth-century industries underwritten by professional-managerial values, American advertising was indeed a "workshop"—and the craft book was its text.

"Mere craftsmanship": Fiction and Poetry Craft Books

Just as advertising craft books peddled the techniques of literary fiction, so did fiction craft books market themselves as useful pedagogies for would-be advertisers, soliciting ad execs and other professionals interested "in story-telling as it relates to [. . .] publicity work in your own line of business."[34] In his 1921 *How To Write Stories*, Columbia journalism professor Walter B. Pitkin offers prospective writers not simply exercises in fiction craftsmanship, but training in literary imagination, cultivating a mode of thought adaptable across professions. Imagination, Pitkin explains, "is indispensable to success in business and all the other practical affairs of life. The manager of a factory is always having to think of tomorrow and next year; where he will find workmen for the new wing that will be completed next March; what he will do in case the machines for the new wing are not delivered on schedule." A prolific author of self-help manuals with titles like *Life Begins at 40* and *The Psychology of Happiness*, Pitkin believed that both the fiction writer and financier "deal[t] in futures," his pun pointing to the ways in which fiction was becoming rapidly professionalized during the first decades of the twentieth century.[35] As in advertising, that process was facilitated by the fiction craft book. As authors like Pitkin well understood, amateur writers wanted access to expanding literary economies, a marketplace of print culture increasingly lucrative not only because advertising allowed for higher payment rates, but because of the potential windfall from film and syndication rights. Such rights held out tantalizing hope for real-life rags-to-riches stories of the kind that, in fictional form, so often filled venues like *Munsey's*, *Ladies' Home Journal*, and *The Saturday Evening Post*. Fiction craft books supplied that access—or claimed to. "Study the fiction market as closely and as persistently as a Wall Street broker studies the stock market," Pitkin recommended.[36] And millions of consumers did.

Geared toward the production of literary commodities destined for mass circulation, fiction craft books insistently invoke metaphors of housing construction to instruct would-be writers in their craft. In his influential *The House of Fiction*, Henry James describes the "radiating and ramifying corridors" in the prose of Honoré de Balzac, contending that to read the French novelist is to "walk with him in the great glazed gallery of his thought."[37] Edith Wharton develops a similar metaphor in her 1925 *The Writing of Fiction*, discussing narrative structure as the "dovetailing of impossible incidents" and suggesting, with respect to point-of-view, that "[i]t should be the story-teller's first care to choose this reflecting mind deliberately, as one would choose a building-site, or decide upon the orientation of one's house."[38] Intriguingly, Wharton reverses this metaphor in her earlier *The Decoration of Houses*, a craft book on architecture and interior design she co-authored with Ogden Codman, Jr. "A large unbroken sheet of plate-glass interrupts the decorative scheme of the room," Wharton writes, "just as in verse, if the distances between the rhymes are so great that the ear cannot connect them, the continuity of sound is interrupted." For proto-modernists like Wharton and James, invocations of housing construction reflect a wider effort to pare away superfluous ornament in favor of a cleaner, more formalistic style; in both architecture and literature, for instance, Wharton values what she calls "fitness of proportion" and "the relation of voids to masses."[39] Though his was a dramatic craft book, George Pierce Baker argued in his 1919 *Dramatic Technique* that "a good scenario bears much the same relation to a completed play that an architect's plans bear to a completed house. Where would the carpenter be without such plans," Baker asks, "yet where is the set of plans which has not been modified or even greatly changed while the building is in construction?"[40]

Such figurations share a distinct historical logic. Throughout the first decades of the twentieth century, "the house as such was being rethought," as Bill Brown has argued, and this rethinking carried over not only into proto-modernist craft books but into craft books produced for popular audiences as well.[41] The latter, of course, invoke housing construction less as part of a stylistic reformation than as an easily comprehensible metaphor, though at times these figurations become so elaborate that vehicle overtakes tenor, comprehension yielding to confusion. "The writer of fiction is doing the same thing as the man who built a house from scattered stones," asserts Hoffman in *The Writing of Fiction*. "Always he must plan and build according to natural laws. He can pile stones one on top of another for walls, but for a roof gravity makes him employ the principle of an arch or use beams. [. . .] Nor can he set causes at work without getting their results; the weight of too many stones over a window-beam will crush it. To keep out the rain he must provide something that, by natural law, will turn the rain aside."[42] It is difficult to discern precisely where Hoffman's metaphor links up with the actual practice of writing. Yet Hoffman concludes his craft book with a remarkable twist on this constructivist ethos. "What we are really doing," he argues, "is building something *within the reader*—creating in him a carefully arranged and controlled flow or movement of interests and feelings, beginning with those aroused by your initial conditions. It is the reader upon whom you are really working, not upon your material and its selection and arrangement. Material and arrangement, plot and structure, are only means to an end—tools. The reader is the clay you model, however much care you must give to the fashioning and using of your tools."[43] Hoffman's is an astounding metaphor. If advertising craft books assert the proximity of advertising to fiction, Hoffman suggests the ways in which mass-market fiction equally attained to advertising's psychic manipulation of the consumer. Metaphors of housing construction thus refer not simply to the brick and mortar of literary structure, but to a virtual structure within the mind of the reader—a mansion of affect and attitude, a house not of fiction but of feeling.[44]

Whereas fiction craft books frame novel and short story writing as rigorous but potentially remunerative labor, craft books in poetry extricate poetic production from broader literary and material economies. As craft books figure it, poetry involves no "mere craftsmanship," but intensive literary labor plus an immaterial spiritual aspect.[45] Embodying an American Arts and Crafts craft ideal, the vision of poetry articulated in poetry craft books balances technical mastery and spiritual expression; like saintly relics, poetry possesses a surplus value beyond its material thingness. Metaphors of labor and laborers, if not of housing construction, play an integral role in such thinking. "Practice poetry all you will," Ethel M. Colson writes in her 1919 *How to Write Poetry*, "indulge in all the poetic craft-work you desire [. . .] but never imagine that you are writing poetry unless the poem insists upon being written, the song, at least in the beginning, insists upon singing itself."[46] In his 1929 *The Craft of Poetry*, Clement Wood maintains that "[v]erse can be manufactured at any time," turned out in "yards and yards [. . .] in any poetic feet desired." "Poetry," Wood stipulates, "comes differently."[47] And writing teacher Brenda Ueland jests in *If You Want to Write* that "at the time of the Renaissance, all gentlemen wrote sonnets. They did not think of getting them in the *Woman's Home Companion*."[48] As Ueland's rhetoric suggests, the effort to cordon off poetry from the literary marketplace renders poetry craft books part of what Janice Radway terms a "discourse of protectionism" prevalent within early twentieth-century cultural pedagogies. Most conspicuous in middlebrow initiatives like the Book of the Month Club, protectionist pedagogies restricted "the definition of the literary" by creating "safe spaces set apart from the commercial hustle and bustle of the workaday world."[49] The poetry craft book occupies precisely that middlebrow space, preserving traditional values while disseminating those values to a mass readership. In this sense, the genre is inherently self-contradictory.

While figurations of poetry as a spiritual proposition were widespread, Canadian poet Bliss Carman's 1908 craft book *The Poetry of Life* offers perhaps the most thorough treatment of poetry as a form of spiritualized labor. To begin with, Carman follows generic convention in extricating poetry from the literary marketplace, describing the "spiritual energy" of poetry as outweighing "the little gain, the jingling reward of gold." For Carman, mass-marketed literature represented "the worthless contrivance of journeymen," cranked out by mere "fabricators," a conviction borne out in Carman's own reliance on reading tours and patronage networks to support himself.[50] Where *The Poetry of Life* moves beyond generic convention is in the systematic taxonomy of labor that Carman develops, a hierarchical classification which positions poetry as the apotheosis of—emerging out of, but fundamentally transforming—other forms of manual labor. At the base of Carman's hierarchy are "primitive industries" like hunting, fishing, and agriculture, occupations that correspond to what Hannah Arendt would later call the labor of "*animal laborans*": strictly utilitarian work bound to the world of necessity.

On the next rung are occupations requiring greater ingenuity, tasks like weaving, housing construction, and metalworking. For Arendt, these skills constitute the work of "*homo faber*," that figure who creates objects of permanence, beauty, and durability.[51] Since this mode of labor, for Carman, "embod[ies] some intentional expression of human life," it contains in inchoate form the essential quality of artistic practices.[52]

As Carman understood it, the degraded character of industrial-corporate labor disrupted this progression from the industrial to the fine arts. "To produce anything worthwhile," he argued, "it is necessary that the worker should not be hurried, and should have some freedom to do his work in his own way." Contemporary workers took "neither pleasure nor pride in [their] work; and consequently that work can have no artistic value." As in Deweyan progressive education, at the heart of Carman's taxonomy was the desire to preserve hand labor as a mode of making and knowing, a craft epistemology. "If a man has never driven a nail in his life, nor built a fire, nor turned a furrow," Carman maintained, "nor picked a barrel of apples, nor fetched home the cows, nor pulled an oar, nor reefed a sail, nor saddled a horse, nor carried home a bundle of groceries from town, nor weeded the garden, nor been lost in the woods, nor nursed a friend, nor barked his shin, nor been thankful for a free lunch, do you think it is likely he will have anything to say to you and me that will be worth listening to?" Carman himself did not. In opposing poetry to the kinds of labor associated with both literary and material commercialism, *The Poetry of Life* translates into a generic and literary historical context that craft ideal first associated with the American Arts and Crafts movement. Meaningful poetry is rooted in "technique" and "execution," Carman argued, but expresses interior, spiritual concerns as well; poetry, as Carman put it, "record[s] for us the noblest aspirations of the human spirit, the ultimate reach of the soul after goodness."[53]

The extrication of poetry from the literary marketplace was not original to early twentieth-century craft books—not by a long shot. One of the earliest poetry craft books engages a similar line of thinking. In his nineteenth-century BC "Ars Poetica," Horace asks his readers whether, "once this rust and care for cash has tainted the soul," they can "hope for poems to be written that deserve preserving with cedar oil and keeping safe in smooth cypress." In "Letter to Augustus," Horace suggests that only "badly-turned verse" belongs in "the quarter where they sell perfumes and scent and pepper and everything else that gets wrapped up in worthless literature."[54] This might easily be a description of the literary marketplace to which poetry craft books like Carman's objected, an ancient corollary for a culture of mass print in which literature and advertising had been drawn increasingly nearer. For Carman, as for Horace, such literature resembled nothing so much as wrapping paper.

Modernist and Postwar Poetry Craft Books

"GRAMMAR MAKES A PARLOR": THE MODERNIST CRAFT BOOK

Part of a middlebrow reaction against the commodification of literary culture, poetry craft books reacted too against an aesthetic mode which ostensibly aligned itself with the literary marketplace. As such craft books maintained, modernist experimentation privileged the merely transitory aspects of human experience over the eternal and spiritual. "Think how much of modern art is characterized by nothing but form," Carman proposed to readers, "how devoid it is of ideas, how lacking in anything like passionate enthusiasm." Ethel M. Colson agreed, describing "strange and sad monstrosities [like] 'cubist' painting and 'toneless' music" which "have been inflicted upon a curious and long-suffering public." Coincident with the extrication of poetry from an evolving industrial-corporate regime, poetry craft books sought to parse the relationship between "genteel" nineteenth-century formalism and poetic modernism, defining these terms in partisan fashion and staking out cultural terrain for them at a time when that terrain was sharply contested.[55]

Despite these efforts, Pound and Stein turned to the craft book to launch an economic critique similar to the one levied in the pages of their middlebrow counterparts. At the same time, modernist craft books depart in significant ways from standard mass-cultural pedagogies, invoking shared metaphors of manual labor while adapting those metaphors to suit uniquely avant-garde imperatives. For Pound, the poetry craft book provided a medium through which to shape and address a kind of counter-public that might preserve Western literary culture within an ever more economistic society. For Stein, the genre served as a platform for a theory of language and literary production irreducible to rationalized modes of language use. Following the lead of Brinkman, Harrington, Rainey, Wicke, and others, I argue in this section that literary modernism constituted less a repudiation of and retreat from a culture of mass print than tactical engagement with mass media, aesthetics, and institutions. The "ambiguous achievement" of modernism, Rainey urges, was "to forge within it a strange and unprecedented space for cultural production, one that [. . .] continued to overlap and intersect with the public realm in a variety of contradictory ways."[56] One site for this intersection was the modernist craft book.

Pound himself addresses the popularity of that genre when he writes in his own craft book, the 1934 *ABC of Reading*, that the "dirtiest book in our language is a quite astute manual telling people how to earn money by writing." The fact that contemporary craft books "advocate the maximum possible intellectual degradation," however, "should not blind one to its constructive merits."[57] For Pound, early twentieth-century craft books may have offered useful lessons in "construction," but they remained tainted with the materialism of the marketplace, an argument that finds expression in Pound's own frequent invocations of housing construction. "A carpenter can put boards together, but a good carpenter would know seasoned wood from green," he insists, adapting Guido Cavalcanti to pun on American money—and perhaps anticipating Josef Albers's notion of "thinking in wood," discussed above. And Pound goes on: "The mere questions of constructing and assembling clauses, of parsing and grammar are not enough. Such study ended in a game of oratory, now parodied in detective stories when they give the learned counsel's summing-up."[58] As his allusion to detective fiction suggests, Pound wishes in *ABC* to preserve poetry from degraded literary habits and stultified ways of thinking, inclinations that entail from the misplaced priorities of a culturally bankrupt civilization. "The modern poet is expected to holloa his verses down a speaking tube to the editors of cheap magazines," Pound writes, decrying a society in which the primary impetus for literary production is economic. "Many writers need or want money," he writes in *ABC*. "These writers could be cured by an application of banknotes."[59]

Of course, *ABC* bills itself as a primer in reading, not as a craft book in literary production. For Pound, however, respectable poetic craftsmanship begins with the careful study of commendable models, so that even when studying literature as such, readers at the same time internalize literary technique. "The proper METHOD for studying poetry," Pound writes, is "COMPARISON of one 'slide' or specimen with another," a methodology he attributes to the empiricism of contemporary biologists like Louis Agassiz.[60] Accordingly, the entire second half of *ABC* consists of "exhibits" implicitly intended for would-be writers. Describing readers' use of these exhibits, Pound once again invokes metaphors of housing construction, explaining that "certain verbal manifestations *can* be employed as measures, T squares, voltmeters" that might "enable a man to estimate writing in general."[61] Once able to "estimate" writing, readers are encouraged in exercises at the end of each section to translate those skills into their own writing. One multistep exercise begins by instructing readers to "write in the meter of any poem [one] likes." After asking them to copy out lyrics to a "well-known tune," Pound then tasks readers with writing new lyrics "in such a way that the words will not be distorted when one sings them." Though Pound employs such exercises in the service of his own cultural project, both exercises and exhibits were common within the craft book genre. And just as craft books invoke physical culture, especially golf, as an analog for literary composition, Pound turns to that other increasingly professional endeavor: tennis. "The writer need no more think about EVERY DETAIL than [William "Big Bill"] Tilden needs to think about the position of every muscle in every stroke of his tennis," Pound reminds readers. "The force, the draw, etc., follow the main intention, without damage to the unity of the act."[62] Despite his protests against the "dirtiest book" that was the literary craft book, Pound clearly appropriated the popular genre in order to carry out a distinctly non-popular cultural and economic project.

Integral to that project, I have suggested, was the opposition of poetry to broader literary and material economies, a war of position Pound wages through metaphors of manual labor. While such rhetoric is widespread in poetry craft books, Pound amplifies the stakes by arguing that the well-wroughtedness of poetry is essential to Western civilization. "If a nation's literature declines," Pound famously writes, "the nation atrophies and decays." In *ABC*, Pound refigures this decay by invoking comparisons to material invention, practices of making by a craft master. If cultural production begins when a "master invents a gadget," as Pound describes, the degradation of that gadget sets in immediately, as apprentices employ it "less skillfully than the master" before it falls into the hands of the "pasteheaded pedagogue or theorist." Then, Pound says, "a bureaucracy is endowed and the pin-headed secretariat attacks every new genius and every form of inventiveness for not obeying the law." Pound concludes by reiterating that "great savants ignore, quite often, the idiocies [. . .] of the teaching profession."[63] A critique of the MFA industry *avant la lettre*, Pound's cultural schematic helps us see *ABC* as an intervention to preserve the clarity and vigor of linguistic craftsmanship. What Pound values in medieval troubadour poetry, for instance, is craft that is superior to the point that it conceals its own labor. "That 'whole art,'" Pound argues, "consisted in putting together about six strophes of poesy so that the words and the tune should be welded together without joint and without wem. The best smith, as Dante called Arnaut Daniel, made the birds SING IN HIS WORDS."[64] Pound's allusion is a subtle in-joke in literary genealogy, for it is Dante's description of Daniel in *Purgatorio*—recycled by Pound as the title for his own chapter on the troubadour in *The Spirit of Romance* (1910)—from which Eliot draws his description of Pound as "*il miglior fabbro*." And neither was Pound's investment in craftsmanship merely metaphorical. After settling into his ground-floor studio in Montparnasse in December of 1921, Pound began construction on a set of armchairs as well as two small tables, bringing with him to Paris another triangular typing table he had built in London. It was around this time that Pound began editing Eliot's typescript copy of "The Waste Land," radically trimming, reshaping, and polishing the poem into final form. Pound earned his reputation as "the better craftsman" on furniture he himself had crafted.[65]

Though Pound's privileging of traditional cultural priorities might be said to resemble the middlebrow "discourse of protectionism" found within more popular literary craft books, *ABC* constitutes not so much part of a middlebrow as an aristocratic, even fascistic, cultural project. Inspired by Mussolini's effective manipulation of the Italian press, Pound looked to the craft book as a way to disseminate his cultural and economic program to a wider audience of elites. In addition to *ABC of Reading*, Pound adopted the genre for his 1933 *ABC of Economics* and employed a similar primer-like title for *Make It New*, an essay collection published in 1934. While biographer Ira Nadel attributes Pound's fascination with the craft book to his interest in A. R. Orage's *An Alphabet of Economics*, published two decades earlier, so keen a cultural critic would no doubt have remarked the contemporary boom in mass-cultural pedagogies, likely lamenting volumes such as *Spade-craft, or How to be a Gardener* (1915), *How to Reduce: New Waistlines for Old* (1920), and *The ABC of Business Insurance Trusts* (1936). Yet the craft book was only one genre among many into which Pound channeled his missionary zeal. His statement that "literature is news that STAYS news," original to *ABC*, merely constitutes a more epigrammatic form of a concern with cultural decline that runs throughout Pound's work from this period, including in essays, operas, radio broadcasts, a newspaper column, and limited-admission lectures. Pound's tone across these various initiatives was hortatory, his didacticism focused on "identifying error," as Nadel describes, and thereby hastening cultural and economic transformation. Pound himself attributes the critical tone of *ABC* to precisely this pedagogical function, explaining that "the present pages should be impersonal enough to serve as a textbook"—one designed specifically, like many other craft books from the era, to supply a course of instruction unavailable in conventional educational settings.[66]

Pound was not alone among modernist writers in turning to the craft book to carry out a project in cultural recuperation. In her 1931 *How to Write*, Gertrude Stein follows generic convention in figuring poetry as a form of labor opposed to more commercial modes of reading and writing. Though metaphors of housing construction are integral to her argument, Stein radically reconceives the implications of these metaphors, refiguring poetry as an architectural practice that proceeds not by reference to predesigned blueprints, but by fidelity to one's self in the moment, what Stein calls an "obedience to intermittence."[67] It is this disciplined, technically rigorous expression of interiority that aligns Stein with an American Arts and Crafts craft ideal, an ethos still very much alive in cultural and economic discourse nearly two decades after the collapse of those institutions that shaped it. Whereas middlebrow poetry craft books spiritualized this ideal, treating expression as sacrosanct, Stein eschews spiritual rhetoric in order to hone a materialist conception of language and literary production, one irreducible to the kinds of language use imaginable under an industrial-corporate regime. In both its middlebrow and modernist guises, this is to say, the poetry craft book intervenes during this period in a broader confrontation between craft epistemologies and those forms of professional-managerial labor which sought to rationalize them.

Published in a limited edition of 1,000 copies, *How to Write* organizes itself along the lines of early twentieth-century grammar textbooks, with successive pedagogical sections dedicated to "Sentences," "Sentences and Paragraphs," "Grammar," and "Forensics." Like much of Stein's writing from this period, the craft book develops an aesthetic of the "continuous present," defining and redefining that and other key terms in a circular form in which ideas recur, build up, and break down across a long, linguistically dense text. Far from an accessible primer for mass audiences, *How to Write* is one of Stein's most challenging works, its idiosyncratic difficulty causing the few critics who engage it to read it as merely a spoof of the craft book genre.[68] In contrast, I argue that the text levels serious and significant claims about labor, language, and the relation of both to broader literary and material economies. Stein's craft book does, however, spoof one popular genre: the sentimental romance. Across Stein's abstract, highly theoretical language runs the faint whisper of a love plot, as *How to Write* follows a newly married couple who pop in and out of a dizzying text in which it is otherwise quite difficult to orient oneself. Stein introduces this love plot in the craft book's opening section, "Saving the Sentence," where we find the couple at the outset of their new life. "Betty is leaving her home or at any rate where she is," Stein writes. "What is it that they would have what is it that they would have gotten if they had it. Hers and his the houses are hers and his the valley is hers and his." Those houses recur throughout *How to Write*, an architectural metaphor for the stability of the couple's union and a symbol of language itself. "No doubt may be with them," Stein declares of her newlyweds.

No doubt may be with them no doubt may be.
May be with them may be. May be they may be.
It is easy to hide a hope.
Have meant.
A little goes a long way.
How many houses are there.
There is a house near where there is a bridge. They were willing to be there.
Hours out of it in adjoining them.[69]

In describing the young couple's houses, Stein is especially fascinated with carpentry joints, those cruxes where the whole edifice—house, couple, language—hold most tightly together. Puns on and versions of jointure fill *How to Write* in the same way that the names of rivers run through the "Anna Livia Plurabelle" chapter of *Finnegans Wake*, often loosed from precise reference or unstable in their signification. "[V]ery to a partly joined disturb," Stein writes, later describing "next how in favor it makes planks for be like taken do join reigned for as likely plating donkcy minded it for meaning." Stein possesses a particular fondness for dovetail joints, as when she writes that "in a case there is unit do for at all peculiar for a polite with all a classing dovetail in totality."[70]

Even in context, such phrases are difficult to parse, but taken cumulatively they suggest a through line concerned with metaphors of housing construction and with the social conditions in which construction takes place. While contemporaneous craft books deploy similar figurations in relatively straightforward fashion—such as housing construction standing in for literary construction—Stein is up to something much more complex. Specifically, the houses that run throughout *How to Write* represent the broader linguistic system, the grammar, that allows for human sociality; for Stein, the house constitutes a space from which speech can emerge. Or, as Stein figures it, "grammar makes a parlor." Stein's newlyweds do not construct their own house, therefore, because "[g]rammar is without their house which has been built without them." As Stein puns, houses may have an "address," but they are first and foremost spaces for an "address," the "parlor" above all a space in which to speak—in French, *parler*.[71] Stein's metaphor is apposite given that her own house at 27 Rue de Fleurus operated as precisely such a space; among Stein's visitors there, as has been abundantly documented, were painters Pablo Picasso and Henri Matisse, socialites Nancy Cunard and Lady Ottoline Morrell, and Lost Generation icons Ernest Hemingway and F. Scott Fitzgerald—a talkative parlor indeed. Moreover, Stein's house was furnished with Renaissance-era pieces that were likely constructed with dovetail joinery, an ancient construction practice that had gained widespread circulation as the art of cabinet-making developed in fifteenth-century Italy.[72] Part of Stein's suspicion of Pound, in fact, who she famously called a "village explainer," owed to a visit he made to the Rue de Fleurus in the spring of 1921, when, gesticulating wildly in the midst of a harangue, he shattered one of Stein's carefully selected armchairs. In London, years earlier, he had done the same thing, leaning back in a "very beautiful cane and gilt chair" until it collapsed beneath him.[73] It may have been out of necessity, it seems, that Pound first developed his considerable skills as a craftsman.

But if grammar is a kind of agentless construction for Stein, a process that happens prior to and envelops the work of the writer, of what does the poet's labor consist? Where exactly does Stein's building take place? To answer those questions, we might first examine Stein's own conception of the poet's work. For Stein, the task of the writer is to "save the sentence" from premeditation, from the tendency of premeditated thought to ossify language or restrict it to well-worn channels. Like Pound, Stein is concerned about keeping language vital, maintaining writing as an event simultaneous with thought and feeling. To "save the sentence," as Stein understands this work, is to preserve the immediacy of language against cliché, sentiment, fustian. *How to Write* offers instruction not necessarily in building with language, then, but in fostering a mode of attention in which language builds through the writer. Not unlike Robert Duncan, Stein argues that the writer's "obedience to intermittence" frees the "indwelling" that is the system of grammar.[74] *How to Write* thus offers instruction in a kind of investigation that takes place during and is made possible by the act of writing. "It is very hard to save the sentence," Stein admits. "Sentences are made wonderfully one at a time. Who makes them. Nobody can make them because nobody can what ever they do see."[75] In addition to the jointure of newlyweds and the houses they occupy, therefore, *How to Write* also meditates on the jointure of thought and feeling with language, and on the manifestation of this jointure in the poetic object—"all at once. / Dove and dove-tail," Stein writes. Or, punning later: "in union there is strength."[76]

Stein's jointure of self and syntax—of interior processes with a prior system of grammar—eventuates in what Stein elsewhere calls the literary "master-piece," naming that object with which apprentices in pre-industrial guilds and workshops proved their mastery of craft practices. For Stein, "master-pieces" eschewed premeditation in favor of the writer's joining herself at the very moment of composition with a broader linguistic matrix. "Now and then a master-piece can escape any one and get to be more and more there," Stein writes in *The Geographical*

History of America, "and any one any one who can write as writing is written can make anything be there again and again."[77] Stein's own esoteric literary style, at its most challenging in a text like *How to Write*, prevents the reader from premeditating how a sentence or bit of syntax will resolve itself. As she figures it, Stein's prose is a way of disrupting the relation between syntax and semantics, as if we were reading one word at a time through a magnifying glass. A "whole thing is not interesting because as a whole well as a whole there has to be remembering and forgetting," Stein asserts. "[B]ut one at a time, oh one at a time is something oh yes definitely something."[78]

Unlike Pound, Stein harbored few reservations about a contemporary culture of mass print, enamored as she was with detective fiction and skilled in manipulating the interstices of that culture for her own ends. Eager, for instance, to boost her profile among cosmopolitan tastemakers, Stein commissioned Mabel Dodge Luhan to publish and distribute a promotional pamphlet at the 1913 Armory Show, a tactic which prompted Maria Jolas to accuse her of "Barnumesque publicity."[79] Stein shares with Pound, though, profound respect for language as a system transcending its local instantiation, figuring language as a form of construction into which we write ourselves, intermittently, moment by moment. If *How to Write* parodies the popular genre of the craft book, as scholars argue, its parody is far from simple tongue-in-cheek spoofing; rather, Stein indicts the genre for its perpetuation of premeditated literary structures and practices to be imitated by a mass audience. While still other scholars note the influence of mass manufacturing on Stein's writing, attention to her little-known craft book, *How to Write*, shows how Stein looked too to earlier forms of pre-industrial labor as a way to understand and articulate the process of poetic composition.[80] Stein describes that labor in a section of *How to Write* called "Arthur a Grammar," arguing that "a grammar makes it easy to change from a factory to a garden. / From working in a factory to working in a garden without distress."[81] It would be inappropriate to read workerist politics into Stein's thinking-through-craft, but this moment does seem to gesture to the wider economic stakes involved in her imbrication of labor and language. Like other early twentieth-century poetry craft books, *How to Write* images a form of labor irreducible to regnant literary and material economies— images it briefly, fleetingly, tentatively; for Stein, it could never be otherwise.

THE POETRY CRAFT BOOK GOES TO SCHOOL

A key step in the expropriation of craft epistemologies, as I have indicated, was the incorporation of the craft book itself into the American university, by midcentury the dominant institution in an evolving industrial-corporate economy. Though the university had been a major economic force since the Morrill Land-Grant Acts of 1862, a number of factors combined around the midcentury to broaden its influence, among them an increase in government research contracts, the expansion of "strategic alliances" between academic departments and corporations, and a boom in corporate endowment of chairs, professorships, and institutes.[82] As sociologist Daniel Bell diagnosed, the university rapidly became the "axial structure" of the midcentury economy, that site where "theoretical knowledge [was] codified and enriched" and where an entrenched professional-managerial class methodically reproduced itself.[83]

For even as the university cemented its authority in American society, and even as GI benefits attracted millions of new students into its orbit, higher education remained largely inaccessible to low-income Americans, particularly those whose parents were not themselves professional-managerial laborers. While women and Black students saw marked gains in college enrollment in the postwar era, working-class students failed to make similar inroads, a failure especially conspicuous at elite institutions. In 1966, only 8 percent of students at private universities came from low-income families, while 32 percent came from families with incomes twice the American average. In contrast, low-income students between 1966 and 1975 increased their representation at two-year colleges from 17 percent to 20 percent, compared with a decrease from 11 percent to 9 percent for wealthier students. As David Karen argues, even though their absolute representation increased, working-class students became "relatively more concentrated in the lowest tier" of American universities.[84] These inequalities endure into the present, as does the concentration of economic and cultural authority in elite institutions and wealthier social classes. From 1970 to 2002, the percentage of low-income students who earned a bachelor's degree by their twenty-fourth birthday held steady at just 6 percent.[85] From 1992 to 2002, while suing to diversify its student body through affirmative action, the University of Michigan reduced the number of low-income students eligible for Pell Grants by an astonishing 48 percent.[86] For Karen, these discrepancies owe to more effective political mobilization on the part of women and Black students, demographics "recognized as official social categories" in ways that low-income students are not.[87] Such discrepancies are also attributable, however, to the university's deliberate prioritization of its own knowledge work and of those classes that perpetuate it, to the point that professional-managerial labor became the fastest growing occupational category following World War II.

It was the reproduction of this class of knowledge workers which led the university to cultivate the abstract discourse of the professional as its *lingua franca*, prioritizing technical and theoretical forms of knowledge over the more concrete, even manual, epistemologies of the craftsman.[88] For Natalia Cecire, these processes, linked with the rise of Big Science, contributed in turn to a "crisis of legitimation" within the arts and humanities, an epistemological break which prompted the emergence of experimental poetic traditions like the Language and Black Mountain schools. Experimental poetries, Cecire argues, "borrow[ed] the language, and frequently the epistemic virtues, of the sciences," simultaneously adapting and critiquing newly corporatized notions of "research."[89] A fundamental claim of this book, however, is that not only experimental but also mainstream academic poetry—what Charles Bernstein designates as "official verse culture"— responded to, facilitated, and in some cases critiqued the academic entrenchment of professional-managerial values.[90] For the university did not simply espouse professional-managerialism in unadulterated form—it rewrote it in the language of craft, invoking manual labor to metaphorize the very ethos which had outmoded manual labor in the first place. As Ethan Schrum summarizes, in what turns out to be an instructive pun, the university "craft[ed] a rhetoric centered on the knowledge economy to promote [its] importance for society." By the postwar era, the poetry craft book and the workshop in which it was used served as key distribution points for those professional-managerial discourses on which a new informational-corporate economy would depend.

But this trajectory was not a foreordained conclusion. Indeed, the first poetry craft book to be employed widely in the writing workshop, Cleanth Brooks and Robert Penn Warren's *Understanding Poetry*, retools the genre's long-running critique of commercialism into a critique of the university itself. Like New Critical ideology writ large, *Understanding Poetry* seeks to train students in forms of language use antithetical to those eventuating from an economistic society; to do so, the text intervenes at the very site where that society reproduces itself, challenging what Allen Tate called "the uncreative money-culture of modern times" and those "attitudes of the *haute bourgeoisie* that support it in the great universities."[91] Hardly the vehicle for a depoliticized aestheticism, as its critics charge, *Understanding Poetry* reads the organic structure of the poem as enacting the ironies, paradoxes, and contradictions papered over in contemporary professional-managerialism; to attend critically to these contradictions, Brooks and Warren believe, is to make visible the limitations of regnant cultural and economic institutions.[92] In levying such a critique, *Understanding Poetry* draws on a tradition of Southern Agrarianism long skeptical of capitalist relations and their effect on American culture, an anti-modern tradition which looked not to pre-industrial craftsman-ship, as the American Arts and Crafts movement did, but to small-scale agricul-ture as an alternative social form. Though agrarianism risked endorsing economic structures every bit as deleterious as those that prevailed under industrial- and informational-corporatism, it remained a potent—and, in the form of *Understand-ing Poetry*, a massively popular—antidote to professional-managerial values.

The merits and limitations of New Critical ideology have been well documented, but rarely acknowledged is how its objection to a rationalized culture revolved around the invocation of labor and laborers. Like its middlebrow and modernist predecessors, *Understanding Poetry* explicitly extricates poetry from the literary and economic marketplace, though its authors are especially concerned about distinguishing the genre from professional-managerial labor. As early as the In-troduction to the first edition, published in 1938, Brooks and Warren figure po-etry as a distinct form of production, drawing up an imaginary scenario involving a hypothetical American worker, in subsequent editions referred to as "Mr. X." "We may do well," Brooks and Warren surmise, "to ask how much of the discourse of an average man in any given day is primarily concerned with information for the sake of information. After he has transacted his business, obeyed his road signs, ordered and eaten his dinner, and read the stock market reports, he might be surprised to reflect on the number of non-practical functions speech had ful-filled for him that day."[93] In later editions this thought experiment is expanded, to the point that by 1960 Mr. X will analyze "stock market quotations [. . .] take inventory of the stock in [his] hardware store," and "follow the directions on a can of weed-killer," all while finding time to "punch the time clock at the factory or give an order to his broker." Brooks and Warren's heuristic is a suggestive articu-lation of New Critical values, locating poetry in a realm of "attitudes and feelings" removed from day-to-day labor and the kinds of language—positivist, practical, utilitarian, all New Critical *bêtes noires*—associated with that labor. In *Understand-ing Poetry*, poetry resembles less the language of Mr. X's workaday experience than the non-informative language with which he "reminded his wife of some lit-tle episode of their early life" or "commented on the fine fall weather to the traffic officer."[94] As did Pound, Stein, and their middlebrow contemporaries, Brooks and Warren attempt to preserve poetic language by disaffiliating such language from wider literary and material economies.

Like Pound's *ABC*, of course, *Understanding Poetry* was intended first and fore-most as instruction in "how to *read* a literary text," its case studies a kind of exe-getical training in "saving the sentence," as Stein put it, from those forces that would reduce language to instrumentality.[95] Implicit in the text, though, is recognition that training in reading functions at the same time as training in writing, fostering as it does the critical discernment integral to literary composition. Moreover, much of the pedagogy in *Understanding Poetry* seems intended for would-be writers, in particular its definition of poetry through reference to metaphors of architecture and housing construction; it is difficult to read Brooks and Warren's discussion of authorial intent, for instance, as merely an interpretive aid. "It is true that sometimes the poet has a pretty clear idea of what he wants his poem to be," they write. "But even in such circumstances, is the process of creation analogous to that of building a house by a blueprint? An architect intends a certain kind of house and he can predict it down to the last nail. The carpenter simply follows the blueprint. But at the best the poet cannot envisage the poem as the architect can envisage the house; and in so far as the poet can envisage the poem, he cannot transfer it into words in a mechanical fashion corresponding to the builder's work on the house."[96] Though such a belabored metaphor may in fact have benefited from blueprinting, the passage is clearly designed as a lesson in how poems come about, and in cultivating the proper attitude toward literary production. In instructing readers in this mentality, *Understanding Poetry* even defines poetry through reference to athletics and physical culture. "Does a finely trained pole-vaulter in the act of making his leap think specifically of each of the different muscles he is employing?" Brooks and Warren ask. "[O]r does a boxer in the middle of a round think of the details of his boxing form?" Echoing middlebrow and modernist craft books, *Understanding Poetry* seems designed as a textbook for the literature classroom as well as a craft book for the writing workshop, the latter an increasingly prominent fixture within the midcentury university. In one of those workshops, a graduate student by the name of Flannery O'Connor understood the text as precisely such a craft book, referring to *Understanding Poetry* as her "Bible"—high praise from the famously devout Catholic.[97]

The adaptability of *Understanding Poetry* to a variety of academic settings reflects not only its authors' marketing savvy, but their familiarity with the institutional constraints under which literary pedagogues labored. At the time they began work on the text, Brooks and Warren were lowly assistant professors in the Department of English at Louisiana State University, tasked with teaching four classes per semester, editing *The Southern Review*, and equipping a culturally deprived student body with the skills of effective language use. Before it became a four-edition mass-market phenomenon, *Understanding Poetry* began its life as a set of lecture notes copied on Ditto machines and circulated among colleagues, a

kind of midcentury academic *samizdat*. It is the entrenchment of this pedagogy—
or its massification as the infinitely reproducible practice of close reading—which
has led critics to find in the New Criticism the very professional-managerial ethos
to which Brooks, Warren, and their associates objected. As Gerald Graff argues,
"as the university increased in size, the need arose for a simplified pedagogy, encouraging the detachment of 'close reading' from the cultural purposes that originally inspired it." Brooks and Warren's "insistence on the disinterested nature of
poetic experience," Graff goes on, "was an implicit rejection of a utilitarian culture and thus a powerfully 'utilitarian' and 'interested' gesture."[98] Edward Brunner
locates this professional-managerial ethos within the "well-wrought" poem itself,
contending that the New Criticism "succeeded in professionalizing that reading
site by claiming a distinct set of interpretive procedures that would do justice to
the literary text."[99] There is certainly merit in such charges—John Crowe Ransom,
after all, called for literary study to be "seriously taken in hand by professionals,"
what he termed a "Criticism, Inc."[100]

This dual face of the New Criticism, however, and of *Understanding Poetry* in
particular, testifies to the text's position as a switching point within the genre of
the poetry craft book. Specifically, *Understanding Poetry* marks the culmination
of a line of thinking, conspicuous in middlebrow and modernist examples of the
genre, which opposes poetry to the professional-managerial values of evolving
industrial- and informational-corporate economies. If New Critics challenged
those values at the site where they were most systematically reproduced, postwar
and contemporary poetry craft books almost universally align themselves with
that very institution; poet Annie Finch recommends her own craft book for use
in the "intermediate or advanced poetry-writing workshop, either undergraduate
or graduate; a beginning undergraduate poetry workshop or a workshop with a
focus predominately on free verse."[101] Not unrelatedly, postwar poetry craft books
depart from Brooks and Warren by figuring poetry as manual labor, transcoding
the university's promotion of professional-managerialism in the language of pre-
industrial craft. At this switching point in literary history, as the craft book takes
up shop within the American university, the manual laborer returns as mascot for
the creative writing workshop, returns as trope and tagline, as that idealized
image so integral for so long to American social and political discourse.

"All was well made": Craft, Inc.

One of the more remarkable figurations of writing as manual labor, Roy Peter
Clark's 2006 *Writing Tools*, demonstrates the importance of craft lexicons to post-

war and contemporary professional-managerial value systems. "The National Commission on Writing has described the disastrous consequences of bad writing in America," Clark writes, "for businesses, professions, educators, consumers, and citizens. Poorly written reports, memos, announcements, and messages cost us time and money. [. . .] The Commission calls for a 'revolution' in the way Americans think about writing. The time is right. [. . .] We need lots of writing tools to build a nation of writers. Here are fifty of them, one for every week of the year. You get two weeks for vacation."[102] Similar figurations recur widely across the late twentieth and early twenty-first centuries, from Iowa Writers' Workshop director Paul Engle's 1964 statement that "a work of art is work" to poet Mary Kinzie's 2013 description of an "apprenticeship" in which, after "mastering [poetry's] rudiments," students begin the "real work of hearing and making rhythm."[103] Indeed, some of the most influential craft books of the MFA era invoke housing construction, in particular, as an analog for poetic composition. In her legendary *A Poetry Handbook*, first published in 1994, Mary Oliver contends that "just as a bricklayer or any worker—even a brain surgeon—improves with study and experience, surely poets become more proficient with study and 'practice.'"[104] In their 1997 *The Poet's Companion*, Kim Addonizio and Dorianne Laux describe poetic making as a "line by line, brick by brick construction," comparing the poet's mastery of detail to the fastidious construction of European architecture. "In the great cathedrals, bridges, and railway stations of our world each block was 'cut smooth and well fitting,'" Addonizio and Laux write, quoting Pound's *usura* Canto.[105] More than ancillary metaphors, such figurations embody core principles within postwar and contemporary writers' otherwise unique poetic ideologies. In his 2004 *Poetry: The Basics*, Jeffrey Wainwright suggests connecting end rhymes with a series of lines running down the margin of the poem, a way for aspiring writers to visualize and imitate poetic structures. "Drawing these arcs and then turning the page through ninety degrees," Wainwright explains, "the rhyming of some elaborate stanza forms [. . .] can be seen to have a nearly architectural structure."[106] In the same way, John Hollander's *Rhyme's Reason* characteristically links form and content: "in couplets, one line often makes a point / Which hinges on its bending, like a joint."[107]

Though postwar poetry craft books depart dramatically from earlier texts, like *Understanding Poetry*, in which poetic production was carefully disaffiliated with labor, in other ways they display a high level of consistency with such texts. Like their predecessors, these craft books are organized by discrete techniques such as line, diction, sound, structure, and image, often with little theoretical or historical framing. Like their predecessors, postwar poetry craft books recommend that writers internalize rather than consciously process these techniques, resorting in many cases to the same metaphors of athletics and physical culture used by earlier authors. "Aspiring golfers swing and miss if they try to remember the thirty or so different elements of an effective golf swing," Clark cautions.[108] Addonizio and Laux note that effective tennis players "aren't thinking 'racket back, step forward, swing, follow through' as [they] rally."[109] Also like their predecessors, postwar poetry craft books mobilize a remarkably consistent set of pedagogical tropes, reminding writers of the pregnant etymologies of "verse,"[110] "sonnet,"[111] and "stanza,"[112] for example, distinguishing between Latinate and Anglo-Saxon diction,[113] and recommending the iambic as that meter which "best suggests the structures of informal speech."[114]

Given these similarities with middlebrow and modernist craft books, why do postwar and contemporary texts so radically revise the relationship between poetry and labor? Why does poetry, we might say, suddenly become so laborious? The most commonly invoked answer to this question is that it is craft alone, as opposed to inspiration or creativity, which can be taught in an institutional setting. As Mark McGurl argues, craft allows literary pedagogues "to separate the question of talent and originality, which cannot be taught, from the question of technique, which can."[115] While cultivating the consciousness of a poet may be an unattainable objective, understanding the relation between vehicle and tenor—or the redirections of poetic movement or the combinative possibilities of alliteration and assonance—is a technique far more easily mastered in the fifteen-week workshop. Tim Mayers reasons similarly: "[b]ecause so many people clung to the notion that writers are born, not made," Mayers explains, "craft became virtually synonymous with the one small aspect of creative composition—technique—that these writers believed could be taught."[116] And though he does not discuss creative writing specifically, Richard Sennett suggests the pedagogical importance of craft techniques, arguing that "there is no art without craft; the idea for a painting is not a painting."[117] This line of thinking may be eminently practical, but it too readily ignores the broader ideological motivations behind the mobilization of craft lexicons; a major contention of this book is that craft constitutes not some lowest common denominator in writing pedagogy, but a deliberately cultivated strategy in the university's promotion of its own knowledge work.

A more convincing answer, it seems to me, as to why postwar poetry craft books consistently link poetic to architectural construction involves the institutional position of creative writing within departments of English. While it is the discipline's encouragement of self-expression that separates creative writing from its departmental neighbors, composition and literature, it is the invocation of manual labor that frames poetry as equal in rigor to the classification of rhetorical topoi or the materialist exegesis of *Ulysses*. In the words of Edward Brunner, craft flaunts the poem as a "labor-intensive" object, an "exquisitely balanced verbal machine crafted by specialists in the language arts."[118] Craft pedagogies convey academic rigor in the same way that, for Thorstein Veblen, Gothic architecture bestows an aura of respectability and permanence on the American university; the "defensive details of a medieval keep" impact "the lay attention directly and convincingly," Veblen argues, "while the pursuit of learning is a relatively obscure matter [. . .] even with the help of the newspapers and the circular literature that issues from the university's publicity bureau."[119] The argument that craft pedagogies stake out disciplinary space for creative writing entails, among other considerations, rethinking Howard Singerman's influential claim that university arts programs train students in theoretical and historical rather than manual skillsets. As Singerman contends, "to be included among the disciplines, art must give up its definition as craft or technique, a fully trainable manual skill on the guild or apprenticeship model."[120] Singerman's argument may hold for visual arts programs, but in extending his claims to creative writing he ignores the rhetorical thrust of craft pedagogies, the ways in which the "apprenticeship model" is strategically deployed within the wider context of a rigorously professional department.

A related ideological motivation for the figuration of poetry as manual labor, then, is that it contributes to a discourse of professionalism which continuously reinforces the authority of the university—craft workshops do not so much produce poets as they produce professionals. Just as craft pedagogies legitimate creative writing as a discipline, craft at the same time provides would-be writers with the credentials necessary to distinguish themselves from county laureate poets and weekend workshoppers. In an era of escalated credentialing and contracting arts economies, craft constitutes one line of force in what Pierre Bourdieu has called a struggle "to impose the dominant definition of the writer," effectively delimiting the population of writers licensed to take part in that struggle.[121] More generally, a degree in creative writing signals the social and symbolic fluency necessary within Peter Sacks's "Human Capital Economy," a professional system in which a worker's value consists less in what he "can make, move, or dig" than in "what the worker knows and the sorts of information over which he or she has command."[122] Whereas craft pedagogies begin, for someone like George Pierce Baker, as a way of disrupting the cultural and material reproduction of an industrial-corporate elite, they function in the postwar period to reinscribe the same utilitarian values that Baker opposed—the creative writing workshop transforms at midnight into a licensing agency.

In a not-unprecedented rhetorical sleight of hand, however, the university conceals its investment in professional-managerial economies with the language of manual labor, part of what Stephen Schryer describes as a wider effort on the part of intellectuals and administrators to "mystify the 'sphere of strategy' within which they work."[123] John Guillory elaborates on this mystification, contending that it is "possible to ground the analysis of intellectuals in the socioeconomic domain by positing a constitutive distinction between intellectual and manual labor, a distinction that for good historical reasons implicates intellectual labor in the system of economic exploitation."[124] Christopher Findeisen puts it even more directly: "the academy's 'symbolic class warfare' necessarily takes place at the level of discourse," he writes, including, as I suggest in this book, the discourse of creative writing craft. Such appeals to workerist language have long been standard within right-wing politics, and Western media have for centuries peddled romantic notions of craft labor as part of a fundamentally hegemonic culture industry. There is dark irony, though, in the fact that, as the university promotes the redistribution of economic resources toward professional-managerial workers, craft books turn back to forms of labor which the university itself has worked to eradicate. "Our culture's most compelling forms of resistance to the business of higher education," Findeisen writes, "are not resistance at all but rather the system's symbolic core."[125] As Jacques Derrida puts it, "desiring to remove the university from 'useful' programs and from professional ends, one may always, willingly or not, find oneself [. . .] reconstituting powers of caste, class, or corporation. We are in an implacable political topography."[126] Postwar writers themselves evince profound regret for the evanescence of manual labor, juxtaposing informational-corporate culture with a lapsed era of craftsmanship. "We sigh—or I do—for the days when whole cultures were infused with noble simplicity," Denise Levertov writes in her own craft essay. "[W]hen though there were cruelty and grief, there was no ugliness; when King Alcinoüs himself stowed the bronze pots for Odysseus under the rowers' benches; when from shepherd's pipe and warrior's sandal to palace door and bard's song, all was *well made*."[127]

Curiously, however, just as craft vanishes as ethos and economic practice, it reappears in appropriated form, not only in the guise of the poetry craft book but in a wider contemporary fascination with craft rhetoric. In the introduction to this book, I discuss how intellectuals such as C. Wright Mills and William H. Whyte invoke craft as a metaphor for the kind of knowledge work involved in sociology and business administration, respectively. Advocating craftsmanship as an idealized model of the sociologist's labor, Mills writes that "there is an inner relation between the craftsman and the thing he makes, from the image he first forms of it through its completion, which [. . .] makes the craftsman's will-to-work spontaneous and even exuberant." Though Mills laments that "none of these aspects are now relevant to modern work experience," he nonetheless urges a rebirth of something like the American Arts and Crafts craft ideal, balancing the sociologist's engaged labor with technical "perfection of his craft."[128] In his 1956 classic *The Organization Man*, likewise, Whyte argues that the task of the properly administered corporation is to "*re-create* the belongingness of the Middle Ages," looking back wistfully on a guild-like sense of corporate purpose.[129] Craft also reappears during this period in the form of luxury consumer products, the enjoyment of which requires both economic and cultural capital. In 1949, the *New York Times* declared "hand-loomed" textiles the "newest look in upholstery fabrics," championing "men and women who create with their hands rather than a pencil."[130] Consumers could, as many did, buy placemats designed by Anni Albers and marketed at department stores such as Macy's and Bloomingdale's. Today, the workshop poem shares discursive space with craft IPAs and "hand-loomed" Pottery Barn rugs, with artisanal donut boutiques and indie video games, retro cassette tapes and YETI coolers. As Bourdieu makes clear, "disguised forms of economic capital [. . .] produce their most specific effects only to the extent that they conceal (not least from their possessors) the fact that economic capital is at their root"—there is no area, including higher education, in which the "stylization of life" might not assert its pressure. Packaged into a haute lifestyle proposition characterized, Bourdieu argues, by the "barbarous reintegration of aesthetic consumption into the world of ordinary consumption," couture craft signals cultural distinction just as the production of a creative writing thesis does.[131] As one group of couture experts describes, craft companies "constantly pursue the right balance between the artistic (creative) soul and the rational (managerial) soul," a description which suggests nothing so much as the creative writing workshop.[132]

To examine the role of the poetry craft book within that workshop is to confront an exhibit in what György Lukács called "the capitalization of the spirit," as the rationalization of American culture extends even into the crafting of the poetic object.[133] So affianced does the poetry craft book become to the broader authority of the university that its erstwhile investment in poetry as a spiritual discipline resurfaces as New Age spiritualism, a kind of haute or couture religios-

ity. Inviting would-be writers to court their own personal muse, Annie Finch recommends filling one's writing space with talismanic figurines organized around
a poetry altar. "My own writing studio is full of figurines or reminders of inspiring
Muses of various cultures," Finch describes, "from Pegasus to the Celtic poetry
goddess Brigid to Sarasvati, Hindu goddess of poetry and music." Finch goes on
to suggest that writers mitigate the anxiety of submitting their work—she calls
it "offering" one's work—by turning the occasion into a festive spiritual séance,
"burning incense or candles and playing music."[134] Redolent of the New Age cult,
such insipid pedagogies belie the quite rationalized function of contemporary
writing craft. It is no accident, after all, that the discipline of creative writing
exploded at precisely the moment during which the university itself, the site of
a newly re-politicized workshop, consolidated its influence over the American
economy—such workshops served efficiently in their dual function of promoting
professional-managerial values while transcoding those values in craft lexicons.

Of course, creative writing also entails far less deleterious consequences, as
my discussion of Richard Hugo will make clear. Within the impersonal and bureaucratic halls of higher education, the writing workshop affords opportunity
for self-expression and individual recognition that may not exist elsewhere—the
workshop table is hardly the amphitheatrically tiered, thousand-person lecture
hall. As the politics of the last decade have impressed upon us, moreover, few skills
are more crucial to the maintenance of democracy than linguistic facility, the kind
of close attention to language use which empowers one, for example, to distinguish between authentic and fraudulent news sources. Indeed, writing workshops
foster creative work which in many cases speaks meaningfully against those very
inequalities the university engenders, including economic stratification. As I tell
my own students, attending to language at the level of line and syntax—or in
terms of plot and trajectory, or shape and structure—can facilitate more ethical
language use across our culture. When we understand poetic rhythm as the movement of a column of air inside us, we learn something too about the rhythms of
our bodies and the revolutions of nations. When we deconstruct literary texts into
formal assemblages, we learn to read other kinds of texts as well, grasping more
fully how systems of injustice perpetuate themselves through rhetorical coercions
and linguistic snares. It is these more positive valences of creative writing that
poet Lisa Jarnot defends when she laments the privileging of "career over craft"
within the contemporary MFA industry. Such programs "highlight the idea that
poetry is a commodity that will allow the poet an academic position, high-visibility
magazine publications, a book contract, and the skills to negotiate through a so-

cial world of academic conferences and publishing house circles," Jarnot diagnoses. "These are all antithetical to the craft of poetry."[135]

While I appreciate the social and cultural merits of the discipline—I graduated from and teach in MFA programs, after all—I have hoped to show in this volume that ethical distinctions like Jarnot's too readily ignore the implication of creative writing craft within a broader informational-corporate economy. The end of craft pedagogies is hardly the well-wrought poem; it is the perpetuation of a system of licensure that literally underwrites the university's cultural and economic capital. Writing craft is a finishing tool for aspiring professionals.

Richard Hugo and Postwar Creative Writing

"INVEST THE FEELING IN THE WORDS": *THE TRIGGERING TOWN*

If craft books like Finch's seem blithely oblivious to the stakes of the rhetoric they peddle, Richard Hugo's 1979 craft book, *The Triggering Town*, unabashedly identifies craft pedagogies as integral to the university's economic authority. "Creative writing belongs in the university for the same reason other subjects do," Hugo makes clear. "[B]ecause people will pay to study them. If you challenge the right of creative writing to be in the university, to be fair you'd have to challenge a long list of other subjects. [. . .] (Not a bad idea, but let's not wreck the economy beyond repair.)"[136]

Hugo understood that economy well. As a young man, he labored at odd jobs in the warehouses, steel mills, and ammunition magazines of West Seattle, and, after earning his degree in English from the University of Washington, worked for twelve years as a technical writer at Boeing. It was at Washington in the fall of 1947, on GI benefits earned as a bomber in World War II, that Hugo studied in the first workshops taught by Theodore Roethke, then on the verge of breakthrough success with his widely acclaimed second collection, *The Lost Son and Other Poems*. Roethke himself was a master poetic craftsman, requiring of his students—among them Carolyn Kizer, William Edgar Stafford, David Wagoner, and James Wright— meticulous craft exercises in forms modeled after Thomas Wyatt, Robert Herrick, Gerard Manley Hopkins, and W. H. Auden.[137] After over a decade at Boeing, Hugo became an assistant professor at the University of Montana in 1965, succeeding in the early 1970s to the directorship of creative writing there, a position he held until his death in 1982.

Hugo, this is to say, is the workshop poet *par excellence*, an upwardly mobile working-class writer from White Center, Washington—"a world outside the mainstream," Hugo wrote, "isolated and ignored"—who marshaled his veteran benefits toward entrée into a postwar professional-managerial class, thereafter disseminating the language of that class to two decades of aspiring writers.[138] Hugo mythologizes this trajectory in his posthumously published autobiography, in which the imposing architecture of neighboring West Seattle prefigures the university into which he would matriculate. There "sat the castle, the hill," Hugo writes, "West Seattle where we would go to high school. The streets were paved, the homes elegant [. . .] Gentility and confidence reigned on that hill. West Seattle was not a district. It was an ideal. [. . .] [I]t towered over the sources of felt debasement, the filthy, loud belching steel mill, the oily slow river, the immigrants hanging on to their odd ways."[139] Despite his sense that his working-class upbringing constituted a source of "debasement," Hugo would return to that source throughout his career as a poet, incorporating both labor and laborers into work centered obsessively on the devastation of working-class communities—the material deterioration, the loss of collective identity, the social and psychological despair. Across this work, Hugo develops a Deep Image poetics characterized by associative imagism and the cultivation of subconscious spiritual and natural values. Whereas iconic Deep Imagists like Robert Bly and W. S. Merwin favor thick description over more expository language, however, Hugo's work possesses a winking postmodern reflexivity. "Try this for obscene development," Hugo writes in his 1977 collection *31 Letters and 13 Dreams*. "[T]hey made me / director of creative writing. Better I'd gone on bleeding / getting whiter and whiter and finally blending / into the snow to be found next spring."[140] Refiguring the whiteness of the page as self-annulling oblivion—an oblivion with racial overtones, as I demonstrate in the coda to this book—Hugo's poetics understands itself *a priori* as a product of postwar institutionality.

The Triggering Town, accordingly, offers a rich diagnostic of the institutional habitus of creative writing. One of the most widely used craft books of all time, the text shares a number of tropes with postwar and contemporary craft books, with Hugo recommending that students write in a "hard-covered notebook with green-lined pages" and advocating internalization of craft techniques through reference to—what else?—the techniques of golf. "Once a spectator said, after Jack Nicklaus had chipped a shot in from the sand trap, 'That's pretty lucky,'" Hugo writes. "Nicklaus is supposed to have replied, 'Right. But I notice the more I practice, the luckier I get.'"[141] Drawing from Hugo's experience teaching at Montana, *The Triggering Town* is a collection of essays on subjects ranging from the economic considerations of writing—"How Poets Make a Living," Hugo titles one essay—to pedagogical strategies and craft techniques, foremost among which are what Hugo calls "triggering" and "generated" subjects. While the poem begins, for Hugo, with a triggering subject that starts or causes its action, it quickly transcends itself to arrive at a generated subject, that idea or feeling "which the poem comes to say or mean" and which is "discovered in the poem during the writing."[142] Though the two writers could hardly be more distinct stylistically, Hugo and Stein share a conception of poetry as a mode of investigation that takes place during and through the act of writing.

For Hugo, the quintessential triggering subject is the deindustrialized mill town, that titular "triggering town" glimpsed as the writer passes through. "It should make impression enough that I can see things in the town [. . .] long after I've left," Hugo writes, but the encounter should be momentary, evocative. The writer must remain unburdened by historical fact and thereby retain the freedom to adapt the triggering town to poetic imperative. "Knowing can be a limiting thing," Hugo writes. "Guessing leaves you more options." As deindustrialized towns recur throughout *The Triggering Town*, the poet's imaginative freedom increasingly comes to resemble an economic relationship. "You owe the details nothing," Hugo advises. "If you have no emotional investment in the town, though you have taken immediate emotional possession of it for the duration of the poem, it may be easier to invest the feeling in the words."[143] The statement, like the poetics to which it gestures, is a fascinating one, ethically complex in the context of postwar creative writing. On the one hand, Hugo asks aspiring poets to reinvest in—to witness and give voice to—those towns left behind in the consolidation of a mid-century informational-corporate regime. On the other hand, Hugo's financial rhetoric frames the writer as a kind of expropriative collections agent, neatly allegorizing the university's promotion of professional-managerial labor—that is, Hugo recommends mining a town for its aesthetic value and redistributing that value among knowledge workers who can make most profitable use of it. Hugo would hardly have been unwitting as to the economic implications of his metaphor. In an essay in *The Triggering Town* titled "In Defense of Creative Writing Classes," he unflinchingly locates creative writing in the context of the research-oriented university. "Today," he writes, "the department budget in most state universities is based on enrollment statistics," noting the importance of creative writing to departments otherwise beset by hiring freezes, financial rollbacks, and departmental consolidation. "The professional administrator is everywhere," Hugo perceives, "and English departments are not above using statistics swelled by people [. . .] for whom knowing is less fun at times than guessing."[144]

Of course, the poverty-stricken mill town does not appear *ex nihilo* on the scene of American literature. From Sherwood Anderson's Winesburg to Edgar Lee Masters' Spoon River, triggering towns have long supplied a rich vein from which American writers have drawn their material. Such towns pop up everywhere in Hugo's writing, to the extent that his tables of contents read like a travelogue—"Graves at Mukilteo," "Mendocino, Like You Said," "The Milltown Union Bar," "Helena, Where Homes Go Mad," "Missoula Softball Tournament," "Why I Think of Dumar Sadly." Perhaps the most iconic of Hugo's triggering towns is Philipsburg, Montana, a former mining and timber town located an hour southeast of Missoula. Memorialized in Hugo's popular "Degrees of Gray in Philipsburg," the town had a population of 820 in the 2010 census and serves as the administrative seat of Granite County, home to more than two dozen ghost towns abandoned when local economies collapsed. Though I do not treat the poem at length, I want to briefly suggest how it embodies Hugo's triggering town poetics, as well as how Hugo meditates therein on the practice of creative writing within the postwar university. For behind the poem's Deep Imagism is a reflexive—and, as its title suggests, ethically nuanced—assessment of those literary and material economies from which poetry, in the postwar era especially, remains inextricable. In "Degrees of Gray," as across his work, Hugo makes it clear how poetic production has migrated discursively in relation to evolving industrial- and informational-corporate regimes; poetry may be work, as postwar craft books figure it, but Hugo shows how this work can adapt without acceding to those terms set for it by a professional-managerial society.

In "Degrees of Gray," Philipsburg's bankrupt mining and timber industries stand in for the speaker's psychic condition, and much of the first half of the poem consists of the description of a town that clearly functions as objective correlative. "The principal supporting business now / is rage," Hugo writes. "Hatred of the various grays / the mountain sends, hatred of the mill, / The Silver Bill repeal, the best liked girls / who leave each year for Butte."[145] One gets a sense in these lines of the highly polished nature of Hugo's craftsmanship; it is a lapidary passage in iambic pentameter, its sliding "il" sounds punctured with plosives that suggest incipient violence. That violence comes not as physical confrontation, however, but as psychic transformation—"Isn't this your life?" Hugo asks in the third stanza, making explicit the link between exterior and interior geographies. It is a striking moment of anagnorisis, the second-person pronoun retaining a kind of psychic distance while also forcing the moment to its crisis. If Hugo's speaker mines the town for what it reveals about his life, Hugo the poet mines the town for its metaphorical potential. Hugo thereby solicits the reader into what becomes a collaborative process of emotional investigation. An equally abrupt turn, moreover, occurs at the beginning of the fourth and final stanza, not a rhetorical question but an imperative command. "Say no to yourself," Hugo pleads, rejecting an equivalence between town and interior condition and, in so doing, undoing the poetic craftsmanship with which the two had been linked. Here in its entirety is the poem's final stanza:

> Say no to yourself. The old man, twenty
> when the jail was built, still laughs
> although his lips collapse. Someday soon,
> he says, I'll go to sleep and not wake up.
> You tell him no. You're talking to yourself.
> The car that brought you here still runs.
> The money you buy lunch with,
> no matter where it's mined, is silver
> and the girl who serves your food
> is slender and her red hair lights the wall.

The ending of the poem certainly possesses a redemptive thrust, its short sentences evoking resilience in the face of economic and emotional collapse, its luminous image suggesting both sexual redemption and artistic grace. Yet Hugo's ending also models the economic complexity of his work at large, as well as the wider institutional context in which it exists. While his poetic attention to detail underwrites the speaker's newfound optimism, Hugo's deployment of that attention points to the expropriative practices so integral to his poetics. Hugo wrenches beauty from a context otherwise shot through by economic scarcity, his own poetic redemption predicated on the labor of an objectified—yet strangely abstracted— server "wall[ed]" in within the constraints of a tourist economy.

One might convict Hugo, therefore, of something like "disaster tourism" or "ruin pornography," or of extracting poetic "surplus value" from Philipsburg's manual laborers. More important, however, is that Hugo discloses these procedures, suggesting poetry's complex position within the postwar university. If Hugo glibly justifies creative writing in economic terms, he also aligns poetry against those forces that would subsume the individual in technocracy. In the same way that the server's luminous red hair suggests, at least from one angle, the redemptive potential of poetic craft, Hugo defends the purpose and objectives of those workshops in which such craft is honed. "What about the student who is not good?" Hugo asks. "Who will never write much? It is possible for a good teacher to get from that student one poem or one story that far exceeds whatever hopes the student had. It may be of no importance to the world of high culture, but it may be very important to the student. It is a small thing, but it is also small and wrong to forget or ignore lives that can use a single microscopic moment of personal triumph." For Hugo, the creative writing workshop constitutes "one of the last places you can go where your life still matters," an alternative to the rationalized regimes that structure postwar experience and that remind us "in dozens of insidious ways that our lives don't matter."[146]

Hugo's ambivalence with respect to the institutional habitus of creative writing—whether to embrace incorporation or struggle to retain autonomy—runs like an undercurrent throughout his poetry, perhaps nowhere more pointedly than in *31 Letters and 13 Dreams*, written contemporaneously with *The Triggering Town*. As should by now be a familiar refrain, Hugo's thinking-through of that ambivalence, the ambivalence of the institutional worker, takes the form of a meditation on labor of various kinds, on work and workers and on the places—bars, mills, towns, trailers, classrooms—within and on behalf of which they labor.

31 LETTERS AND 13 DREAMS

In the winter of 1970–71, while serving as a visiting instructor at the Iowa Writers' Workshop, Hugo suffered a breakdown that forced him to resign his post and retreat, with some degree of public shame, to psychiatric treatment in Seattle. Hugo had been living in a trailer at the time and drinking heavily, and, while the details of what he called his "crack-up" are inconsistent, his collapse seems to have involved charged sexual encounters with several women and personal flare-ups with colleagues.[147]

31 Letters and 13 Dreams opens in the aftermath of this collapse, as Hugo skulks back to Seattle and eventually to the Department of English at Montana. All of this is established in the opening "Letter to Kizer from Seattle," in which Hugo confesses to fellow Roethke student Carolyn Kizer that "I suddenly went ape / in the Iowa tulips. [. . .] Ten successive days I alienated women / I liked best. I told a coed why her poems were bad / (they weren't) and didn't understand a word I said."[148] Given the traumatic context of the collection, it is unsurprising that the book possesses an emotional intensity and serious sense of introspection sometimes lacking in Hugo's earlier work. In *31 Letters*, Hugo moves from a Deep Image mode influenced by Roethke to a mature Confessionalist mode which, in the wake of Robert Lowell's 1959 *Life Studies*, would come to dominate midcentury workshop poetry. Gone are Hugo's idiosyncratic turns of phrase and objective correlatives drawn from mining and timber towns. In their place, Hugo cultivates an expository, statement-driven voice housed in a looser line that tends toward the colloquial. The tone in *31 Letters* is the tone of recovery. Hugo is clear-eyed but wounded, tentative, as if gingerly wandering out into the world for the first time. This formal shift, I argue, pries apart two aspects of what I have called an American Arts and Crafts craft ideal: engaged, expressive labor and fastidious adherence to technical standards. For in *31 Letters*, Hugo not only jettisons his previous Deep Image mode, but a consciously crafted style—lapidary, polished, controlled— in order to develop a more expressive, emotion-driven poetics. Hugo's ambivalence about the institutional habitus of creative writing registers in a formal shift that finds him tentatively rejecting both workshop craft and the institution that houses it.

As Hugo retreats from Iowa, the epistolary poems of *31 Letters and 13 Dreams* serve to reestablish the personal and professional networks essential to Hugo's literal and literary health. Like the highways, rivers, and rail lines that run through his earlier work, these letters reconnect Hugo to a world outside his own turmoil, integrating him with a support system represented in writers like Kizer, Marvin Bell, Robert Bly, and even the young Albert Goldbarth, Hugo's student at Iowa. Relatedly, the places from which Hugo writes are often cities and university towns to which Hugo has been invited to read, the book mapping his reincorporation into professional circuits of academic achievement. As much as *31 Letters* functions as a narrative of personal redemption, it is also an Algeresque class narrative, one that culminates in Hugo being named "director / of Creative Writing" at Montana.[149] Yet Hugo's is no straightforward trajectory toward the ivory heights of Missoula. For every "31 letters" forward, the collection offers "13 dreams" in which, as the inverted number suggests, Hugo's traumatic past resurfaces. Written in a second-person perspective that functions, I have argued, to maintain an insulating psychic distance, the collection's dream poems exhibit the return of repressed anxieties, from the drinking, insecurity, and misogynistic violence that loomed so threateningly at Iowa to older anxieties revolving around Hugo's experience in World War II and his childhood fear of authority figures. Moreover, Hugo's quasi-mythological ascent from the depths of his Iowa City trailer is accompanied, as in *The Triggering Town*, by profound ambivalence about his reincorporation into the professional culture of the university.

In *31 Letters*, that ambivalence registers in part in the speaker's relation to work, workers, and workplaces. "What a relief that was from school," Hugo says of the Milltown Union Bar in "Letter to [William] Logan from Milltown," "from that smelly / student-teacher crap and those dreary committees / where people actually say 'considering the lateness / of the hour.'"[150] Such ambivalence aesthetically instantiates C. Wright Mills's classic postwar account of "cross-pressured" professional-managerial laborers. "Internally, they are split, fragmented," Mills writes; "externally, they are dependent on larger forces."[151] Time and again, *31 Letters* details Hugo's felt disconnect from a vanished past associated with small-town manual laborers. In "Letter to Reed from Lolo," Hugo laments that "The Dixon Bar is off personal limits / since they misread our *New Yorker* poems and found them / derogating, not the acts of love we meant."[152] In "Letter to Levertov from Butte," Hugo goes further: "On one hand, no matter what my salary is / or title, I remain a common laborer," he writes, "stained by the perpetual / dust from loading flour or coal. I stay humble, inadequate / inside." On the other hand, he goes on, "I know the cruelty of poverty," and "I don't want / to be part of it. I want to be what I am, a writer good enough / to teach with you and Gold and Singer, even if only in / some conference leader's imagination." That poem concludes with a striking passage instructive in assessing Hugo's "triggering town" poetics, a passage which suggests that, whatever its faults, the poetic mining of deindustrialized mill towns served deep psychic needs:

> And I want my life
> inside to go on long as I do, though I only populate bare
> landscape with surrogate suffering, with lame men
> crippled by more disease, and create finally
> a simple grief I can deal with, a pain the indigent can find
> acceptable. I do go on.[153]

Poetic craftsmanship may arrogate economic and cultural authority to the postwar university, but it also allows a poet like Hugo to objectify interior trauma in the form of the well-wrought aesthetic object. Just as Hugo's personal health depends on his reintegration into academic networks, so does his professional health depend on his ability to master the discourse of writing craft. As Hugo puts it, "we create our prison and we earn parole each poem."[154]

Accordingly, much of *31 Letters* lavishes attention on various forms of craftsmanship, acts of care in making that testify, for Hugo, to an overcoming of interior trauma and exterior chaos. In "Letter to Mantsch from Havre," the only poem addressed to a non-writer, Hugo recalls his admiration for his teammate in Missoula's recreational softball league:

I want to tell him style in anything,
pitching, hitting, cutting hair, is worth our trying even
if we fail. And when that style, the graceful compact swing
leaves the home crowd hearing its blood and the ball roars off
in night like determined moon, it is our pleasure
to care about something well done.

As in many of his poems, Hugo makes explicit the associative leap to poetry. "The ball jumps / from your bat over and over. I want my poems to jump / like that," the jump between lines testifying to Hugo's own master craftsmanship.[155] Yet while Hugo professes admiration for craftsmanship, poetic and otherwise—and while his earlier Deep Image mode certainly embodies such craftsmanship—much of *31 Letters* is written in a newly developed expressive mode evident even in the passages I have quoted. In *31 Letters*, Hugo pries apart a craft ideal that fuses expression and technical mastery. The interplay of these two aspects of craftsmanship is neatly suggested in "Letter to Wright from Gooseprairie," where technical mastery resurfaces in the form of a cautionary editorial voice which interrupts the more expressive parataxis. "And people seemed uglier," Hugo writes of the past, "more like the Bedfords were and probably aren't anymore / and more like people in war. I'm using too many r's."[156] For Hugo, this probing movement toward a more expressive mode formally enacts a growing skepticism toward the postwar university and its commodification of craft discourses.

Hugo offers a concise articulation of this line of thinking in "Letter to Mayo from Missoula," in which he entertains a series of retirement fantasies that encapsulate his ambivalence toward the university and the wider technocratic culture of which it is a part. In one fantasy, "the speeches ring / in the sunlight."

All my students, twenty-five years of them
cheer me as I rise to accept their acclaim. Some of them
are famous poets and they stand up and say, 'It's all because
of him,' pointing to me. I sob like Mr. Chips and their
applause booms through my tears. I walk alone down the campus,
their voices yelling my name behind me. I am crying
in the car (new Lincoln) and my wife (28, lovely)
comforts me as we speed to our vine and moss covered home
on the lake where I plan to write an even more brilliant
book than my last one, 'Me and John Keats,' which won the NBA,

Pulitzer, APR, Shelley, Bollingen and numerous
other awards and made me a solid contender for
the Nobel.[157]

One would be hard-pressed to imagine a scenario more emblematic of literary institutionality, from the invocation of the 1934 campus novella *Goodbye, Mr. Chips* to the iconic new Lincoln—which materially embodies the cultural capital in Hugo's cornucopia of literary prizes—to the feedback loop established as Hugo's students, now "famous poets," point back at him in a tight cipher for the pyramid scheme that is the MFA. In this fantasy, Hugo becomes a "contender" at last, his rise to administrative power symbolized in the literal ivy that envelops his suburban home. If Hugo binds himself to an institution he elsewhere figures as a "prison," however, he quickly settles on a more pragmatic retirement fantasy. "O.K. then this," he writes.

> I want to retire kind and hardheaded as you, to know
> not once did I leave the art, not once did I fail to accept
> the new, not once did I forget that seminal coursing
> of sound in poems and that lines are really the veins of men
> whether men know it or not.

It is here, in parataxis that perhaps reads like "seminal coursing," that Hugo most fully evinces an expressivist ethos, that aspect of the craft ideal which someone like Mike Gold described as "jets of exasperated feeling" issuing from proletarian writers.[158] In the poem's closing signatory, Hugo doubles down on this ethos, rejecting poetic craftsmanship and extricating poetry from professional networks of exchange. "Leave labor to slaves," he closes the poem. "Give my best to / Myra and show this letter only to trustworthy friends. Luck. Dick."

"Lunch with J. Hillis Miller": On the McPoem

The poems of *31 Letters and 13 Dreams* not only offer a formal allegory for the institutional habitus of creative writing, then, but help rebut the widespread charge that the institutionalization of creative writing leads *ipso facto* to the commodification of American poetry.

Joshua Clover and Juliana Spahr level a particularly compelling version of this charge in their 2010 essay "The 95cent Skool." Excoriating writing programs organized around "niche marketing of the well-made object," Clover and Spahr insist that "craft is not what's at stake. So, no endless condensing. No polishing bannisters. No lapidary work at all." While they offer little by way of an alternative, Clover and Spahr reject "the incontestable object with the slack removed and the jointures hidden," contending that the disarticulation of craft from overarching critical and theoretical discourses merely perpetuates "the division of labor in the academic factory."[159] Such criticism has been as common from the avant-garde left, of which Clover and Spahr are part, as it has from the literary establishment. Avant-gardist Barrett Watten, for instance, argues that the "professionalization" of creative writing reinforces the "poetics and politics of a threatened petit-bourgeois personal life," while a poet of official verse culture such as Geoffrey Hill laments that contemporary poetry more closely resembles "home movies" than a sophisticated aesthetic practicum.[160]

Though I am sympathetic to such critiques, Hugo helps us rethink the conviction that the practice of craft in the postwar university signals the inevitable entrenchment of the "workshop lyric" or "McPoem"—the poems of *31 Letters* are hardly the lapidary aesthetic gems or the self-fascinated plaints that such critiques most frequently stereotype.[161] In fact, Hugo's poetry represents exactly the kind of "critical art practice" that Watten advocates, "laying bare the device of its construction," albeit in a style all but illegible to the literary avant garde.[162] "I eat lunch with J. Hillis Miller," Hugo gushes in "Letter to Kizer from Seattle," "brilliant and nice / as they come, in the faculty club, overlooking the lake, much of it now filled in."[163] As Hugo's name-drop suggests, the contemporary workshop poem deconstructs its own craftedness. In Hugo, the alignment of poetry and university opens discursive space for a postmodernist poetics characterized neither by abstract theoretical positioning—nor by the experimental scientism of the avant-garde, nor by outdated notions of aesthetic autonomy—but by reflexive attention to its own institutionality: to its craft.

Coda

A Grindstone Does Its Job; Or, What about Iowa?

In a scholarly project purporting to uncover a distinct genealogy for the discipline of creative writing, one name may seem curiously absent.

Invoked by my count on fewer than half a dozen occasions, the Iowa Writers' Workshop (IWW) has played a bit part within a historical drama in which it typically commands the starring role. Though histories of creative writing from Katherine H. Adams and D. G. Myers, for example, trace the discipline to turn-of-the-century composition courses at Harvard, both devote significant space to the workshop at Iowa City, a radical reorientation, these scholars contend, in creative writing theory and practice.[1] More recently, Mark McGurl reads the Iowa Writers' Workshop as a "case study in [the] dialectical conjoining of opposites" that characterizes the institutionalization of creative writing. On the one hand, McGurl explains, the workshop at Iowa embodied "a new hospitality to self-expressive creativity on the part of progressive-minded universities"; on the other hand, workshop founders "rationalized their presence in a scholarly environment by asserting their own disciplinary rigor."[2] For McGurl, Iowa serves as the epicenter for an aesthetic and institutional habitus—"programmatic self-expression," he terms it—which I have traced instead to the American Arts and Crafts movement and its maintenance of a craft ideal.

If Iowa has occupied an outsized position in histories of creative writing, that position deserves reassessment less for the relative importance of Iowa itself—certainly the workshop there was and is an influential one—than for its tendency to conceal from scholarly hindsight those other institutions and ideologies that have shaped the discipline. This book has been an attempt to tell another story about creative writing, one that bypasses Iowa City in order to track the practice to an Arts and Crafts culture with which the first creative writing workshop, so called, was closely affiliated. In telling this story, I have focused on sites where the relation between work and writing was explicitly contested, from George Pierce Baker's 47 Workshop to institutions such as the Minnesota Labor School and Black Mountain College to the evolving genre of the poetry craft book. At each of these sites, creative writing craft facilitated multiple aesthetic, institutional, and ideological objectives. Not only did craft supply a set of values by which to reorient institutions of higher education and reimagine American literature in the process, but the mobilization of literary craftsmanship allowed writers to stage a wider social intervention, helping them rethink the meaning and ramifications of labor at moments when both seemed unstable. While scholars of creative writing largely demur on assessing the broader economic consequences of the discipline, this book has traversed wide historical terrain in order to demonstrate how craft lexicons migrated discursively from an alternative and non-rationalized mode of labor to a value system integral to the economic hegemony of American higher education. Exploring these stakes has meant asking what the discipline looks like without its most iconic institution, without Iowa.

In this closing coda, however, I gesture to the implications of literary craftsmanship at the first and most prestigious of the postwar programs in creative writing. For "the Workshop," as it is known, was hardly the first to use that name, and scholars of the program have overlooked the importance of writing craft in facilitating what was, at Iowa, nothing less than an institutional and ideological coup. Specifically, I contend that creative writing craft provided the legitimating language for an insurgent attempt—Irving Babbitt's New Humanism—to transform literary study at the university level and to reconceive the relation between literary study and Western democracy. At the Iowa Writers' Workshop, "workshop" worked double-time, figuring creative writing as a rigorous discipline while disciplining writers toward responsible civic participation. New Humanists like Babbitt, therefore, could be said to prioritize that aspect of an American Arts and Crafts craft ideal which tempered the craftsman's expression with rigorous adherence to technical standards; for Babbitt, those standards were supplied not by modernist aesthetics (as they were for John Dos Passos) nor by the resistances of craft material (as they were at Black Mountain), but by an inherited literary tradition and the cultural values that entailed from it. To New Humanists, those values mattered more than ever during the first half of the twentieth century, a time when democracy and American-style capitalism seemed increasingly imperiled by totalitarianisms on both the Left and Right. Extending the work of creative writing historian Eric Bennett, I show here how Iowa's "workshop of empire" was undergirded by craft rhetoric. Though Bennett devotes significant attention to Iowa as a bastion of liberal individualism in the Cold War era, his cursory treatment of New Humanist ideology causes him to overlook the important fact that at the heart of the vast international project that became "the Workshop" was a workshop. The maintenance of New Humanist ideology, whether educational or imperial, literary or geopolitical, entailed a complex of rhetorical and material strategies linking work and writing.

Perhaps unsurprisingly, the New Humanist iteration of an American Arts and Crafts craft ideal figures prominently in the work of two poets who studied at Iowa at the height of New Humanist influence there. For Workshop director Paul Engle, poetic craftsmanship both aesthetically enacts and constitutes a kind of training toward the self-discipline necessary to maintaining cultural, political, and moral superiority in the Cold War era. Mobilizing New Humanist thought in the service of a postwar liberal consensus, Engle's writing posits a lossless translation from the work of the poet to the work of mental and manual laborers, workers who carry out "the daily acts / Of life in work and word" that underwrite American civilization.[3] Less sanguine about the virtues of poetic and civic discipline, Engle's advisee Margaret Walker examines in her master of fine arts (MFA) thesis *For My People* how New Humanist thought, including narrowly conceived notions of poetic craftsmanship, inhibits the well-being of writers and workers alike, particularly writers and workers of color. Balancing technique with meaningful self-expression, Walker's critically neglected poetry draws on and updates American Arts and Crafts values for the Cold War era.

Irving Babbitt and Norman Foerster
"The power of restraint": New Humanist Craft

Perhaps no arts institution outside of the Bauhaus has generated a greater number of retrospective memoirs and reminiscences than the Iowa Writers' Workshop. From anthologies of alumni recollections[4] to quasi-official Workshop-endorsed histories[5] to the legions of literary biographies in which successful graduates recall their time at Iowa with the wistfulness of childhood reverie, the program has hatched a veritable cottage industry of firsthand accounts of "life, love, and literature at the Iowa Writers' Workshop."[6] Each of these accounts illuminates a slightly different aspect of the Iowa experience. In *We Wanted to be Writers*, Eric Olsen and Glenn Schaeffer use interviews with Iowa alums as the basis for their own memoiristic recollection of social life in Iowa City: the bohemian dance parties, Thursday nights at the Foxhead, and drunk readings from Pulitzer Prize winners, suggesting a consciously curated depiction of what Olsen and Schaeffer regard as the writer's life. In contrast, Robert Dana's anthology *A Community of Writers* sounds a more professional note, gathering accounts from Philip Levine on the pedagogy of John Berryman, for example, from Hualing Nieh Engle on the International Writing Project, and from Dana himself on the practice of writing craft at Iowa.

One anthology in particular, though, speaks closely to the endurance of New Humanist values there, including the broader ideological importance of craft-based pedagogies. In his introduction to *The Workshop: Seven Decades of the Iowa Writers' Workshop*, novelist Tom Grimes recalls learning quickly around the workshop table that "Romanticism's deification of the writer is the single most idiot aberration in the history of literature." As Grimes states, echoing a common New Humanist metaphor, "[w]riters are craftsmen, and as such all of our apprentice work is rough, inelegant, flawed. [. . .] We enter the program possessing the skills of fledgling carpenters—if we're lucky—yet hoping to build palaces."[7] Though published in 1999, Grimes's introduction invokes pedagogical values established in the earliest days of the Workshop, when craft lexicons served to undergird New Humanists' intervention in literary study as well as their systematic rethinking of the relation between literature and democracy. Recovering the importance of craft rhetoric and pedagogies at Iowa thus requires understanding the multifaceted and often contentious cultural intervention that was the New Humanism.

Centered around the polemical figure of Irving Babbitt, the New Humanism's objectives were twofold. In the first place, Babbitt and his partisans sought to overturn regnant regimes of literary scholarship dedicated to philology and literary biography, modes of inquiry New Humanists perceived as overly scientific and contributive to a growing "separatism" in literary life.[8] Modeled after Germanic scholasticism, philology and biography exacerbated a critical dissociation of sensibility, neglecting the integrative, spiritual aspect of literary experience and its sustenance of the individual in his entirety. Alternatively, New Humanists taught literature in a more "literary" manner, advocating the kind of broadly cultural criticism which Myers and his mentor Gerald Graff associate with the origins of academic creative writing. "The goal—an educational one—was to reform and redefine the academic study of literature," Myers argues, "establishing a means for approaching it 'creatively'; that is, by some other means than it had been approached before that time, which was historically and linguistically."[9] Rather than accumulating facts, literary study should help preserve traditional cultural values, provide an intellectual foundation for educated decision-making, and cultivate sprezzatura-like good sense in both civic and cultural contexts. "The urgent need of the time," Babbitt disciple Norman Foerster wrote, "is a centripetal effort, a pulling together toward a common center as the condition of clear purpose."[10] A second objective of the New Humanism, alluded to in Grimes's craft rhetoric above, was to counteract what Babbitt and others perceived as the deleterious effects of Romantic expressionism—or, as Babbitt put it, "the eagerness of a man to get his own uniqueness uttered." To New Humanists, a doctrine like William Wordsworth's "spontaneous overflow of powerful feelings" constituted reckless submission to emotion and the self-fascinated privileging of individual experience. Writers should strive not for individuality, New Humanists believed, but universality, to be representative. In his 1919 polemic *Rousseau and Romanticism*, Babbitt argued that the "*primary concern*" of the writer was the problem "not of expressing but of humanizing himself," and writers could do so, Babbitt maintained, only "by constant reference to the accepted standard of what the normal man should be." Accordingly, New Humanist pedagogy de-emphasized values like creativity, genius, and originality in order to prioritize aesthetic discipline and rigorous self-restraint. "Genuine culture," Babbitt summarized, "is difficult and disciplinary."[11]

It is easy to see how such objectives led to the adoption of creative writing craft as principle and practice. One of the most effective ways of studying literature in a distinctly literary manner, for New Humanists, was to develop more imaginative or cultural forms of scholarship, among them creative writing. To appreciate literature properly, Foerster argued, one must also understand how to write it, since "the act of writing—the selection of materials, the shaping of them, the recasting and revising—enables the student to repeat what the makers of literature have done, to see the processes and the problems of authorship from the inside."[12] Within the context of established literary curricula, moreover, craft rhetoric like Foerster's—shaping, casting, making—helped promote creative writing as an intellectual pursuit as rigorous as philological source-hunting and as meaningful as biographical historicism. When the term "workshop" first appears in Iowa course catalogs in 1939, with its connotations of stolid, respectable labor, it replaces the more fanciful-sounding "Imaginative Writing," and a promotional piece from *The Daily Iowan* of that year frames the Workshop as serious professional inquiry, describing a "writers' workshop where students can do work to-ward publication."[13] Babbitt himself speaks to this function of creative writing craft—that is, as disciplinary intervention—in his 1908 *Literature and the American College*, where he imagines the kind of curricular overhaul his disciple Foerster will later implement at Iowa. "Any plan for rehabilitating the humanities [must entail] the finding of a substitute for the existing doctorate," Babbitt wrote. "What is wanted is a training that shall be literary, and at the same time free from suspicion of softness or relaxation; a degree that shall stand for discipline in ideas, and not merely for a discipline in facts."[14] That degree would become the MFA.

Coextensive with its projection of disciplinary rigor, craft served as a form of discipline in its own right, providing what Babbitt called an "inner check" or "restraint" on the expressive tendency of the egoistic self. "The permanent or ethical element in himself towards which [the writer] should strive to move," Babbitt describes, "is known to him practically as a power of inhibition or inner check upon expansive desire. Vital impulse (*élan vital*) may be subjected to vital control (*frein vital*)." Foerster reiterates Babbitt's formulation in 1930, insisting that "those who throw down the reins are simply abandoning their humanity to the course of animal life or the complacency of vegetables."[15] As with John Dos Passos's technician or the student-craftsmen of Black Mountain College, immediate engagement with the materials of literary construction worked effectively to shape, channel, and curtail the ever-present specter of self-expression. Just as in Baker's 47 Workshop, moreover, the collective labor of the classroom community ensured that individual expression would be tempered through the workshop process, subjected—if not to specific committees for staging, set design, or music—to a range of voices that would overlap with, dampen, drown out, and otherwise mitigate the writer's expression. Though New Humanists like Babbitt understood artistic production to involve a tension between self-expression and technical discipline, the curricular revolution they promoted carried forward an anti-expressivist ethos integral to, if critically neglected within, the history of creative writing.

But the New Humanism was more than merely a curricular intervention. It was also an attempt to stake out a distinct public role for poets, writers, and literary pedagogues. For New Humanists, the disciplining of self-expression—along with the education of the individual in his entirety, relying on traditional cultural values—was integral to the maintenance of American democracy; just as the post-war MFA produced professionals more than it did poets, New Humanists aimed to shape not simply student-writers, but responsible citizens. The workshop represented a key step in this production process, offering training in miniature for citizenship within democratic institutions that likewise "act[ed] as checks on the immediate will of the people."[16] In *Rousseau and Romanticism*, Babbitt makes explicit the larger stakes for New Humanist pedagogies, contending that "the design of higher education, so far as it deserves the name, is to produce leaders" and that the "success or failure of democracy" depended on the ability of universities to do so.[17] At the time, of course, the success of democracy seemed very much in question. Published in 1919, two years after the Russian Revolution, *Rousseau and Romanticism* opposes responsible liberal citizens to socialist ideologues who would shift social responsibility to the wealthy. For Babbitt, Rousseau seemed "very close to our most recent agitators. If a working girl falls from chastity," he mimed, "do not blame her, blame her employer. She would have remained a model of purity if he had only added a dollar or two a week to her wage." Romantic expressionism was deleterious not only in its own right, then—and not only for the individual writer—but because it encouraged an evasion of civic duty, a tendency to excuse oneself from and shirk responsibility for collective life. As instituted at Iowa, writing craft buttressed a society made up of "sound individualists who look up imaginatively to standards set above their ordinary selves," making it nothing less than a bulwark against the Red Menace.[18]

Bound up in New Humanist ideology, therefore, was an argument about American work and workers, about whose labor should be valued and whose discounted, about which classes should be singled out for social promotion and why. Specifically, Babbitt's opposition to socialist thinking frequently registered as a critique of what he perceived as the overestimation of manual labor, the tendency—common to Romantic and socialist thought alike—to falsely dignify such labor in ways that reduced work to its lowest terms. Rather than rhetorically inflating the worth of manual labor, Babbitt held that educational institutions should promote the "higher forms of working"—mental labor and laborers—over and against those Americans who worked with their hands. "From the point of view of civilization," Babbitt argues, "it is of the highest moment that certain individuals should in every community be relieved from the necessity of working with their hands in order that they may engage in the higher forms of working and so qualify for leadership."[19] New Humanists' investment in the language of craft should thus be distinguished from both an American Arts and Crafts craft ideal and the kinds of socialist thought promoted by original Arts and Crafts adherents such as William Morris and John Ruskin; Babbitt and his associates may have emphasized literary craftsmanship as a form of discipline, but they radically reconceived the social and political implications of such discipline. Though Foerster's statement that "the common man" should be more than "a mere worker" has the ring of egalitarianism, in fact the New Humanism constituted a deeply conservative, even aristocratic, cultural ideology.[20]

Indeed, his elitist impulse dwarfing even that of Babbitt, Foerster played the social eugenicist in arguing that "in its healthy estate, higher education is concerned with the fit, the large number of robust young men and women who are able to think, able to feel, able to liberate themselves." Acknowledging that universities should "serve state and nation" by providing education "in accord with a constitutional democracy," Foerster nonetheless intended such education to be the privilege of the elite, invoking notions of a Jeffersonian aristocracy whose excellence would be imitated by the masses. In the increasing openness of American public universities, Foerster found troubling instantiation of Romantic ideology, lambasting the idea that all Americans deserved a forum and opportunity for self-expression. "The state universities are accepting every manner of student, including many only slightly above the level of the defective, delinquent, and dependent," Foerster bemoaned. "They are acting upon the devastating assumption, inherited from the romantic conception of the individual genius, that the special aptitude of each unique individual, no matter how pitiful it may be, should be given every opportunity to express itself. [. . .] If this continues to be our ideal of well-being, the downward course of the state university will be swift."[21] Echoing Ezra Pound's contempt for a "deliquescence" of cultural standards, Foerster suggests how the New Humanism reconceived the relation among literature, labor, and American democracy, in the process promoting certain forms of work as inherently more meaningful to the maintenance of American values.[22] The New Humanist bid for curricular and cultural influence thus makes explicit the advancement of a professional-managerial ethos which elsewhere proceeds more clandestinely under the cover of craft lexicons. New Humanists like Babbitt and Foerster perceived the privileges of professional-managerialism not as a democratic birthright, however, but as the prerogative of a cultural and economic elite, the perquisite of those white-collar classes most essential to past and future civilization.

"WHAT THE NORMAL MAN SHOULD BE": THE WORK OF WORKSHOP

If Babbitt was the New Humanism's founder, theoretician, and polemicist, Norman Foerster (pronounced "Firster") was its bureaucrat and bulldog, the figure most responsible for putting New Humanist values into practice. While the changes Foerster implemented at Iowa were hardly as draconian as his rhetoric might lead one to expect, they were nonetheless sweeping. Arriving from the University of North Carolina in 1930, Foerster immediately reorganized the departments of English, German, Classics, and Romance languages under his own administrative aegis in the School of Letters and Science, a means of attacking scholarly specialization. Additionally, Foerster added a wide range of courses in the liberal arts, including offerings in classical literature, Theory and Practice of Literary Criticism, and Readings in the History of Humanism. In a move toward studying literature in more literary fashion, moreover, Foerster permitted the production of creative writing rather than scholarly research in fulfillment of certain doctoral requirements.[23] The Iowa Writers' Workshop was a direct result of this administrative restructuring, an effort to cultivate what Foerster identified as "aesthetic sensitivity" and to offer "rigorous discipline in the specialized types of literary activity."[24] As I have suggested, the craft pedagogies undergirding the Workshop at Iowa ensured that writers would not so much express as "humanize" themselves, the workshop supplying a model of—and rigorously enforcing— "what the normal man should be."[25] At Iowa, the delicate balance between self-expression and technical rigor that had comprised the American Arts and Crafts craft ideal was dramatically recalibrated to minimize writers' individuality. In this light, the perennial debate as to whether or not graduate programs in creative writing constrain writers' individual genius—whether, that is, such programs produce mere minor variations of the house style, the "workshop lyric"—seems moot. As Iowa indicates, this is their *raison d'être*.

Though McGurl rightly contends that the Workshop at Iowa was founded on "the imposition of [. . .] institutional constraints upon unfettered creativity," in attributing such constraints to modernist and New Critical impersonality, he leaves unexamined the role that New Humanist literary craftsmanship played in the curricular and cultural intervention there.[26] To be sure, there were many links between the New Humanism and New Criticism, links especially strong between Babbitt and his student T. S. Eliot. Babbitt echoes Eliot's "Tradition and the Individual Talent," for instance, in subordinating the modern writer to tradition, defining that term as "a completion and enrichment of present experience by that of the past," what Eliot calls an "ideal order."[27] Eliot, in turn, found in New Humanist discipline the same "*inner* control" he admired in Anglicanism.[28] But in addition to castigating modernist writing as mere "sociological documents," New Humanists eschewed New Critical aestheticism in favor of a moralistic and socially oriented cultural criticism; New Humanists approached Cleanth Brooks's well-wrought poem not as an autotelic object, but as the urn-like container of moral and cultural values. It was this orientation, more than an affinity for modernist impersonality, that influenced the early years of the Workshop at Iowa.[29]

If the New Humanism entailed the production of more than "mere worker[s]," as I have shown, representations of manual laborers would prove integral to the poetry and pedagogy of perhaps the most influential director of the Workshop: Paul Engle. Director at Iowa from 1940 to 1965, Engle was also an Iowa alum, earning one of the first advanced degrees in creative writing for his Foerster-supervised thesis *Worn Earth*, a collection later selected by Stephen Vincent Benét for the prestigious Yale Series of Younger Poets. Yet despite the dynamism of his roaring American laborers, Engle in fact solidifies the New Humanist circuit between literary discipline and democratic citizenship, de-emphasizing the writer's self-expression in order to imagine a culture "useful to the writer, friendly for the businessman, and healthy for the university."[30] As I will demonstrate, Engle's poetry and administrative work constitute an effort to marshal New Humanist values toward a postwar liberal consensus—no arbitrary or inevitable ideological formation, but, like so much at Iowa, a consciously crafted phenomenon.

Paul Engle

"PLOW[ING] THE DEEP FURROWS OF THE HEART": ENGLE AND THE NEW HUMANISM

In his 1934 blank-verse polemic, "Complaint to Sad Poets," Paul Engle, then only 26 years old, sounds every bit the tradition-bound New Humanist curmudgeon, objecting to an expressivist strain in American poetry which had caused modernist writers to turn their backs on meaningful civic engagement. "Will you never be done with barking at the moon / Through the bleak hours of silver-blackened night?" Engle implores.

> Will you
> Always fear the world until you pour
> The strong wine of self-pity down your throats,
> Wiping your lips with trembling hands, and then,
> Drunk with the sickening liquor of yourselves,
> Find the yellow courage to stand up
> A feeble hour?

Part of his acclaimed second collection, *American Song*, the poem finds in bacchanalian expression a betrayal of the poet's social obligation, urging erstwhile "sad poets" to "reach upward to embrace / The wide, wind-trampled archway of the sky."[31]

True to form, *American Song* models precisely the kind of civic-minded poetics that Engle advocates, its Whitmanic anaphora and Homeric epithets establishing a vision of American civilization as an irrepressible, westward-tending empire. Peopled throughout with stock figures from American mythology—cowboys, Conestoga-borne pioneers, buffalo, fur-trappers, American Indians, outlaws—Engle's New Humanist poetics rely to a large extent on a rhetorical trope I have been tracking throughout this book: the figuration of writing as manual labor. In the "Troubadour of Eze," written from Eze, Switzerland, where Engle had spent part of the previous summer, the budding New Humanist poet equates literary production with the "greater building" of civic improvement. "[W]ith the blue steel chisel of the mind," Engle writes, "Shaped by the hammer of a new world's dream, / And tempered in the clear frame of the heart, / There can be carved, from the quarried stone of time / A proud and shining symbol of new life."[32] The conceit reveals a great deal about Engle's incorporation of New Humanist values into his poetry, pedagogy, and administrative work at Iowa. Whereas New Humanists like Babbitt and Foerster looked contemptuously on manual labor and laborers, Engle idealizes such work as a corollary for the poetic process; Engle's depiction of poetic introspection as a chiseling, shaping, hammering, and tempering, however, suggests his endorsement of the self-restraint so pivotal to New Humanist thinking. In Engle's figuration, the work of the poet is less *con*-structive than *de*-structive, a cutting through or planing away of emotional and intellectual dross within the "quarried stone of time" that is the poem. Moreover, the discipline of poetic labor matters for Engle because of its role in helping to produce responsible citizens. In this passage and throughout Engle's poetry, self-making aligns metaphorically and materially with civilization-making, so that the vocation of poet entails both work on oneself and training toward democratic citizenship. "There is a mighty fate that hammers out / The iron form of continents," Engle declares, "breaking / The stubborn back of nations, bending kings, / Shaping the whole bright world in its hands."[33] For Engle, poetry is that breaking.

While Engle has attracted significant attention in recent years, much of this scholarship has focused in sensationalized fashion on his work as director at Iowa, in particular his transformation of the Workshop into an instrument of US cultural diplomacy in the postwar era.[34] Engle's critical writing certainly licenses such an approach. In an article published in the June 1937 issue of *The English Journal*, Engle maintains that "in these days of universal conscription a poet must be interested in an armament bill in Washington or Westminster and in the foreign policy of his own and all other nations." Similarly, Engle dedicates his 1964 craft book *On Creative Writing* to a "heartening variety of individuals, foundations, and corporations who have refused to believe" in the "alienation of the writer from his times and country." Under Engle's tenure, the Workshop would prove no hermetically sealed cloister, but an apparatus of American empire—or, as Engle put it, "an international community of the imagination."[35] Despite scholarly focus on his administrative work, however, Engle is nowhere treated in the context of Babbitt and Foerster's New Humanism. Nor is Engle's poetry, much of it produced under Foerster's aegis, given anything other than short critical shrift, with the lone scholar to examine Engle's poetic output maintaining that "serious scholars don't care about his oeuvre." "In an age of compression, obliquity, obscure allusion, and experimental technique," Bennett argues, Engle "wrote in plain language and used old forms. [. . .] A Helen Vendler or a Harold Bloom has no reason to attend to his legacy."[36] Yet Engle's poetry was not only widely acclaimed in his time, but frequently featured at the center of midcentury debates about the proper relation of the poet to his culture. If his work seems dated to our eyes—turgid, sentimental, jingoistic— its outmodedness has led scholars to underestimate both the intellectual development that takes place therein as well as the influence Engle's writing had on his students and peers. For in Engle's mid-career trilogy—*American Song* (1934), *Break the Heart's Anger* (1936), and *Corn* (1939)—we find ideological scaffolding that will help construct the Workshop into a powerful force for postwar democracy, scaffolding braced and buttressed throughout with figurations of writing as work. Engle's trilogy models in both form and content his evolving relationship with New Humanist thought, especially as it bears upon his own and others' poetic output.

Engle himself was no stranger to work. Born in Cedar Rapids to a farming family of German descent, Engle apprenticed from a young age in the training and selling of livestock, moonlighting in high school as a chauffeur, gardener, newspaper salesman, and drugstore clerk.[37] After graduating from nearby Coe College in 1931—where, like some Dickensian waif, he was supported by a secret benefactor— Engle took his master of arts (MA) under Foerster at the university in Iowa City, eventually earning a three-year Rhodes Scholarship to Oxford. There, he worked with poet and professor Edmund Blunden and became a close acquaintance of W. H. Auden, Cecil Day-Lewis, and Stephen Spender, all of whom would have a profound influence on his writing. It was during Engle's time at Oxford that *American Song* appeared in the United States to widespread acclaim, earning Engle, among other plaudits, a full front-page review in the *New York Times Book Review*.

In the above-the-fold photograph that accompanies the piece, a boyish Engle sports both a crew cut and a crew-neck sweatshirt, looking every bit the respectable New Humanist acolyte turned Rhodes Scholar. Reviewer J. Donald Adams hails Engle's expansive American optimism, finding in his muscular cadences and patriotic myth-making "an indicator of changing mood and temper among creative writers of the youngest generation."[38] Though widely lauded, *American Song* also generated its fair share of critical responses. In *Poetry*, John Gould Fletcher derided Engle's faith in the "magnificent walking dream that somehow made this country," chalking such civic boosterism up to the misguided exuberance of youth.[39] Similarly, leftist writer Malcolm Cowley argued in *The New Republic* that Engle was not so much a poet as an "eagle orator." "He says all the proper things for a congressman to say when he wants to make his constituents forget about high prices and low wages and remember only that they are free-born Americans."[40] To millions of other Americans, however, Engle's red-white-and-blue-tinted lyricism seemed a welcome antidote to Great Depression-era ennui, to the point that the collection briefly attained bestseller status, as difficult a feat for a poet in the 1930s as it remains today.

The opening proem to *American Song* gives clear indication of the collection's can-do ideological investments. Invoking a distinctly American *genius loci* in the manner of Hart Crane's *The Bridge*, Engle hails in characteristic parataxis the "Land of the Iowa cornfields endlessly rising," of "Missouri hills where every man / Plows the deep furrows of his heart alone." Though he draws here on the etymology of "verse" in order to figure poetry as a form of interior cultivation, Engle idealizes not only agricultural labor but industrial work as well, describing the United States as a "great glowing open hearth." "In you we will heat the cold steel of our speech," Engle proclaims,

> Rolling it molten out into a mold,
> Polish it to a shining length, and straddling
> The continent, with hands that have been fashioned,
> One from the prairie, one from the ocean, winds,
> Draw back a brawny arm with a shout and hurl
> The fiery spear-shaft of American song [. . .][41]

Like his metaphoric plowman, Engle's industrial bard borrows his authority from the land, an autochthonous figure whose body spans and gathers to itself the entire continent. Engle's metaphor is also, of course, patently sexual in nature, as his Leviathan-like worker straddles the continent while gripping the "shining length" or "spear-shaft" of his language. If such a figure seems to recall Mike Gold's self-expressive proletarian, however—who wrote in "jets of exasperated feeling," akin to Richard Hugo's later "seminal coursing"—the work of Engle's industrial worker-bard is far more disciplined.[42] No mere expressivist venting, Engle's ideal poetry is "polish[ed]" to a hard shine, stamped out in the kind of mold that a New Humanist like Babbitt, with his overriding concern for the normal, would no doubt have appreciated.

Engle's thinking-through of New Humanist values carries over to his 1936 collection *Break the Heart's Anger*, where he once again links poetic production to the production of democratic citizens. "You are the makers of another world," Engle exhorts his readers in "Epilogue at the Core of the Earth."

> You with your mortal hands. Build with fire,
> Desperation and blue tempered steel,
> The durable, dark stone that is the mind,
> Till the skyscrapers flower on their huge stalks,
> Your eyes become but clear intensities [. . .][43]

As is seen throughout Engle's poetry, the forging of self is coextensive with the forging of society, Engle's widely used adjectives—"tempered," "clear," "durable"—suggesting his characteristically New Humanist emphasis on sobriety and restraint. Where *American Song* celebrated the limitless potential of American laborers, however, *Break the Heart's Anger* reveals those laborers as fundamentally betrayed by rigged economic structures; specifically, Engle laments that workers have been sold out to financial interests whose speculative practices lead to underemployment, economic contraction, and spiritual lassitude. While manual labor remains meaningful, the "humble right to work" has been stolen.[44] Influenced by Engle's association with the Auden Group, *Break the Heart's Anger* is emphatically leftist in outlook, its social invective peppered throughout with references to Karl Marx, Vladimir Lenin, Leon Trotsky, and Abraham Lincoln, the latter invoked as an indefatigable champion of the working classes. In mode, too, *Break the Heart's Anger* evinces values seemingly at odds with the roaring exceptionalism of a book like *American Song*; the poems in Engle's third collection are economic jeremiads in the proletarian tradition: beginning in plaint and ending in prophesy, heavily paratactic, and employing an accusatory second-person in which "you" denotes those financial interests that have betrayed American workers.

In a high-altitude flyover of Engle's poetry, Bennett reads *Break the Heart's Anger* as a dramatic departure, therefore, from the main line of his work. "In the 1920s, when he was a teenager, [Engle's] politics were one thing," Bennett argues. "[I]n the 1930s, another; in the 1940s, 1950s, 1960s, something else yet again. In each phase, his poetry changed too."[45] In fact, Engle's mid-career trilogy reveals a consistent, if evolving, relationship with New Humanist thought, a relationship which certainly takes distinct political hues, but which nonetheless remains committed to self-discipline as constitutive of American democracy. Contemporary reviewers recognized the consistency between *Break the Heart's Anger* and its more patriotic predecessor. Cowley argues that Engle "remains the orator rather than the poet. He delivers his orations on May Day now, instead of Fourth of July, but he delivers them in the same loose style bespangled with generalities" and "mixes his metaphors in a concrete mixer."[46] In *New Masses*, poet Ruth Lechlitner found herself wishing that Engle would "make a clean break from the romantic, I-suffer-for-my-country, adolescent attitude." Engle's "love of rhetoric," Lechlitner writes, "of emotional forensics, runs away with him."[47] Despite leftist overtones, these reviewers recognized, *Break the Heart's Anger* remained rooted in traditional New Humanist values, its workers lauded not in their own right—and certainly not as harbingers of some future socialist state—but because the discipline of their labor constituted a form of edification necessary to democracy.

And yet the language employed by these reviewers points to dramatic fissures within Engle's ostensibly New Humanist poetics. If Engle's subject matter models an ideal democratic discipline, his form betrays the restrictive nature of this discipline, with Engle's loose blank verse—not to mention his reliance on anaphora, epithet, parataxis, and other expansive techniques—"run[ning] away" from the formal and social restraint he sought to impose. Identifying Engle's poetics as both "emotional" and "romantic," Lechlitner suggests that authentic democratic experience may indeed be too boundless to be tempered by New Humanist discipline—that the form of Engle's poetry betrays an expressivist impulse its subject matter attempts to deny. As if to paper over this fissure, Engle insists again and again that to work the furrow of the poetic line or tend the dynamo of American speech really is to edify oneself for civic participation. Engle is speaking just as much about poetic as manual labors, for instance, when he hails "you givers of shape to all the vague and void, / Carpenters of the human, real creation, / Builders in the immortal ways of men."[48] The poet, it seems, doth protest too much, for the discrepancy in Engle's work between an expressive form and disciplined content reveals, more than a fissure within New Humanism, a problem in translating aesthetic into social values—as at Black Mountain, the ancient homology between writing and work proves faulty.

Engle doubles down on this metaphor in his 1939 collection *Corn*, extending his labor imagery to incorporate the work of the literary pedagogue as well as the poet. As Engle returns from Oxford to take over as director at Iowa, he announces a kind of mission statement for the pedagogical and administrative work that will become his primary focus. "Too long I went / With a great urge and shouting into life," Engle writes in the collection's title poem. "Now I will let it, like a change of season, / Come to me here. A grindstone does its job / By a perpetual turning in one place / Wearing itself down slower than the steel."[49] Figuring literary pedagogy as a sharpening of other implements, Engle explicitly echoes one of Western culture's earliest creative writing pedagogues, refashioning Horace's ambition to "play the part of the whetstone, that can sharpen the knife though it can't itself cut." Without writing himself, Horace would "teach function and duty—where the poet's resources come from, what nurtures and forms him, what is proper and what not, in what directions excellence and error lead."[50] Trumpeting New Humanist discipline *avant la lettre*, Horace suggests just how rooted in tradition such values were, including the craft-based pedagogy of the Iowa Writers' Workshop.

Far from apprentice work, Engle's poetic output reveals how that pedagogy was undergirded by the linking of labor and literature, a rhetorical figuration which for New Humanists entailed profound social and political consequences. While fuller assessment of Engle's pedagogical and administrative work lies beyond the scope of this coda, it bears emphasizing—especially as scholars have neglected it—that Engle explicitly conceived this work in relation to a New Humanist craft ideal. Effective writing, Engle instilled in his students, should hardly resemble "the uninhibited confession from the psychiatrist's couch, sodium amytal cheerfully flowing"; rather, students should "rewrite again and again as a fine craftsman polishes over and over the same increasingly brilliant piece of maple or mahogany."[51] Reassessing Engle's own poetic craftsmanship helps us understand both the attitudes he would bring to his subsequent work as IWW's director, as well as how New Humanist priorities informed a school of poetry that would become, at Iowa, nothing less than America's official verse culture.

Margaret Walker

"A ten-poun' hammer ki-ilt John Henry": *For My People*

While Engle's mid-career trilogy demonstrates the importance of craft rhetoric to the New Humanist mission, another Iowa poet would challenge precisely that rhetoric, undoing the circuit between literary discipline and democratic citizenship that Foerster and Engle hardwired into their curricula. In doing so, Margaret

Walker makes explicit the revealing fissure—between form and content, workers' expression and the discipline of labor—that cuts through Engle's work. A graduate student at Iowa during the first years of Engle's directorship, Walker rethinks the New Humanist belief that disciplined labor eventuates in civic flourishing; specifically, she populates her MA thesis and Yale-winning collection, *For My People*, with workers whose lives have been maimed, impaired, and sometimes destroyed by the discipline of their work, insisting as she does that workers and writers alike should maintain an appropriate balance between expression and technical discipline. Walker's poetry thus constitutes the first in a long line of alumni disavowals of the Workshop, in particular its reliance on what Walker figures as the stultifying and dehumanizing practice of writing craft. Though New Humanists like Babbitt and Foerster sought to enforce aesthetic and cultural discipline, not all Iowa writers proved as receptive to that discipline as the famously monastic Flannery O'Connor.

Born in 1915 to a Methodist minister and music teacher—the embodiment of a dialectic between discipline and expression that runs throughout her work—Margaret Walker came of age as a writer in the charged atmosphere of the 1930s, graduating from Northwestern University in 1935 and taking a job soon afterward with the Works Progress Administration (WPA)-directed Federal Writers' Project. Earning $85 per month as a junior writer, Walker produced news stories, reported on arts and cultural events, and contributed, as had Meridel Le Sueur in Minnesota, to the WPA's state guide to Illinois. Walker was also introduced during this time to socialist and cultural nationalist ideals through Chicago chapters of the Communist Party and the National Negro Congress. As she describes to her biographer, "[i]n Chicago, home to one of the largest urban populations and distinctively black and southern in character, the Depression fueled the activities of the Communist Party, which drew a host of writers into its orbit."[52] Walker would go on to become a leading figure in the Chicago Renaissance, a member of the famed South Side Writers Group whose acquaintances would include Arna Bontemps, Gwendolyn Brooks, Fenton Johnson, Richard Wright, and others. Before she rose to national prominence with her 1966 novel *Jubilee*, Walker earned an MA in creative writing at the University of Iowa, her 1940 thesis *For My People*, produced under Engle's supervision, winning the Yale Series of Younger Poets Prize two years later.

While Walker acknowledges that Engle "reawakened [her] interest" in the kind of folk ballads that appear in her thesis, it was Northwestern professor Edward Buell Hungerford who inducted Walker into what she calls the "discipline" of writing craft. "Professor Hungerford drilled me in types and forms of English prosody and made me seek to master versification and scansion," Walker relates. To Hungerford, she goes on, "sonnets furnish[ed] the same discipline for the poet as five-finger exercises for the musician."[53] Walker's brief account of her coming of age as a writer, included as a preface to the collected edition of her poetry, also features several encounters that served to encode the broader disciplinary structures of literary life: with Harriet Monroe at Northwestern, with Muriel Rukeyser at a cocktail party at the Chicago offices of *Poetry*, and with an unscrupulous vanity publisher who sought out Walker at a young age. "My mother [. . .] paid to have four of my poems published," Walker writes. "At Northwestern I was shamed into the knowledge that I should never do that again."[54] Just as poet Richard Hugo found in creative writing a form of upward mobility into a midcentury professional-managerial class, Walker's career—at Northwestern, Iowa, Yaddo, and as winner of the Yale Prize—testifies to how the mastery of writing craft can provide entrée into the charmed circles of the properly professional writer.

Readers who expected from *For My People* a tight, quasi-New Humanist linkage of discipline and democracy, however, found instead a pointed critique of that line of thinking. Indeed, Walker puts self-expression and technical discipline in dynamic interrelation in order to pry apart what she saw as a stilted and one-sided New Humanist craft ideal. To New Humanists, as I have shown, the discipline of poetic and manual labor was intended to yield those "sound individualists" on which an American Century might be built. In *For My People*, in contrast, Walker explores how the discipline of labor yields little more than economic insecurity, intraracial violence, and death, stifling the very individuals who might most contribute to and benefit from a revitalized American democracy. Walker makes explicit this challenge to New Humanist values in the preface to her collected poems. Whereas the New Humanist canon was restricted to Western and primarily Greco-Roman tradition, Walker acknowledges wide-ranging influences on her work, from the Egyptian *Book of the Dead* to the Sumerian epic *Gilgamesh* to the *Mahabharata* and *Bhagavad Gita* from India. As Walker explained, "all of these are pre-Homeric epics which my white professors denied existed."[55] Similarly, Walker's preface frames *For My People* as a self-expressive account of her experience as a Black woman in the American South; to the extent that her personal narrative approaches what Babbitt advocated as "normal" experience, it does so as a document of the particular oppression faced by Walker and other Black Americans. Walker's poems "express my ideas and emotions about being a woman and a black person in these United States—Land of the *Free* and Home of the Brave?"[56]

Though written four decades after her time at Iowa, Walker's statements offer sharp refutation of the kind of Cold War patriotism so carefully crafted under the banner of the New Humanism.

Despite its importance in the history of midcentury American poetry, *For My People* has received little scholarly attention.[57] This coda will not do justice to the complexity of that text, but I do want to gesture to how the collection questions craft discourses not only as they contribute to the mission and identity of the Iowa Writers' Workshop, but as they buttress the broader cultural and political intervention New Humanists proposed. Walker herself was uniquely positioned to think through the implications of this intervention. A graduate student at Iowa in the late 1930s and early 1940s, she witnessed firsthand a bout of departmental infighting over New Humanist influence there; though the conflict would grow to encompass much of the English and creative writing faculty, it centered on Foerster and the man who would disassemble his broad New Humanist curriculum: recently appointed dean and progressive educator Harry K. Newburn. Marshaling scholastically conservative faculty long opposed to Foerster's directorship, Newburn advocated for even further specialization than had previously existed at Iowa, undoing departmental requirements and more closely tailoring its curricula to students' individual interests. Newburn's counterrevolution, of sorts, would have a significant impact on the theory and practice of writing craft at Iowa, and his influence resulted in the short term in Foerster's resignation from the School of Letters and Science which he had established.[58] Walker's own work refracts institutional tensions that must have been very much a part of the Workshop experience during her time at Iowa.

As a collection, *For My People* is divided by form into three sections. The poems in the first, including the well-known title poem, employ long-lined free-verse strophes that rely to a large extent on anaphoric invocation. The fact that Walker credits Richard Wright with helping her to develop this strophic form suggests the necessity of looking outside the strictures of the Iowa Writers' Workshop for a poetics expressive of Black experience. In contrast, the second and third sections of *For My People* consist of traditionally metrical verse, featuring character-sketch folk ballads in African-American dialect and tightly crafted sonnets steeped in Walker's childhood reminiscences. The collection's formal heteroglossia—what Cary Nelson has called its "plural textuality"—therefore embodies in miniature a craft ideal which, as I establish in previous chapters, joins together expression and restraint, aesthetic freedom and technical discipline.[59] Though New Humanists like Babbitt and Foerster did not conceive their work in relation to the American Arts and Crafts movement, such an ideal nonetheless loomed large in their thinking. Contemporary commentators identified this same ideal in *For My People*. In his foreword to the collection, Yale judge Stephen Vincent Benét noted its combination of expressive "straightforwardness" and "controlled intensity of emotion."[60] Writing in *The Saturday Review*, George Zabriskie found the collection's free-verse strophes reminiscent of evangelical "exhorters," while its ballads and sonnets established Walker's reputation as a "technical virtuoso."[61] On the surface, *For My People* exhibits strong similarities with Engle's own poetry, since the latter's loose blank verse housed an irrepressible, even self-expressive, voice akin to that of Walt Whitman. In other ways, too, Walker's poetry resembles that of her supervisor, Engle's influence evident in everything from Walker's use of anaphora to the prominence of agrarian imagery in the collection to her repeated linkage of poetry and manual labor. "I want to walk along with sacks of seed to drop in fallow ground," Walker confesses in the poem "Sorrow Home," sounding very much the Iowa horse-trader turned pedagogue. "I want the cotton fields, tobacco and the cane."[62]

A poem like "Big John Henry," however, reveals how Walker draws on Engle's poetics in order to reconsider its implications. Just as Engle's poetry comes peopled throughout with stock figures from American mythology, "Big John Henry" narrates in rough ballad form the "tale of a sho-nuff man" who "useta work for Uncle Sam." As Walker's metonymy suggests, Henry's labor on farm, steamboat, and rail line is essential to the construction of American empire. In Walker's treatment, though, Henry's work is also destructive of his own raced and classed body. At the poem's conclusion, its lilting ballad meter breaks down into lines half the length of those that precede them, a formal instantiation of Henry's physical breakdown: "But a ten-poun' hammer ki-ilt John Henry, / Bust him open, wide Lawd! / Drapped him ovah, wide Lawd! / Po' John Henry, he cold and dead."[63] Here, as throughout *For My People*, the discipline of manual labor, enacted formally in the discipline of Walker's poetic line, produces not so much a responsible liberal citizen as an expended—because expendable—American worker. Walker herself was thoroughly acquainted with such discipline. Prior to joining the WPA, she had signed on alongside her sister to work in a pecan factory on Chicago's West Side, a gig that lasted one day before both women were mercifully fired. As she relates in her biography, Walker "thought Mercedes would ruin her hands and not be able to play the piano," while her sister feared that "I would cut my hands and be unable to type." In another failed attempt to find employment, Walker "walked twelve miles [. . .] and all I got that day was a pair of fallen arches."[64]

Similar experiences—characters maimed, stunted, or killed by the discipline to which they are subjected—recur throughout the ballads in *For My People*, to the point that the collection seems a kind of tabulation of the victims of industrial-corporate work.

So too do Walker's first-person lyrics levy a sharp critique of the promise that Engle finds in manual labor. Most explicitly, a set of paired sonnets near the end of the collection indicts Engle's idealization of agrarian work and workers. The first, "Iowa Farmer," opens with the pastoralism we might expect from an Engle apprentice, the eponymous farmer's work evincing his close union with and stewardship of his land. At the poem's volta, however, Walker complicates this pastoral mode, writing that "in the Middle West where wheat was plentiful; / where grain grew golden under sunny skies / and cattle fattened through the summer heat / I could remember more familiar sights." It is an abrupt, somewhat riddling conclusion to the poem, one that gestures obliquely to a critique made more explicit on the facing page. There, in an accompanying sonnet titled "Memory," Walker juxtaposes to the previous poem's amber waves of grain a set of images drawn from Black urban life, including "wind-swept streets of cities / on cold and blustery nights" and "hurt bewilderment on poor faces, / smelling a deep and sinister unrest." For Walker, it is these "more familiar sights" that constitute the true legacy of American democracy, as the "living distress" of tenement dwellers, homeless vagrants, and un- and underemployed workers stands in stark contrast to an ever more incredible "Iowa farmer."[65] Serving as the structural and emotional apogee of *For My People*, the pair of sonnets offers a masterful reassessment of the New Humanist craft ideal, in particular its tendency to idealize discipline as a mode of spiritual and social uplift. While the sonnets' technical virtuosity points to Walker's mastery of poetic craft, their rhetorical treatment of labor and laborers suggests how the New Humanist vision extends only to certain forms of work—and certain workers.

The Machinery of Certification: Craft and Race

Throughout *For My People*, and especially in the sonnets that conclude the collection, Walker makes visible the incipient aristocratic tendencies in a New Humanist craft ideal, showing how such thinking is predicated on the evasion of those material realities that determine the experience of the majority of American workers, especially workers of color. That New Humanists might not have conceived of such workers, much less conceived of them as potential mental laborers, is concisely suggested in Walker's first encounter with Foerster upon arriving in Iowa City in the fall of 1938. As Walker recounts in her unpublished autobiography, Foerster "stared at me as if he could not believe his eyes. 'You're Margaret Walker?' he asked, incredulously." Walker continues: "For a long while I was puzzled and only after much reflection did I realize he did not expect a black person."[66]

Gesturing to the elitist assumptions undergirding New Humanist thought, Walker's anecdote points equally to the uneasy relation between creative writing craft and the literary expression of racial experience. For if craft discourses rely in part on the mediation of individual expression—always shaped by, channeled through, and articulated via disciplinary techniques—such discourses necessarily abstract from and homogenize embodied experience, processes which have major implications for more expressive, identity-based writing. "First person may have been suspect [. . .] for its seemingly inherent lack of impersonality," McGurl explains, "but the appeal of *speaking for oneself*, or of *having one's voice heard*, is obvious when it is considered as an act primarily of political self-representation."[67] In *Craft in the Real World*, Matthew Salesses suggests that "the challenge is this: to take craft out of some imaginary vacuum [. . .] and return it to its cultural and historical context. Race, gender, sexuality, etc. affect our lives and so must affect our fiction."[68] As McGurl and Salesses help us recognize, the workshop has at times seemed less a platform for diverse expression than a chamber within which to discipline that expression into form. Though MFA programs have long enjoined their students to "find your voice," what they have in fact meant is "let us *provide* you your voice"—or, potentially more deleterious, "let us provide you ours." While scholars such as Natalia Cecire and Cathy Park Hong have identified a kind of race blindness at the heart of postwar avant-garde and experimental poetries, Walker's work helps us see how mainstream academic poetry has evolved too as a literally generic white discourse.[69] Junot Díaz describes this discourse in his widely cited polemic "MFA vs. POC," where he explains that "in my workshop we never talked about race except on the rare occasion someone wanted to argue that 'race discussions' were exactly the discussion a serious writer should not be having."[70] Though such discussions remain peripheral to MFA workshops, they no doubt constituted an even more negligible portion of those workshops organized around New Humanist thought—this book, it turns out, has been tracking not merely the incorporation of craft lexicons into an over-arching professional-managerialism, but the establishment of a particular mode of literary whiteness.

Indeed, Walker anticipates Díaz's critique in the poem "Childhood," another finely wrought sonnet meditating on her upbringing in Alabama. Specifically, the poem describes Walker's daily encounters with a group of miners employed by the Tennessee Coal, Iron and Railroad Company, operator of the Ishkooda Iron Mines near Birmingham. "When I was a child I knew red miners," Walker writes.

> dressed raggedly and wearing carbide lamps.
> I saw them come down red hills to their camps
> dyed with red dust from old Ishkooda mines.
> Night after night I met them on the roads,
> or on the streets in town I caught their glance;
> the swing of dinner buckets in their hands,
> and grumbling undermining all their words.[71]

Punning on the term "undermining," Walker suggests how the discipline of labor inhibits the expression of working-class experience. For though the Ishkooda Mines operated in segregated fashion, and though the workers Walker encountered were in all likelihood Black, their individual identity is effaced as their skin is covered over in the iron-rich dust of their work; what Babbitt champions as the "sound individualists" integral to democracy here possess no individuality at all. In "Childhood," Walker repurposes disciplined poetic craftsmanship—and her pentameter is flawless—in order to expose the deleterious effects not necessarily of aesthetic but of the broader social and economic discipline for which New Humanists advocated.

That, anyway, is one way of reading the poem. It is also possible to find in Walker's MFA thesis precisely the kind of multiculturalism that has functioned within educational institutions to manage and anesthetize more radical forms of anti-racism. As Jodi Melamed explains, in the postwar era, "racial liberalism's governing narrative of race reform was to institute a massive and multifaceted program of national education designed to dispel prejudiced belief, replace it with accurate knowledge about African-American lives and conditions, and popularize new images, histories, and narratives attesting to the racially inclusive nature of U.S. citizenship." In doing so, American higher education channeled racial experience through its "machinery of validation, certification, and legibility to generate forms that augmented, enhanced, and developed hegemony rather than disrupted it."[72] There existed no more efficient machinery for such certification than the Iowa Writers' Workshop, in particular as that institution functioned under the administrative aegis of Paul Engle. Financed by the Rockefeller and Ford Foundations, as well as by the State Department, US Steel, and Maytag, the Workshop at Iowa constituted the epitome of what Juliana Spahr and Stephanie

Young term an "ecosystem of privatization and institutionalization," incorporating racialized expression into a multiculturalism far less radical, in the end, than midcentury workshops affiliated with socialist and cultural nationalist causes, like Berkeley-based Quinto Sol.[73] In the context of liberal multiculturalism, then, Walker's writing might be said to function as a window onto an appropriately diverse American experience, a window framed up in the white mansion in which the Iowa Writers' Workshop is quite literally housed.

It is hardly the purview of this book to adjudicate whether or not Walker's writing instances what Michael Omi and Howard Winant call "the expanding involvement of the state in the racial formation process."[74] Walker's later work as a professor at Jackson State University, however, certainly levels a significant critique of postwar racial, cultural, and educational frameworks. There, in 1968, Walker founded the Institute for the Study of the History, Life, and Culture of Black People, known today as the Margaret Walker Alexander National Research Center and a major focal point at the time for Black radicalism and other cultural nationalisms. Establishing one of the nation's earliest Black Studies programs, Walker designed a curriculum that included courses on Black literature, literary criticism, race in the modern world, creative writing, and the Bible as literature, among other subjects. As Walker perceived, "just as there are Anglo-Saxon and white American standards by virtue of our inequitable systems of education [. . .] there are, of necessity, a Black standard, a set of Black value judgments and, what is more, a history of traditions of Black idioms and Black conceptualizations." Walker attached this curriculum to a radical social and economic project, contending that "All America needs to become acquainted with this literature. White America still does not seem to understand that no people can enslave others' bodies and save their own souls. When every human being is holy in the eyes of another, then begins the millennium. Meanwhile, prepare for Armageddon."[75] Walker's administrative and pedagogical work, including her writing workshops at Jackson State, marshaled literary study toward fuller realization of those democratic values so stridently promoted by Babbitt, Foerster, Engle, and by a postwar liberal consensus which each of them, in their own way, helped to craft.

Such work constitutes an important foundation, therefore, for contemporary poets working within and without the academy toward racial and economic justice. In the writing and community work of figures like Tyehimba Jess, Mark Nowak, and Claudia Rankine, and in the race-based advocacy of organizations like CantoMundo, Kundiman, and Cave Canem, we find a reminder not necessarily of the discriminatory legacy of the New Humanism but of how the very idea of writing craft, especially as disseminated within institutional settings, can lead to the suppression of underrepresented voices. As Walker puts it, "we tend the crop and gather the harvest, / but not for ourselves do we labor."[76]

"The Iowa Writers' Workshop nearly broke me"; or, The Disavowal

Neither in her poetry nor in her public statements did Walker indict Engle, Foerster, or the Iowa Writers' Workshop as contributing to the stultification of American democracy, nor did she express misgivings about her own experiences in Iowa City. As I demonstrate above, however, the graduate thesis she produced there serves as a document of disavowal of both the Workshop and those discourses that sought to link poetic and manual labor to responsible citizenship.

Read this way, *For My People* constitutes the first in what would become a long line of alumni disavowals of the Iowa Writers' Workshop and other postwar MFA programs, disavowals particularly common among writers of color. "[W]e got the craft thing at Iowa," Sandra Cisneros explains, "but we didn't learn about the *why*, why we write what we write, or for whom. [. . .] [W]e learned the 'how,' but not the 'why.' I mean, all the things about craft are important, but they're secondary to who we write for and why."[77] More recently, Díaz has revealed that he "didn't have a great workshop experience" at Cornell, citing "the standard problem of MFA programs. That shit was too white."[78] And Yale-winning poet Eduardo C. Corral stated in 2017 that "the Iowa Writers' workshop nearly broke me. My talent was dismissed. My doubts were amplified."[79] Such disavowals point to the fissures within the New Humanist-turned-professional-managerial discourse that is creative writing craft, revealing how the language of the writing professional, like the closed guild in which it is disseminated, encodes its own fraught racial politics.

Of course, these disavowals are themselves carefully crafted pieces of rhetoric. Downplaying the influence of professionally enabling institutions like Iowa, they portray the literary artist as a resilient "talent" whose deserved success comes despite, not because of, his participation in bureaucratic systems of literary licensure. The "professional disavowal," as Shannon Jackson identifies this maneuver, is "symptomatic of a broader thought-structure in late-twentieth century disciplinary discussions," one in which "the language of subversion co-exists uneasily next to the language of institutionalization."[80] Frances Ferguson traces the disavowal to the Romantic privileging of individual expression, describing "a series of self-delusions that involved a mystification of making, as if by calling oneself a genius one could achieve a blissful schizophrenia in which one could imagine that one's own production was one's own accident."[81] For Pierre Bourdieu, a similar "disavowal of power" exists within contemporary cultural production. "[P]roducers tend, as we have seen, to think of themselves as intellectuals or artists by divine right," Bourdieu contends, "as 'creators,' that is as *auctors* 'claiming authority by virtue of their charisma' and attempting to impose an *auctoritas* that recognizes no other principle of legitimation than itself. [. . .] They cannot but resist, moreover, the institutional authority which the educational system, as a consecratory institution, opposes to their competing claims."[82] For Bourdieu, these writers yearn secretly for the official accreditation which they publicly reject. Ironically, in their reliance on a stereotype of the expressive artist hampered by disciplinary constraints, such writers activate a craft ideal which testifies unwittingly to the ideological power of the very institutions they disavow.

Situating these rhetorical gestures within an institutional and cultural history of the workshop, however, allows us to envision with renewed clarity the ambit and argumentative sweep of this book as a whole. For I have demonstrated, I hope, how creative writing craft migrates discursively in relation to industrial- and informational-corporate economies, evolving from an alternative, non-rationalized discourse and labor practice to a language which works, quite materially, to subordinate individuals to those institutions that administer postwar life.

The Iowa Writers' Workshop was one such institution, but to name it—to fix it in time and place, as if it were an isolable phenomenon—is to imagine that we could ever exist outside of those institutions, to imagine that we are not, even now, the real class they are crafting.

Notes

Introduction

1. My use of the term "professional-managerial class" derives from the definition first proposed by economic historians Barbara and John Ehrenreich. See especially Ehrenreich and Ehrenreich, "The Professional-Managerial Class."

2. For more on Burnham's "managerial revolution," see Burnham, *The Managerial Revolution*. For Chandler's description of "the visible hand," see *The Visible Hand*. For well-informed economic histories of the late nineteenth and early twentieth centuries, see Dubofsky, *Industrialism and the American Worker*; Lears, *No Place of Grace*, 7–10; and Lind, *Land of Promise*, 151–249.

3. For excellent overviews of the US labor movement, see Dubofsky and Dulles, *Labor in America*, and Faue, *Rethinking the American Labor Movement*. On the American Arts and Crafts movements, see Bowman, *American Arts and Crafts*; Clark, ed., *The Arts and Crafts Movement in America*; and Lucie-Smith, *The Story of Craft*.

4. Plato, *The Republic*, 10.596–7, in Russell and Winterbottom, eds., *Classical Literary Criticism*, 37, 39. Aristotle, *Poetics*, 25.1460b8, 6.1450b32, in McKeon, ed., *The Basic Works of Aristotle*, 1483, 1462.

5. Horace, "The Art of Poetry," in Russell and Winterbottom, eds., *Classical Literary Criticism*, 109, 105, 106. Horace, "Ode IV.2," in Rudd, trans., *Odes and Epodes*, 223, 225.

6. Young, *Conjectures on Original Composition*, 7, 13 (emphasis in original). For further discussion of medieval scriptoria, see Efland, *A History of Art Education*, 21.

7. Veblen, *The Higher Learning in America*, 39, 43. See also Veblen, *The Instinct of Workmanship*, 33.

8. Society of Arts and Crafts, *Handicraft*, vol. 1, no. 1. See also The United Crafts at Eastwood New York, "Foreword," ii, and Ross, "The Arts and Crafts: A Diagnosis," 237.

9. Baker, "The 47 Workshop," 187.

10. See Drucker, *The Age of Discontinuity*, 263–86.

11. McGurl, *The Program Era*, 93.

12. Though he focuses on the curricular relationship between creative writing and composition, Tim Mayers bucks the trend in creative writing scholarship in arguing that "craft, by virtue of its seeming ubiquity, is one of the most important words in the discourse about creative writing in America." See Mayers, *(Re)Writing Craft*, 33.

13. Veysey, *The Emergence of the American University*, 142.

14. Adams, *A History of Professional Writing Instruction*, 61–2.

15. Graff, *Professing Literature*, 85.

16. Myers, *The Elephants Teach*, 5.

17. McGurl, *The Program Era*, 83.

18. Ibid., 93.

19. My notion of a "constructivist ethos" derives from Barrett Watten's use of the term. See Watten, *The Constructivist Moment*, xv–xxx.

20. Sennett, *The Craftsman*, 10.

21. On the stereotypical "workshop lyric," see Dooley, "The Contemporary Workshop Aesthetic." For more on the "McPoem," see Hall, "Poetry and Ambition."

22. Graff, *Professing Literature*, 14.

23. Risatti, *A Theory of Craft*, 168.

24. Sennett, *The Craftsman*, 9, 20 (emphasis in original). For related definitions of craft, see Adamson, *Thinking Through Craft*, 4, and Risatti, *A Theory of Craft*, 108.

25. Mills, *White Collar*, 220.

26. Palmer, "The Workshop: type of building or method of work?," in Barnwell, Palmer, and Airs, eds., *The Vernacular Workshop*, 2. On the transitional nature of historical workshops, see Barnwell, "Workshops, Industrial Production and the Landscape," in *The Vernacular Workshop*, 172–82; Rigal, *The American Manufactory*, 14; and Swanson, *Medieval Artisans*, 122–45.

27. Marx, *Capital*, 371, 404.

28. Veblen, *The Instinct of Workmanship*, 232.

29. Lucie-Smith, *The Story of Craft*, 14, 13.

30. Adamson, *The Invention of Craft*, 184.

31. Morris, "Art Under Plutocracy," in Morton, ed., *Political Writings of William Morris*, 71.

32. Lears, *No Place of Grace*, 79.

33. Bowman, *American Arts and Crafts*, 3–4. See also Boris, "'Dreams of Brotherhood and Beauty': The Social Ideas of the Arts and Crafts Movement," in Kaplan, ed., '*The Art that is Life*', 209.

34. Lears, *No Place of Grace*, 64–5.

35. See Greenblatt, *Shakespearean Negotiations*, 21–65.

36. Chandler, *The Visible Hand*, 1. See also Mills, *White Collar*, 106.

37. Denning, *The Cultural Front*, 38.

38. Braverman, *Labor and Monopoly Capital*, 60, 443. For further discussion of the expropriation of craft skills, see Donkin, *The History of Work*, 28–32.

39. In Helen Clifford's view, craft books served less as codices of craft mysteries than as promotional material to impress potential clients. See Clifford, "Making Luxuries: The Image and Reality of Luxury Workshops in 18th-Century London," in *The Vernacular Workshop*, 20.

40. Adamson, *The Invention of Craft*, 59.

41. Quoted in Cesare Pastorini, "The Philosopher and the Craftsman," 754.

42. Quoted in Clifford, "Making Luxuries," 20.

43. Moxon, *Mechanick exercises*, NP.

44. Laughton, "Moxon, Joseph," NP.

45. Moxon, *Mechanick exercises*, NP.

46. Ibid., NP.

47. See Biddick, *The Shock of Medievalism*, 34.

48. Clifford, "Making Luxuries," 20.

49. Quoted in Pastorini, "The Philosopher and the Craftsman," 755. John Darling suggests the stakes of this moment when he declares in his 1685 *The carpenters rule made easie* that it was amateur workmen "for whose sake chiefly I have this time exposed [craft secrets] to publick view." See Darling, *The carpenters rule made easie*, A4v.

50. *Oxford English Dictionary*, s.v. "traduce, v.," accessed February 21, 2020.

51. Adamson, *The Invention of Craft*, 57.

52. For further discussion of the "instrumental" university, see Schrum, *The Instrumental University*.

53. Ehrenreich and Ehrenreich, "The Professional-Managerial Class," 33. See also Jackson, *Professing Performance*, 16, and Bell, *The Coming of Post-Industrial Society*, 26, 28.

54. See Kleinman, "The Commercialization of Academic Culture and the Future of the University," in Radder, ed., *The Commodification of Academic Research*, 28.

55. Sennett, *The Craftsman*, 54.

56. Ibid., 80.

57. Bourdieu, *The Field of Cultural Production*, 23.

58. On the inhospitality of higher education to low-income students, see especially Sacks, *Tearing Down the Gates*, 118–79.

59. See Findeisen, "Injuries of Class," 284–98, and Spahr and Young, "The Program Era and the Mainly White Room," NP.

60. Sacks, *Tearing Down the Gates*, 130.

61. Bourdieu, *Distinction*, 5.

62. Cecire, *Experimental*, 3.

63. Mills, *The Sociological Imagination*, 224, 196, 195.

64. Whyte, *The Organization Man*, 36, 36–37 (emphasis in original).

65. Bardach, *Getting Agencies to Work Together*, 33 (emphasis in original).

66. Adamson, "Gatherings: Creating the Studio Craft Movement," in Falino, ed., *Crafting Modernism*, 38.

67. Quoted in Adamson, "Gatherings," 38.

68. Hannah, "An 'Exploding Craft Market,' 1945–1969," in *Crafting Modernism*, 120. On the evolution of craft, see Adamson, *Thinking Through Craft*, 4–7, and Falino, "Craft Is Art Is Craft," in *Crafting Modernism*, 16–31.

69. On the renaming of the American Craft Museum, see Lauria and Fenton, *Craft in America*, 32, and Risatti, *A Theory of Craft*, 153.

70. Brown, *Other Things*, 146.

71. Quoted in Pratt, "Woman Writer in the CP," 252.

72. Robert Duncan to Denise Levertov, October 19, 1971, in Bertholf and Gelpi, eds., *The Letters of Robert Duncan and Denise Levertov*, 665.

73. Colson, *How To Write Poetry*, 20.

74. Hugo, *The Triggering Town*, 54.

75. Engle, *Corn*, 27.

76. See Foley, *Radical Representations*; Marsh, *Hog Butchers, Beggars, and Busboys*;

Nealon, *The Matter of Capital*; Nelson, *Revolutionary Memory*; and Rabinowitz, *Labor and Desire*.

77. Harrington, *Poetry and the Public*, 55. See also Rainey, *Institutions of Modernism*, 4.

78. Nelson, *Repression and Recovery*, 244.

79. de Botton, *The Pleasure and Sorrows of Work*, 35.

80. Sacks, *Tearing Down the Gates*, 289. See also Coiner, *Better Red*, 4–5 (emphasis in original).

81. Virgil, *Georgics*, 10.

CHAPTER ONE. **The Play's a Thing**

1. Excerpts from this chapter appear previously under the same title in *American Literary History*, vol. 32, no. 2, 2020, pp. 243–72.

2. Quoted in Kinne, *George Pierce Baker*, 166.

3. See Kinne, *George Pierce Baker*, 164.

4. Quoted in Kinne, *George Pierce Baker*, 167.

5. Baker, "The 47 Workshop," 185.

6. Elizabeth McFadden to George Pierce Baker (January 31, 1910), George Pierce Baker Papers.

7. Baker, *Dramatic Technique*, 15.

8. Baker, "The theater during this century" (unpublished lecture notes), George Pierce Baker Papers.

9. See Miller and Frazer, *American Drama Between the Wars*, 1–25.

10. My discussion of workshop as a "laboring force in American culture" echoes Laura Rigal's contention that American labor emerged as "the artifact of myriad representational structures," what she calls "the cultural production of production." See Rigal, *The American Manufactory*, 8–25.

11. Lears, *No Place of Grace*, 69.

12. McGurl, *The Program Era*, 149.

13. Society of Arts and Crafts, Boston, *Handicraft*, vol. 1, no. 1, NP.

14. Baker, "The 47 Workshop," 194.

15. Society of Arts and Crafts, Boston, *Handicraft*, vol. 1, no. 1, NP.

16. Quoted in Kinne, *George Pierce Baker*, 1.

17. For further overview of the American Arts and Crafts movement, see Clark, ed., *The Arts and Crafts Movement*.

18. On the American Arts and Crafts movement in Boston, see Koplos and Metcalf, *Makers*. On SACB as an exercise in cultural capital, see Cooke, Jr., "Talking or Working: The Conundrum of Moral Aesthetics in Boston's Arts and Crafts Movement," in Meyer, ed., *Inspiring Reform*.

19. Quoted in Kinne, *George Pierce Baker*, 86.

20. See Ross, "The Arts and Crafts: A Diagnosis," pp. 229–43.

21. Society of Arts and Crafts, *Handicraft*, vol. 3, no. 1, pp. 34–5.

22. Boris, "'Dreams of Brotherhood and Beauty': The Social Ideas of the Arts and Crafts Movement," in Kaplan, ed., '*The Art that is Life*,' 209.

23. Bowman, *American Arts and Crafts*, 3.

24. Cooke, Jr., "Talking or Working," 24.

25. Boris, "Dreams of Brotherhood and Beauty," 209.

26. See Lears, *No Place of Grace*, 59–96.

27. For elaboration of Veblen's "instinct of workmanship" and the "instinct for idle curiosity," see Veblen, *The Instinct of Workmanship*, 1–38, and *The Higher Learning in America*, 39–43.

28. Carey, "The Past Year and Its Lessons," 4, 9.

29. On SACB aesthetic standards, including the role of art critics in defining standards of beauty and utility, see especially Brandt, *The Craftsman and the Critic*, 47–54.

30. Quoted in Brandt, *The Craftsman and the Critic*, 49.

31. See Baker, Untitled lighting plan (unpublished), George Pierce Baker Papers.

32. Lears, *No Place of Grace*, 77.

33. Kaplan, "The Lamp of British Precedent: An Introduction to the Arts and Crafts Movement," in Kaplan, ed., 'The Art that is Life,' 59.

34. Quoted in Kinne, *George Pierce Baker*, 102.

35. Veysey, *The Emergence of the American University*, 60.

36. For the effects of Harvard's elective system on secondary education, see Hawkins, *Between Harvard and America*, 95–6.

37. Eliot, "Eliot on the Scientific Schools," in Hofstadter and Smith, eds., *American Higher Education*, 638.

38. Veysey, *The Emergence of the American University*, 67.

39. Eliot, "The New Education," 218.

40. Veblen, *The Engineers and the Price System*, 52.

41. Eliot, "Scientific Schools," 638. See also the comments of Eliot's biographer, Henry James, on the elective system in James, *Charles W. Eliot*, 347.

42. See Adams, *A History of Professional Writing Instruction*, 61–2.

43. Eliot, "Inaugural Address as President of Harvard, 1869," in Hofstadter and Smith, eds., *American Higher Education*, 603.

44. Quoted in Veysey, *The Emergence of the American University*, 61.

45. Eliot, "The Changes Needed in American Secondary Education," in *A Late Harvest*, 107. Quoted in Kinne, *George Pierce Baker*, 102.

46. Lowell, "Inaugural Address of the President of Harvard University," 499.

47. For an otherwise probing account of the history of literary education, see Graff, *Professing Literature*.

48. "Account of expenses of *Lina Amuses Herself*," George Pierce Baker Papers.

49. Kinne, *George Pierce Baker*, 67.

50. Berkowitz, *American Drama of the Twentieth Century*, 11.

51. Gardner, "How Prof Baker Made Place for His Work—if Not at Harvard," 40.

52. On popular theater during the first decades of the twentieth century, see especially Bigsby, *A Critical Introduction*, 1–9; Fahy, *Staging Modern American Life*, 1–15; and Miller and Frazer, *American Drama*, 1–2.

53. Baker, "The theater during this century," 7–14.

54. For more on theatrical experimentation as a "stretching device," see Berkowitz, *American Drama*, 31.

55. Baker, *Dramatic Technique*, 7, 15.

56. Miller and Frazer, *American Drama*, 30.

57. Baker, "The Theatre and the University," 104.

58. Greenberg, "Towards a Newer Laocoon," 42.

59. Baker, "The theater during this century," 9–10.

60. For other readings of the influence of early modern stagecraft on dramatic form, see especially Baker, *The Development of Shakespeare as a Dramatist*, 71–96.

61. Quoted in Kinne, *George Pierce Baker*, 283 (emphasis in original).

62. Wagner, "The Art-Work of the Future," in Ellis, ed., *Richard Wagner's Prose Works, Volume I*, 184 (emphasis in original).

63. Wagner, "Art and Revolution," in Ellis, ed., *Richard Wagner's Prose Works, Volume I*, 33. Wagner, "Art-Work," 191.

64. Wagner, "Art-Work," 95. Wagner, "Art and Revolution," 61.

65. Wagner, "Art-Work," 185 (emphasis in original).

66. Kinne, *George Pierce Baker*, 90.

67. "The 47 Workshop Constitution," [1921], George Pierce Baker Papers.

68. "Interpretation of the play by the scenery," (unpublished lecture notes), George Pierce Baker Papers.

69. "Program for *Lina Amuses Herself*," George Pierce Baker Papers.

70. Mrs. Walter B. Kahn to George Pierce Baker, undated, George Pierce Baker Papers.

71. "Attendance card," George Pierce Baker Papers.

72. [Illegible] to George Pierce Baker, undated, George Pierce Baker Papers.

73. Quoted in "Baker of Harvard, Maker of Dramatists."

74. Baker, "The 47 Workshop," 423.

75. Sennett, *The Craftsman*, 54.

76. Ibid., 120.

77. See Glassberg, *American Historical Pageantry*, 4–5.

78. Ibid., 110. See also Prevots, *American Pageantry*, 1–12.

79. Sayler, "The Return of the Pilgrim," 302.

80. See Philpott, "Final Performance of Pilgrim Pageant," *Boston Daily Globe*, August 14, 1921.

81. Hutton, *A History of the American Society of Mechanical Engineers*, 10.

82. Ibid., 1.

83. Society of Arts and Crafts, Boston, *Handicraft*, vol. 1, no. 1, NP.

84. "Explosion Kills 53; Many Are Missing," *New York Times*, 21 March 1905. "Died Sitting in His Chair," *Salt Lake Herald*, 22 March 1905. "Fifty Perish in Factory Fire; Boiler Explosion Wrecks Plant," *The Evening Statesman*, 20 March 1905.

85. Untitled, *Science*, vol. 71, no. 1839, 1930, 334–5.

86. Baker, *Control*, 55.

87. Ibid., 49.

88. Ibid., 59.

89. Ibid., v.

90. Ibid., 7.

91. Ibid., 60–1.

92. Ibid., 63.

93. Ibid., 41, x.

94. McGurl, *The Program Era*, 94.

95. Ibid., 23, 11.

96. Ibid., 135.

97. On advanced composition at Harvard, an alternative origin story for creative writing, see Adams, *History*, 16–60.

98. Baker, "The theater during this century," 7.

99. Dos Passos, "The American Theatre: Is the Whole Show on the Skids?," in *Three Plays*, xx.

100. Dos Passos, "Introduction to *The Garbage Man*," in *Three Plays*, 75.

101. See Dowling, *Eugene O'Neill*, 504; Johnson, "The Yale Rep Goes to Harvard," and Myers, *The Elephants Teach*, 68.

102. Dos Passos, "The American Theatre," xxi.

103. Ibid., xxi–xxii.

104. Dos Passos, "Is the 'Realistic' Theatre Obsolete,' in Pizer, ed., *John Dos Passos*, 76. Dos Passos advances similar characterizations of Broadway theater in *Manhattan Transfer*, describing the preference of audiences for "detective melodrama or a rotten French farce." See Dos Passos, *Manhattan Transfer*, 261–2.

105. Dos Passos, "Towards a Revolutionary Theatre," 20.

106. Ibid., 20. Distinguishing between theatricality and absorption in French painting of the eighteenth century, Fried writes that "the recognition that the art of painting was inescapably addressed to an audience that must be gathered corresponds to the exactly concurrent recognition that the theater's audience was inescapably a gathering not simply of auditors but beholders." See Fried, *Absorption and Theatricality*, 93.

107. Dos Passos, "'Realistic' Theatre," 77.

108. Dos Passos, "Did the New Playwrights Theatre Fail?," 13.

109. Dos Passos, *Airways, Inc.*, in *Three Plays*, 98.

110. Ibid., 81–2.

111. Ibid., 84.

112. Bilstein, "The Airplane and the American Experience," in Pisano, ed., *The Airplane in American Culture*, 24.

113. Dos Passos, *Airways, Inc.*, 125, 150, 125.

114. Ibid., 125.

115. Bilstein, "The Airplane and the American Experience," 21. See also Serling, *Legend and Legacy*, 7.

116. Quoted in Bilstein, "The Airplane and the American Experience," 21.

117. Ibid., 22.

118. Dos Passos, *Airways, Inc.*, 125.

119. Ibid., 133.

120. Ibid., 128, 149.

121. Foley, *Radical Representations*, 327.

122. See especially Carr, *Dos Passos*, 251.

123. Gold, "The Education of John Dos Passos," 95.

124. Wilson, "Dahlberg, Dos Passos, and Wilder," 157.

125. Dos Passos, *Airways, Inc.*, 115.

126. Ibid., 152.

127. Ibid., 93.

128. Ibid., 155.

129. Dos Passos, "The Writer as Technician," in Hart, ed., *American Writers' Congress*, 79.

130. Ibid., 78.

CHAPTER TWO. **A Vast University of the Common People**

1. Excerpts from this chapter appear under the same title in *English Literary History*, vol. 88, no. 1, 2021, pp. 225–50.

2. Le Sueur, "I Was Marching," 17.

3. My description of the Minneapolis Truckers' Strike is informed by two incisive studies. See Faue, *Rethinking the American Labor Movement*, and Palmer, *Revolutionary Teamsters*.

4. Cannon, "Minneapolis and its Meaning," NP.

5. Quoted in Palmer, *Revolutionary Teamsters*, 85.

6. Ibid., 222.

7. Palmer, *Revolutionary Teamsters*, 3.

8. Ross, "The Arts and Crafts: A Diagnosis," 243.

9. Dos Passos, "The Writer as Technician," in Hart, ed., *American Writers' Congress*, 80.

10. Ibid., 81. See also Gold, "Go Left, Young Writers!," 4.

11. See Allred, *American Modernism*; Clark, "The Popular Front and the Corporate Appropriation of Modernism," in Brown, Gudis, and Moskowitz, eds., *Cultures of Commerce*, 51–74; Cooney, *Balancing Acts*; and Rigal, *The American Manufactory*, 8.

12. *Oxford English Dictionary,* s.v., "craft, n.," accessed February 21, 2020.

13. Denning, *The Cultural Front*, 96.

14. See especially McGurl, *The Program Era*, 127–82.

15. See especially Foley, *Radical Representations*, 136–67.

16. Gold, "Notes of the Month," 23.

17. See Foley, *Radical Representations*; Nelson, *Revolutionary Memory*; and Rabinowitz, *Labor and Desire*.

18. The most sustained and insightful engagement with Le Sueur's work comes from Constance Coiner and Julia Mickenberg. See Coiner, *Better Red*, and Mickenberg, "Writing the Midwest: Meridel Le Sueur and the Making of a Radical Regional Tradition," in Inness and Royer, eds., *Breaking Boundaries*, 143–61. For other helpful readings of Le Sueur's work, see Denning, *The Cultural Front*, 200–29, and Rabinowitz, *Labor and Desire*, 17–62.

19. Dos Passos to Edmund Wilson, March 1929, in *The Fourteenth Chronicle*, 391.

20. Le Sueur, "Proletarian Literature and the Middle West," in Hart, ed., *American Writers' Congress*, 135.

21. Quoted in Ludington, *John Dos Passos*, 342.

22. Ibid., 342.

23. Dos Passos, "Technician," 80.

24. Ibid., 81.

25. Quoted in Alfred Corn, "Hemingway & Co. in Key West," *New York Times*, November 20, 1988.

26. Society of Arts and Crafts, Boston, *Handicraft*, vol. 1, no. 1, 1902, NP.

27. Brandt, *Craftsman and the Critic*, 47.

28. Dos Passos, "Technician," 82.

29. Dos Passos, "What Makes a Novelist," in Pizer, ed., *John Dos Passos*, 273.

30. Dos Passos, "Technician," 79.

31. Ibid., 79.

32. Veblen, *Engineers and the Price System*, 69–70.

33. Allred, *American Modernism*, 42.

34. In his 1930 essay "Whom Can We Appeal To?," Dos Passos parrots Veblen's technocracy almost verbatim and without attribution. See Dos Passos, "Whom Can We Appeal To?," in Pizer, ed., *John Dos Passos*, 131–3.

35. John Dos Passos, "A Farewell to Arms," in Pizer, ed., *John Dos Passos*, 121.

36. Ibid., 122.

37. For a compelling account of how Dos Passos's increasing conservatism manifested in his "melancholia" over the demise of the literary Left, see Moglen, *Mourning Modernity*.

38. Dos Passos, "A Farewell," 122.

39. Ibid., 122.

40. Dos Passos, *U.S.A.*, 812–3.

41. Ibid., 814, 1006 (emphasis in original).

42. Quoted in Hart, "Introduction," in Hart, ed., *American Writers' Congress*, 15, 16.

43. Aragon, "From Dada to Red Front," in Hart, ed., *American Writers' Congress*, 34.

44. Dos Passos, "Technician," 80. See also Conroy, "The Worker as Writer," in Hart, ed., *American Writers' Congress*, 83.

45. Burke, "Revolutionary Symbolism in America," in Hart, ed., *American Writers' Congress*, 88. For a more elaborate treatment of Burke's response to Dos Passos, see Allred, *American Modernism*, 29–42.

46. Le Sueur, "Proletarian," 137.

47. Gold, "Go Left, Young Writers!," 4.

48. Le Sueur, "Proletarian," 136.

49. Quoted in Brandt, *The Craftsman and the Critic*, 54.

50. Ibid,. 54.

51. Gold, "Notes of the Month," 5 (emphasis in original).

52. Gold, "Go Left, Young Writers!," 4.

53. Gold, "Papa Partisan and Mother Anvil," 22.

54. Gold, "Migratory Intellectuals," 27.

55. Gold, "Gertrude Stein: A Literary Idiot," in *Change the World*, 25.

56. Ibid., 23. See also Gold, "Notes of the Month," 5.

57. Phelps and Rahv, "Criticism," 20.

58. Phillips, "The Aesthetic of the Founding Fathers," 19.

59. Dos Passos, "Novelist," 272.

60. Ross, "The Arts and Crafts: A Diagnosis," 232.

61. Dennett, "Aesthetics and Ethics," 29.

62. Henry Hart, "Discussion and Proceedings," in Hart, ed., *American Writers' Congress*, 192.

63. McGurl, *The Program Era*, 147.

64. Ibid., 230. See also Dos Passos, "Technician," 81.

65. Quoted in Foley, *Radical Representations*, 138.

66. Ibid., 277.

67. Nelson, *Repression and Recovery*, 234.

68. Bloom, *Left Letters*, 6–7.

69. Foley, *Radical Representations*, 167, 3, 6.

70. Le Sueur, *Worker Writers*, §2.

71. Ibid., §2.

72. Quoted in Pratt, "Woman Writer in the CP," 252. See also Le Sueur, *Worker Writers*, §2.

73. Ibid., §4.

74. Le Sueur, "Biography of My Daughter," in *Worker Writers*, NP.

75. Le Sueur, "Biography," NP.

76. Ibid., NP.

77. Le Sueur, *Worker Writers*, §2. See also Le Sueur, "Biography," NP, and Le Sueur, *Worker Writers*, §4.

78. McGurl, *The Program Era*, 230.

79. Accounts of the actual demographic reach of the WEP vary. See Denning, *The Cultural Front*, 69–73, and Kornbluh, *New Deal*, 4–5.

80. For a broader discussion of WEP course offerings, see Denning, *The Cultural Front*, 69; Kornbluh, *New Deal*, 5; and Ware, *Labor Education*, 5.

81. For procedures involved in administering the WEP, see Kornbluh, *New Deal*, 3–5, and Ware, *Labor Education*, 5.

82. Le Sueur, *North Star Country*, 219.

83. Denning, *The Cultural Front*, 73.

84. See especially Kornbluh, *New Deal*, 12–6, and Ware, *Labor Education*, 5.

85. Dewey, *Democracy and Education*, 249, 302, 307.

86. Ibid., 302, 307.

87. For further discussion of the WEP controversy between the AFL and CIO, see especially Kornbluh, *New Deal*, 54–6, and Dubofsky and Dulles, *Labor in America*, 250–85.

88. Le Sueur, *Worker Writers*, §5.

89. Ibid., §1.

90. Le Sueur, "Women are Hungry," in Hedges, ed., *Ripenings: Selected Work*, 152.

91. Ibid., 153–4.

92. On the right-wing assault against WEP initiatives, see Kornbluh, *New Deal*, 100–2.

93. See especially Ware, *Labor Education*, 8–131.

94. For the classic study in New Left pedagogy, see Freire, *Pedagogy of the Oppressed*.

95. Le Sueur, *Worker Writers*, §1. See also Le Sueur, "The Fetish of Being Outside," 22.

96. For Le Sueur's personal account of her parents' teaching work, see Le Sueur, *Crusaders*.

97. Wharton, *Plain English*, 30, 19, 50, 31.

98. See Allen, "'Dear Comrade,'" 123–4.

99. Wharton, *Plain English*, 413. Le Sueur, *Worker Writers*, §1.

100. Le Sueur, "Fetish," 22.

101. Le Sueur, *Worker Writers*, §5.

102. Le Sueur, "Fetish," 23.

103. On FWP oversight of the American Guide series, see Bold, *The WPA Guides*, 12–35.

104. WPA, *Minnesota: A State Guide*, 3.

105. Ibid., 36.

106. Quoted in Meltzer, *Violins & Shovels*, 109.

107. Bold, *The WPA Guides*, xv, 11.

108. Allred, *American Modernism*, 14.

109. Le Sueur, *North Star Country*, 321.

110. Ibid., 52–4.

111. Austin, *How to Do Things with Words*, 25–38.

112. Le Sueur, *North Star Country*, 230.

113. Ibid., 205.

114. Holbrook, "Six Months of Good Sledding," 3.

115. Jones, "'Folklore' and the Upper Middlewest," 11.

116. Stott, *Documentary Expression*, 62.

117. Le Sueur, *Worker Writers*, §4.

118. Le Sueur, "Fetish," 22.

119. Le Sueur, *I Hear Men Talking*, 102.

120. Le Sueur, "Afterword," in *The Girl*, 133.

121. Ibid., 133.

122. Le Sueur, *I Hear Men Talking*, 113.

123. Le Sueur, *The Girl*, 118.

124. Ibid., 122, 125.

125. Ibid., 126.

126. Ibid., 120.

127. Ibid., 130.

128. See especially Coiner, *Better Red*, 108–9, and Rabinowitz, *Labor and Desire*, 3–15.

129. Le Sueur, *The Girl*, 131.

130. Le Sueur, "Afterword," 133.

131. Schleuning, "Untitled," in *The Girl*, 135. See also Crawford, "The Book's Progress: The Making of *The Girl*," in *The Girl*, 139.

132. Le Sueur, *The Girl*, 72.

133. Le Sueur, "Marching," 158.

134. Le Sueur, *I Hear Men Talking*, 59.
135. Ibid., 43, 78.
136. Le Sueur, *Worker Writers*, §5.
137. Ibid., §5.
138. Le Sueur, *I Hear Men Talking*, 94.
139. Le Sueur, "Afterword," in *I Hear Men Talking*, 241.
140. Le Sueur, *I Hear Men Talking*, 73.
141. Gold, "Notes," 5.
142. For further discussion of how labor and working-class experience influenced literary modernism, see Marsh, *Hog Butchers, Beggars, and Busboys.*
143. Le Sueur, *I Hear Men Talking*, 2.
144. Ibid., 47.
145. *Oxford English Dictionary, s.v.,* "craft, n. 4," accessed March 3, 2019.
146. Le Sueur, *North Star Country*, 141–2.
147. Ibid., 142.

CHAPTER THREE. **Significant Craft**

1. Quoted in Reynolds, *Visions and Vanities*, 124.
2. See Clark, "The Eastern Seaboard," in Clark, ed., *The Arts and Crafts Movement*, 9–10, and Lambourne, *Utopian Craftsman*, 162. Jonathan Leo Fairbanks, in contrast, dates the decline of American Arts and Crafts to the rise of modernist design in the 1940s. See Fairbanks, "Shaping Craft in an American Framework," in Lauria and Fenton, eds., *Craft in America*, 276.
3. "An Art Event," 72.
4. For examples of the resurgence of craft communities in the Great Depression, see Lauria and Fenton, eds., *Craft in America*.
5. Foremost among rural craft institutions were the Highlander Folk School in eastern Tennessee and the Penland School of Craft in western North Carolina. In contrast, more elite coastal institutions included the Rhode Island School of Design and the California College of the Arts in Oakland.
6. Dewey, *Democracy and Education*, 264. See also Dewey, *Art as Experience*, 9.
7. Duncan, "Introduction to *Bending the Bow*," in Quartermain, ed., *Robert Duncan: The Collected Later Poems and Plays*, 297. Duncan to Denise Levertov, October 19, 1971, in Bertholf and Gelpi, eds., *The Letters of Robert Duncan and Denise Levertov*, 665.
8. Albers, "Conversations with Artists," in Danilowitz, ed., *Anni Albers*, 53.
9. Sennett, *The Craftsman*, 120.
10. Albers, "Werklicher formunterricht [Teaching Form Through Practice]," NP.
11. Albers, "Designing as Visual Organization," in Danilowitz, ed., *Anni Albers*, 60.
12. Albers, "Design: Anonymous and Timeless." See also Albers, "Material as Metaphor."
13. Albers, "On Education and Art Education," NP.
14. Albers, "Work with Material," NP.
15. Urbain, "Class notes from Albers," Black Mountain College Project Collection.

16. Adamic, *My America*, 625.

17. Dreier, "Lake Eden Construction Journal," Theodore and Barbara Loines Dreier Black Mountain College Collection.

18. Horace, "The Art of Poetry," in Russell and Winterbottom, eds., *Classical Literary Criticism*, 109.

19. Quoted in Adamic, "Black Mountain," 633.

20. Olson, "Projective Verse," in Allen and Friedlander, eds., *Collected Prose*, 244 (emphasis in original).

21. Gropius, "The Theory and Organization of the Bauhaus," in Bayer, Gropius, and Gropius, eds., *Bauhaus 1919–1928*, 25.

22. See Borchardt-Hume, "Two Bauhaus Histories," in *Albers and Moholy-Nagy*, 69, and Lucie-Smith, *The Story of Craft*, 252.

23. Troy, *The Modernist Textile*, 117.

24. Albers, "Weaving at the Bauhaus." See also Albers, "Handweaving Today: Textile Work at Black Mountain College."

25. Albers, "Designing," in Danilowitz, ed., *Anni Albers*, 20. See also Albers, "Design: Anonymous and Timeless," NP.

26. Quoted in Borchardt-Hume, "Two Bauhaus Histories," 69.

27. For further discussion of the relationship between Bauhaus craft and industry, see especially Bayer, "The Role of Handicrafts at the Bauhaus," in Bayer, Gropius, and Gropius, eds., *Bauhaus 1919–1928*; Darwent, *Josef Albers*; Hochman, *Bauhaus: Crucible of Modernism*; Lucie-Smith, *The Story of Craft*; and Smith, *Bauhaus Weaving Theory*.

28. On resistance to the Bauhaus among German workers, see Hochman, *Bauhaus: Crucible of Modernism*, 193–200.

29. Barron et al., *Exiles + Emigrés*, 213.

30. On the Appalachian crafts revival, see Lauria and Fenton, *Craft in America*, 16–20, and Troy, *Anni Albers*, 3–5.

31. Quoted in Scanlan, "Handmade Modernism: Craft in Industry in the Postwar Period," in Falino, ed., *Crafting Modernism*, 102.

32. Albers, "Handweaving Today: Textile Work at Black Mountain College," NP. For more on Anni Albers's dispute with the Southern Highland Craft Guild, see Auther, "From Design for Production to Off-Loom Sculpture," in Falino, ed., *Crafting Modernism*, 144–63, and Albers, "Constructing Textiles," in Danilowitz, ed., *Anni Albers*, 29.

33. Smith, *Bauhaus Weaving Theory*, 157, 158.

34. Troy, *Anni Albers*, 4.

35. See Diaz, *The Experimenters*, and Cecire, *Experimental*.

36. Darwent, *Josef Albers*, 213.

37. Albers, "Tactile Sensibility," in Danilowitz, ed., *Anni Albers*, 71. For consideration of *matière* studies alongside the pedagogies of other avant-garde artists at Black Mountain, see Lehmann, "Pedagogical Practices and Models of Creativity at Black Mountain College," in Blume, Felix, Knapstein, and Nichols, eds., *Black Mountain College*, 98–109.

38. See Fer, "Black Mountain College Exercises," in Coxon, Fer, and Müller-Schareck, eds., *Anni Albers*, 65.

39. On the Alberses' *material* studies, see Harris, *The Arts at Black Mountain College*, 76–79, and Horowitz and Danilowitz, *Josef Albers*, 73–129.

40. Albers, "Concerning Art Instruction," NP.

41. "Course Outline," in Blume, Felix, Knapstein, and Nichols, eds., *Black Mountain*, 144. See also Albers, "Concerning Art Instruction," NP.

42. Albers, "On Education and Art Education," NP. For Josef's elaboration of his retraining of perception, see Albers, *Interaction of Color*.

43. Albers, "Art at BMC," NP.

44. Albers, "Work with Material," NP.

45. Dewey, *Art as Experience*, 58–63.

46. For more on Josef's career as a schoolteacher in Germany, see Horowitz and Danilowitz, *Josef Albers*, 7–11.

47. Readers interested in how notions of play influence twentieth-century artistic experimentation might consult Getsy, ed., *From Diversion to Subversion*; Obniski and Alfred, eds., *Serious Play*; and Sutton-Smith, *The Ambiguity of Play*.

48. On Dewey's revolutionizing of industrial production, see Dewey, *Democracy and Education*, 188–98; Dewey, *Art as Experience*, 4–49; and Cremin, *Transformation*, 183–207. On Rugg and Shumaker's expressive education, see Rugg and Shumaker, *The Child-Centered School*.

49. Albers, "On Education and Art Education," NP. See also Albers, *Interaction of Color*, 72.

50. Albers, "The Meaning of Art," NP.

51. Horowitz and Danilowitz, *Josef Albers*, 178.

52. Albers, "Designing as Visual Organization," 68.

53. Brown, *Other Things*, 125.

54. For comparison between Cage and the Alberses, see Lehmann, "Pedagogical Practices," 102–7.

55. Whitehead, *Process and Reality*, 71.

56. Ibid., 127–38, 325, 130 (emphasis in original).

57. Urbain, "Class notes . . .," NP.

58. See "Library catalog," Black Mountain Miscellaneous Collection.

59. Albers to Franz Perdekamp, June 10, 1933, in Liesbrock, ed., *Josef Albers*, 105–6.

60. Ibid., 106.

61. On Albers's Catholicism, see Darwent, "From the Church to the Plaza: Josef Albers, Artist and Catholic," in Liesbrock, ed., *Josef Albers*, 230–9, and Darwent, *Josef Albers*, 254–9.

62. Quoted in Darwent, *Josef Albers*, 257. Quoted in Liesbrock, "The Spiritual Artist," in Liesbrock, ed., *Josef Albers*, 244.

63. Olson, "Projective Verse," 239. For more on Josef's "breathing line," see Horowitz and Danilowitz, *Josef Albers*, 154.

64. For more detailed discussion, see Finkelstein, "Albers' 'Graphic Tectonics,'" 10–15.

65. For further discussion of Josef's *Transformation of a Scheme* series, see Redensek,

"*Farbenfabeln*: On the Origins and Development of the 'Homage to the Square,' in Liesbrock, ed., *Josef Albers*, 173–4, and "The Interaction of Color: Op Art," in Kentgens-Craig, *The Bauhaus and America*, 156.

66. Quoted in Coxon and Müller-Schareck, "Anni Albers: A Many-Sided Artist," in Coxon, Fer, and Müller-Schareck, eds., *Anni Albers*, 13.

67. My description of Anni's weaving techniques is especially informed by Troy, *The Modernist Textile*, 120–2.

68. On Anni's interest in Andean weaving, see Troy, *Anni Albers*, 1–12 and 30–9.

69. On inscribing with floating wefts, see Minera, "Discovering Monte Albán," in Coxon, Fer, and Müller-Schareck, eds., *Anni Albers*, 74–85, and Troy, *Anni Albers*, 117–21.

70. For further discussion of Anni's medium specificity and her move from abstract to pictorial weaving, see Smith, *Bauhaus Weaving Theory*, 41–78.

71. Duncan, "Towards an Open Universe," in Maynard, ed., *Collected Essays and Other Prose*, 129 (emphasis in original).

72. Weitzer, "Memoir," Black Mountain College Project Collection.

73. "Newsletter Number 11 (February, 1941)," Black Mountain College Project Collection.

74. Kocher, "The Building Project and Work Program," Black Mountain College Research Project.

75. Ricc, "Kitchen form," Black Mountain College Project Collection.

76. Dewey, *Democracy and Education*, 264, 298 (emphasis in original).

77. For detailed discussion of the manual training movement, see Cremin, *Transformation*, 25–34.

78. Dreier, "The Question of Evaluating Community Work at Black Mountain College," in Theodore and Barbara Loines Dreier Black Mountain College Collection.

79. Dreier, "Revised Draft of Questionnaire about Lake Eden Work Program," in Theodore and Barbara Loines Dreier Black Mountain College Collection.

80. On Katherine S. Dreier's instrumental role in bringing modernism to the United States, see especially Kentgens-Craig, *The Bauhaus and America*, 68–81.

81. Quoted in Duberman, *Black Mountain*, 42–3.

82. For specs on the Studies Building, see Harris, *The Arts at Black Mountain College*, 60, and Felix, "Constructing Experience: Architecture at Black Mountain College," in Blume, Felix, Knapstein, and Nichols, eds., *Black Mountain*, 196–207.

83. Quoted in Felix, "Constructing Experience," 203.

84. Quoted in Lane, ed., *Black Mountain College*, 31, 32. Dreier recounts the story in similar fashion in a 1946 letter to Earlene Wight. See Dreier, "Letter to Earlene Wight, March 21, 1946," in Blume, Felix, Knapstein, and Nichols, eds., *Black Mountain*, 210–4.

85. American Friends Service Committee, *Work Camps*, NP.

86. For detailed consideration of the work camp movement, see Nichols and Glaser, *Work Camps for America*. American Friends Service Committee, *Work Camps*, NP.

87. Steere, "Work and Contemplation," in Theodore and Barbara Loines Dreier Black Mountain College Collection.

88. Ibid., NP.

89. Jimmie Jamieson, "Senior Division Examination," in Black Mountain College Project Collection.

90. Quoted in Lane, ed., *Black Mountain College*, 80–1 (emphasis in original).

91. Ibid., 146–7.

92. Quoted in Duberman, *Black Mountain*, 257, 158.

93. DeVoto, "Another Consociate Family," 606.

94. Dewey, *Democracy and Education*, 198. For more on Dewey's conception of drudgery, see Dewey, *Art as Experience*, 145.

95. Duberman, *Black Mountain*, 82. See also Harris, *The Arts at Black Mountain College*, 64.

96. "Notes and Recommendations for Farm Plan," in Black Mountain College Project Collection.

97. Quoted in Harris, *The Arts at Black Mountain College*, 175. For further examination of Olson's role as rector, see Clark, *Charles Olson*, 211–39.

98. Clark, *Charles Olson*, 239. On the decline of Black Mountain in its final years, see Harris, *The Arts at Black Mountain College*, 168–80.

99. Duberman, *Black Mountain*, 364.

100. Rumaker, *Robert Duncan in San Francisco*, 4.

101. Quoted in Katz, "Black Mountain College: Experiment in Art," in Katz, ed., *Black Mountain College*, 211.

102. Duncan, "Man's Fulfillment in Order and Strife," in Maynard, ed., *Collected Essays and Other Prose*, 213 (emphasis in original).

103. Duncan to Denise Levertov, October 4, 1971, in Bertholf and Gelpi, eds., *The Letters of Robert Duncan and Denise Levertov*, 662 (emphasis in original).

104. "Black Mountain School," in Preminger and Brogan, eds., *The New Princeton Encyclopedia of Poetry and Poetics*, 137.

105. For more on Olson's management of the Black Mountain budget, see Clark, *Charles Olson*, 240.

106. See Allen, ed., *The New American Poetry*; Von Hallberg, *American Poetry and Culture*, 31; Conte, *Unending Design*; and Dewey, *Beyond Maximus*. For two other influential accounts stressing the association between Duncan and Olson, see Collis and Lyons, eds., *Reading Duncan Reading*, and Foster, *Understanding the Black Mountain Poets*.

107. Quoted in Jarnot, *Robert Duncan*, 154.

108. Duncan, "Introduction to *Bending the Bow*," in Quartermain, ed., *Robert Duncan: The Collected Later Poems and Plays*, 297.

109. Duncan, "From Notes on the Structure of Rime," in Maynard, ed., *Robert Duncan*, 291.

110. Duncan, "The Lasting Contribution of Ezra Pound," in Maynard, ed., *Robert Duncan*, 100.

111. Duncan to Denise Levertov, February, 26, 1965, in Bertholf and Gelpi, eds., *The Letters of Robert Duncan and Denise Levertov*, 489.

112. Duncan, "Man's Fulfillment," in Maynard, ed., *Robert Duncan*, 204.

113. Whitehead, *Process and Reality*, 125.

114. Bergson, *Matter and Memory*, 294, 113.

115. On Duncan's relation to process philosophy, see Davidson, "A Book of First Things: *The Opening of the Field*," in Bertholf and Reid, eds., *Robert Duncan*, 56–84; Maynard, *Robert Duncan*; and Von Hallberg, *Charles Olson*, 72–103.

116. Duncan, "At the Loom," in Quartermain, ed., *Robert Duncan: The Collected Later Poems and Plays*, 307–9.

117. Albers, "Art—A Constant," in Danilowitz, ed., *Anni Albers*, 14.

118. See especially Dewey, *Beyond Maximus*, 124–31. For other political interpretations of "At the Loom," see Gibbons, "Simultaneities: The Bow, the Lyre, the Loom," in *How Poems Think*, 174–5, and Michelson, "A Materialist Critique of Duncan's Grand Collage," 38–9.

119. Duncan, "At the Loom," 309.

120. Duncan, "Introduction to *Bending the Bow*," 298.

121. Ibid., 298, 297.

122. Maynard, *Robert Duncan*, 2 (emphasis in original).

123. Duncan to Denise Levertov, December 3, 1965, in Bertholf and Gelpi, eds., *The Letters of Robert Duncan and Denise Levertov*, 516.

124. Duncan, "The Structure of Rime XXII," in Quartermain, ed., *Robert Duncan: The Collected Later Poems and Plays*, 301.

125. Urbain, "Class notes. . .," NP.

126. Genesis 3:19, *The New American Bible*.

127. Duncan to Denise Levertov, January 12, 1964, in Bertholf and Gelpi, eds., *The Letters of Robert Duncan and Denise Levertov*, 448.

128. Duncan to Denise Levertov, November 3, 1971, in Bertholf and Gelpi, eds., *The Letters of Robert Duncan and Denise Levertov*, 669.

129. Duncan, "Introduction to *Bending the Bow*," 298.

130. Duncan to Denise Levertov, November 3, 1971, in Bertholf and Gelpi, eds., *The Letters of Robert Duncan and Denise Levertov*, 669.

131. Duncan, "Introduction to *Bending the Bow*," 298.

132. Quoted in Koplos and Metcalf, *Makers*, 75.

133. Quoted in Jarnot, *Robert Duncan*, 33.

134. For more on the influence of Duncan's parents on his poetics, see Davidson, "Foreword," in Jarnot, ed., *Robert Duncan*, xix, and Jarnot, *Robert Duncan*, 12–33.

135. Duncan, *The Opening of the Field*, 36.

136. Bachelard, *The Poetics of Space*, 4.

137. Ibid., 3. See also Heidegger, "Building Dwelling Thinking," in Hofstadter, trans., *Poetry, Language, Thought*, 161.

138. Wagstaff, "'This Here Other World': The Art of Robert Duncan and Jess," in Duncan and Wagstaff, eds., *An Opening of the Field*, 54.

139. On Duncan's living arrangements, see Duncan, "An Opening of the Field: Jess, Robert Duncan, and Their Circle," in Duncan and Wagstaff, eds., *An Opening of the Field*, 9–39, and Quartermain, "Introduction," in Quartermain, ed., *Robert Duncan: The Collected Later Poems and Plays*, xxix.

140. Quoted in Katz, "Black Mountain College: Experiment in Art," in Katz, ed., *Black Mountain College*, 211.

141. Beach, *Poetic Culture*, 8.

CHAPTER FOUR. **The Better Craftsmanship**

1. Quoted in Ezell, "Martin Duberman's Queer Historiography and Pedagogy."

2. See Duberman, *Black Mountain*, 225–7, and Harris, *The Arts at Black Mountain College*, 105.

3. McGurl, *The Program Era*, 158, 157.

4. Wunsch and Smith, *Studies in Creative Writing*, 7.

5. Clark, *Charles Olson*, 239.

6. Harrington, *Poetry and the Public*, 4.

7. Colson, *How To Write Poetry*, 20.

8. Denning, *The Cultural Front*, 38.

9. See Harrington, *Poetry and the Public*; Rainey, *Institutions of Modernism*; and Wicke, *Advertising Fictions*, especially 1–11.

10. Brooks and Warren, *Understanding Poetry*, 335. I quote here and throughout from the second edition of *Understanding Poetry*, largely unchanged from the first.

11. McGurl, *The Program Era*, 93.

12. See Dooley, "The Contemporary Workshop Aesthetic," 260.

13. Pound, "How to Read," in Eliot, ed., *Literary Essays*, 15.

14. Lardner, *How to Write Short Stories*, v.

15. Brinkman, *Poetic Modernism*, 7.

16. See Ellsworth, *Creative Writing*.

17. Hoffman, *The Writing of Fiction*, 8.

18. Rainey, *Institutions of Modernism*, 4.

19. Hotchkiss, *Advertising Copy*, 220. See also Barton, *How to Write Advertising*, 124.

20. Wildman, *Writing to Sell*, 212. See also Calkins, *The Advertising Man*, 123.

21. Wildman, *Writing to Sell*, 274.

22. Andrews, *The Writing and Reading of Verse*, 79. See also Hoffman, *The Writing of Fiction*, 348.

23. Hawley and Zabin, *Understanding Advertising*, 55.

24. On early twentieth-century advertising, see Lears, *Fables of Abundance*; Marchand, *Advertising the American Dream*; and Ohmann, *Selling Culture*.

25. On the idea of "knowledge work," see Drucker, *Landmarks of Tomorrow*. See also Ehrenreich and Ehrenreich, "The Professional-Managerial Class."

26. Quoted in Ohmann, *Selling Culture*, 109.

27. Quoted in Brown, "Rationalizing Consumption," in Brown, Gudis, and Moskowitz, eds., *Cultures of Commerce*, 82.

28. Hotchkiss, *Advertising Copy*, 427–8.

29. Ibid., 11.

30. Ibid., 406, 407.

31. Pound, "A Retrospect," in Davis, ed., *Praising It New*, 185. See also Barton, *How to Write Advertising*, 38.

32. Pound, "A Retrospect," 185. See also Goode, *Manual of Modern Advertising*, 142.

33. Barton, *How to Write Advertising*, 53.

34. Pitkin, *How To Write Stories*, 3.

35. Ibid., 18.

36. Ibid., 289.

37. James, *The House of Fiction*, 72, 74.

38. Wharton, *The Writing of Fiction*, 46.

39. Wharton and Codman, Jr., *The Decoration of Houses*, 67, 19, xix.

40. Baker, *Dramatic Technique*, 462.

41. Brown, *A Sense of Things*, 143.

42. Hoffman, *The Writing of Fiction*, 46.

43. Ibid., 214 (emphasis mine).

44. Hoffman even imagines rationalizing fiction through the same kind of market research pioneered by agencies like BBDO. "Comprehensive data on actual reader reaction would be particularly valuable," Hoffman muses, "in adding to our knowledge of the degree of power of visualizing, and of other sensory responses of the imagination." See Hoffman, *The Writing of Fiction*, xvii.

45. Colson, *How to Write Poetry*, 20.

46. Ibid., 120.

47. Wood, *The Craft of Poetry*, 22–3.

48. Ueland, *If You Want to Write . . .*, 17.

49. Radway, *A Feeling for Books*, 139–40.

50. Carman, *The Poetry of Life*, 3–4, 7.

51. See Arendt, *The Human Condition*, 144–52, 153–8.

52. Carman, *The Poetry of Life*, 17.

53. Ibid., 36, 68–9, 117.

54. Horace, "The Art of Poetry," in Russell and Winterbottom, eds., *Classical Literary Criticism*, 106. Horace, "Letter to Augustus," in Russell and Winterbottom, eds., *Classical Literary Criticism*, 97.

55. Carman, *The Poetry of Life*, 34. See also Colson, *How to Write Poetry*, 46. My description of nineteenth-century formalism is informed by David Perkins's description of the mode as a "genteel tradition." See Perkins, *A History of Modern Poetry*, 100–33.

56. Rainey, *Institutions of Modernism*, 3.

57. Pound, *ABC of Reading*, 89.

58. Ibid., 73.

59. Pound, "A Retrospect," 189. See also Pound, *ABC of Reading*, 194.

60. Ibid., 17.

61. Ibid., 87 (emphasis in original).

62. Ibid., 68, 75.

63. Ibid., 200.

64. Ibid., 53.

65. See Nadel, *Ezra Pound*, 95–6.

66. Nadel, *Ezra Pound*, 149. Pound, *ABC of Reading*, 11.

67. Stein, *How to Write*, 30.

68. See Kirsch, "'Suppose a grammar uses invention,'" 294, and Miller, *Gertrude Stein*, 11.

69. Stein, *How to Write*, 20.

70. Ibid., 44, 46, 45.

71. Ibid., 56, 96, 61.

72. For discussion of Stein's furniture, see Hobhouse, *Everybody Who Was Anybody*, 102–3. On dovetail joints in Renaissance-era furniture, see Diehl and Donnelly, *Medieval & Renaissance Furniture*, 188.

73. On Pound's hapless relation to Stein's furniture, see Mikriammos, "Ezra Pound in Paris (1921–1924)," 385–6.

74. Stein, *How to Write*, 71. See also Duncan, *The Opening of the Field*, 36.

75. Ibid., 30, 34.

76. Ibid., 174, 260.

77. Stein, *The Geographical History of America*, 204.

78. Ibid., 115.

79. Hobhouse, *Everybody Who Was Anybody*, 165.

80. On Stein's literary style and the techniques of mass manufacturing, see Watten, *The Constructivist Moment*, especially 118–25.

81. Stein, *How to Write*, 88.

82. See Radder, "The Commodification of Academic Research," in Radder, ed., *The Commodification of Academic Research*, 7.

83. Bell, *The Coming of Post-Industrial Society*, 26. On the role of the postwar university in facilitating the rise of professional-managerialism, see Ehrenreich and Ehrenreich, "The Professional-Managerial Class," 26–33, and Schryer, *Fantasies of the New Class*.

84. Karen, "The Politics of Class," 220.

85. Sacks, *Tearing Down the Gates*, 118.

86. Findeisen, "Injuries of Class," 293.

87. Karen, "The Politics of Class," 210.

88. Drucker, *Landmarks of Tomorrow*, 69.

89. Cecire, *Experimental*, 3.

90. See Bernstein, *Content's Dream*.

91. Tate, "The Present Function of Criticism," 9.

92. For a similar interpretation of New Critical cultural politics, see Graff, *Professing Literature*, 216–7, and Jancovich, *Cultural Politics of the New Criticism*.

93. Brooks and Warren, *Understanding Poetry*, xlii.

94. Brooks and Warren, *Understanding Poetry*, 5–6.

95. Brooks, "Forty Years of *Understanding Poetry*," in Sewell and Rogers, eds., *Confronting Crisis*, 168 (emphasis mine).

96. Brooks and Warren, *Understanding Poetry*, 606.

97. See McGurl, *The Program Era*, 133.

98. Graff, *Professing Literature*, 145, 149.

99. Brunner, *Cold War Poetry*, 6.

100. Ransom, "Criticism, Inc.," in Davis, ed., *Praising It New*, 50.

101. Finch, *A Poet's Craft*, viii.

102. Clark, *Writing Tools*, 8.

103. Engle, "The Writer on Writing," in Engle, ed., *On Creative Writing*, 12. See also Kinzie, *A Poet's Guide to Poetry*, 214.

104. Oliver, *A Poetry Handbook*, 28.

105. Addonizio and Laux, *The Poet's Companion*, 104, 186.

106. Wainwright, *Poetry: The Basics*, 24.

107. Hollander, *Rhyme's Reason*, 11.

108. Clark, *Writing Tools*, 6.

109. Addonizio and Laux, *The Poet's Companion*, 183.

110. See Oliver, *A Poetry Handbook*, 35, and Pinsky, *The Sounds of Poetry*, 25.

111. See Beum and Shapiro, *The Prosody Handbook*, 136.

112. See Hollander, *Rhyme's Reason*, 18–9.

113. See Clark, *Writing Tools*, 61, and Redmond, *How to Write a Poem*, 92.

114. Beum and Shapiro, *The Prosody Handbook*, 34–5. See also Hollander, *Rhyme's Reason*, 10.

115. McGurl, *The Program Era*, 93.

116. Mayers, *(Re)Writing Craft*, 67.

117. Sennett, *The Craftsman*, 65.

118. Brunner, *Cold War Poetry*, 6.

119. Veblen, *The Higher Learning in America*, 135, 132.

120. Singerman, *Art Subjects*, 6.

121. Bourdieu, *The Field of Cultural Production*, 42.

122. Sacks, *Tearing Down the Gates*, 134.

123. Schryer, *Fantasies of the New Class*, 7.

124. Guillory, "Literary Critics as Intellectuals," in Dimock and Gilmore, eds., *Rethinking Class*, 110.

125. Findeisen, "'The One Place,'" 78.

126. Derrida, "The Principle of Reason," 18.

127. Levertov, "A Note on the Work of the Imagination," in *The Poet in the World*, 205 (emphasis in original).

128. Mills, *White Collar*, 220, 224, 196.

129. Whyte, Jr., *The Organization Man*, 36–7 (emphasis in original).

130. Quoted in Scanlan, "Handmade Modernism," in Falino, ed., *Crafting Modernism*, 102.

131. Bourdieu, "The Forms of Capital," in Richardson, ed., *Handbook of Theory and Research*, 252. See also Bourdieu, *Distinction*, 5, 6. For further discussion of couture craft in the late twentieth century, see Adamson, *The Invention of Craft*, 35–60.

132. Amatulli, De Angelis, Costabile, and Guido, *Sustainable Luxury Brands*, 10–11.

133. Quoted in Mills, *White Collar*, 156.

134. Finch, *A Poet's Craft*, 15, 608.

135. Lisa Jarnot, "Why I Hate MFA Programs," in Wilkinson, ed., *Poets on Teaching*, 181.

136. Hugo, *The Triggering Town*, 54.

137. For these and other details of Hugo's biography, see Allen, *We Are Called Human*, 3.

138. Hugo, *The Real West Marginal Way*, 14.

139. Ibid., 8.

140. Hugo, *Making Certain It Goes On*, 297.

141. Hugo, *The Triggering Town*, 37, 17.

142. Ibid., 4.

143. Ibid., 5–6, 13.

144. Ibid., 59, 54.

145. This and all subsequent quotations of the poem come from Hugo, *Making Certain*, 216–7.

146. Hugo, *The Triggering Town*, 64, 65.

147. See Allen, *We Are Called Human*, 113–4.

148. Hugo, *Making Certain*, 275.

149. Ibid., 304.

150. Ibid., 297.

151. Mills, *White Collar*, ix. For a more recent account of professional-managerial laborers being "cross-pressured" in their relation to their employers, see McAdams, *The New Class in Post-Industrial Society*.

152. Hugo, *Making Certain*, 288.

153. Ibid., 308.

154. Ibid., 313.

155. Ibid., 286–7.

156. Ibid., 303.

157. This and all subsequent quotations of the poem come from Hugo, *Making Certain*, 306–7.

158. Gold, "Go Left, Young Writers!," 4.

159. Clover and Spahr, "The 95cent Skool," in Wilkinson, ed., *Poets on Teaching*), 185, 186.

160. Quoted in Beach, *Poetic Culture*, 32. Also quoted in McLoughlin, "Paradigms, Fables and Notes," NP. Hill's critique finds fuller expression in Jed Rasula's invocation of "home movie" poetry in "Poetry Systems Incorporated." See Rasula, *Syncopations*, 155. More conservative critics, such as Joseph Epstein and Dana Gioia, critique workshop poetics through the poetry *post mortem*, with Epstein asking "Who killed poetry?" and Gioia lamenting that poetry can hardly "matter" in the age of the MFA. See Epstein, "Who Killed Poetry?," *Commentary*, and Gioia, *Can Poetry Matter?*.

161. See Dooley, "The Contemporary Workshop Aesthetic," 260, and Hall, "Poetry and Ambition."

162. Watten, *Questions of Poetics*, 8. See also Watten, *The Constructivist Moment*, xxiii.

163. Hugo, *Making Certain*, 276.

CODA. **A Grindstone Does Its Job; Or, What about Iowa?**

1. In *A History of Professional Writing Instruction in American Colleges*, Adams identifies several Iowa-based precursors to the Iowa Writers' Workshop, including student writing clubs and workshop-style courses in poetics and "verse-making." Myers, meanwhile, reads the entrenchment of creative writing at Iowa as part of a broader New

Humanist intervention in literary study, a claim I refine and expand upon in this coda. See Adams, *A History*, 85–133, and Myers, *The Elephants Teach*, 124–60.

2. McGurl, *The Program Era*, 129–30.

3. Engle, *Corn*, 27.

4. See, for example, Dana, ed., *A Community of Writers*; Grimes, ed., *The Workshop*; and Olsen and Schaeffer, *We Wanted to be Writers*.

5. See Wilbers, *The Iowa Writers' Workshop*.

6. Olsen and Schaeffer, *We Wanted to be Writers*, NP.

7. Grimes, ed., *The Workshop*, 5.

8. Myers, *The Elephants Teach*, 139.

9. Ibid., 4.

10. Foerster, "The Study of Letters," in Foerster et al., ed., *Literary Scholarship*, 29.

11. Babbitt, *Rousseau and Romanticism*, 46, 55, 63 (emphasis in original). Of course, the New Humanist characterization of Romanticism relied to a large extent on carica-ture. As Michael Löwy and Robert Sayre point out, Romantic "individualism" is "fun-damentally different from that of modern liberalism," since it embodies the revolt of human subjectivity from the repressions of capitalist relations. Jerome McGann reads Romantic expressionism as an attempt to transcend the "corrupting appropriation" of the world under capitalism. See Löwy and Sayre, *Romanticism Against the Tide of Modernity*, 25, and McGann, *The Romantic Ideology*, 13.

12. Foerster, "The Study of Letters," 26.

13. Quoted in Wilbers, *The Iowa Writers' Workshop*, 52.

14. Babbitt, *Literature and the American College*, 132.

15. Babbitt, *Rousseau and Romanticism*, 150. See also Foerster, *Humanism and America*, xiii.

16. Babbitt, *On Being Creative and Other Essays*, 206.

17. Babbitt, *Rousseau and Romanticism*, 294.

18. Ibid., 129, 286.

19. Babbitt, *Democracy and Leadership*, 203.

20. Foerster, *The Humanities and the Common Man*, vi.

21. Foerster, *The American State University*, 184, 6, 198.

22. Pound, *ABC of Reading*, 89.

23. For more on Foerster's administrative shakeup at Iowa, see Hoeveler, *The New Humanism*, 120–1.

24. Foerster, "The Study of Letters," 20.

25. Babbitt, *Rousseau and Romanticism*, 55.

26. McGurl, *The Program Era*, 131.

27. Babbitt, *On Being Creative*, 27.

28. Babbitt, *On Being Creative*, 27. See also Eliot, "Tradition and the Individual Talent," and Eliot, "The Humanism of Irving Babbitt," in Dickey, Formichelli, and Schuchard, eds., *The Complete Prose of T. S. Eliot*, 454–62 (emphasis in original).

29. Babbitt, *On Being Creative*, 219.

30. Engle, "Dedication," in Engle, ed., *On Creative Writing*, vii.

31. Engle, *American Song*, 80, 81.

32. Ibid., 62.

33. Ibid., 55.

34. Both Greg Barnhisel and Eric Bennett, for example, explore how Engle marshaled state department and Rockefeller Foundation financing to promote a postwar liberal consensus and wage a "cold war" via cultural programming. In similar fashion, Evan Kindley reads figures like Engle as "administrators of culture" whose institutional work "help[ed] legitimate the floundering enterprises of American capitalism and liberalism." Relatedly, Mike Chasar argues that Engle's work for the Iowa Writers' Workshop and Hallmark makes him an "aesthetic mediator" between high and low aesthetics. Finally, McGurl focuses on Engle's work as a teacher of Flannery O'Connor, framing him as the hard-edged disciplinarian from whom O'Connor learned her impersonal style. See Barnhisel, "Modernism and the MFA," in Glass, ed., *After the Program Era*, 55–66; Bennett, *Workshops of Empire*; Kindley, *Poet-Critics*, 7; Chasar, *Everyday Reading*, 188–219; and McGurl, *The Program Era*, 127–79.

35. Engle, "Poetry in a Machine Age," 436. See also Engle, "Dedication," vii.

36. Bennett, *Workshops of Empire*, 72.

37. See Chasar, *Everyday Reading*, 194.

38. Adams, "A New Voice in American Poetry," *The New York Times*, 29 July 1934, 31.

39. Fletcher, "The American Dream," 288.

40. Cowley, "Eagle Orator," in Hicks et al., ed., *Proletarian Literature*, 346.

41. Engle, *American Song*, xii.

42. Gold, "Go Left, Young Writers!," 4.

43. Engle, *Break the Heart's Anger*, 189.

44. Ibid., 87.

45. Bennett, *Workshops of Empire*, 73.

46. Cowley, "Public Speakers," 226.

47. Lechlitner, "American Song, Revised," 23–4.

48. Engle, *Break the Heart's Anger*, 126.

49. Engle, *Corn*, 36.

50. Horace, "Letter to Augustus," in Russell and Winterbottom, eds., *Classical Literary Criticism*, 106.

51. Engle, "The Writer on Writing," in Engle, ed., *On Creative Writing*, 6, 7.

52. Quoted in Brown, *Song of My Life*, 27.

53. Walker, *This Is My Century*, xiii, xv.

54. Ibid., xii.

55. Walker, Ibid., xvii.

56. Ibid., xvi (emphasis in original).

57. Among the few scholars to deal with Walker's poetry, Derek Furr positions *For My People* alongside the anthropological work of Alan Lomax, reading its ballad forms for their performance of African-American "folk" identity. Similarly, William Scott explores Walker's investment in "what it means, historically, to *be* and to *belong to* a people." See Furr, "Re-Sounding Folk Voice," 232–59, and Scott, "Belonging to History," 1083–106.

58. On Newburn's influence at Iowa, see Hoeveler, *The New Humanism*, 121, and Wilbers, *The Iowa Writers' Workshop*, 75.

59. Nelson, *Repression and Recovery*, 178.

60. Benét, "Foreword to *For My People*," in *This is My Century*, 3.

61. Zabriskie, "The Poetry of Margaret Walker," 19.

62. Walker, *This Is My Century*, 12.

63. Ibid., 44, 45.

64. Quoted in Brown, *Song of My Life*, 25.

65. Walker, *This Is My Century*, 48, 49.

66. Quoted in Brown, *Song of My Life*, 40.

67. McGurl, *The Program Era*, 260 (emphasis in original).

68. Salesses, *Craft in the Real World*, xii.

69. As Hong puts it, "The avant-garde's 'delusion of whiteness,' is the specious belief that renouncing subject and voice is anti-authoritarian, when in fact such wholesale pronouncements are clueless that the disenfranchised need such bourgeois niceties like voice to alter conditions forged in history." See Hong, "Delusions of Whiteness in the Avant-Garde." See also Cecire, *Experimental*, 36–7.

70. Díaz, "MFA vs. POC," NP.

71. Walker, *This Is My Century*, 46.

72. Melamed, *Represent and Destroy*, 22, 31.

73. Spahr and Young, "The Program Era and the Mainly White Room," NP.

74. Omi and Winant, *Racial Formation in the United States*, 76.

75. Walker, "Some Aspects of the Black Aesthetic," in *How I Wrote Jubilee*, 132. For further discussion of Walker's work at Jackson State, see Brown, *Song of My Life*, 67–73, and Walker, "Black Women in Academia," in *How I Wrote Jubilee*, 26–32.

76. Walker, *This Is My Century*, 17.

77. Quoted in Olsen and Schaeffer, *We Wanted to be Writers*, 217.

78. Díaz, "MFA vs. POC," NP.

79. Corral, Twitter post, December 5, 2017, 5:32 PM.

80. Jackson, *Professing Performance*, 30.

81. Ferguson, *Solitude and the Sublime*, 88.

82. Bourdieu, *The Field of Cultural Production*, 105, 124.

Bibliography

Adamic, Louis. *My America*. Harper & Brothers Publishers, 1938.

———. "Black Mountain: An Experiment in Education." *My America*. Harper & Brothers Publishers, 1938, pp. 612–45.

Adams, J. Donald. "A New Voice in American Poetry: Paul Engle's *American Song* May Prove a Literary Landmark." *The New York Times*, 29 July 1934, pp. 31.

Adams, Katherine H. *A History of Professional Writing Instruction in American Colleges*. Southern Methodist University Press, 1993.

Adamson, Glenn. "Gatherings: Creating the Studio Craft Movement." *Crafting Modernism: Midcentury American Art and Design*, edited by Jeannine Falino, Abrams (in association with MAD / Museum of Arts and Design), 2011, pp. 32–55.

———. *The Invention of Craft*. Bloomsbury, 2013.

———. *Thinking Through Craft*. Berg, 2007.

Addonizio, Kim, and Dorianne Laux. *The Poet's Companion: A Guide to the Pleasures of Writing Poetry*. W.W. Norton & Company, 1997.

Albers, Anni. "Art—A Constant." *Anni Albers: Selected Writings on Design*, edited by Brenda Danilowitz, Wesleyan University Press, 2000, pp. 10–16.

———. "Constructing Textiles." *Anni Albers: Selected Writings on Design*, edited by Brenda Danilowitz, Wesleyan University Press, 2000, pp. 29–33.

———. "Conversations with Artists." *Anni Albers: Selected Writings on Design*, edited by Brenda Danilowitz, Wesleyan University Press, 2000, pp. 52–4.

———. "Design: Anonymous and Timeless." *The Joseph & Anni Albers Foundation*, https://albersfoundation.org/artists/selected-writings/anni-albers/#tab3. Accessed 10 June 2019.

———. "Designing as Visual Organization." *Anni Albers: Selected Writings on Design*, edited by Brenda Danilowitz, Wesleyan University Press, 2000, pp. 58–68.

———. "Handweaving Today: Textile Work at Black Mountain College." *The Joseph & Anni Albers Foundation*, http://albersfoundation.org/teaching/anni-albers/texts/. Accessed 10 June 2019.

———. "Material as Metaphor." *The Joseph & Anni Albers Foundation*, https://albersfoundation.org/teaching/anni-albers/lectures/#tab5. Accessed 10 June 2019.

———. "Tactile Sensibility." *Anni Albers: Selected Writings on Design*, edited by Brenda Danilowitz, Wesleyan University Press, 2000, pp. 69–72.

———. "Weaving at the Bauhaus." *The Joseph & Anni Albers Foundation*, https://albersfoundation.org/artists/selected-writings/anni-albers/#tab1. Accessed 30 January 2020.

———. "Work With Material." *The Joseph & Anni Albers Foundation*, https://albersfoun dation.org/artists/selected-writings/anni-albers/#. Accessed 10 June 2019.

Albers, Josef. "Art at BMC." *The Joseph & Anni Albers Foundation*, https://albersfoun dation.org/teaching/josef-albers/texts/#tab4. Accessed 10 June 2019.

———. "Concerning Art Instruction." *The Joseph & Anni Albers Foundation*, https:// albersfoundation.org/teaching/josef-albers/texts/#tab1. Accessed 10 June 2019.

———. *Interaction of Color*. Yale University Press, 1963.

———. Letter to Franz Perdekamp from Berlin, June 10, 1933. *Josef Albers: Interaction*, edited by Heinz Liesbrock, Yale University Press, 2018, pp. 105–6.

———. "The Meaning of Art." *The Josef & Anni Albers Foundation*, https://albersfoun dation.org/teaching/josef-albers/lectures/#tab2. Accessed 27 January 2020.

———. "On Education and Art Education." *The Joseph & Anni Albers Foundation*, https:// albersfoundation.org/teaching/josef-albers/lectures/#tab1. Accessed 10 June 2019.

———. "Werklicher formunterricht [Teaching Form Through Practice]." *The Joseph & Anni Albers Foundation*, https://albersfoundation.org/teaching/josef-albers/texts/#. Accessed 10 June 2019.

Allen, Donald M. *The New American Poetry, 1945–1960*. University of California Press, 1960.

Allen, Julia M. "'Dear Comrade': Marian Wharton of the People's College, Fort Scott, Kansas, 1914–1917." *Women's Studies Quarterly*, vol. 22, no. 1/2, 1994, pp. 119–33.

Allen, Michael S. *We Are Called Human: The Poetry of Richard Hugo*. The University of Arkansas Press, 1982.

Allred, Jeff. *American Modernism and Depression Documentary*. Oxford University Press, 2010.

Amatulli, Cesare, Matteo De Angelis, Michele Costabile, and Gianluigi Guido. *Sustain able Luxury Brands: Evidence from Research and Implications for Managers*. Palgrave Macmillan, 2017.

American Friends Service Committee. *Work Camps*. American Friends Service Commit tee, 1941.

"An Art Event." *The Craftsman*, vol. 23, no. 6, 1913, p. 72.

Andrews, C.E. *The Writing and Reading of Verse*. D. Appleton and Company, 1929.

Aragon, Louis. "From Dada to Red Front." *American Writers' Congress*, edited by Henry Hart, International Publishers, 1935, pp. 33–8.

Arendt, Hannah. *The Human Condition*. The University of Chicago Press, 1998.

Aristotle. *Poetics. The Basic Works of Aristotle*, edited by Richard McKeon and translated by Ingram Bywater, The Modern Library, 2001, pp. 1453–87.

Austin, J. L. *How to Do Things with Words*. Oxford University Press, 1962.

Auther, Elissa. "From Design for Production to Off-Loom Sculpture." *Crafting Modern ism: Midcentury American Art and Design*, edited by Jeannine Falino, Abrams (in asso ciation with MAD / Museum of Arts and Design), 2011, pp. 144–63.

Babbitt, Irving. *Democracy and Leadership*. Houghton Mifflin Company, 1924.

———. *Literature and the American College*. The Riverside Press, 1908.

———. *On Being Creative and Other Essays*. Houghton Mifflin Company, 1932.

———. *Rousseau and Romanticism*. University of Texas Press, 1977.

Bachelard, Gaston. *The Poetics of Space*. Beacon Press, 1964.

Baker, George Pierce. *Control: A Pageant of Engineering Progress*. The American Society of Mechanical Engineers, 1930.

——. *The Development of Shakespeare as a Dramatist*. The Macmillan Company, 1907.

——. *Dramatic Technique*. Houghton Mifflin Company, 1947.

——. "The 47 Workshop." *The Quarterly Journal of Speech Education*, vol. 5, no. 3, 1919, pp. 185–95.

——. Papers, Harvard University Library.

——. "The Theatre and the University." *Theatre Arts*, vol. 9, no. 2, 1925, pp. 103–7.

Baker, George Pierce, editor. *Plays of the 47 Workshop, Third Series*. Brentano's, 1922.

"Baker of Harvard, Maker of Dramatists." *New York Tribune*. 13 February 1916.

Bardach, Eugene. *Getting Agencies to Work Together: The Practice and Theory of Managerial Craftsmanship*. Brookings Institutions Press, 1998.

Barnhisel, Greg. "Modernism and the MFA." *After the Program Era: The Past, Present, and Future of Creative Writing in the University*, edited by Loren Glass, University of Iowa Press, 2016, pp. 55–66.

Barnwell, P. S. "Workshops, Industrial Production and the Landscape." *The Vernacular Workshop: From Craft to Industry, 1400–1900*, edited by P. S. Barnwell, Marilyn Palmer, and Malcolm Airs, Council for British Archaeology, 2004, pp. 179–82.

Barron, Stephanie, et al. *Exiles + Emigrés: The Flight of European Artists from Hitler*. H. N. Abrams, 1997.

Barton, Howard Allan. *How to Write Advertising*. J.B. Lippincott Company, 1925.

Bayer, Herbert. "The Role of Handicrafts at the Bauhaus." *Bauhaus 1919–1928*, edited by Herbert Bayer, Walter Gropius, and Ise Gropius, The Museum of Modern Art, 1938, p. 40.

Beach, Christopher. *Poetic Culture: Contemporary American Poetry Between Community and Institution*. Northwestern University Press, 1999.

Bell, Daniel. *The Coming of Post-Industrial Society: A Venture in Social Forecasting*. Basic Books, 1973.

Benét, Stephen Vincent. "Foreword to *For My People*." *This Is My Century: New and Collected Poems*, by Margaret Walker, The University of Georgia Press, 1989.

Bennett, Eric. *Workshops of Empire: Stegner, Engle, and American Creative Writing During the Cold War*. University of Iowa Press, 2015.

Bergson, Henri. *Matter and Memory*. The Macmillan Company, 1913.

Berkowitz, Gerald M. *American Drama of the Twentieth Century*. Longman, 1992.

Bernstein, Charles. *Content's Dream: Essays 1975–1984*. Sun and Moon Press, 1986.

Bertholf, Robert J., and Albert Gelpi, editors. *The Letters of Robert Duncan and Denise Levertov*. Stanford University Press, 2004.

Beum, Robert, and Karl Shapiro. *The Prosody Handbook: A Guide to Poetic Form*. Dover Publications, 2006.

Biddick, Kathleen. *The Shock of Medievalism*. Duke University Press, 1998.

Bigsby, C.W.E. *A Critical Introduction to Twentieth-Century American Drama*. Cambridge University Press, 1982.

Bilstein, Roger. "The Airplane and the American Experience." *The Airplane in American*

Culture, edited by Dominick A. Pisano, The University of Michigan Press, 2003, pp. 16–35.

Black Mountain College Project Collection. State Archives of North Carolina, Western Regional Archives, Asheville, NC, USA.

Black Mountain College Research Project. State Archives of North Carolina, Western Regional Archives, Asheville, NC, USA.

Black Mountain Miscellaneous Collection. State Archives of North Carolina, Western Regional Archives, Asheville, NC, USA.

Black Mountain College. "Course Outline." *Black Mountain: An Interdisciplinary Experiment: 1933–1957*, edited by Eugen Blume, Matilda Felix, Gabriele Knapstein, and Catherine Nichols, Spector Books, 2015, pp. 144–9.

"Black Mountain School." *The New Princeton Encyclopedia of Poetry and Poetics*, edited by Alex Preminger and T.V.F. Brogan, Princeton University Press, 1993, p. 137.

Bloom, James. *Left Letters: The Culture Wars of Mike Gold and Joseph Freeman*. Columbia University Press, 1992.

Bold, Christine. *The WPA Guides: Mapping America*. University Press of Mississippi, 1999.

Borchardt-Hume, Achim. "Two Bauhaus Histories." *Albers and Moholy-Nagy: From the Bauhaus to the New World*, edited by Achim Borchardt-Hume, Tate Publishing, 2006, pp. 92–102.

Boris, Eileen. "'Dreams of Brotherhood and Beauty': The Social Ideas of the Arts and Crafts Movement." *'The Art that is Life': The Arts & Crafts Movement in America, 1875–1920*, edited by Wendy Kaplan, Museum of Fine Arts Boston, 1987, pp. 208–22.

Bourdieu, Pierre. *Distinction: A Social Critique of the Judgement of Taste*. Translated by Richard Nice. Harvard University Press, 1984.

———. *The Field of Cultural Production*. Columbia University Press, 1993.

———. "The Forms of Capital." *Handbook of Theory and Research for the Sociology of Education*, edited by J. G. Richardson, Greenwood Press, 1986, pp. 241–58.

Bowman, Leslie Greene. *American Arts and Crafts: Virtue in Design*. The American Federation of Arts, 1994.

Brandt, Beverly K. *The Craftsman and the Critic: Defining Usefulness and Beauty in Arts and Crafts-Era Boston*. The University of Massachusetts Press, 2009.

Braverman, Harry. *Labor and Monopoly Capital: The Degradation of Work in the Twentieth Century*. Monthly Review Press, 1974.

Brinkman, Bartholomew. *Poetic Modernism in the Culture of Mass Print*. Johns Hopkins University Press, 2017.

Brooks, Cleanth. "Forty Years of *Understanding Poetry*." *Confronting Crisis: Teachers in America*, edited by Ernestine P. Sewell and Billi M. Rogers, University of Texas at Arlington Press, 1979, pp. 167–78.

———. *The Well Wrought Urn: Studies in the Structure of Poetry*. Harcourt, 1970.

Brooks, Cleanth, and Robert Penn Warren. *Understanding Poetry*. Revised ed., Henry Holt and Company, 1950.

———. *Understanding Poetry*. Holt, Rinehart and Winston, 1960.

Brown, Bill. *Other Things*. The University of Chicago Press, 2015.

———. *A Sense of Things: The Object Matter of American Literature*. The University of Chicago Press, 2003.

Brown, Carolyn J. *Song of My Life: A Biography of Margaret Walker*. University Press of Mississippi, 2014.

Brown, Elspeth. "Rationalizing Consumption: Lejaren à Hiller and the Origins of American Advertising Photograph, 1913–1924." *Cultures of Commerce: Representation and American Business Culture, 1877–1960*, edited by Elspeth H. Brown, Catherine Gudis, and Marina Moskowitz, Palgrave Macmillan, 2006, pp. 75–90.

Brunner, Edward. *Cold War Poetry*. University of Illinois Press, 2001.

Burke, Kenneth. "Revolutionary Symbolism in America." *American Writers' Congress*, edited by Henry Hart, International Publishers, 1935, pp. 87–94.

Burnham, James. *The Managerial Revolution*. Indiana University Press, 1960.

Calkins, Earnest Elmo. *The Advertising Man*. Charles Scribner's Sons, 1922.

Cannon, James P. "Minneapolis and its Meaning." *The New International*, vol. 1, no. 1, 1934, NP.

Carey, Arthur A. "The Past Year and Its Lessons." *Handicraft*, vol. 1, no. 1, 1902, pp. 4–9.

Carman, Bliss. *The Poetry of Life*. L.C. Page & Company, 1908.

Carr, Virginia Spencer. *Dos Passos: A Life*. Doubleday & Company, 1984.

Carruth, William Herbert. *Verse Writing: A Practical Handbook for College Classes and Private Guidance*. The MacMillan Company, 1925.

Cecire, Natalia. *Experimental: American Literature and the Aesthetics of Knowledge*. Johns Hopkins University Press, 2019.

Chandler, Alfred D. *The Visible Hand: The Managerial Revolution in American Business*. Belknap Press (Harvard University Press), 1977.

Chasar, Mike. *Everyday Reading: Poetry and Popular Culture in Modern America*. Columbia University Press, 2012.

Clark, Robert Judson, editor. *The Arts and Crafts Movement in America, 1876–1916*. Princeton University Press, 1972.

Clark, Roy Peter. *Writing Tools: 50 Essential Strategies for Every Writer*. Little, Brown and Company, 2006.

Clark, Shannan. "The Popular Front and the Corporate Appropriation of Modernism." *Cultures of Commerce: Representation and American Business Culture, 1877–1960*, edited by Elspeth H. Brown, Catherine Gudis, and Marina Moskowitz, Palgrave Macmillan, 2006, pp. 51–74.

Clark, Tom. *Charles Olson: The Allegory of a Poet's Life*. W.W. Norton & Company, 1991.

Clifford, Helen. "Making Luxuries: The Image and Reality of Luxury Workshops in 18th-Century London." *The Vernacular Workshop: From Craft to Industry, 1400–1900*, edited by P. S. Barnwell, Marilyn Palmer, and Malcolm Airs, Council for British Archaeology, 2004, pp. 17–27.

Clover, Joshua, and Juliana Spahr. "The 95cent Skool." *Poets on Teaching: A Sourcebook*, edited by Joshua Marie Wilkinson, University of Iowa Press, 2010, pp. 185–7.

Coiner, Constance. *Better Red: The Writing and Resistance of Tillie Olsen and Meridel Le Sueur*. Oxford University Press, 1995.

Collis, Stephen, and Graham Lyons, editors. *Reading Duncan Reading: Robert Duncan and the Poetics of Derivation*. University of Iowa Press, 2012.

Colson, Ethel M. *How to Write Poetry*. A.C. McClure & Co., 1919.

Conroy, Jack. "The Worker as Writer." *American Writers' Congress*, edited by Henry Hart, International Publishers, 1935, pp. 83–6.

Conte, Joseph. *Unending Design: The Forms of Postmodern Poetry*. Cornell University Press, 1991.

Cooke, Edward S., Jr. "Talking or Working: The Conundrum of Moral Aesthetics in Boston's Arts and Crafts Movement." *Inspiring Reform: Boston's Arts and Craft Movement*, edited by Marilee Boyd Meyer, Abrams / Davis Museum and Cultural Center, 1997, pp. 19–24.

Cooney, Terry A. *Balancing Acts: American Thought and Culture in the 1930s*. Twayne Publishers, 1995.

Corn, Alfred. "Hemingway & Co. in Key West." *New York Times*. 20 November 1988, pp. 5–15.

@EduardoCCorral. "Okay, I can't let it go! The Iowa Writers' Workshop nearly broke me. My talent was dismissed. My doubts were amplified. I felt like a token. But I survived. Hell, I'm thriving. Eat it, Iowa Writers' Workshop." *Twitter*, 5 December 2017, 5:32 p.m., https://twitter.com/EduardoCCorral/status/938219487974662144.

Cowley, Malcolm. "Eagle Orator." *Proletarian Literature in the United States: An Anthology*, edited by Granville Hicks, Joseph North, Michael Gold, Paul Peters, Isidor Schneider, and Alan Calmer, International Publishers, 1935, pp. 346–9.

———. "Public Speakers," *The New Republic*, vol. 86, no. 1113, 1936, p. 226.

Coxon, Ann, and Maria Müller-Schareck. "Anni Albers: A Many-Sided Artist." *Anni Albers*, edited by Ann Coxon, Briony Fer, and Maria Müller-Schareck, Tate Modern, 2018, pp. 12–19.

Crawford, John. "The Book's Progress: The Making of *The Girl*." *The Girl*, by Meridel Le Sueur, West End Press, 1978, pp. 137–46.

Cremin, Lawrence A. *The Transformation of the School: Progressivism in American Education, 1876–1957*. Alfred A. Knopf, 1961.

Dana, Robert, editor. *A Community of Writers: Paul Engle and the Iowa Writers' Workshop*. University of Iowa Press, 1999.

Darling, John. *The carpenters rule made easie: Or, The art of measuring superficies and solids*. George Sawbridge, 1694.

Darwent, Charles. "From the Church to the Plaza: Josef Albers, Artist and Catholic." *Josef Albers: Interaction*, edited by Heinz Liesbrock, Yale University Press, 2018, pp. 230–9.

———. *Josef Albers: Life and Work*. Thames & Hudson, 2018.

Davidson, Michael. "A Book of First Things: *The Opening of the Field*." *Robert Duncan: Scales of the Marvelous*, edited by Robert J. Bertholf and Ian W. Reid, New Directions, 1979, pp. 56–84.

———. "Foreword." *Robert Duncan: The Ambassador from Venus*, edited by Lisa Jarnot, University of California Press, 2012.

de Botton, Alain. *The Pleasures and Sorrows of Work*. Pantheon Books, 2009.

Dennett, Mary Ware. "Aesthetics and Ethics." *Handicraft*, vol. 1, no. 11, 1902, pp. 29–47.

Denning, Michael. *The Cultural Front: The Laboring of American Culture in the Twentieth Century*. Verso, 1996.

Derrida, Jacques, et al. "The Principle of Reason: The University in the Eyes of Its Pupils." *Diacritics*, vol. 13, no. 3, 1983, pp. 3–20.

DeVoto, Bernard. "Another Consociate Family." *Harper's Monthly Magazine*, 1 December 1935, pp. 605–8.

Dewey, Anne Day. *Beyond Maximus: The Construction of Public Voice in Black Mountain Poetry*. Stanford University Press, 2007.

Dewey, John. *Art as Experience*. Perigee Books, 1934.

———. *Democracy and Education*. Dover Publications, Inc., 1916.

Diaz, Eva. *The Experimenters: Chance and Design at Black Mountain College*. The University of Chicago Press, 2015.

Diaz, Junot. "MFA vs. POC." *The New Yorker*, 30 April 2014, https://www.newyorker.com/books/page-turner/mfa-vs-poc. Accessed 3 February 2018.

"Died Sitting in His Chair." *Salt Lake Herald*, 22 March 1905, pp. 3.

Diehl, Daniel, and Mark P. Donnelly. *Medieval & Renaissance Furniture: Plans & Instructions for Historical Reproductions*. Stackpole Books, 2012.

Donkin, Richard. *The History of Work*. Palgrave Macmillan, 2010.

Dooley, David. "The Contemporary Workshop Aesthetic." *The Hudson Review*, vol. 43, no. 2, 1990, 259–80.

Dos Passos, John. *Airways. Inc. Three Plays*. Harcourt, Brace and Company, 1934.

———. "The American Theatre: Is the Whole Show on the Skids?' *Three Plays*. Harcourt, Brace and Company, 1934.

———. "Did the New Playwrights Theatre Fail?" *New Masses*, vol. 5, no. 3, 1929, p. 13.

———. "A Farewell to Arms." *John Dos Passos: The Major Nonfictional Prose*, edited by Donald Pizer, Wayne State University Press, 1988, pp. 121–2.

———. *The Fourteenth Chronicle: Letters and Diaries of John Dos Passos*, edited by Townsend Ludington, Gambit, 1973.

———. "Introduction to *The Garbage Man*." *Three Plays*. Harcourt, Brace and Company, 1934.

———. "Is the 'Realistic' Theatre Obsolete." *John Dos Passos: The Major Nonfictional Prose*, edited by Donald Pizer, Wayne State University Press, 1988, pp. 75–8.

———. *Manhattan Transfer*. Houghton Mifflin Company, 1925.

———. "Towards a Revolutionary Theatre." *New Masses*, vol. 3, no. 8, 1927, p. 20.

———. *U.S.A.* Library of America, 1996.

———. "What Makes a Novelist." *John Dos Passos: The Major Nonfictional Prose*, edited by Donald Pizer, Wayne State University Press, 1988, pp. 268–75.

———. "Whom Can We Appeal To?" *John Dos Passos: The Major Nonfictional Prose*, edited by Donald Pizer, Wayne State University Press, 1988, pp. 131–3.

———. "The Writer as Technician." *American Writers Congress*, edited by Henry Hart, International Publishers, 1935, pp. 78–82.

Dowling, Robert M. *Eugene O'Neill: A Life in Four Acts*. Yale University Press, 2014.

Dreier, Theodore. "Farm Plan for 1933–34." Theodore and Barbara Loines Dreier Black

Mountain College Collection. PC.1956 (Box 38). State Archives of North Carolina, Western Regional Archives, Asheville, NC, USA.

———. "Lake Eden Construction Journal." Theodore and Barbara Loines Dreier Black Mountain College Collection. PC.1956 (Box 39). State Archives of North Carolina, Western Regional Archives, Asheville, NC, USA.

———. Letter to Earlene Wight, March 21, 1946. *Black Mountain: An Interdisciplinary Experiment: 1933–1957*, edited by Eugen Blume, Matilda Felix, Gabriele Knapstein, and Catherine Nichols, Spector Books, 2015, pp. 210–4.

———. "The Question of Evaluating Community Work at Black Mountain College." Theodore and Barbara Loines Dreier Black Mountain College Collection. PC.1956 (Box 38). State Archives of North Carolina, Western Regional Archives, Asheville, NC, USA.

———. "Revised Draft of Questionnaire about Lake Eden Work Program." Theodore and Barbara Loines Dreier Black Mountain College Collection. PC.1956 (Box 38). State Archives of North Carolina, Western Regional Archives, Asheville, NC, USA.

Drucker, Peter. *The Age of Discontinuity: Guidelines to Our Changing Society*. 2nd ed., Routledge, 2017.

———. *Landmarks of Tomorrow*. Harper & Brothers, 1959.

Duberman, Martin. *Black Mountain: An Exploration in Community*. E. P. Dutton, 1972.

Dubofsky, Melvyn. *Industrialism and the American Worker, 1865–1920*. Harlan Davidson, 1985.

Dubofsky, Melvyn, and Foster Rhea Dulles. *Labor in America: A History*. Harlan Davidson, 2004.

Duncan, Michael. "An Opening of the Field: Jess, Robert Duncan, and Their Circle." *An Opening of the Field: Jess, Robert Duncan, and Their Circle*, edited by Michael Duncan and Christopher Wagstaff, Crocker Art Museum, 2013, pp. 9–50.

Duncan, Robert. *The Collected Later Poems and Plays*, edited by Peter Quartermain, University of California Press, 2014.

———. "From Notes on the Structure of Rime." *Robert Duncan: Collected Essays and Other Prose*, edited by James Maynard, University of California Press, 2014, pp. 290–301.

———. "The Lasting Contribution of Ezra Pound." *Robert Duncan: Collected Essays and Other Prose*, edited by James Maynard, University of California Press, 2014, pp. 99–102.

———. "Man's Fulfillment in Order and Strife." *Robert Duncan: Collected Essays and Other Prose*, edited by James Maynard, University of California Press, 2014, pp. 202–29.

———. *The Opening of the Field*. New Directions, 1973.

———. "Towards an Open Universe." *Robert Duncan: Collected Essays and Other Prose*, edited by James Maynard, University of California Press, 2014, pp. 127–38.

Efland, Arthur D. *A History of Art Education: Intellectual and Social Currents in Teaching the Visual Arts*. Teachers College Press, 1990.

Ehrenreich, Barbara, and John Ehrenreich. "The Professional-Managerial Class." *Between Labor and Capital*, edited by Pat Walker, South End Press, 1979, pp. 5–45.

Eliot, Charles W. "The Changes Needed in American Secondary Education." *A Late Harvest*. Atlantic Monthly Press, 1924.

———. "Eliot on the Scientific Schools." *American Higher Education: A Documentary*

History, edited by Richard Hofstadter and Wilson Smith, vol. 2, The University of Chicago Press, 1961, pp. 624–41.

——. "Inaugural Address as President of Harvard, 1869." *American Higher Education: A Documentary History*, edited by Richard Hofstadter and Wilson Smith, vol. 2, The University of Chicago Press, 1961, pp. 601–24.

——. "The New Education." *The Atlantic Monthly*, no. XXIII, 1869, pp. 302–66.

Eliot, T. S. "The Humanism of Irving Babbitt." *The Complete Prose of T. S. Eliot: The Critical Edition: Literature, Politics, Belief, 1927–1929*, edited by Frances Dickey, Jennifer Formichelli, and Ronald Schuchard, Johns Hopkins University Press, 2015, pp. 454–62.

——. "Tradition and the Individual Talent." *Poetry Foundation*, 13 October 2009, https://www.poetryfoundation.org/articles/69400/tradition-and-the-individual-talent. Accessed 17 July 2018.

Ellsworth, William Webster. *Creative Writing: A Guide for Those Who Aspire to Authorship*. Funk & Wagnalls Company, 1929.

Engle, Paul. *American Song*. Doubleday, Doran & Company, Inc., 1934.

——. *Break the Heart's Anger*. Doubleday, Doran & Co. Inc., 1936.

——. *Corn*. Doubleday, Doran & Co., Inc., 1939.

——. "Poetry in a Machine Age." *The English Journal*, vol. 26, no. 6, 1937, pp. 429–39.

——. "The Writer on Writing." *On Creative Writing*, edited by Paul Engle, E.P. Dutton, 1964, pp. 5–13.

Engle, Paul, editor. *On Creative Writing*. E. P. Dutton, 1964.

Epstein, Joseph. "Who Killed Poetry?" *Commentary*, 1 August 1988, https://www.commentarymagazine.com/articles/joseph-epstein/who-killed-poetry/. Accessed 27 March 2018.

"Explosion Kills 53; Many Are Missing." *New York Times*, 21 March 1905, pp. 1.

Ezell, Jason. "Martin Duberman's Queer Historiography and Pedagogy." *Black Mountain Studies Journal* 1, http://www.blackmountainstudiesjournal.org/volume1/1-4-jason-ezell/. Accessed 1 November 2017.

Fahy, Thomas. *Staging Modern American Life: Popular Culture in the Experimental Theatre of Millay, Cummings, and Dos Passos*. Palgrave Macmillan, 2011.

——. "Up in the Air: Technology and the Suburban Nightmare in John Dos Passos's *Airways Inc.*" *The Journal Of American Culture*, vol. 34, no. 2, 2011, pp. 124–40.

Fairbanks, Jonathan Leo. "Shaping Craft in an American Framework." *Craft in America: Celebrating Two Centuries of Artists and Objects*, edited by Jo Lauria and Steve Fenton, Clarkson Potter, 2007, pp. 269–76.

Falino, Jeannine. "Craft Is Art Is Craft." *Crafting Modernism: Midcentury American Art and Design*, edited by Jeannine Falino, Abrams (in association with MAD / Museum of Arts and Design), 2011, pp. 16–31.

Faue, Elizabeth. *Rethinking the American Labor Movement*. Routledge, 2017.

Felix, Matilda. "Constructing Experience: Architecture at Black Mountain College." *Black Mountain: An Interdisciplinary Experiment: 1933–1957*, edited by Eugen Blume, Matilda Felix, Gabriele Knapstein, and Catherine Nichols, Spector Books, 2015, pp. 196–207.

Fer, Briony. "Black Mountain College Exercises." *Anni Albers*, edited by Ann Coxon, Briony Fer, and Maria Müller-Schareck, Tate Modern, 2018, pp. 64–73.

Ferguson, Frances. *Solitude and the Sublime: Romanticism and the Aesthetics of Individuation.* Routledge, 1992.

"Fifty Perish in Factory Fire; Boiler Explosion Wrecks Plant." *The Evening Statesman,* 20 March 1905, pp. 1.

Finch, Annie. *A Poet's Craft: A Comprehensive Guide to Making and Sharing Your Poetry.* University of Michigan Press, 2012.

Findeisen, Christopher. "Injuries of Class: Mass Education and the American Campus Novel." *PMLA*, vol. 130, no. 2, 2015, pp. 284–98.

———. "'The One Place Where Money Makes No Difference': The Campus Novel from *Stover at Yale* through *The Art of Fielding*." *American Literature*, vol. 88, no. 1, 2016, pp. 67–91.

Finkelstein, Irving. "Albers' 'Graphic Tectonics.'" *Form*, no. 4, 1967, pp. 10–15.

Fletcher, John Gould. "The American Dream." *Poetry*, vol. 45, no. 5, 1935, pp. 285–8.

Foerster, Norman. *The American State University: Its Relation to Democracy.* The University of North Carolina Press, 1937.

———. *Humanism and America: Essays on the Outlook of Modern Civilization.* Farrar and Rinehart, 1930.

———. *The Humanities and The Common Man: The Democratic Role of the State Universities.* The University of North Carolina Press, 1946.

———. "The Study of Letters." *Literary Scholarship: Its Aims and Methods*, edited by Norman Foerster et al., The University of North Carolina Press, 1941, pp. 3–32.

Foley, Barbara. *Radical Representations: Politics and Form in U.S. Proletarian Fiction, 1929–1941.* Duke University Press, 1993.

Foster, Edward Halsey. *Understanding the Black Mountain Poets.* University of South Carolina Press, 1995.

Freeman, Joseph. "Introduction." *Proletarian Literature in the United States: An Anthology*, edited by Granville Hicks, Joseph North, Michael Gold, Paul Peters, Isidor Schneider, and Alan Calmer, International Publishers, 1935, pp. 9–28.

Fried, Michael. *Absorption and Theatricality: Painting and Beholder in the Age of Diderot.* University of California Press, 1980.

Freire, Paulo. *Pedagogy of the Oppressed.* Continuum, 1999.

Furr, Derek. "Re-Sounding Folk Voice, Remaking the Ballad: Alan Lomax, Margaret Walker, and the New Criticism." *Twentieth Century Literature*, vol. 59, no. 2, 2013, pp. 232–59.

Gardner, Jackson. "How Prof Baker Made Place for His Work—if Not at Harvard." *Boston Daily Globe*, 30 November 1924, p. 40.

Getsy, David J. *From Diversion to Subversion: Games, Play, and Twentieth-Century Art.* Penn State University Press, 2011.

Gibbons, Reginald. *How Poems Think.* University of Chicago Press, 2015.

Gioia, Dana. *Can Poetry Matter?: Essays on Poetry and American Culture.* Graywolf Press, 1992.

Glassberg, David. *American Historical Pageantry: The Uses of Tradition in the Early Twentieth Century*. The University of North Carolina Press, 1990.

Gold, Michael. "The Education of John Dos Passos." *English Journal*, vol. 22, no. 2, 1933, pp. 87–97.

———. "Gertrude Stein: A Literary Idiot." *Change the World!*, International Publishers, 1936, pp. 23–6.

———. "Go Left, Young Writers!" *New Masses*, vol. 4, no. 8, 1929, pp. 3–4.

———. "Migratory Intellectuals." *New Masses*, vol. 21, no. 12, 1936, pp. 27–9.

———. "Notes of the Month." *New Masses*, vol. 5, no. 4, 1930, pp. 3–5.

———. "Papa Partisan and Mother Anvil." *New Masses*, vol. 18, no. 8, 1936, pp. 22–3.

———. "Towards a Proletarian Art." *Mike Gold: A Literary Anthology*, edited by Michael Folsom, International Publishers, 1972, pp. 62–70.

Goode, Kenneth M. *Manual of Modern Advertising*. Greenberg, 1932.

Graff, Gerald. *Professing Literature: An Institutional History*. The University of Chicago Press, 1987.

Greenberg, Clement. "Towards a Newer Laocoon." *Pollock and After: The Critical Debate*, edited by Francis Frascina, Routledge, 2000, pp. 35–46.

Greenblatt, Stephen. *Shakespearean Negotiations: The Circulation of Social Energy in Renaissance England*. University of California Press, 1989.

Greer, Jane. "Refiguring Authorship, Ownership, and Textual Commodities: Meridel Le Sueur's Pedagogical Legacy." *College English*, vol. 65, no. 6, 2003, pp. 607–25.

Grimes, Tom, editor. *The Workshop: Seven Decades of the Iowa Writers' Workshop*. Hyperion, 1999.

Gropius, Walter. "The Theory and Organization of the Bauhaus." *Bauhaus 1919–1928*, edited by Herbert Bayer, Walter Gropius, and Ise Gropius, The Museum of Modern Art, 1938, pp. 20–9.

Guillory, John. "Literary Critics as Intellectuals." *Rethinking Class: Literary Studies and Social Formations*, edited by Wai Chee Dimock and Michael T. Gilmore, Columbia University Press, 1994, pp. 107–48.

Hall, Donald. "Poetry and Ambition." *Poets.org*, 8 March 2005, https://poets.org/text/poetry-and-ambition. Accessed 3 February 2018.

Hannah, Caroline M. "An 'Exploding Craft Market,' 1945–1969." *Crafting Modernism: Midcentury American Art and Design*, edited by Jeannine Falino, Abrams (in association with MAD / Museum of Arts and Design), 2011, pp. 120–43.

Harrington, Joseph. *Poetry and the Public: The Social Form of Modern U.S. Poetics*. Wesleyan University Press, 2002.

Harris, Mary Emma. *The Arts at Black Mountain College*. The MIT Press, 1987.

Harrod, Tanya. "Craft Over and Over Again." *Craft*, edited by Tanya Harrod, The MIT Press, 2018, pp. 12–6.

Hart, Henry. "Discussion and Proceedings." *American Writers' Congress*, edited by Henry Hart, International Publishers, 1935, pp. 165–92.

———. "Introduction." *American Writers' Congress*, edited by Henry Hart, International Publishers, 1935, pp. 9–17.

Hawkins, Hugh. *Between Harvard and America: The Educational Leadership of Charles W. Eliot.* Oxford University Press, 1972.

Hawley, Raymond, and James Barton Zabin. *Understanding Advertising.* Gregg Publishing Company, 1931.

Hedges, Elaine. "Introduction." *Ripenings: Selected Work*, edited by Elaine Hedges, The Feminist Press, 1990, pp. 1–28.

Heidegger, Martin. "Building Dwelling Thinking." *Poetry, Language, Thought*, translated by Albert Hofstadter, Harper & Row, 1971, pp. 143–62.

Hobhouse, Janet. *Everybody Who Was Anybody: A Biography of Gertrude Stein.* G.P. Putnam's Sons, 1975.

Hochman, Elaine S. *Bauhaus: Crucible of Modernism.* Fromm, 1997.

Hoeveler, J. David. *The New Humanism: A Critique of Modern America, 1900–1940.* University Press of Virginia, 1977.

Hoffman, Arthur Sullivant. *The Writing of Fiction.* W.W. Norton & Company, 1934.

Holbrook, Stewart. "Six Months of Good Sledding." *New York Herald Tribune Weekly Book Review*, no. VII, 1945.

Hollander, John. *Rhyme's Reason: A Guide to English Verse.* 3rd ed., Yale University Press, 2001.

Hong, Cathy Park. "Delusions of Whiteness in the Avant-Garde." *Lana Turner*, no. 7, 2014.

Horace. "The Art of Poetry." *Classical Literary Criticism*, edited by D. A. Russell and Michael Winterbottom, Oxford University Press, 2008, pp. 98–110.

———. "Letter to Augustus." *Classical Literary Criticism*, edited by D.A. Russell and Michael Winterbottom, Oxford University Press, 2008, pp. 98–110.

———. "Ode IV.2." *Odes and Epodes*, translated by Niall Rudd, Harvard University Press, 2004, pp. 222–5.

Horowitz, Frederick A., and Brenda Danilowitz. *Josef Albers: To Open Eyes.* Phaidon Press, 2006.

Hotchkiss, George Burton. *Advertising Copy.* Harper & Brothers, 1949.

Hugo, Richard. *Making Certain It Goes On: The Collected Poems of Richard Hugo.* W.W. Norton & Company, 1984.

———. *The Real West Marginal Way: A Poet's Autobiography.* W.W. Norton & Company, 1986.

———. *The Triggering Town: Lectures and Essays on Poetry and Writing.* W.W. Norton & Company, 1979.

Hutton, Frederick Remsen. *A History of the American Society of Mechanical Engineers.* ASME, 1915.

Jackson, Shannon. *Professing Performance: Theatre in the Academy from Philology to Performativity.* Cambridge University Press, 2004.

James, Henry. "The Art of Fiction." *Partial Portraits*, The Macmillan Company, 1888, pp. 386–404.

———. *Charles W. Eliot, President of Harvard University 1869–1909.* Houghton Mifflin Company, 1930. 2 vols.

———. *The House of Fiction: Essays on the Novel.* Rupert Hart-Davis, 1957.

Jancovich, Mark. *The Cultural Politics of the New Criticism*. Cambridge University Press, 1993.

Jarnot, Lisa. *Robert Duncan: The Ambassador from Venus*. University of California Press, 2012.

J.G. "Review of *Minnesota: A State Guide*." *The Saturday Review of Literature*, no. 19, 1938, p. 22.

Johnson, Malcolm. "The Yale Rep Goes to Harvard." *New York Times*, 9 September 1979.

Jones, Howard Mumford. "'Folklore' and the Upper Middlewest." *The Saturday Review of Books*, no. 29, 1946, p. 11.

Kaplan, Wendy. "The Lamp of British Precedent: An Introduction to the Arts and Crafts Movement." *'The Art that is Life': The Arts & Crafts Movement in America, 1875–1920*, edited by Wendy Kaplan, Museum of Fine Arts Boston, 1987, pp. 52–61.

Karen, David. "The Politics of Class, Race, and Gender: Access to Higher Education in the United States, 1960–1986." *American Journal of Education*, vol. 99, no. 2, 1991, pp. 208–37.

Katz, Vincent. "Black Mountain College: Experiment in Art." *Black Mountain College: Experiment in Art*, edited by Vincent Katz, The MIT Press, 2002, pp. 13–236.

Kentgens-Craig, Margret. *The Bauhaus and America: First Contacts, 1919–1936*. The MIT Press, 1999.

Kindley, Evan. *Poet-Critics and the Administration of Culture*. Harvard University Press, 2017.

Kinne, Wisner Payne. *George Pierce Baker and the American Theatre*. Harvard University Press, 1954.

Kinzie, Mary. *A Poet's Guide to Poetry*. 2nd ed., The University of Chicago Press, 2013.

Kirsch, Sharon J. "'Suppose a grammar uses invention': Gertrude Stein's Theory of Rhetorical Grammar." *Rhetoric Society Quarterly*, vol. 38, no. 3, 2008, pp. 283–310.

Kleinman, Daniel Lee. "The Commercialization of Academic Culture and the Future of the University." *The Commodification of Academic Research: Science and the Modern University*, edited by Hans Radder, University of Pittsburgh Press, 2010, pp. 24–43.

Klevar, Harvey L. *Erskine Caldwell: A Biography*. The University of Tennessee Press, 1993.

Kocher, Alfred Lawrence. "The Building Project and Work Program." Black Mountain College Research Project. Series VI (Box 75). State Archives of North Carolina, Western Regional Archives, Asheville, NC, USA.

Koplos, Janet, and Bruce Metcalf. *Makers: A History of American Studio Craft*. The University of North Carolina Press, 2010.

Kornbluh, Joyce L. *A New Deal for Workers' Education*. University of Illinois Press, 1987.

Lambourne, Lionel. *Utopian Craftsmen: The Arts and Crafts Movement from the Cotswolds to Chicago*. Peregrine Smith, 1980.

Lane, Mervin, editor. *Black Mountain College: Sprouted Seeds, an Anthology of Personal Accounts*. The University of Tennessee Press, 1990.

Lardner, Ring. *How to Write Short Stories*. Charles Scribner's Sons, 1924.

Laughton, John Knox. "Moxon, Joseph." *Oxford Dictionary of National Biography*, 23 September 2004, https://www.oxforddnb.com/view/10.1093/ref:odnb/9780198614128

.001.0001/odnb-9780198614128-e-19466?rskey=hodjJZ&result=2. Accessed 9 December 2019.

Lauria, Jo, and Steve Fenton. *Craft in America: Celebrating Two Centuries of Artists and Objects*. Clarkson Potter, 2007.

Lears, T.J. Jackson. *Fables of Abundance: A Cultural History of Advertising in America*. Basic Books, 1994.

———. *No Place of Grace: Antimodernism and the Transformation of American Culture, 1880–1920*. The University of Chicago Press, 1994.

Lechlitner, Ruth. "American Song, Revised." *New Masses*, vol. 19, no. 8, 1936, pp. 23–4.

Lehmann, Annette Jael. "Pedagogical Practices and Models of Creativity at Black Mountain College." *Black Mountain: An Interdisciplinary Experiment: 1933–1957*, edited by Eugen Blume, Matilda Felix, Gabriele Knapstein, and Catherine Nichols, Spector Books, 2015, pp. 98–109.

Le Sueur, Meridel. "Afterward." *I Hear Men Talking*, West End Press, 1984, pp. 237–43.

———. "Biography of My Daughter." *Worker Writers*, West End Press, 1982, NP.

———. *Crusaders: The Radical Legacy of Marian and Arthur Le Sueur*. Minnesota Historical Society Press, 1984.

———. "The Fetish of Being Outside." *New Masses*, vol. 14, no. 9, 1935, pp. 22–3.

———. *The Girl*. West End Press, 1978.

———. *I Hear Men Talking*. West End Press, 1984.

———. "I Was Marching." *New Masses*, vol. 12, no. 12, 1934, pp. 16–18.

———. *North Star Country*. Book Find Club, 1945.

———. "Proletarian Literature and the Middle West." *American Writers' Congress*, edited by Henry Hart, International Publishers, 1935, pp. 135–8.

———. "Women are Hungry." *Ripenings: Selected Work*, edited by Elaine Hedges, The Feminist Press, 1990, pp. 144–57.

———. *Worker Writers*. West End Press, 1982.

Levertov, Denise. "A Note on the Work of the Imagination." *The Poet in the World*, edited by Denise Levertov, New Directions, 1973, pp. 202–6.

Liesbrock, Heinz. "The Spiritual Artist." *Josef Albers: Interaction*, edited by Heinz Liesbrock, Yale University Press, 2018, pp. 241–4.

———, editor. *Josef Albers: Interaction*. Yale University Press, 2018.

Lind, Michael. *Land of Promise: An Economic History of the United States*. HarperCollins, 2012.

Lowell, A. Lawrence. "Inaugural Address of the President of Harvard University." *Science*, vol. 30, no. 772, 1909, pp. 497–505.

Löwy, Michael, and Robert Sayre. *Romanticism Against the Tide of Modernity*. Translated by Catherine Porter, Duke University Press, 2001.

Lucie-Smith, Edward. *The Story of Craft: The Craftsman's Role in Society*. Cornell University Press, 1981.

Ludington, Townsend. *John Dos Passos: A Twentieth Century Odyssey*. E.P. Dutton, 1980.

Lull, Herbert Galen. *The Manual Labor Movement in the United States*. Bulletin of the University of Washington, 1914.

Marchand, Roland. *Advertising the American Dream: Making Way for Modernity, 1920–1940*. University of California Press, 1985.

Marsh, John. *Hog Butchers, Beggars, and Busboys: Poverty, Labor, and the Making of American Poetry*. The University of Michigan Press, 2011.

Marx, Karl. *Capital: A Critique of Political Economy*. Vol. 1, Random House, 1906.

Mayers, Tim. *(Re)Writing Craft: Composition, Creative Writing, and the Future of English Studies*. University of Pittsburgh Press, 2005.

Maynard, James. *Robert Duncan and the Pragmatist Sublime*. University of New Mexico Press, 2018.

McAdams, John. *The New Class in Post-Industrial Society*. Palgrave Macmillan, 2015.

McGann, Jerome J. *The Romantic Ideology: A Critical Investigation*. The University of Chicago Press, 1983.

McGurl, Mark. *The Program Era: Postwar Fiction and the Rise of Creative Writing*. Harvard University Press, 2009.

McLoughlin, Paul. "Paradigms, Fables and Notes." *PN Review*, vol. 13, no. 2, 1986, NP.

Melamed, Jodi. *Represent and Destroy: Rationalizing Violence in the New Racial Capitalism*. University of Minnesota Press, 2011.

Meltzer, Milton. *Violins & Shovels: The WPA Arts Projects*. Delacorte Press, 1976.

Michelson, P. "A Materialist Critique of Duncan's Grand Collage." *Boundary 2: A Journal of Postmodern Literature*, vol. 8, no. 2, 1980, pp. 21–43.

Mickenberg, Julia. "Writing the Midwest: Meridel Le Sueur and the Making of a Radical Regional Tradition." *Breaking Boundaries: New Perspectives on Women's Regional Writing*, edited by Sherrie A. Inness and Diana Royer, University of Iowa Press, 1997, pp. 143–61.

Mikriammos, Philippe. "Ezra Pound in Paris (1921–1924): A Cure of Youthfulness." *Paideuma: Modern and Contemporary Poetry and Poetics*, vol. 14, no. 2/3, 1985, pp. 385–93.

Miller, Jordan Y. and Winifred L. Frazer. *American Drama Between the Wars: A Critical History*. Twayne Publishers, 1991.

Miller, Rosalind. *Gertrude Stein: Form and Intelligibility*. Exposition Press, 1949.

Mills, C. Wright. *The Sociological Imagination*. Oxford University Press, 1959.

———. *White Collar: The American Middle Classes*. Oxford University Press, 1951.

Minera, María. "Discovering Monte Albán." *Anni Albers*, edited by Ann Coxon, Briony Fer, and Maria Müller-Schareck, Tate Modern, 2018, pp. 74–85.

Moglen, Seth. *Mourning Modernity: Literary Modernism and the Injuries of American Capitalism*. Stanford University Press, 2007.

Morris, William. "Art Under Plutocracy." *Political Writings of William Morris*, edited by A. L. Morton, International Publishers, 1973, pp. 59–72.

Moxon, Joseph. *Mechanick exercises: or, The doctrine of handy-works*. Daniel Midwinter and Thomas Leigh, 1703.

Myers, D.G. *The Elephants Teach: Creative Writing Since 1880*. The University of Chicago Press, 2006.

Nadel, Ira. *Ezra Pound: A Literary Life*. Palgrave Macmillan, 2004.

Nealon, Christopher. *The Matter of Capital: Poetry and Crisis in the American Century*. Harvard University Press, 2011.

Nelson, Cary. *Repression and Recovery: Modern American Poetry and the Politics of Cultural Memory, 1910–1945*. The University of Wisconsin Press, 1989.

———. *Revolutionary Memory: Recovering the Poetry of the American Left*. Routledge, 2001.

The New American Bible: Translated from the Original Languages with Critical Use of All the Ancient Sources by Members of the Catholic Biblical Association of America. Catholic Book Publishing Co., 1970.

Nichols, Osgood, and Kurt Glaser. *Work Camps for America: The German Experience and the American Opportunity*. John Day Company, 1933.

Obniski, Monica, and Darrin Alfred, editors. *Serious Play: Design in Midcentury America*. Yale University Press, 2018.

OED Online. Oxford University Press, 2015, https://www.oed.com.

Ohmann, Richard. *Selling Culture: Magazines, Markets, and Class at the Turn of the Century*. Verso, 1996.

Oliver, Mary. *A Poetry Handbook: A Prose Guide to Understanding and Writing Poetry*. Harcourt, Brace and Company, 1994.

Olsen, Eric, and Glenn Schaeffer. *We Wanted to be Writers: Life, Love, and Literature at the Iowa Writers' Workshop*. Skyhorse Publishing, 2011.

Olson, Charles. "Projective Verse." *Collected Prose*, edited by Donald Allen and Benjamin Friedlander, University of California Press, 1997, pp. 239–49.

Omi, Michael, and Howard Winant. *Racial Formation in the United States: From the 1960s to the 1980s*. Routledge & Kegan Paul, 1986.

Palmer, Bryan D. *Revolutionary Teamsters: The Minneapolis Truckers' Strikes of 1934*. Brill, 2013.

Palmer, Marilyn. "The Workshop: type of building or method of work?" *The Vernacular Workshop: From Craft to Industry, 1400–1900*, edited by P. S. Barnwell, Marilyn Palmer, and Malcolm Airs, Council for British Archaeology, 2004, pp. 1–16.

Pastorini, Cesare. "The Philosopher and the Craftsman: Francis Bacon's Notion of Experiment and Its Debt to Early Stuart Inventors." *Isis*, vol. 108, no. 4, 2017, pp. 749–68.

Perkins, David. *A History of Modern Poetry, Volume I: From the 1890s to the High Modernist Mode*. Belknap Press (Harvard University Press), 1976.

Phelps, Wallace, and Philip Rahv. "Criticism." *Partisan Review*, vol. 2, no. 7, 1935, pp. 16–25.

Phillips, William. "The Aesthetic of the Founding Fathers." *Partisan Review*, vol. 4, no. 4, 1938, 11–21.

Philpott, A.J. "Final Performance of Pilgrim Pageant." *Boston Daily Globe*, 14 August 1921, pp. 10.

Pinsky, Robert. *The Sounds of Poetry: A Brief Guide*. Farrar, Straus, and Giroux, 1998.

Pitkin, Walter B. *How to Write Stories*. Harcourt, Brace and Company, 1921.

Plato. *The Republic* 10. *Classical Literary Criticism*, edited by D. A. Russell and Michael Winterbottom, Oxford University Press, 2008, pp. 36–50.

Pound, Ezra. *ABC of Reading*. New Directions, 1934.

———. "How to Read." *Literary Essays of Ezra Pound*, edited by T. S. Eliot, New Directions, 1954, pp. 15–40.

———. "A Retrospect." *Praising It New: The Best of the New Criticism*, edited by Garrick Davis, Swallow Press/Ohio University Press, 2008, pp. 185–94.

Pratt, Linda Ray. "Woman Writer in the CP: The Case of Meridel Le Sueur." *Women's Studies*, vol. 14, no. 3, 1988, pp. 247–64.

Prevots, Naima. *American Pageantry: A Movement for Art and Democracy*. UMI Research Press, 1990.

Quartermain, Peter. "Introduction." *Robert Duncan: The Collected Later Poems and Plays*, edited by Peter Quartermain, University of California Press, 2014, pp. xxv–lii.

Rabinowitz, Paula. *Labor and Desire: Women's Revolutionary Fiction in Depression America*. The University of North Carolina Press, 1991.

———. *They Must Be Represented: The Politics of Documentary*. Verso, 1994.

Radder, Hans. "The Commodification of Academic Research." *The Commodification of Academic Research: Science and the Modern University*, edited by Hans Radder, University of Pittsburgh Press, 2010, pp. 1–23.

Radway, Janice. *A Feeling for Books: The Book-of-the-Month Club, Literary Taste, and Middle-Class Desire*. The University of North Carolina Press, 1997.

Rainey, Lawrence. *Institutions of Modernism: Literary Elites and Public Culture*. Yale University Press, 1998.

Ransom, John Crowe. "Criticism, Inc." *Praising It New: The Best of the New Criticism*, edited by Garrick Davis, Swallow Press/Ohio University Press, 2008, pp. 49–60.

Rasula, Jed. *Syncopations: The Stress of Innovation in Contemporary American Poetry*. University of Alabama Press, 2004.

Redensek, Jeannette. "*Farbenfabeln*: On the Origins and Development of the 'Homage to the Square.'" *Josef Albers: Interaction*, edited by Heinz Liesbrock, Yale University Press, 2018, pp. 172–91.

Redmond, John. *How to Write a Poem*. Blackwell Publishing, 2006.

Reynolds, Katherine C. *Visions and Vanities: John Andrew Rice of Black Mountain College*. Louisiana State University Press, 1998.

Rice, Frank. "Kitchen form." Black Mountain College Project Collection. PC.7008 (Box 20). State Archives of North Carolina, Western Regional Archives, Asheville, NC, USA.

Rice, John A. "Fundamentalism and the Higher Learning." *Harper's Monthly Magazine*, 1 December 1936, pp. 587–96.

Rigal, Laura. *The American Manufactory: Art, Labor, and the World of Things in the Early Republic*. Princeton University Press, 1998.

Risatti, Howard. *A Theory of Craft: Function and Aesthetic Expression*. The University of North Carolina Press, 2007.

Ross, Denman. "The Arts and Crafts: A Diagnosis." *Handicraft*, vol. 1, no. 10, 1903, pp. 229–43.

Rugg, Harold and Ann Shumaker. *The Child-Centered School: An Appraisal of the New Education*. World Book Company, 1928.

Rumaker, Michael. *Robert Duncan in San Francisco*. City Lights/Grey Fox, 2013.

Sacks, Peter. *Tearing Down the Gates: Confronting the Class Divide in American Education.* University of California Press, 2007.

Salesses, Matthew. *Craft in the Real World: Rethinking Fiction Writing and Workshopping.* Catapult, 2021.

Sayler, Oliver M. "The Return of the Pilgrim." *The New Republic*, vol. XXVII, 1921, pp. 302–3.

Scanlan, Jennifer. "Handmade Modernism: Craft in Industry in the Postwar Period." *Crafting Modernism: Midcentury American Art and Design*, edited by Jeannine Falino, Abrams (in association with MAD / Museum of Arts and Design), 2011, pp. 98–119.

Schleuning, Neala. "Untitled." *The Girl*, by Meridel Le Sueur, West End Press, 1978, pp. 134–5.

Schrum, Ethan. *The Instrumental University: Education in the Service of the National Agenda After World War II.* Cornell University Press, 2019.

Schryer, Stephen. *Fantasies of the New Class: Ideologies of Professionalism in Post-World War II American Fiction.* Columbia University Press, 2011.

Scott, William. "Belonging to History: Margaret Walker's *For My People.*" *MLN*, vol. 121, no. 5, 2006, pp. 1083–106.

Sennett, Richard. *The Craftsman.* Yale University Press, 2008.

Serling, Robert J. *Legend and Legacy: The Story of Boeing and Its People.* St. Martin's Press, 1992.

Singerman, Howard. *Art Subjects: Making Artists in the American University.* University of California Press, 1999.

Smith, T'ai. *Bauhaus Weaving Theory: From Feminine Craft to Mode of Design.* University of Minnesota Press, 2014.

Society of Arts and Crafts Boston. *Handicraft*, vol. 1, no. 1, 1902.

———. *Handicraft*, vol. 3, no. 1, 1919.

Spahr, Juliana, and Stephanie Young. "The Program Era and the Mainly White Room." *The Los Angeles Review of Books*, 20 September 2015, NP.

Steere, Douglas V. "Work and Contemplation." Theodore and Barbara Loines Dreier Black Mountain College Collection. PC.1956 (Box 39). State Archives of North Carolina, Western Regional Archives, Asheville, NC, USA.

Stein, Gertrude. *The Geographical History of America or the Relation of Human Nature to the Human Mind.* Random House, 1936.

———. *How to Write.* Dover Publications, Inc., 1975.

Stott, William. *Documentary Expression and Thirties America.* Oxford University Press, 1973.

Sutton-Smith, Brian. *The Ambiguity of Play.* Harvard University Press, 2001.

Swanson, Heather. *Medieval Artisans: An Urban Class in Late Medieval England.* Basil Blackwell, 1989.

Tate, Allen. "The Present Function of Criticism." *Reason in Madness: Critical Essays*, G. P. Putnam's Sons, 1941, pp. 3–19.

Troy, Virginia Gardner. *Anni Albers and Ancient American Textiles: From Bauhaus to Black Mountain.* Ashgate, 2002.

———. *The Modernist Textile: Europe and America, 1890–1940.* Lund Humphries, 2006.

Ueland, Branda. *If You Want to Write . . .* The Schubert Club, 1984.

United Crafts of Eastwood, N.Y. "Foreword." *The Craftsman*, vol. 1, no. 1, 1901, i–ii.

Untitled. *Science*, vol. 71, no. 1839, 1930, pp. 334–5.

———. *Science*, vol. 71, no. 1841, 1930, p. 382.

Urbain, John. "Class notes from Albers." Black Mountain College Project Collection. PC.7008 (Box 19). State Archives of North Carolina, Western Regional Archives, Asheville, NC, USA.

Veblen, Thorstein. *The Engineers and the Price System*. The Viking Press, Inc., 1921.

———. *The Higher Learning in America: A Memorandum on the Conduct of Universities by Business Men*. Edited by Richard F. Teichgraeber III, Johns Hopkins University Press, 2015.

———. *The Instinct of Workmanship: And The State of Industrial Arts*. The Macmillan Company, 1914.

Veysey, Laurence R. *The Emergence of the American University*. The University of Chicago Press, 1965.

Virgil. *Georgics*. Translated by Kristina Chew, Hackett Publishing Company, 2002.

Von Hallberg, Robert. *American Poetry and Culture, 1945–1980*. Harvard University Press, 1985.

———. *Charles Olson: The Scholar's Art*. Harvard University Press, 1978.

Wagner, Richard. "Art and Revolution." *Richard Wagner's Prose Works, Volume I: The Art-Work of the Future*, edited and translated by William Ashton Ellis, Broude Brothers, 1966, pp. 21–68.

———. "The Art-Work of the Future." *Richard Wagner's Prose Works, Volume I: The Art-Work of the Future*, edited and translated by William Ashton Ellis, Broude Brothers, 1966, pp. 21–68.

Wagstaff, Christopher. "'This Here Other World': The Art of Robert Duncan and Jess." *An Opening of the Field: Jess, Robert Duncan, and Their Circle*, edited by Michael Duncan and Christopher Wagstaff, Crocker Art Museum, 2013, pp. 51–88.

Wainwright, Jeffrey. *Poetry: The Basics*. Routledge, 2004.

Walker, Margaret. *How I Wrote Jubilee and Other Essays on Life and Literature*. The Feminist Press of the City University of New York, 1990.

———. *This Is My Century: New and Collected Poems*. The University of Georgia Press, 1989.

Ware, Caroline F. *Labor Education in Universities*. American Labor Education Service, Inc., 1946.

Watten, Barrett. *The Constructivist Moment: From Material Text to Cultural Poetics*. Wesleyan University Press, 2003.

———. *Questions of Poetics: Language Writing and Consequences*. University of Iowa Press, 2016.

Weitzer, Harry. "Memoir." Black Mountain College Project Collection. PC.7008 (Box 16). State Archives of North Carolina, Western Regional Archives, Asheville, NC, USA.

Wharton, Edith. *The Writing of Fiction*. Charles Scribner's Sons, 1925.

Wharton, Edith, and Ogden Codman, Jr. *The Decoration of Houses*. Charles Scribner's Sons, 1902.

Wharton, Marian. *Plain English: For the Education of the Workers by the Workers*. The People's College, 1917.

Whitehead, Alfred North. *Process and Reality: An Essay in Cosmology*. The Macmillan Company, 1929.

Whyte, William H., Jr. *The Organization Man*. Doubleday & Company, Inc., 1956.

Wicke, Jennifer. *Advertising Fictions: Literature, Advertisement, and Social Reading*. Columbia University Press, 1988.

Wilbers, Stephen. *The Iowa Writers' Workshop: Origins, Emergence, & Growth*. University of Iowa Press, 1980.

Wildman, Edwin. *Writing to Sell*. D. Appleton and Company, 1923.

Wilson, Edmund. "Dahlberg, Dos Passos, and Wilder." *The New Republic*, vol. XXXVI, no. 62, 1930, pp. 156–8.

Wood, Clement. *The Craft of Poetry*. E.P. Dutton & Company, Inc., 1929.

WPA. *Minneapolis: The Story of a City*. Minnesota Department of Education, 1940.

——. *Minnesota: A State Guide*. The Viking Press, 1938.

Wunsch, William Robert, and Mary Reade Smith. *Studies in Creative Writing*. Henry Holt and Company, 1933.

Young, Edward. *Conjectures on Original Composition*. Edited by Edith J. Morley, Longmans, Green & Co., 1918.

Zabriskie, George. "The Poetry of Margaret Walker." *The Saturday Review*, 11 September 1943, p. 19.

Index